THE CLASSICS OF WESTERN SPIRITUALITY
A Library of the Great Spiritual Masters

President and Publisher
Kevin A. Lynch, C.S.P.

EDITORIAL BOARD

Theatine Spirituality
SELECTED WRITINGS

TRANSLATED, EDITED AND WITH AN INTRODUCTION AND NOTES BY
WILLIAM V. HUDON

PREFACE BY
GIGLIOLA FRAGNITO

PAULIST PRESS
NEW YORK • MAHWAH

Cover Art: GERARD QUIGLEY is a New York native who for many years has created art with religious themes in various media. He executed this illustration, inspired by seventeenth-century woodcuts and frontispieces appearing in editions of early Theatine writings, in acrylics on canvas. His work depicts Lorenzo Scupoli and Theatine spirituality between two worlds: that of the cloister and that of the Catholic hierarchy, as the church reached outward from the Vatican in the age of the Tridentine Reformation.

The publisher and translator gratefully acknowledge the Vatican Library and its prefect, Leonard E. Boyle, O.P., for permission to translate the letters of Gaetano da Thiene.

Library of Congress Cataloging-in-Publication Data

Theatine spirituality : selected writings / translated, edited, and
   with an introduction and notes by William V. Hudon.
      p.   cm. — (The classics of Western spirituality ; #87)
   Includes bibliographical references and index.
   ISBN 0-8091-0479-2 (alk. paper). — ISBN 0-8091-3637-6 (alk.
paper)
      1. Theatines—Spiritual life.   I. Hudon, William V., 1956–
II. Series.
BX4085.T47   1996
255'.51—dc20   96-33711
                                                    CIP

Published by Paulist Press
997 Macarthur Boulevard
Mahwah, New Jersey 07430

Printed and bound in the United States of America

Contents

Editor and Translator of this Volume

WILLIAM V. HUDON, department chair, is professor of history at Bloomsburg University, where he has taught since 1989. A specialist in early modern Italian studies, he received his B.A. in history and philosophy from Fordham University (1980) and an M.A. (1983) and Ph.D. (1987) in history from the University of Chicago. He is the author of *Marcello Cervini and Ecclesiastical Government in Tridentine Italy* (DeKalb, IL: Northern Illinois University Press, 1992). His other recently published works include eleven entries in the *Encyclopedia of the Reformation* (New York: Oxford University Press, 1995) and "Countering 'the Turk': Papal and Genoese Naval Policy, 1535–1536," *Archivum historiae pontificiae* 30 (1992): 351–62.

Author of the Preface

GIGLIOLA FRAGNITO, professor of early modern history at Parma University, is a specialist in studies of Italian religious and cultural history in the Renaissance and the Counter-Reformation. She received her *Laurea* from the University of Rome, *La Sapienza*. She has been assistant professor and associate professor in the Department of History and Civilization at the European University Institute of Florence and associate professor at the Faculty of Letters and Philosophy of the University of Florence. She is the author of *Memoria individuale e costruzione biografica, Beccadelli, Della Casa, Vettori alle origini di un mito* (Urbino, 1979); *In museo e in villa, Saggi sul Rinascimento perduto* (Venezia, 1988); and *Gasparo Contarini, Un magistrato veneziano al servizio della cristianità* (Firenze, 1988). Her most recent scholarly works include: "La trattatistica cinque e seicentesca sulla corte cardinalizia. «Il vero ritratto d'una bellissima e ben governata corte»," *Annali dell'Istituto storico italo-germanico in Trento* 17 (1991); "Intorno alla «religione» dell'Ariosto," *Lettere italiane* 44 (1992); "Gli Ordini religiosi tra Riforma e Controriforma," in *Clero e società nell'Italia moderna*, edited by Mario Rosa (Bari, 1992); "Cardinals' Courts in Sixteenth-Century Rome," *The Journal of Modern History* 65 (1993); and "Le contraddizioni di un censore: Ludovico Beccadelli di fronte al Panormita ed al Boccaccio," in *Studi in memoria di Paola Medioli Masotti*, edited by Franca Magnani (Napoli, 1995).

FOR QUIN

. . . ti amo sempre

Acknowledgments

*I*n researching the history of the Theatine order and in editing and translating some of its spiritual writings, I have incurred a number of debts, both intellectual and personal. I am grateful for the generous assistance of a number of scholars and friends—among them Ken Jorgensen, Elisabeth Gleason and Craig Harline—who read portions of the introduction at different stages of composition and provided numerous suggestions for improvement. They saved me from even more numerous errors. Ken went above and beyond "generosity" by providing me photocopies of obscure secondary literature he procured during his own research on the Theatines. Francesco Andreu, C.R., provided valuable bibliographic assistance and kind willingness to help a new student of the order. Members of my honors seminar at Bloomsburg University on the Reformation and Counter-Reformation, like Karol Weaver, Andy Shively, Chris Corley, and Matt Smith, patiently waited, listened and questioned as I developed some of my initial ideas on the unique Theatine spirituality. Comments received at sessions in the 1992 and 1993 *Sixteenth Century Studies Conference*, where I presented portions of the work that follows in an earlier draft, gave substantial assistance. Aaron Polonsky performed innumerable O.C.L.C. searches, and not only tolerated my continual interruptions of his own work but always used them deftly as occasions to exercise his inimitable sense of humor. Bernard McGinn provided not only the translation of Carafa's Rule for the Theatines, but also invaluable encouragement throughout the project. His comments and suggestions on the content of earlier drafts as well as his time-consuming, careful editing improved this work immensely. Lydia Cochrane sprang willingly to my aid and undertook the arduous task of checking my translations of Scupoli's excruciating prose. A word of thanks to all, but with my recognition that it will never repay the debt or truly express my gratitude.

The Faculty Professional Development Committee and the Office of the Provost at Bloomsburg University provided two one-quarter course reductions in the form of released-time awards during the spring and fall semesters, 1993. Those awards permitted much more concentrated effort at a crucial stage. Jo Crossley, who coordinates interlibrary loan at Bloomsburg, fielded continual requests and handled them expeditiously. The chairman of the department of history, James R. Sperry, and the dean of the College of Arts and Sciences, Hsien-tung Liu, also provided consistent support and encouragement. Projects like this, undertaken while simultaneously teaching, can rarely be completed without such assistance, and I am grateful.

My family, as always, contributed great moral and material support. My parents, Vincent B. and C. Elizabeth Hudon, and my mother and father-in-law, Norman E. and Betty R. Toft, are unwavering in love, encouragement and support that make my life a great deal happier and my work a great deal easier. The model of family commitment that they have lived and taught through example will forever be mine. The devotion, love and generosity of my wife, Wendy, sustains me. All that I am, all that I do is because of her and belongs to her.

And then there's Quin. Product of the love and pain his mother and I experienced over our three years in the Bronx, he reflects it all: delighting and exasperating, testing and rewarding, loving without question and challenging at every turn. Being a father may rarely be simple, but it's never easy to be a son, and he has grown into a fine young man in whom I take enormous pride. I dedicate this book to him in the hope that he will find his own path and his own goals, experience the same kind of happiness and love that he has showered upon me, and that I will be lucky enough to see it all.

Preface

(TRANSLATED BY WILLIAM V. HUDON)

*T*his anthology of texts, which illustrates the spirituality of the first two generations of Theatines and is presented for a large, English-speaking audience, is meritorious for a number of different reasons.

Above all, anyone familiar with the often convoluted and dense language in which the religious uncertainties and mystical experiences of women and men are dressed in an age of profound spiritual and cultural upheaval like the sixteenth century can have no trouble imagining the difficulty this translator has met and resolved in rendering the works in English. He has offered us a version in plain and clear language that makes the testimony of intense religious experience in Theatine writings accessible to a nonspecialized audience.

Although this is a noteworthy accomplishment in itself, it is not the only valuable element in this volume. The rich, developed introduction and the wise selection of texts permit us, in fact, to more fully understand the birth of the first congregation of regular clerics, which obtained official ecclesiastical recognition with Clement VII's apostolic letter *Exponi nobis* in 1524. Considering that amid the origins of the new congregation we find two profoundly different personalities—Gaetano da Thiene and Gian Pietro Carafa—it was a most complex beginning. For although these two founders appear so disparate in geographic origin, social extraction, and their religious and cultural formation, still they were connected by a common objective: the religious renewal of Christian society. In fact, nothing seemed to link Thiene and Carafa. It would seem difficult to believe that they could manage to live together in the newborn congregation—let alone to expand its membership, though in a very contained manner—if from the beginning the determining role of Carafa did not emerge to guide the congregation. He did so with a firm and inflexible hand, even reorienting its scope and refocusing its mystical, ascetic tendencies. Thus, it was not by chance that the clerics gained their nickname from his episcopal see of Chieti. The letter included here that Carafa wrote around 1526 is significant in this regard. That letter regulated the Theatine manner of life until the approbation of formal constitutions in 1604, which in many ways merely absorbed its contents.

It is impossible to determine to what extent Gaetano approved of the vertical and rigidly hierarchical organization that Carafa imposed on the congregation or to what degree he shared Carafa's rigorously enunciated principle of obedience and total submission to the superior. But when the future pope ruled on Theatine rapport with women (to limit themselves to cases of extreme necessity and only with the authorization of the superior), he stood clearly against the important function that "illumined" women—teachers with prophetic spirits and thaumaturgic powers—had developed and continued to develop in those years when they served as charismatic guides to persons seeking interior perfection. His ruling was, in fact, an implicit rejection of the rapport, characterized by veneration and total subordination (as illustrated in the letters edited here), that linked Gaetano to the Brescian nun Laura Mignani.

The desire to control and contain the expression of a religiosity that in the restless search for mystical union with God could easily degenerate into quietist practices of dubious orthodoxy is, on the other hand, evident also in Carafa's rigid and schematic division of time dedicated to liturgical services and to chanting of the Divine Office in choir. In fact, the "rule" of Carafa reduced the opportunities of Theatines to practice and dedicate themselves to more intimate and personal piety. He thereby shifted the central position that such piety held at the heart of the Oratory of Divine Love, from which the first Theatines came and by which they were mainly formed. A similar restriction in the "rule" against commentary by the clerics on Holy Scripture and the fathers of the church read during meals and attribution of this task exclusively to the superior revealed the plan of Carafa in all its coherence and lucidity. The "rule" was tight, to constrain and direct efflorescent late medieval spirituality—the kind that had matured inside the confraternities—within rigidly outlined channels and to limit the risk of religious subjectivism that could not be conducted into the stream of orthodoxy and ecclesiastical discipline.

Carafa did not, however, limit himself to composing a "rule" that would at least block, if not impede, those dangerous deviations of the road toward complete Christian perfection trod by the first followers of Gaetano da Thiene. Neither did he stop at considerable modification of their original, predominant dedication to works of mercy and imitation of

PREFACE

Christ, which progressively was flanked by their zeal for the renovation of ecclesiastical institutions, from the formation of clergy to the direction of convents to the governance of dioceses. Carafa took actions that follow from the "rule" and that, to some degree, help to illuminate its guidelines. It is sufficient to consider the premature suspicion that the future Pope Paul IV "hatched" against the teachings of the Dominican friar Battista Carioni da Crema, who was the confessor and spiritual director of Gaetano da Thiene in his arduous path toward penitential asceticism and mystical illumination, and whose guidance left profound impressions in the spirituality and writings of the saint, as Dr. Hudon explains in the introduction. Carafa had, in fact, expressed misgivings regarding these teachings in a 1532 letter to Carioni. Immediately after the death of the friar in January 1534, Carafa clearly indicated that he had died "outside the flock of the Church." Convinced that the old spiritualist and mystical heresy of the "free spirit" had reemerged in the devotional teachings of the Dominican, Carafa—who in 1536 probably urged investigation of the Lombard conventicles of Battista's disciples—did not hesitate, once he was cardinal inquisitor, to condemn the teaching of Fra Battista as "scandalous in several matters, in others truly reckless and in many things heretical" or to include all Battista's written works on the *Index of Prohibited Books* published in 1559, once he had ascended the papal throne.

In the space of those twenty-five years that passed between composition of the "rule" and the condemnation of Battista da Crema, the more disquieting elements of the religious experience of Gaetano da Thiene and his companions were absorbed by the energetic disciplinary actions of Carafa. The "divine mothers," who at the beginning of the century had encouraged the mystical "adventures" of their "spiritual sons," now left the job to "spiritual fathers." At the beginning of the 1530s, Gian Pietro Carafa gave Gaetano charge of the spiritual direction of his sister, Maria Carafa, and of her monastic community at the *Sapienza* in Naples. Still later, Lorenzo Scupoli wrote, at the request of a nun and for a female audience, *Il combattimento spirituale*, a text on spiritual direction destined to become a huge editorial success. There were some 600 editions generated after the author's death in 1610. Carafa's distrust of the function of "divine mothers" as inspiring spiritual guides for groups restless with religious tension was already manifest in his "rule" of 1526. From that beginning, he provoked a painless reversal of roles at the heart of this congregation that elsewhere would be imposed by more traumatic, violent means that tore others asunder.

In this light, vicissitudes in the early history of the Barnabite order, which were recently reconstructed by Massimo Firpo ("Paola Antonia Negri da 'divine madre maestra' a 'spirito diabolico,' " *Barnabiti studi* 7 [1990]:6–66), are nicely illuminated, for the changes possess many similarities with the Theatine experience. The Barnabite regular clerics of St. Paul took their first steps not only under the direction of Battista da Crema, the spiritual father of their founder, Antonio Maria Zaccaria, but also under the direction of a sister of the *Angeliche* congregation, Paola Antonia Negri. No differently from Gaetano da Thiene—who had singled out Laura Mignani as his "master" of spirituality—Zaccaria entrusted himself to the mystical teaching of Negri, the heir of Fra Battista. She wound up governing both the Barnabites and the *Angeliche* with indisputable authority for about fifteen years, and by doing so she attracted inquisitorial investigation to both groups in 1550. The investigation concluded two years later with the previously mentioned condemnation of the teachings of Battista, a meticulous apostolic visitation of their Milanese houses, the approbation of new constitutions, the clear separation of the Barnabites from the *Angeliche*, the transformation of the latter into a cloistered order, and the compulsory seclusion of Negri in the convent of Santa Chiara in Milan.

A member of the Roman Congregation of the Holy Office that conducted the inquest, Carafa was no outsider to this crisis that profoundly shook the Barnabites and the *Angeliche*. The role he played on that occasion throws light retrospectively on his timely and lucid interventions in the Theatine congregation. Through these actions he took the young group on a radical turn, blocking its fall into dangerous heterodox deviations and saving it from inquisitorial trials.

But that premature reconciliation of the diverging lines of the first founders was not without cost, as it led to what appears—at least from the sources edited here—to be progressive impoverishment of Theatine religiosity. The documentation reveals, in fact, the distance that separates the restless, suffering spirituality found in the letters of Gaetano to Mignani from the prosaic, commonplace nature of his succinct notes to Maria Carafa and from the cautious practicality of the *Spiritual Combat* of Scupoli.

Through his erudite introduction and the selected texts, Dr. Hudon has reasserted—and rightly so, no doubt—the necessity of analyzing the first years of the Theatine order in a more articulate and developed manner than has been characteristic in the past. Two complementary requirements for that better analysis emerge from these pages. First, it is necessary to avoid isolating consideration of the creation of one congregation from that of the others, since they flourished in an identical religious climate. They rose from analogous instances of personal and collective renewal, while their tormented beginnings had no small number of points in common, as the misfortunes of the first Jesuits before the Spanish and Roman Inquisitions demonstrate. Second, it is necessary to avoid projecting onto the beginning of what many have commonly called the "new congregations of the Counter-Reformation" the doctrinal and disciplinary certainties that appeared in the era of their maturity. One must keep in mind that "in the doctrinal confusion and in the yearnings for reform" that characterized the years in which the regular clerics were born, "the language and the ideas, the practices and the spirituality of those who preached 'reform' were not easily distinguishable from the disciplinary and dogmatic watershed of orthodoxy" (Carlo Ossola, "Rilettura degli 'Esercizi spirituali,' " *RSLR* 21 [1985]:279). Only then can one fully comprehend how two of the founders, Antonio Maria Zaccaria and Gaetano da Thiene, were able to follow the teaching of someone like Battista da Crema, who was so soon thereafter condemned for heresy. One can also come to understand how spiritual journeys begun together in that climate of theological uncertainty could come to such profoundly different ends. It was not by chance, after all, that Bartolomeo Stella (one of the first companions of Gaetano da Thiene) and Marcantonio Flaminio (who in 1533 requested and was refused entry into the Theatine order) both found themselves welcomed into the *familia* of Cardinal Reginald Pole, a man Carafa considered to be the master of every heresy.

Abbreviations

AfR	*Archiv für Reformationsgeschichte*
AGT	Archivum Generale dei Teatini, Rome, Italy
AHP	*Archivum Historiae Pontificiae*
AHR	*American Historical Review*
AIGT	*Annali dell' Istituto storico italo-germanico in Trento*
CHR	*Catholic Historical Review*
CnS	*Cristianesimo nella storia*
CS	*Critica storica*
CT	*Concilium Tridentinum. Diariorum Actorum Epistularum Tractatuum nova collectio,* 13 vols. (Freiburg, 1901–1938).
DBI	*Dizionario biografico degli italiani* (Rome, 1958–)
DIP	*Dizionario degli istituti di perfezione* (Rome, 1974–)
DS	*Dictionnaire de spiritualité ascétique et mystique doctrine et histoire* (Paris, 1937–)
DTC	*Dictionnaire de Théologie Catholique,* 15 vols. (Paris, 1909–1950)
JEH	*Journal of Ecclesiastical History*
JMH	*Journal of Modern History*
RAM	*Revue d'ascétique et mystique*
RD	*Regnum dei*
RR	*Renaissance and Reformation*
RSCI	*Rivista di storia della chiesa in Italia*
RSI	*Rivista storica italiana*
RSLR	*Rivista di storia e letteratura religiosa*
SCJ	*Sixteenth Century Journal*

A Note on the Translations

*I*n the translations, I have struggled to remain as literal as possible throughout. I am well aware that this policy results in a more archaic rendering, but I am convinced this is required in order to present a better sense of the author and audience. I have tried to intercede, at times, mostly to simplify what I consider excessive archaism in the form of convoluted prose and tortured syntax, but only when absolutely necessary. The prose of Scupoli required a good deal more intervention than that of Gaetano. My goal overall has been to retain a firm sense of what appears to me undeniable: that these authors, Scupoli in particular, were not especially critical—or maybe even fully "literate"—writers.

Introduction

GENERAL BACKGROUND

O ver the first generations of the Theatine order (1524-1600), the western world experienced intense and vibrant change in virtually every element of its culture. According to differing schools of historical interpretation, the conclusion of the fifteenth, the sixteenth and early-seventeenth centuries stood as the degenerative demise of a better Middle Ages; or as the expansive growth of capitalist economic institutions and competitive, mercantilist empires; or as the rich harvest of a Middle Ages that provided seed for modernity; or as the very foundation of the modern world. Still, learned analysts all agree on one thing: this era can be characterized as one of profound change. Without adopting the terms of historical periodization used by any one of them, examples of shifting outlooks, economic change, political consolidation, religious rethinking and social upheaval are legion.[1]

It was, after all, the age of the intellectual movement known as the Renaissance. The suggestion that suddenly in the fifteenth century the Middle Ages were over and Renaissance methods of thought completely reshaped the way human beings thought about themselves and their society may be oversimplistic, but intellectual life did gradually change to reflect some discounting of the scholastic methodology typical of medieval universities and the increasing importance of a different methodology known as humanism. While medieval intellectuals did not totally or comprehensively reject Greek and Roman classical literature and culture, the early-modern educated elite placed increasing emphasis upon the importance of that literature and culture in systems of learning and thought. Committed to the recovery and publication of ancient sources that might contain a guide to life and action in their contemporary world, they came to understand classical culture on its own terms. They valued it not as a model to be slavishly

1

imitated, but as a set of practical examples that might have relevance to the intellectual, moral, political and social issues of their own day, as they struggled to surpass the achievements of the ancients in all those matters. Some practitioners of the early-modern brand of humanism also engaged a set of religious, Christian concerns through the same methodology, and they were not confined to the northern end of the European continent either. Convinced that the ancient sources of Christianity—that is, the books of the New Testament—contained a model worth pursuing in the interest of imitating and surpassing the religiosity and devotion of ancient Christians, Italians familiar with humanistic methodology, from Francesco Petrarca (1304–1374) through the Theatine authors edited here, struggled to apply their understanding of the Christian past in the interest of creating a better religious future.[2]

For the average person, however, the term "Renaissance" signifies and refers to activity in the sphere of the plastic arts, not literature and education. Painting, sculpture, music and architecture underwent dramatic and continual change from the end of the fifteenth through the beginning of the seventeenth centuries. Most view the early portion of the period as that of "high Renaissance," when the techniques and methods of ancient Greek and Roman artists, so zealously exhumed, both literally and figuratively, by their mainly Italian followers in the late fourteenth and early-fifteenth centuries, became a cultural standard. Imitators seeking to surpass one another (and the ancients themselves, in the process) gradually turned to play, rethinking, reinventing, and in some cases, temporarily demolishing the models, through the "mannerist" style identified by analysts of seventeenth-century art. Employing innovation and humor, mannerists helped to create a national style that was faithful to the methodology of Renaissance humanism while rejecting idealization of both methods and subjects. They even helped to transform the discipline of architecture into a vehicle toward that thoroughly "modern" goal of urban planning. It was best exemplified in new cities, but also in old yet newly expanded and reorganized ones like Turin under the administration of Carlo Emanuele I (1580–1630) and the Rome of Pope Alexander VII (1655–1667).[3]

In economic and geographical terms, the era inspires and deserves continual reinvestigation as the "age of discovery." Economic change in the medieval period, driven by a twelfth-century movement called the "commercial revolution," set the terms for similar growth in the early-modern period, as both turned on the expansion of trading routes and the development of systems we associate with the term "capitalism." The overland expansion of medieval, town-based trade was followed by overseas expansion of the early-modern economy along increasingly "national" lines, as western European governments vied with one another for materials and markets in the "New World" opened by explorers and imperialists.[4]

Historians identify the beginnings of that other intellectual readjustment known as the Scientific Revolution in this period. Humanist study of ancient philosophers and scientists demonstrated that their views were not accepted in an unquestioned fashion even in the ancient world, and thus provided justification for contemporary re-evaluation. Scientists shifted from the reading and interpretation of classic texts to the creation, reading and interpretation of experimental results in the process of explaining and answering standard questions in physics, astronomy and anatomy. The shift is exemplified nicely in two works published in 1543: Nicolaus Copernicus's *On the Revolutions of the Heavenly Bodies*, and *The Structure of the Human Body* by Andreas Vesalius. The work of Galileo Galilei (1564–1642) and that of other physicists like Johannes Kepler (1571–1630) and Isaac Newton (1642–1727) stand at the heart of the popular image of the Scientific Revolution, but often without adequate reference to the humanism that served as inspiration. Historians often make an unfortunate link between this scientific work and a confrontation early-modern scientists were presumed to have with the religious culture they allegedly rejected. Undue focus upon astronomical and physical discoveries as the heart of science in this era often leads to neglect of other significant works. Incorporation of contemporary contributions to mathematics, natural history, botany and chemistry within the story of the Scientific Revolution might permit a fuller understanding of this third major shift.[5]

Dramatic change came also in the form of political consolidation. In Italy, warring Renaissance *condottieri* dominated the essentially localized political picture that emerged from the vigorous efforts of various German, Spanish and French overlords to control particular regions and the equally vigorous efforts of some Italian states to push them out. These characters only gradually, and often contentiously, gave way to a process of political consolidation based upon the foreign policy that Holy Roman Emperor Charles V (1519–1556) delivered through his ambassadors to the lands he occupied, like Milan, Naples and Palermo. The consolidation was also based upon the more-or-less independent rule of states loosely allied to him that acted through *signori* transformed into either dynastic monarchs or intransigent oligarchs. Among the former were persons like Andrea Doria (1466–1560) in Genoa and Cosimo de' Medici (1520–1574) in Florence (two mostly dependable imperial allies), while among the latter were the landowning and upper-middle classes in places like Lucca, where unacceptable candidates for civic office and violent worker revolts were repressed with equal vigor.

Outside of Italy, monarchs expressing disaffection with the standard, medieval form of kingship—weak and dependent—worked hard to counteract dependence through centralization of power and administration. In the process, they created what has at times been called "new monarchy." They also generated considerable contention, perhaps nowhere better illustrated than that between emperors like Charles V and the conglomeration of fiercely independent electors, dukes and princes of Germany. Consolidation outside of Italy, in addition to administrative centralization in the Papal States, provided the first steps toward the construction of absolute government characteristic of Europe from the middle of the seventeenth century until the age of revolution.[6]

Germany served as the site for the beginning of another contention, in part political, that triggered what was arguably the most dramatic change of all for the early-modern world: the Protestant Reformation. Most consider the argument between what came to be the "Protestant" and "Catholic" definitions of proper Christian devotion to be the essence of this contention. It is dangerous, however, to focus too completely here, as one can ignore the precedents necessary to comprehend fully the early-modern contention. The dispute and its ultimate significance are wrapped up in the larger context already described, and although initiated by a German Augustinian at the university in Wittenberg named Martin Luther (1483–1546), the movement gained success in large part due to the political upheaval of the early-modern age, particularly the challenge to imperial authority represented by German nobles. The movement also possessed a rich, variegated religious legacy and stood in continuity with earlier controversy over proper devotion in and legitimate leadership of "the church" throughout its ancient and medieval history.

Jesus of Nazareth, after all, stood as the model for all Christian "reformers." As a popular critic of contemporary Judaic behavior, he targeted the elite religious authorities of his own time, the Sadducees and Pharisees, calling them to reform and to genuine religiosity. As portrayed in the Gospels, he preached a message directly and deliberately opposite to theirs and directed it at a popular audience. He exhibited at least righteous indignation at, if not real intolerance of, those he considered deaf to the "real" message of God concerning salvation. And he struggled with questions on the relative importance of religious authority and secular political power in an age notorious for violence and injustice.[7]

When Christianity became tolerated, then a privileged religious institution, and finally a permanent fixture in western medieval culture, these issues and problems did not recede, but rather, the stage was set for more intense and more hotly contested arguments. When persecution ended and imperial law gradually granted privileges to Christians and their clergy, they transformed themselves from the persecuted to persecutors. That fascinating process was largely complete by the time of the publication of the Justinian Code of civil law in the sixth century, as the already harsh punishments for engaging in pagan practices from late fourth and fifth-century legislation were made even more severe and included capital punishment. A complicated mixing of Christian religious authority with secular political power then took place, one that was encouraged by theologians such as Augustine (354–430), who hoped that, in general terms, the church would direct the state and the state would uphold the church. On the one hand, monasteries and papal initiatives provided security from and then conversion of "barbarian" peoples in the early Middle Ages, and in the absence of imperial determination fully to control events in the west, they acquired independent political and legal leverage. On the other hand, the monasteries that represented outposts of Christian civilization became to a degree dependent upon both female and male members of the laity who first settled in the vicinity for practical reasons and then served as sources of additional property through charitable bequests. Moreover, like Roman emperors before who took an interest in episcopal appointments for the bit of territorial and community stability they might provide, newly Christianized Germanic kings looked to control papal succession and relied on church figures to perform a good deal of the actual work of governing Germany.[8]

Medieval reformers and reform movements that stood as precursors to Luther and his initiative challenged three basic themes: clerical decay, the distasteful self-assurance of official Christendom, and the longstanding mixture of political and religious authority wielded by bishops and abbots. The tenth-century Cluniac reform called both regular and secular clerics to a higher moral standard through adherence to the canon laws and monastic rules under which they lived. The eleventh-century actions taken by both Franconian kings and Pope Gregory VII (1073–1085), which led to the "investiture conflict," all had the motivation of reform and a desire to re-spiritualize the church administration behind them, even if their long-range significance was to begin to define modern western political discourse on the separation of church and state. The Cistercian, Dominican and Franciscan movements in the later half of the twelfth and the early-thirteenth centuries all sketched heroic, even elitist, images of what real Christian devotion ought to be like in answering the decay of Benedictine monasticism and in criticizing both clerical and non-clerical pursuit of the goods of this world. The thirteenth and fourteenth-century critics who wrote in the vernacular for popular audiences, like Dante Alighieri (1265–1321) and Walther von der Vogelweide (c.1170-c.1230), vilified overblown papal claims to political and economic influence in the form of monarchical government. In his poems, Vogelweide even sounded like Luther, ridiculing a bishop with curial loyalties as a money-grubbing "Lord Money Box," one who represented policies of Innocent III (1198–1216) that threatened to impoverish the German people through inordinate taxes and simultaneously to destroy true Christian belief. The fourteenth and fifteenth-century conciliarist movement and those calling for personal and institutional change in the church, like Marsilio of Padua (c.1290–c.1343) and Catherine of Siena (1347–1380), questioned the veracity of the Christian commitment of certain popes and the legitimacy of maintaining a governmental structure in which only popes could call councils into being.[9]

Hence, when Luther issued his 1517 challenge on the topic of indulgences and then engaged a host of questions concerning fundamental elements of the Christian faith, he looked for all the world like another in a long line of medieval reformers. As bad as his predecessors painted the papacy and curia, one could argue that Luther had even more to complain about in the very recent past. Popes like Sixtus IV (1471–1484), Innocent VIII (1484–1492), Alexander VI (1492–1503) and Julius II (1503–1513) exhibited flagrant immorality and headed administrations that were consumed with nepotism, rivalry, intrigue and "worldly" considerations associated with Renaissance culture in Italy. Luther likely considered all of their careers to have found a culmination in that of the Medici pope Leo X (1513–1521). The Augustinian had visited Leo's Rome and was repulsed by what he found there in 1510, even though recent analysis indicates that the city was not quite so lavish as we might expect. Roman curialists reacted in a lackadaisical fashion to Luther's original reforming message, convinced that sooner or later, like the others before him, he would just go away.[10]

Of course, Luther and his message did no such thing, and tremendous change emerged as the result. As important as his theological contribution was, especially the doctrine of "justification by faith alone," the method of independent scriptural interpretation behind it and the implications that it held for the definition of the relationship between individual Christians and religio-political authorities was an equally significant part of his message. Luther and that message stood behind the creation of a multiplicity of churches, all critical of the Roman church and all claiming, to one degree or another, possession of the truth concerning Christianity.

Luther and other Protestant leaders made heavy use of the rapidly organizing printing industry and created the prototype of modern exploitation of information media for propagandistic purposes. Adherents to his message and recommendations employed them for other, nonreligious ends. German peasants, for example, utilized Scripture in 1524 and 1525 to justify social and political rebellion against their feudal overlords. Theological discourse at universities changed to become even more polemical than medieval scholastic debate. Indeed, even the problem medieval reformers seemed to criticize most—that false but self-assured institutional conviction of religious truth (albeit held by a new set of institutions and their leaders)—spilled over into intolerance in many forms, particularly "religious" civil war.[11] In the sixteenth, and through the first half of the seventeenth century, it spawned a rather bloody set of conflicts with European-wide dimensions.[12]

TRIDENTINE REFORMATION

Alongside the dramatic change known as the Protestant Reformation stands another movement, called sometimes the "Catholic Reformation," at other times the "Counter-Reformation," but I think best described by the term "Tridentine Reformation." The problem over historiographical terminology attributed to Catholic action in this period possesses a rich and interesting history of its own. Analysts of the Reformation era politicized and polemicized its history from the beginning, when the vituperative *Magdeburg Centuries* compiled by Protestants between 1559 and 1574 under the direction of Matthias Flacius Illyricus (1520–1575) received a better researched, but still partisan answer in Cesare Baronio's *Annales ecclesiastici*, published between 1598 and 1607. Only much later, in the nineteenth century, did Protestant historians coin the term "Counter-Reformation" to describe Catholic attempts to reconvert areas in Germany where rulers and people were loyal to Lutheranism. Originally intended to describe a particular sort of Catholic reaction, the term has come into popular use as descriptive of all Catholic action in the period, summarizing it as conservative, violent repression of progressive, positive innovation.

Catholic historians from the same era matched this pejorative title with a term of their own—"Catholic Reform"—to focus attention on the efforts toward ecclesiastical renewal, especially in Spain and Italy, that pre-dated the Lutheran initiative. In a sense, these terms repeated and revived the polemics of the very era they were created to describe, and now in the late-twentieth century the debate rages on. Interest in such Catholic institutions as the Roman and Spanish inquisitions and the *Index of Prohibited Books* has led some to assert that, in reality, the Catholic church in the sixteenth century reflected only one thing—repression—and that the "Catholic Reform" was a myth created by fearful, militant post-World War II Catholic historians. A growing number of other scholars contradict this view, convinced that episodes of what sixteenth-century persons would have considered unwarranted, extra-legal repressive activity were limited exceptions to the long-term trend in Catholic action.[13]

Using the term "Tridentine Reformation" will perhaps defuse and refocus the debate toward a more carefully nuanced outcome. It may help us to see the individual prelates in the Roman church, like Gasparo Contarini (1483–1542), Marcello Cervini (1501–1555), Rodolfo Pio da Carpi (1500–1564) and Giovanni Morone (1509–1580), previously identified as either "lenient" toward or "repressive" of Protestantism, as they really were—churchmen with a common background whose particular and fascinating circumstances, experiences and interests led them toward a variety of pastoral policies. It may help us to understand how these and others fit into the general thrust of Catholic action throughout the early-modern period, a thrust that was consistent with late-medieval initiatives and that culminated in the decrees of the Council of Trent (1545–1563). Finally, it may help us to explain and understand those others, like Gian Pietro Carafa (1476–1559) and Michele Ghislieri (1504–1572), whose policies were so inconsistent and personally motivated as to demonstrate their difference from the others, as they really were—the individuals responsible for repressive "Counter Reformation" initiatives.[14]

The Tridentine Reformation, standing alongside the same set of situations and conditions that served as context for the Protestant Reformation, represented no less dramatic a change. Although enmeshed with medieval institutions and precedents that Protestantism seemed to reject, the Tridentine Reformation, like the Protestant, was still a bold, spiritual revival. That revival and change can be identified in any number of individuals, from priests, prelates and popes like Ignatius of Loyola (1491–1556), Gian Matteo Giberti (Bishop of Verona, 1525–1543), and Paul III (1534–1549), to laywomen, laymen and the confraternities they established, like Catherine of Genoa (1447–1510), Ettore Vernazza (ca. 1470–1524) and the Oratory of Divine Love. Members of religious orders who pursued direct and personal communication with God and encouraged such pursuit in others, like Teresa of Avila (1515–1582), Roberto Bellarmino (1542–1621) and John of the Cross (1542–1591), were also prominent among the proponents of religious revival. The institutional church also provided evidence of the revival, from the decrees of the Council of Trent to Catholic outreach and evangelization, by way of missionary activity, in the New World. It is important to investigate the ideas and institutions that motivated all this action, primarily the humanist outlook and intellectual method inherited from the Renaissance, in both its Italian and extra-alpine versions.

The increased importance and development of late-medieval lay confraternities exemplifies both the continuity and change implicit in the Tridentine Reformation. The confraternities were traditional institutions in urban centers during the Middle Ages, with a long history not unlike that of the religious orders. At the end of the fifteenth and during the sixteenth century, old confraternities were reformed and new ones founded, all in the pursuit of two goals: the greater devotional perfection of individual members, and heroic charitable service to nonmembers. To those ends, old confraternities revised their organizational procedures and sought confirmation by local bishops, if not by the papacy itself. New foundations, including even those relatively few that limited or rejected clerical membership altogether, similarly sought confirmation and utilized some priest or priests as spiritual directors and chaplains. Naturally, founders and reformers tied the devotional life of these institutions to the traditional sacraments and prayers of the church. In fact, many confraternity leaders were also leaders in particular parishes, and hence, the confraternities were not substitutes for the parish or in opposition to its life and activities. Responding to the pressing poverty characteristic of portions of all early-modern urban populations, they also required that their institutions be infused with charitable activities. Designed to meet some unfulfilled need in the larger communities of which each was a part, confraternities assumed functions that contributed to the ideals of brotherhood and social equality and also promoted social stability.

These institutions dedicated themselves either to some event in salvation history (like the annunciation), to the Eucharist, or to a patron saint (St. Jerome was one of the most popular). Members, both male and female, made such dedication efficacious by staffing homes for repentent prostitutes, lepers' hospitals and schools teaching reading and writing to poor children, among other activities. The best known of all the confraternities was the Oratory of Divine Love, founded in Genoa in 1497 by Ettore Vernazza. Its *Rule* required a fixed program of prayers that included recitation of the divine office in common, a weekly fast and reception of communion at what was then a saintly pace: at least four times per year. Copying the charitable activities of Catherine of Genoa (Caterina Fieschi Adorno), who was known to spring suddenly from contemplative prayer whenever some patient required care in the Pammatone hospital she administered with her husband, the members staffed the hospital during her tenure and after her death. Vernazza helped to found numerous branches of the Oratory in other Italian cities he visited, among them Rome, Venice and Naples.[15]

Clerics within various levels of the church hierarchy reflected significant change, specifically in their outlook and behavior. In part, they did so due to inspiration derived from the public, popular activities of confraternity members. Even high-ranking prelates went to work in hospitals serving the poor, at least on a part-time basis, in the centers of Italian urban life. Some bishops, seeking the same self-sanctification, but also the fulfillment of their canonical responsibilities in the dioceses to which they had been appointed, turned away from the pursuit of higher office in Rome—typical of their colleagues and many others who held the title of bishop in the Middle Ages—and took up residency in their sees. The change was startling to the faithful, who were familiar with the long precedents of dispensation from the residency requirement of all those holding the care of souls (or *cura animarum*) and the appointment of uneducated, even illiterate, vicars. In the process, bishops like Giberti, who left a lucrative curial office, and others before and after him, like Pietro Barozzi (Bishop of Padua, 1487–1507), became models for the Tridentine expectations of bishops defined and codified in the reform decrees of Trent. They served as models also for those who eventually implemented the decrees through systematic organization of diocesan devotions, creation of seminaries for better education of clergy, preaching that taught the basic elements of faith, and above all, example, which was only possible with episcopal residence.

Clerics at the bottom as well as at the pinnacle of the ecclesiastical structure reflected the change as well. Priests of no special prominence either initiated or participated in the foundation of movements that exerted wide influence well beyond the sixteenth century. The Jesuit order, for example, received its inspiration from an obscure and initially uneducated Basque named Ignatius of Loyola. Wounded in a battle at Pamplona in 1491 and then spiritually transformed through meditative and mystical experiences in a cave near Manresa in Spain, he wrote one of the devotional classics of this period, the *Spiritual Exercises*. With a focus on the personal choices a Christian could make to engage actively in the service of God, and never intended exclusively for his own followers, it became the center of more than the individual spirituality of Jesuits: it also stands at the heart of a retreat movement still popular among Christians today. The work of Ignatius's followers helped to set the terms of Catholic theological orthodoxy at the Council of Trent, to spread the faith in extensive missionary and pastoral activities, and to encourage learning and culture through dynamic educational institutions like the Roman College.[16]

Another obscure cleric, and one of the principal subjects of this volume, Gaetano da Thiene (c.1480–1547), rocketed to prominence from his native Vicenza in much the same manner, as one of the co-founders of the Theatine order. The work of his followers went a long way toward encouraging the revival of a more pastoral, spiritual outlook in parish priests and in bishops throughout the sixteenth and seventeenth centuries. Dynamic reform through the creation of other new orders and the improvement of established ones can be seen in the history of the Barnabites (founded by Antonio Maria Zaccaria, 1502–1537), the Somascans (founded by Jerome Aemiliani, 1481–1537) and the Oratorians (founded by Philip Neri, 1515–1595), in addition to the Capuchin reform movement in the Franciscan order and the initiatives carried out in the Dominican and Augustinian orders. Female religious life also underwent change and renewal, best exemplified, perhaps, in the work of Angela Merici (1474–1540), who established the Company of the Servants of St. Ursula (or the Ursulines) for the education of girls.[17]

At the opposite end of the clerical order, popes also provided indications (although mixed) that the religious life and institutions of western "Catholic" Christendom would be different in the sixteenth and seventeenth centuries than in the several preceding. Paul III usually receives credit for commencing serious reform activity in this era, and in fact he added prominent humanists like Marcello Cervini, Gasparo Contarini, Reginald Pole (1500–1558), Giovanni Morone and Gian Pietro Carafa to reformers already seated in the college of cardinals, while supporting new and renewed religious orders, reviving the Roman Inquisition and convening the Council of Trent. Paul nonetheless retained elements of the simoniac, patronistic, Renaissance approach to ecclesiastical government, which died hard in the early-modern era. In addition to the humanists and reformers mentioned above, he appointed two grandsons to the position of cardinal, maintained a foreign policy linked as clearly to the medieval crusading spirit as to the pragmatism of early-modern politics, and shocked virtually everyone with his gift of Parma and Piacenza from the papal domain to his son Pier Luigi Farnese (1503–1547). Julius III (1550–1555), Marcellus II (1555), Paul IV (1555–1559), Pius IV (1559–1565), Pius V (1566–1572) and Gregory XIII (1572–1585) all demonstrated commitment, to one degree or another, to the general push toward ecclesiastical renewal and revival.[18]

Something of an explosion of mysticism also provided evidence of vitality and change in the early-modern Catholic world. We frequently associate reports of direct communication and union with God in this era with persons like Teresa of Avila and John of the Cross. As important as they were, numerous others contributed as well and can help to fill out the picture. Women felt this highest of spiritual experiences more often than men, and they came from all social strata. Members of the nobility of Brescia, like Paola Gambara (1463–1505), as well as members of its underclass, like the orphan and house servant Stefana Quinzani (1457–1530), became famous for their penances, austerity and holiness, as well as for their reported prophetic gifts and messages from God. While some, like Lucretia de León (b.1568), relayed information with a decidedly political content, most of the others gave spiritual advice to lay and religious persons, or advice on activities that might result in the improvement of religious life and institutions, like Paola Antonia Negri (1508–1555), Chiara Bugni (1471–1514) and Osanna Andreasi (1449–1505). Unlike many of their medieval counterparts, they pursued charitable work in the world rather than in an isolated monastic setting. They also served as a focus of attention, and even civic pride, for the citizens of the town or region in which they lived and experienced their heavenly favors.[19]

The activity of this multifaceted reform effort culminated in the decrees of the Council of Trent. With its principal goals the clarification of dogma and the reform of clerical behavior, this council met in sessions stretching over three basic periods: 1545–1547, 1551–1552, and 1562–1563. A compromise between Charles V, who wanted to see clerical reform discussed and laid down first, and Paul III, who wished doctrinal definition to take precedence, gave the decrees their particular structure. For each substantive session or subdivision within the published decrees, first a particular doctrine (justification, for example) was stated, and then teaching on the reform issues ostensibly related to it (episcopal residence, for example). As a result of the sometimes heated discussions, the medieval doctrinal lack of clarity that stood in part behind Luther's theological challenge disintegrated, and the fathers gathered at Trent revived and buttressed the powers of individual bishops that had been subverted through generations of nonresidence and privileges bestowed upon religious orders and cathedral chapters. In the process, they provided efficient and more centralized church government. The order established at Trent, no matter how hard the fathers attempted to assert its traditional, patristic history, remained "new," if only from the perspective of the recent, unreformed past. It became the fundamental structure of the institutional Catholic church until Vatican Council II (1962–1965). Perhaps the best proof of the novelty of the Tridentine formulations was the long process of implementation required to create such dramatic change as the establishment of a seminary for the education of clergy in every diocese, to mention just one of Trent's orders.[20]

Wide-ranging missionary activity disseminated the Catholic religious revival of this period. Like the confraternities, this activity also represented a vehicle for persons to engage in the active life and to imitate Christians of the apostolic era. Like the religious wars, it provided an outlet for millennialist dreams, as most medieval prophecy, at least from the era of Joachim of Fiore (1135–1202), included the conviction that the whole world would be converted to Christianity just prior to a millennium of peace and the second coming of Christ. Still, zeal and the desire to act heroically in the service of God infused the members of religious orders and congregations who devoted themselves to this work. Initial activities organized by the Spanish and Portuguese crowns, and the explorers who worked for them early in the sixteenth century, stood upon rights of patronage granted by the papacy for the nomination of persons to sees and benefices in the New World. Massive, superficial conversions and baptisms followed, as those rights were abused. Increasingly, individual religious orders, like the Jesuits, came to direct missionary activity in the sixteenth century, although that arrangement also generated problems. Rivalry between the orders and disagreements over missionary policies ensued. Perhaps the most famous example involved Jesuit missions in the East, as Roberto de Nobili (1577–1656) and Matteo Ricci (1552–1610) revised the approach of the famous Francis Xavier (1506–1552) and adapted themselves to the cultures of the persons they sought to convert (in India and China, respectively) in order to gain more lasting success. When Ricci approved continued "honoring" of ancestors by Chinese Christians, the stage was set for the "Chinese rites" controversy that resulted in withdrawal of the approbation and the demise of the Catholic mission in China. Popes learned a collective lesson from all of this, and eventually a new curial administrative body, the Congregation for the Propagation of the Faith, coordinated the activity, beginning in 1622. The body pursued a goal quite different from the royal houses that initially led the process: to

13

develop an indigenous Christianity rather than a transplanted European one. The congregation based the plan upon central, Roman control of all missions, colleges for the training of missionaries and recruitment of native clergy.[21]

All of this action found justification in the humanist methodology and outlook derived from both Italian and northern European practitioners in the fifteenth and sixteenth centuries, a method and outlook adopted by the contemporary papacy. It was only with appeal to a more authentic, ancient Christianity, after all, that religious enthusiasts of the Tridentine era could support rejection of medieval precedents that had encouraged church corruption. It was one of the princes of Renaissance culture, Francesco Petrarca, who could provide a model for pursuit of a more direct, personal affiliation with God, the goal of so many in the sixteenth century. In the *Secretum*, while examining his apparently paralyzing self-doubt over the value of learning and literary prominence, Petrarca mentally engaged the ghost of Augustine, whom this age considered just as "ancient" (and hence, authoritative) an author as Cicero. Desiderius Erasmus (1469–1536), the leading figure among northern humanists, had promoted a similar piety based upon northern European spiritual classics like the *Imitation of Christ* and his own pursuit of Christian truth through philological analysis of the Scriptures. An important connection between "popular" and "elite" cultures was made on the basis of the study of Scripture by both clerics and lay persons, and it flourished, at least for a time, in the early-sixteenth century Viterbo circle of Reginald Pole. That center and its members later sustained attack, but an attack motivated by the person and outlook of Pope Paul IV, a man whose interest in humanism and its utilization by the church declined dramatically as his career progressed. The reading of Scripture and the Latin Church Fathers, plus the recovery of the writings of the Greek Church Fathers by clerics in Italy, all utilizing humanist philology, contributed to more than just a general rethinking of medieval theology. It also led to whole new schools of interpretation, like the one centered on the concept of restoration of human nature that was favored by the Benedictines of Santa Giustina of Padua. It also provided the raw material for the deliberations at Trent and the decrees that emanated from them.[22]

Lest the Tridentine Reformation be seen unilaterally as one of purely positive, revivalist development and progress, it is important to recognize the excesses and degenerative elements of the movement. Along with a more efficient and more highly organized form of ecclesiastical government, Tridentine reformers created bureaucracies that at times took on lives of their own and could be manipulated by influential persons. The two most notoriously repressive institutions in the Catholic administration, the congregation organized to draft the *Index of Prohibited Books* and the Roman inquisition, are perfect examples. The congregation of the inquisition first drafted an *Index* to be published under Roman authority in 1557. This reflected the doctrinal uncertainty of the period, as well as the local nature of indexes created and published earlier in specific territories. It repeated, for example, condemnations from earlier Parisian, Spanish, Venetian and Milanese lists. In 1558 and 1559, Paul IV dominated the congregation, and in 1559 it produced a much broader *Index*, with many more "first class" condemnations that proscribed the complete writings of a particular author. The document he influenced also issued broad condemnations against many printers: viewing sixty-one of them as disseminators of heresy, Paul sought to effect a complete boycott of all their publications, no matter who the author or what the subject. That kind of action generated such opposition that Paul's successor, Pius IV, gave the job to a larger committee, more representative of the church at large, which modified and radically toned down the earlier list in an *Index* published in 1564.[23]

The Roman inquisition had a similar history in this period. Recreating it in 1542 to unify action against Protestantism taken by local Italian tribunals, Paul III apparently intended that it operate in a cautious manner that some historians have even described as "mild," especially in relation to the Spanish inquisition of the same period. When Paul IV became pope, however, he steered the tribunal toward investigations motivated more by his personal animosities and his own definition of orthodoxy. He pursued investigations of two prominent members of the college of cardinals, Reginald Pole and Giovanni Morone. Morone underwent trial and a lengthy imprisonment, while Pole seemed to avoid these only through his absence from Rome and his death in 1558. Those actions, as well as Paul's manipulation of the *Index* and the violent intolerance he exhibited toward the Jewish community in Rome, along with his failure to pursue any continuation of the Council of Trent, so distinguished and distanced him from his immediate predecessors and successors as to establish him as an exception to the Tridentine movement. His bold nepotism and disastrous military escapades against Spain provoked the opposition of many members of the hierarchy. They also provoked the rage of a Roman mob, which attacked the symbols of his administration—the palace which housed his inquisition and his self-erected statue on the Quirinale—upon news of his death in 1559. The Roman inquisition maintained similar policies only during the pontificate of a man who originally served as

Paul's hand-picked successor in the administration of the tribunal, Antonio Ghislieri (Pius V, 1566–1572).[24]

In its later history, the court provided further evidence of the corruption inherently possible, if not always actual, in Roman curial bureaucracies. The persecution of Galileo Galilei (1564–1642) revolved around the jealousy of his academic rivals at least as much as it did around matters of theology and scriptural interpretation. Seeking to discredit him intellectually, they chose the method which promised greatest success in the seventeenth century—the accusation of heresy. They used their influence with bureaucrats working for the Roman tribunal in order to secure the investigation of Galileo, and ultimately, his public abjuration of the "errors" of Copernicanism. The physicist's second trial in 1633, which turned on a piece of unverifiable, probably forged evidence, and which was marked by the refusal of three judges to sign the sentence, constituted proof of two things: that his enemies would stop at nothing; and that unwarranted procedures by the tribunal, even if explicit "condemnation" were avoided (as in this case), were no more acceptable to everyone in 1633 than in 1558.[25]

Further evidence suggesting that the Tridentine Reformation was something other than a uniformly positive and popular movement comes from the history of its implementation. It was extraordinarily difficult to create and sustain the institutions necessary to undertake the dramatic changes necessitated by the decrees of the Council of Trent. Members of the hierarchy faced an even greater challenge in the effort to change ways of thinking about elements in ecclesiastical organization as basic as the episcopacy and priesthood. The first of the challenges can even be understood in economic terms that are simple and obvious: the seemingly innumerable poor dioceses of western Europe were hard put to create just the buildings, let alone faculties, for the seminaries required by the decrees. Less obvious, but no less real, was the challenge inherent in changing minds: encouraging clerical office holders, some of whom were members of families who had possessed them for generations, to begin looking at those offices as opportunities for service rather than as portions of a family patrimony to be protected.[26]

THE THEATINE ORDER

The Theatines and their spirituality are right at the heart of the debate over the actual or presumed existence of "Catholic Reform," "Counter-Reformation" and "Tridentine Reformation," for they stood simultaneously at the culmination of a long medieval tradition and at the birth of a new religious age in the history of western culture.

The importance of the order for this issue in the history of western Christianity can be clearly seen in the circumstances of its foundation. Four members of the Roman branch of the Oratory of Divine Love— Gaetano da Thiene, Gian Pietro Carafa, Bonifacio de' Colli (d. 1558) and Paolo Ghislieri (1499–1557)—came together to create the organization in 1524. Their common convictions, inspiration and original goals derived from one of the first institutions dedicated to promotion of ecclesiastical renewal among laypersons and clerics through return to ancient Christian models derived from both traditional and scriptural sources. They perceived their new organization as one dedicated to both their own individual sanctification and the service of others through active, Christian charity. The group at its origin, therefore, had everything in common with late-medieval religiosity. Groups like the fourteenth- and fifteenth-century *disciplinati* had earlier sought the appeasement of God's wrath over the sins of society through self-imposed penances and extreme mortifications. The "observant" Franciscan movement, embodied in persons like Bernardino da Feltre (d. 1494), also urged rigorous self-discipline. Medieval confraternities sought to put revived religious determination at the service of the needy through charitable activity.

The Oratory, from which the Theatines sprang, reflected all of this. Its original inspiration was focused on work undertaken on behalf of the sick, following the example of Catherine of Genoa, as understood by her disciple, Ettore Vernazza. Her own asceticism and the gift she had allegedly received through "divine love"—a vision of Christ's passion—helped to drive not just the members' view of the importance of service to others, but also their idea of the need for penance in a sinful society that endured punishment through incomprehensible, "incurable" illnesses. The mystifying *mal francese*, or syphilis, whose very contagion was only imperfectly understood, now ranked alongside recurrent episodes of the plague as a prime example of the wrath of God. In seeking to answer the needs of those afflicted while simultaneously contributing to the salvation of its members the Oratory, and the Theatines that emerged from it, had a good deal in common with the other new Catholic religious orders of the period, like the Barnabites, Ursulines, Somascans, Jesuits and Oratorians. The Oratory and the Theatines were also institutions whose early development spanned the traditionally supposed dividing line between "Catholic Reform" and "Counter-Reformation" in 1542.

Members of the Oratory of Divine Love, first founded in Genoa in

INTRODUCTION

1497 and approved by papal legislation in 1514, became famous for their devotions, but especially for their charitable work, despite an intense effort to guard the secrecy of their organization and membership. The Roman branch possessed a broad spectrum of members, including both laymen and clerics. There was even a group of women with close ties to its work, headed by Angela Merici. These later became the backbone of the Ursuline order. When Vernazza helped to form the Roman branch sometime between 1514 and 1517, the undertaking must have made perfect sense both to him and to those who knew him in Rome. As the capital city of a now worldwide Christianity, it was a magnet for Christians both inside and outside Italy. Many of them arrived seeking employment and a better way of life but found neither. As a result, they required, or at least sought, charitable assistance from ecclesiastical persons and organizations. Work for the amelioration of their condition through assistance was justified by those persons and institutions with the phrase "for the love of God." Miraculous compounding of charitable resources was even attributed to the new Oratory, and it had a lasting significance for two reasons. First, it served the sixteenth-century contribution to the development of organized welfare, and second, it also nurtured the religious sensibilities of persons who later became prominent in the Tridentine Reformation. Gian Matteo Giberti, Luigi Lippomano (1500–1559) and Gasparo Contarini, in addition to Gaetano and Carafa, were among its members. But historians have most often tied the significance of the Roman Oratory to its role as the inspiration of the Theatine order. This came about mainly through two members of the confraternity, Gaetano da Thiene and Gian Pietro Carafa.[27]

Gaetano da Thiene is the lesser known of the two. Born in Vicenza in 1480, he was named after an uncle who was a prominent professor of philosophy and theology at the University of Padua. Gaetano grew up in not only a well-educated, but also a pious, noble family. He received his early education at the hands of his father, Gaspare, in accord with standard noble practice in early-modern Italy. When Gaspare died, his wife, Maria da Porto, assumed tutelage of Gaetano and his two brothers. She and the boys frequented the Dominican church of S. Corona, and she endowed the attached convent with a portion of her dowry. She apparently decided on an intellectual career for Gaetano, as he studied philosophy and law at Padua. He received degrees there in both civil and canon law in 1505, and among his fellow students were persons who went on to prominence in the Roman church, like Gasparo Contarini and Paolo Giustiniani. Gaetano then began his own pursuit of an ecclesiastical career by taking up residence in Rome. He purchased the office of *scrittore* (scribe or writer) of apostolic letters in 1508, during the administration of Julius II (1503–1513). Julius favored him with parish benefices in the diocese of Vicenza, and he eventually became apostolic notary. He spent the next ten years, arguably the height of Renaissance culture in Rome, as an employee of the papal curia.[28]

The years 1516 and 1517 were ones that dramatically changed Gaetano's life. In late September 1516, he passed through the minor clerical orders, then the subdeaconate and the deaconate, and finally received ordination as a priest at the hands of François Berthelay, who served as titular bishop of Milopotamos (Crete) between 1499 and 1538. Gaetano did this against the wishes of his mother, because as the only surviving of her three sons, it was his duty to protect the patrimony and interests of the family. As seems to have been customary in this period among new priests with a fervent devotional life, he delayed the celebration of his first Mass considerably, until the feast of the Epiphany (6 January), 1517. He said that Mass at the altar of the manger in the Roman basilica of S. Maria Maggiore. He experienced a vision there on Christmas day, 1517, that he related in one of his letters.[29] Either late in 1516 or early in 1517, he also decided to join the Roman Oratory, then forming at the church of Ss. Sylvestro e Dorothea in Trastevere, and became one of its most active members. In March 1517, Gaetano met the Brescian cleric Bartolomeo Stella (1488–1554), whom he brought into the Oratory, and through whom he heard of the Brescian nun Laura Mignani (1480–1525). Stella had come to Rome as procurator of the convent in which she lived, and later, upon his return to Brescia, he founded both another Oratory cell and a hospital for incurables. After speaking with Stella about her, Gaetano entered into correspondence with the nun, and the two exchanged letters between 1517 and 1521. The letters of Gaetano are all that survives of this correspondence, but they contain evidence of a rich relationship of mutual spiritual direction.[30]

In 1518, Gaetano left Rome, not to return for any length of time until 1523. Over the course of these years, he certainly visited Vicenza, Verona and Venice, and perhaps Brescia. He departed Rome in April for Vicenza, to visit his ailing mother, who probably died in 1520. While there, he joined another branch of the Oratory, the company of S. Girolamo. Epistolary evidence indicates that he desired to go to Brescia in order to meet and consult with Mignani, and he may have done so in the fall of 1518. In 1519, he found himself briefly in Verona, where he became a member of the company of the Most Holy Sacrament and helped to revise its governance statutes. The group was linked to the Oratory cell in Vicenza, to which he returned in the same year.

In Vicenza, Gaetano placed himself under the spiritual direction of Battista Carioni da Crema (c.1460–1534), a Dominican in the convent Maria da Porto endowed. In 1533, Battista helped Antonio Maria Zaccaria to found the Barnabites (so called because of their center at the monastery of S. Barnaba in Milan), but he attained his real prominence as the prolific author of treatises on devotional topics like confession, communion and control of the passions. He took a rather practical approach to the spiritual life, focusing on the struggle of the Christian against the enemies of vice and concupiscence. He can be considered one of the first to formulate and express the idea of spiritual combat, which became so generally characteristic of Italian spirituality in the sixteenth century and of Theatine spirituality in particular. The followers he encouraged and the apparently excessive mortifications he undertook aroused suspicion on the part of some Dominicans, but an inquisitorial trial against him in Milan in 1530 resulted in his vindication. Battista's ideas and their interpretation by later followers, like Paola Antonia Negri, eventually resulted in the condemnation of his writings in 1552, after his death. From him, Gaetano adopted the practice of more frequent communion and learned of the teachings of John Cassian (c. 365–c. 435) concerning monastic organization.[31]

Gaetano made a final trip prior to his return to Rome, this time to Venice. He went there in 1522 at the suggestion of Battista and founded another hospital for incurables. He seemed disappointed by the lack of religious zeal he detected in the Venetian population, and he returned to Rome toward the end of that same year. Back at the Roman Oratory and the hospital affiliated with it, he probably first met Bonifacio de' Colli, who became one of the four founders of the Theatine order, in 1524.

Along with Gaetano, the other major figure in the foundation was Gian Pietro Carafa. The fact that he served as Pope Paul IV would be reason enough for him to be more widely known than Gaetano, but the self-assurance and violent nature of this man, to whom words like "hot-blooded," "volcanic" and "intransigent" are most often applied, cinched his place in history. Carafa was born in 1476 in Carpriglio, in the region of Abruzzi. He displayed the beginnings of his fervent religiosity at age fourteen, when he attempted to enter the Dominican convent of S. Domenico Maggiore in Naples. He and his older sister Maria (1468–1552) had hatched a plot to run away from home and enter religious life, but only she was successful. After a humanistic education typical of Italian nobles in the Renaissance, he became an equally typical Renaissance churchman. Promoted through the good offices of his uncle, Oliviero Carafa (d. 1511), the cardinal bishop of Chieti, he served in the curia of Alexander VI, and, in 1505, succeeded his uncle in that Abruzzi diocese which had virtually become Carafa family property. He travelled as legate to England and later to Spain during the pontificate of Leo X. He became famous for his humanism, zeal and devotion during those journeys, earning even the praise of Desiderius Erasmus. He returned to Rome in 1520, at which time he may have joined the Oratory, although the precise date of his initiation is uncertain. After visits between December 1521 and August 1522 to Chieti and to Brindisi, another diocese to which he was appointed, Carafa voiced insistent calls for clerical reform during the reign of Clement VII. He bound himself with the other three in the Theatine foundation in order to do something concrete about the need for the reform he considered so urgent.

There exists no clear indication of how these two, Gaetano and Carafa, plus Bonifacio de' Colli and Paolo Consiglieri actually first met and developed the idea of establishing a new order. Older studies tend to attribute the conception of the idea to Gaetano and Bonifacio, although it is improbable that the two met before 1524. At any rate, they decided to create a group of "clerics regular" in imitation of a Christian practice considered "ancient" in their day: the common life established for the clergy in the diocese of Hippo by St. Augustine in the fifth century. A life of intense pastoral and charitable work, as well as an equally intense interior spirituality, they believed, would help to counteract the intellectual and moral decay common in the contemporary clergy.

Like other institutions promoting religious renewal in the period, the four sought papal approbation. They did not receive it, however, until after considerable difficulties over the financial resources of the founders and how they would be used were resolved. In an audience with Clement VII on 3 May 1524, it became clear that Carafa would be required to give up his bishoprics in order to participate in the foundation. Gaetano had foreseen this problem and apparently recognized how difficult any such renunciation would be under the circumstances of Carafa's career and the expectations of his family at large. Gaetano was impressed with the prelate's willingness to renounce these possessions and his tenacious determination to carry out the plan, but remained unconvinced that in the long run it could end the worldly ambitions of Carafa. Gaetano may have sensed that Carafa wished to control the shape of the new foundation. His continuing worries over Carafa's curial prominence are evident in the letters he wrote to the prelate's sister much later.[32] Carafa renounced the bishoprics into the hands of the pope, who allowed him to retain his episcopal status and the pontifical faculties associated with it, such as the authority to ordain priests.

Gaetano faced similar problems of his own, as he still held the curial office of *scrittore apostolico* in 1524. He decided to resign from it, but the new holder, a cleric from Cambrai, paid him for the office. These facts clearly indicate the tenacity with which the view of church office as property was held; even a dedicated "reformer" like Gaetano was unable to see past what he must have viewed as the recovery of his original capital to the implicit simony represented in the transaction. Neither did the founders appear to grasp the irony of the history of a new foundation dedicated to the reform of clerical abuses commencing with a dispensation like that accorded to Carafa. The funds that accrued to Gaetano through his office, as well as the proceeds from the sale of the founders' other possessions, came to enrich the new congregation.[33]

Final papal approbation in 1524 came only after still other questions were raised by curialists attempting to block the foundation. Members of the papal curia always exerted considerable influence over the decisions concerning new and established religious orders. Even though in 1524 the curia contained some cardinals in favor of the push for reform, there was also a strong faction opposed to any change whatever in the status quo. Among the leaders of this latter group was Cardinal Lorenzo Pucci (+1531), head of the curial office known as the Penitentiary, a papal tribunal established in the fourteenth century that adjudicated matters of conscience and controlled the granting of indulgences. A multiple benefice holder himself, he vigorously opposed Clement's interest in the Theatines, and would likely have thwarted the plans of the four altogether, if it had not been for the intervention of another curialist, Gian Matteo Giberti. Giberti had served Clement even before his papal election. In 1524 he held the lucrative and responsible position of Datary, at the head of the administrative body that conferred benefices and controlled dispensations from excommunication. In a letter he wrote in 1533, Carafa indicated that it was Giberti's urgent advocacy that secured papal approbation in the brief *Exponi nobis*, dated 24 June 1524.[34]

In the brief, Clement suggested that he was consciously creating a new form of religious life, that of "clerics regular." The members received authorization to take vows of poverty, chastity and obedience, and to live a common life in either a "religious" place (i.e., a monastery) or in a "secular" one (i.e., a private house). They gained permission to elect their own superiors for three-year terms, and rather than reporting to the bishop of the diocese in which they lived, they were placed under the immediate supervision of the papacy. Through the brief, Clement also empowered the members to draft constitutions to govern their conduct, devotion and common life, with the understanding that none of these would contradict canon law, but would rather reflect a reformed, corrected version of what was then considered "religious" life. In addition, Clement clearly recognized one of the primary intentions of the four: to first reform clerics generally and then, through these, to revive the religious devotion of Christians at large. This last point he underlined in a passage permitting them to receive as novices either lay persons or secular clerics who were inspired by God toward the Theatine common life.[35]

Later that same year, the four founders began to carry out the brief and utilize the privileges extended. On 14 September they gathered early in the morning in St. Peter's basilica and heard Mass in the chapel of St. Andrew, said by a papal representative and notary, Giovanni Battista Bonciani (+1532), the bishop of Caserta. After communion, they moved to the main altar, where Bonciani read *Exponi nobis* aloud and received the vows of the four members. They stepped aside from the altar and chose Carafa as their first *preposito* (superior general), and Bonciani ratified the vows and election. Carafa held the office of superior until 1527, being reelected in the two succeeding "general congregation" meetings they began to hold on each anniversary of the vows that represented their foundation. They took up residence in the house of Bonifacio, worked as priests in a local church, continued to labor at San Giacomo (the Roman hospital for incurables) and still frequented the meetings of the Oratory. They received their first novices, Bernardino Scotti, Girolamo Consiglieri and Andrea Verso, in the spring of 1525, as well as five others soon thereafter.[36]

The original members, strangely, never exercised their power to draft a formal set of constitutions. Here, the Theatines represent a departure from traditional practice. Founders of other institutions tended to write rules of their own, though sometimes against their will, as in the case of Francis of Assisi in the early thirteenth century. Still other founders took up rules already in existence, as did the Cistercians, who adopted rigorous Benedictinism in the early twelfth century. The most recent analyst of the early Theatines attributes their failure to construct a rule to a decision to retain their common background in the Oratory and to rely upon the continuing direction of their own superiors. There is no direct evidence, however, to confirm this thesis.[37] Although formal Theatine constitutions were published only in 1628, a document considered the "original" rule of the group does exist. It was likely composed by Carafa between 1525 and

1526. Here, he described the practices of the early members, a description that came to be included in a letter sent by Bonifacio to Gian Matteo Giberti.

The document contains few absolute decrees beyond the assertion that none of the Theatine practices was to be taken as a precept binding the conscience. The major rule for prayer was to recite the divine office and to celebrate Mass according to the practices of the Roman church. In regard to fasts, members similarly were to follow scrupulously those prescribed by the church. Restrictions on leaving the house seemed important to Carafa, who indicated that members who did so must pray beforehand, seek the permission of the superior, and always go with a companion. They possessed no distinctive habit, but they did maintain an unusual understanding of the vow of poverty. In Carafa's view, poverty did not exclude the holding of annual ecclesiastical incomes, although they were to be held "in common." If he intended to give any priority to specific items, they probably were two: strict preliminary testing for new members, and the importance of obedience and self-denial for all. Novices were not even admitted to probation without a two- or three-year preparation and testing period, and admission required the unanimous consent of the membership, meeting in general chapter. Obedience seemed to be, for Carafa, the key to self-mastery and to the goal of charitable assistance toward others. He stressed this point by utilizing the image of the passion contained in Christ's admonition, "If anyone wishes to come after me, let him deny himself and take up his cross and follow me." These latter themes— obedience, self-mastery, self-denial and imitation of Christ in his passion— recur frequently in Theatine devotional writings.[38]

Little more is known of the group as it continued its activities in the city until the infamous "Sack of Rome" in early May 1527. Clement VII fled the German and Spanish troops and took refuge in Castel Sant'Angelo, in which he became a prisoner for some seven months. The Theatines remained in the city from the beginning of the sack on 6 May until 25 May, and they endured two separate attacks, one by German soldiers and the other by Spanish troops. Gaetano apparently received the worst treatment of any of them, tortured in an attempt to force him to turn over money the soldiers believed they were hiding. How Carafa, whose wealth logically would have been the principal target of the attack, escaped torture is not known. On 25 May, some unknown individual provided them with a boat and the safe conduct necessary for escape through the papal port of Civitavecchia. They proceeded to Venice, undoubtedly grateful to be alive.[39]

INTRODUCTION

In Venice, their work changed little. They received use of the church and residence of S. Nicola da Tolentino from Venetian civic authorities, formed an Oratory and worked at a hospital for incurables. They promoted eucharistic devotions and remained exceedingly cautious about the admission of new members. They held a second general chapter in Venice during September 1527, and Gaetano became the new *preposito*. The records of this and the other early Theatine chapters tell us little, as they consist of summaries apparently put together after the fact, thus seeming to reflect continued determination to maintain relative secrecy about the organization, as in the Oratory. The members also continued their close association with Gian Matteo Giberti, who, after accompanying Clement VII in his imprisonment, returned to his assigned diocese of Verona to become one of the Tridentine models for episcopal residence. A Theatine house was even established in Verona, but it lasted only a short time.

Venetian residency brought the Theatines into contact with still other persons interested in ecclesiastical reform. They maintained contact with Pietro Lippomano (bishop of Bergamo, 1517–1548), to whom Gasparo Contarini had addressed his famous text on the episcopal office entitled *De officio viri boni ac probi episcopi* (1517). Gaetano exchanged letters with and provided spiritual guidance to a cell of the Oratory in Salò, on Lake Garda in the diocese of Brescia, founded by Stefano Bertacciolo and his cousins Giambattista and Bartolomeo Scaini. He and Carafa did the same for a cell in Padua. The Theatines encountered the prominent poet Marcantonio Flaminio (1498–1550) through their association with Giberti, and Flaminio, impressed with their devotion and religiosity, eventually sought admission to the order, albeit in vain. In these years, Carafa also encouraged the Venetian patrician Girolamo Miani (or Emiliani) in his dedication to the service of orphans and abandoned children. Miani's work in the 1530s is generally considered the beginning of another group of "clerics regular," known as the Somascans.[40]

Venetian residency in the 1530s was of crucial importance to the history of the group in another way: it brought the first Theatine contacts with heterodoxy. Here again, Carafa held the preeminent position. Early in 1530, he took up the duties associated with the trial of a conventual Franciscan and suspected heretic, Girolamo Galateo (c.1490–1541), at the request of the papal nuncio, Altobello Averoldo (+1531, bishop of Poli 1497–1514). Carafa issued a condemnation after the conclusion of the trial in Padova, on 16 January, but Venetian authorities refused to carry out the execution and Galateo died in prison. The Theatine bishop received high praise from Clement VII for his handling of the matter. Carafa apparently became increasingly concerned with this sort of anti-heretical, pro-Roman activity, demonstrating this in his 1532 memorandum to Clement. Citing the earlier work against Galateo, he indicated intense hatred of heresy and those he considered responsible for its spread, "apostates and conventual friars." He urged the pope to "shake up the ordinaries" and send a legate who would "punish or at least put to flight the wicked heretics." He also expressed his belief that books and popular preaching, both so common-place in early-modern Italian cities, especially Venice, were the main vehicles for dissemination of heresy. One could argue that all of this focus and the increasing vehemence with which Carafa pursued it, and for which he became famous, sprang from the central Theatine goal of improving clerical behavior. There can be no doubt, however, that the experience of the sack and then of urban life in Venice profoundly affected Carafa's view of what the Roman church needed. Indeed, his later career as inquisitor and as pope-inquisitor is inexplicable without consideration of those influences. Other Theatines also played influential roles in the history of inquisitions in this period, but it cannot be said that they typically dominated such institutions.[41]

At about the same time, Carafa secured a number of papal privileges for the order and received a second term as *preposito*. The papal concessions of 1529 were concerned with celebration of the Mass and the divine office in Theatine houses, as well as a general permission for Theatines to preach. Under certain circumstances, specifically when engaged in extensive charitable works and during illness, the general was given permission to allow abbreviation of the divine office. After Carafa's new election as general in September 1530, additional favors were decreed. On 10 February 1533, Clement gave an extended dispensation from the office and a general permission for Theatine priests to hear confessions and grant absolutions, even of sins typically reserved to pontifical authority. A separate brief on 7 March 1533 confirmed the earlier foundation of the order and all the recently acquired privileges. Although he solicited and received the assistance of Giberti in procuring the concessions, Carafa proved quite proficient in gaining them, even over the continued opposition of influential curial administrators like Pucci.[42]

The Theatines grew in numbers and spread geographically, although not rapidly. Clement requested the establishment of a house in Naples, one that became, after Rome, their most important headquarters. Gaetano and another member, Giovanni Marinoni (b. 1490) arrived there at the end of September 1533, and they were successful in setting up a residence. In that city they worked at a hospital for incurables, encouraged devotion to the nativity of Christ, and initiated Theatine contact with Carafa's sister, Maria, who had left her Franciscan convent with some other nuns to adopt a stricter rule. Gaetano also came into contact with the Neapolitan circle that gathered around Juan de Valdés and included the Capuchin Bernardino Ochino. Gaetano is credited with being among the first to identify and expose their heresy. The Neapolitan Theatines obtained possession of the church that is still their southern headquarters, S. Paolo Maggiore, in May 1538. This house, plus the Venetian one, were the only Theatine establishments until well after the death of Gaetano in 1547. Later houses were established in Rome (1555), Padua and Cremona (1565), Piacenza (1569) and Milan (1570). Over the next century, their numbers grew to about a thousand members.[43]

During the sixteenth and seventeenth centuries, Theatines operated in close collaboration with the Roman hierarchy on a variety of different projects. Briefs by Clement VII in 1529 empowering Carafa to conduct visitations of monasteries in Vicenza could perhaps be considered the beginning of direct papal sponsorship of Theatine clerical reform. The focus of the order shifted gradually and steadily toward Rome, as Carafa was called there in 1536 to participate in the group that drafted the famous reform proposal known as the *Consilium de emendanda ecclesia*. He was promoted to the college of cardinals late in the same year. The establishment of a Theatine house in Rome and the election of Carafa as Pope Paul IV, both in 1555, cemented the relationship among the order, the city and the curia. Paul assigned them the church of S. Silvestro al Quirinale, which became their central headquarters. During the pontificates of Pius V, Sixtus V and Clement VIII, Theatines were active in the revision and re-edition of the Roman breviary and missal, as well as the Vulgate edition of the Bible. One of them, Paolo Burali d'Arezzo (1511–1578), undertook distinguished service in the early process of implementation of the decrees of Trent under Gregory XIII, first as bishop of Piacenza and later as cardinal archbishop of Naples.[44]

The Theatines' link with the Roman hierarchy also expanded through their activity as bishops. Two members besides Carafa and Burali received episcopal appointments in the early history of the order. Thomas Goldwell, the first member of English origin, became the bishop of St. Asaph in Wales in 1553, and Bernardino Scotti became the bishop of Trani in 1555. The trend of Theatine appointments continued and expanded dramatically in the seventeenth century, to such an extent that Ludwig von Pastor referred to the new order as a "seminary" for bishops. This is a strange conclusion, especially considering the fact that the Theatines set up no seminary at all in this period, not even an educational establishment for the formation and priestly training of their own members. Still, these early and continuing appointments constitute one of the reasons why Theatines shifted their apostolic activities from a beginning in continuity with the tradition of the Oratory at the service of the sick poor to far more general parochial and pastoral activities, in concert with the Roman hierarchy, throughout Italy, Germany, Austria and Spain in the sixteenth and seventeenth centuries. It seems that any significance the Theatines held for the revision and improvement of early-modern clerical practices must have come not from the creation of any formal or informal "seminary," but from their reputation for holiness and devotion to personal reform and the promotion of the same in others through parish work. That was the main reason popes increasingly chose them to serve in episcopal administration. There remains, nonetheless, something of a contradiction here. The expansion of the work of Theatines as bishops suggests that, as time went on, members no longer considered commitment to episcopal administration and the privileges and income derived therefrom as contrary to their original ideals. This change represents a break from the way Gaetano viewed such office in 1524 and even later, when he expressed uneasiness over the offices and ecclesiastical honors received by Carafa.[45]

In these centuries as well, Theatines participated in the growing missionary activity of the Roman church. Members held important offices in the Collegio Urbano di Propaganda Fide (founded by Urban VIII for the education of missionaries), including Marco Romano delle Grottaglie, who served as the first rector of the college. The Congregation for the Propagation of the Faith authorized the sending of Theatine missionaries to Georgia in the Caucasus in 1626. They took vows to remain there for ten years and successfully worked to return a number of schismatic Christian leaders to the Roman faith. Four Theatine missionaries went to India in 1640, and their successors helped to open a seminary for the training of indigenous clergy in Goa in 1721. Theatines were sent to Borneo in 1692, again by the Congregation for the Propagation of the Faith, although that mission produced only mixed results. Theatines served in other portions of the Indian archipelago later in the eighteenth century, including Sumatra and Java.[46]

Toward the end of the eighteenth century, the order experienced decline, like so many other religious institutions in the period, but the group has survived into the twentieth century, maintaining its headquarters in Rome. Their motto comes from Matthew 6:33—"Quaerite [ergo] primum Regnum Dei" ("Seek first the Kingdom of God").[47] They remain a rather small order, with approximately two hundred members. The Theatines have one location in the United States, in Denver, Colorado, where they staff St. Cajetan's Parish and maintain a novitiate and seminary. The name of the order, "Theatine," derives from the nickname "Teatino" or "Chietino," which they received in the sixteenth century, a name referring to the bishopric of Chieti in southern Italy held by Carafa. The name thus highlights his influence on the order and its first members. Although Carafa's role undoubtedly was crucial, the relative permanence of the institution and its survival into the modern period are at least as much the result of its distinctive spirituality, as developed by other early Theatines, specifically Gaetano da Thiene and Lorenzo Scupoli (c. 1530–1610).

GAETANO DA THIENE AND HIS *LETTERS*

Over the course of their history as a religious order, Theatines have led an active literary life, producing and publishing works on a variety of topics, from works of history, philosophy, mathematics and academic theology to collections of sermons, prayers and other devotional tracts.[48] Certainly none is closer, chronologically, to the origin of the order than the *Letters* of Gaetano. Most of the original manuscripts are venerated, both as relics, because they were drafted by a canonized saint, and because of the significance of their message. They are also close to the origin of the order in another way: they represent clearly both the influences that shaped Theatine history and those that motivated its unique activity in the life of the Roman church.

The documents by Gaetano that I have translated consist mainly of letters, plus a brief summary of directions for the spiritual life and a prayer. Gaetano composed them between 1517 and 1547. I have selected these from the critical edition produced by the Theatine historian Francesco Andreu, *Le lettere di San Gaetano da Thiene*, Studi e testi, #177 (Vatican City, 1954). I have chosen to omit a few letters because they seem unrelated to spirituality. (Three others omitted are notarial documents relating to Gaetano's alienation of his patrimony and his decision to turn over certain property to his cousins. These documents come from the period in which his religious fervor was growing and he became increasingly concerned with religious poverty.)

Gaetano addressed his letters to a variety of audiences. Theatine historians have generally considered those he wrote to Laura Mignani between 1517 and 1521 to be the most significant and revealing. This is due in part to their relative length in comparison with letters addressed to other correspondents. The shortest letter to Mignani is still about two hundred words, while the longest goes on for some twelve hundred. His letters to others, like Maria Carafa, were at times very brief, sometimes only a sentence or two. Gaetano addressed letters to Mignani as his "spiritual mother" and filled them with references to himself as her son. He seemed even more anxious to cement this relationship after the death of his natural mother in 1520. In a postscript to a letter in which he related the circumstances of her death to Mignani, he begged the other sisters of her convent to "compel [your] mother, sister Laura, to take me as her son, since the soul of my mother has departed."[49] It also seems clear that he looked for her guidance, advice and intercession. He expressed hope that she would experience a closer relationship with Christ in order that the blessing given to her might result in spiritual assistance to him: a set of "running streams" that would "extinguish" his interest in human, earthly matters, so that "everything in the world [might] become bitter" to him.[50] He viewed her as one who had attained that highest of spiritual gifts, status as the "spouse" of Christ, and perhaps with a bit of false humility expressed amazement at her interest in him. "He is husband to you," Gaetano wrote in 1518, adding, "he loves you, while I am His dwelling place and treasurer, and yet you love me. Oh, who can understand this?"[51] He frequently linked such statements to additional appeals for assistance for himself, members of his family and their common friends.

Still, there are passages in some of the letters to Mignani that suggest Gaetano gave her advice, and that perhaps she may even have solicited such from him. In his letter of 28 January 1518, he indicated that he prayed for her every day at Mass, and he expressed concern for her in the context of the apparent death of a relative of one of her other "spiritual sons." He advised her to give up her sorrow in favor of confidence in Christ. "I am certain," he wrote, "that our pleasure and firmness of soul more quickly render thanks to God than our sadness."[52] In 1520 he advised her to be willing to take more concerns of others upon herself out of the desire to imitate Christ, suggesting that she possessed a saintly, almost salvific, power of intercession. "Have in your heart St. Paul and St. Martin," he told her, adding that "you must . . . forget yourself in everything for Jesus Christ, and . . . desire, as I know you have, that all the world may be thrown upon you, so that they may be saved."[53] He even sought Mignani's intercession in embarrassing and desperate circumstances: in one letter he suggested that Bartolomeo Stella had contracted venereal disease in the context of his work on behalf of the *incurabili*.[54] Mignani's side of this correspondence has unfortunately been lost. Only its recovery would fill in the picture of the complex and apparently mutual relationship of spiritual counsel between her and Gaetano.

Among the other addressees of these documents were Elisabetta Porto (his niece) and Paolo Giustiniani (1476–1528), as well as Bartolomeo and Giambattista Scaini, who were members of the confraternity of San Girolamo in Vicenza. Gaetano provided Elisabetta a dowry for her marriage in 1521, and he wrote to her in 1522 as she prepared for childbirth. In what might arguably be the most beautiful prose he wrote, Gaetano advised her to dedicate herself to Mary and Jesus for the health and well-being of both herself and the baby. He drew upon the story of Mary's visit to Elizabeth and encouraged her to seek union with Christ through the intercession of the Virgin and through the sacraments, especially the Eucharist. He told her to urge her husband to do the same, and hoped they would seek the guidance of his own spiritual director, Battista da Crema, in confession.[55] He wrote to Giustiniani, with whom he was a fellow student at Padua, in response to a letter in which Giustiniani apparently indicated that he had heard of Gaetano's good work and devotion. Worried that he could not live up to the characteristics attributed to him by the third party, Gaetano praised Giustiniani's renown at Padua and at Rome, while describing himself as a "miserable soul." Here again he may have been guilty of a little false humility, as he sought the monk's assistance through prayer, but he certainly underlined his belief that a recluse like Giustiniani "remains [in a monastery] in order to help those who are battling in the field."[56]

Bartolomeo and Giambattista Scaini received a number of letters, like others who sought Gaetano's advice. Such correspondents all desired to emulate his work and that of his fellow Theatines. The Scaini brothers were part of the predominantly lay group who sought enhanced individual devotion, charitable activity and radical ecclesiastical reform in the town of Salò, on Lake Garda, in the diocese of Brescia. They even urged the establishment of a Theatine house in the town. Gaetano wrote them five letters between 1529 and 1542. The most interesting and revealing is the first, in which Gaetano discussed what ought to be done about a layman in their number named Bernardo da Todi, who had preached, in violation of canon law, and had been corrected by Carafa. Gaetano expressed uncertainty about the sincerity of his conversion, convinced that the behavior itself was evidence of a dangerous arrogance, and stated, "I believe this poor man is not of the opinion that he is a rebel against the holy Church."

He urged all of the members of the group to bind themselves "with humility to holy Church of Christ," warning Bartolomeo to avoid the temptation to try to understand the message of Christ without any reference to ordained clergy and their teaching. Gaetano also indicated a conviction that this was the reason why "every day we are finding more false messengers of Christ in the world." His defense of clerical leadership was anything but blind, however, as he admitted that part of the reason for the temptation lay in the church itself, for "prostitutes are among its ministers."[57]

Gaetano addressed a substantial portion of this group of documents to Maria Carafa and the other women she lived with in the Neapolitan convent known as the *Sapienza*. Most were letters to Maria, but there was also one written to her niece and fellow nun, Caterina, as well as a summary or compendium on the spiritual life addressed to the full community. Through the intervention of her brother, Maria and some of her colleagues in a Franciscan monastery in the heart of Naples received authorization from Lorenzo Pucci at the Penitentiary to exchange their Franciscan rule and habit for the Dominican. They intended to observe the new rule in the strictest fashion possible. Their foundation was entrusted to the archbishop of Naples and solemnized on 25 June 1530.[58] When Gaetano came to Naples from Venice in 1532, he undertook spiritual direction of the convent. The letters, written between 1533 and 1552, proceed from that relationship.[59]

The contents of these letters range from recommendations for frequent use of the sacraments and information concerning the dates of his upcoming visits to administer the same, to guidance on the problems of individual sisters and a request for a loan for unspecified purposes. Gaetano clearly took on the role of director in this correspondence, and the tone he adopted reflects this. He issued firm correction, for example, over what he viewed as their improper practice of the divine office and the danger implicit in preferential treatment for particular sisters.[60] But his confidence in these women and in their ability to lead the spiritual life is also apparent. He described himself and them "united as one" in a common prison, and encouraged Maria to give comfort to the daughters she had been given by Christ. He seemed to view them as persons engaged in a spiritual struggle identical to his own; he frequently indicated his own failings and encouraged them to the same sort of humility that he apparently sought himself. Expressing his longing for "the beautiful and only true light," he suddenly stopped to say, "I am not suited to raise my eyes to such a light, but rather to cry out upon the earth, . . . 'truly I am dung and not a man.' " He urged Maria to be so humble as not to "attribute even a dot" to herself and asked her to intercede with the Virgin Mary on his behalf "so that she might cover me, with her humility, from the just anger of her son." In one letter, he reminded Maria of her status as a spiritual mother, and explained that such persons "conceive with fear and sorrow and give birth with joy."[61]

GAETANO'S SPIRITUALITY

In these letters Gaetano's character and spirituality, as well as the influences upon him, shine through. Battista da Crema's role is preeminent. Promotion of frequent communion may be the teaching most commonly associated with Battista, but the focus he placed on the absolute necessity of grace, on individual struggle to overcome oneself through humility, and on defeating Satan through spiritual combat is central to the spirituality of Gaetano and the members of the first two Theatine generations. Battista served as his confessor and spiritual director, and Gaetano conveyed what he learned from the Dominican in his letters and other writings.

For example, he recommended the pursuit of humility to virtually all his correspondents, and he made recognition and acceptance of one's place and duties in the religious community the center of his advice to the nuns of the *Sapienza*. Hell can be avoided, he said, "if one does not attain satisfaction of self-will and does not miss Purgatory, thus purging and purifying one's own will."[62] He suggested the difficulty he perceived in the acquisition of worldly influence in his letter informing Maria and her fellow nuns of the promotion of her brother to the college of cardinals. He said they all should try "to comfort him whenever [possible]," so that they might try to "share this weight he has." He expressed his hope that the new cardinal could see beyond the "temporary exaltation," to the "responsibility implied," and eventually "find the eternal reward beyond that burden."[63]

Gaetano even reflected the practicality of Battista, as he identified solutions to some spiritual desires through "worldly" means. His letter of 15 February 1530 contains evidence of this, as he encouraged Bartolomeo Scaini to solicit a major gift from the typographer Paganino Paganini (+1538). He described Paganini as "worn out by the world," and he invited him to come to Venice to set up a printing press that would operate under Theatine direction. One spiritual contribution that could result from this would be the publication of evangelical and anti-heretical literature. In addition, Gaetano suggested, Paganini's monetary contribution and printing activities in Venice could provide a solution to the printer's weariness with the business world. It might also provide work and sustinence for the growing number of persons under the care of the Theatines in Venice.[64]

The second main influence on Gaetano's spirituality was the humanist culture and intellectual methodology of the Renaissance in Italy. He, like many others in this period, turned the pursuit of ancient sources to a Christian devotional purpose, specifically the imitation of Christ as the essence of real, "reformed" Christianity. Long identified in northern Europe with the *devotio moderna*—that is, the Brethren of the Common Life and the devotional texts that emerged from that school—the same theme of imitation can be found in Gaetano and other Italian writers. His focus on Christ is particularly evident in the extensive use he made of Scripture throughout these letters. Gaetano sought the Christ he hoped to emulate through the Gospels, and by alluding to gospel stories familiar to his audiences, recommended the same to them. He most frequently cited three books of the New Testament: the Gospels of Luke, Matthew, and John. It was to Christ as he suffered in the passion, as he taught in parables, as he called persons to follow him and as he rewarded humility that the Theatine most frequently referred.[65]

The spiritual message of Gaetano was above all Christocentric. He stated this most directly in his brief compendium on the spiritual life, apparently addressed to his fellow Theatines, although the date and place of origin of the document are uncertain. "The true and inestimably spiritual delight of men," he wrote, "is to strive after likeness to the heart and person of Jesus, expecting no other prize." He urged them to be willing, like St. Paul before them, to suffer imprisonment and death "for the name of the Lord." He applied this Christocentric approach to more practical matters as well. When explaining his determination to renounce financial concerns and to cede property rights in favor of his cousins, he committed himself to the pursuit of poverty in imitation of Christ. "I see that Christ was poor and I am rich, He reviled and I honored, He in pain and I enjoying delight," Gaetano explained, adding, "I long for still one day before I die to take some step toward Him." That was the reason, he continued, "that I have decided to reduce my possessions and no longer be so rich." Gaetano provided another Christ-centered appeal in his prayer for peace during civil unrest in Naples in 1547. He begged God the Father to "hear the voice of the blood of our brother Jesus," crying out "from the cross," and to grant the Neapolitans his mercy.[66]

INTRODUCTION

Gaetano's spirituality also expressed other traditional themes and imagery. He frequently employed the image of fire as a metaphor descriptive of the love of God and the sort of love he himself hoped to possess for God. In letters to Laura Mignani and Paolo Giustiniani between 1517 and 1523 he used the fire motif in both a positive and a negative sense. Most often, he described the flame as an aspect of divine love that produced the light and ardor necessary for the spiritual prowess that he admired in Mignani. He often contrasted it with the tepidity, or even coldness, of his own response to God. For Gaetano, divine love could also be understood as a "fiery knife" that cut out and simultaneously burned up sin, purifying the soul.[67] He also used the image twice in a strangely opposite, if not contradictory, sense. An "ardent flame" represented to him on one occasion the intensity of his attachment to the world. When describing this, in the very same sentence, in fact, he expressed hope that a "running stream" of life would burst forth from Mignani to extinguish his worldliness, so that he would then realize the importance of the "illuminating fire" of the Eucharist. In another letter to Mignani, after expressing desire for the heat and light of the fire Christ sought to spread upon earth, he lamented the condition of his "bruised, burning soul." In his use of the love-as-fire imagery in the letter to the learned Giustiniani, he may have been utilizing its Neoplatonic overtones.[68]

Gaetano made allusions to the notion of spiritual combat, but he did not develop the theme as highly as earlier authors of devotional materials, like Battista da Crema, or authors who came later, like Scupoli. In fact, the concept has ancient roots in the Christian tradition and is frequently traced from St. Paul through theologians like Augustine and John Cassian when identifying precedents to the Italian interest in the theme during the sixteenth and seventeenth centuries. Paul's references to spiritual combat in the letters to Timothy and 1 Corinthinans exhort the faithful to fight against self and in defense of one's own faith, in order to "take hold of the eternal life" open to them as confessing believers. Paul urged them to accomplish this through self-control, holding his own behavior up as an example, explaining how he would "pummel . . . and subdue" his own body. Gaetano delivered his clearest expression on the theme of spiritual combat, like so many of his other principal points, in letters to Mignani. In the opening paragraph of his second letter to her, Gaetano indicated his desire to "undertake constant warfare against [his] . . . pestiferous enemies," referring to his attachments to "the flesh" and other "affections of this miserable life." In a letter from the summer of 1518, he asked for her assistance on behalf of himself and Bartolomeo Stella, his "spiritual brother," who had originally told him of Mignani and encouraged their correspondence. "We are novices," he said, "devoid of [spiritual] arms, and clothed with worldly attachments. On you, Mother, I call, so that the enemies be put to flight, . . . otherwise evil will be done to us."[69]

While acknowledging the importance of both Mignani's intercession and God's grace, Gaetano voiced here also a commitment to the necessity of human action and determination in leading the spiritual life and in pursuit of salvation. He reiterated this in the letter to his niece, in which he sought to "remind" her "that even all the saints are unable to make you as beloved by Christ as you yourself are able." He urged her to make an act of the will, for although "we can no longer obtain" eternal life "here because of what we have lost through our sins," we must "desire . . . to receive Him," and he advised her to "make a gift of herself" to Christ. Gaetano made these implicit rejections of contemporary challenges to the value of human free acts explicit in a letter from about the same time addressed to Mignani. He complained that "works" were then "the subject of little concern by miserable mortals," and added his own promise to "work gratefully" for Christ, "even if . . . by the means of sinners." It is interesting to note that in the same letter he indicated his adherence to two other beliefs increasingly coming under attack at the beginning of the Reformation. He referred to those in purgatory, "that limited, but still most cruel fire," as among the few who truly understood the value of the passion of Christ. He also described the cloistered, monastic life as a "sweet wood" representing "a defensive weapon for all mortals against invisible and inaccessible enemies."[70]

Gaetano also developed a spirituality with a decidedly Marian focus. The visions he experienced, his spiritual counsel to his correspondents and his image of Mignani as "spiritual mother" all revolve around this theme. In a plea to Mignani for assistance in overcoming what he perceived to be a cold devotional life and unwillingness to engage in spiritual warfare, he credited Mary for "some lofty gifts," particularly for a series of remarkable visionary experiences around Christmas of 1517. He described the visions in intense, physical detail. "I found myself in that real and most holy manger," he related. This first vision allegedly took place on Christmas, in the church of Santa Maria Maggiore in Rome. Not only did he observe persons and actions at that scene, but he also became an active participant. "With the confidence of vigilant Joseph," he added, "I took that tender child, incarnation of the Eternal Word, from the hand of the cautious Virgin, newly my mother Patroness." He did not follow descriptions like this with much relation of joy or delight over the blessing given, but instead with continual self-correction. Expressing disappointment over finding himself unmoved by this first vision, he said, "The fact that [my heart] was not melted at that moment is a sign that it is truly hardened." The occasion of mystical experience, it seems, represented to Gaetano just one thing: a call to a higher level of spiritual commitment and practice. Similar visions on the feast of the Circumcision and the Epiphany left him with the same reaction. "Still my senses are not circumcised," he said, and "nothing other than iron, waste and useless gifts was found in me." He indicated that he expected another vision five days later, on the feast of the Purification, "to hear that sweet canticle of old Simeon and his tough and bitter words of prophecy." These visionary experiences, with their focus on the episodes in the life of Christ where Mary played a central role, are the only ones Gaetano related in his letters.[71]

Gaetano often utilized Marian themes in the spiritual advice he gave to women, such as Elisabetta Porto and Maria Carafa. In the 1522 letter to Porto he developed this theme extensively, and quite logically, as his niece was about to become a mother herself. "Pray frequently to the Virgin Mary," he told her, "that she may visit you with her glorious Son. She will give Him to you willingly, and He will come more willingly to fortify you and your children in this journey through the dark forest." In one of his letters to Carafa, he urged her to adopt the humility and obedience of Mary. Vanity was a vice whose corrective could be found in the person and attitude of Mary, he believed; vanity was particularly dangerous, since he saw "vain, lofty ones falling into the depths of the sea." In both cases he evoked standard, conventional beliefs about the importance of Mary and her place in Christian devotion.[72]

Gaetano also conceived and described his relationship with his "spiritual mother," Laura Mignani, in Marian terms. In the same letter in which he explained his visionary experiences, he spoke of Mignani's role in his own devotional life. For him, she served as an intercessor with Jesus, just as Mary did for Christians generally, in standard Christian theology then and in Catholic theology now. Throughout the letter he seemed to identify his "Patroness" as the Virgin Mary, but at the conclusion of a paragraph requesting "the ability" to hold himself in contempt "and the desire to be scorned," he asked Mignani to beg Mary for the blessing, seeking a kind of dual intercession. "It is to hope I turn," he wrote, "that my Patroness and Star will be begged by you [for the gift], making a bond and assurance [out] of me."[73] Gaetano directly compared Mignani to Mary in another letter seeking her intercession. "May your Charity," he wrote, "take this concern from me, and for that purpose have recourse to urge [your]

Spouse Jesus." He added a reference to the story of the wedding feast at Cana and concluded, "For even if it is not the hour, if the Queen wishes it, Jesus will do it all."[74]

Gaetano thus developed a complex spirituality much affected by his relationships with women. Those relationships were further affected and influenced by the status of women in the religious culture of sixteenth-century Italy. The impact that women made upon that culture is the focus of extensive historical analysis today. This analysis has become increasingly complex, and its results often fascinating.[75] Gaetano addressed most of his spiritual message to women in convents frequently assumed to have been filled with *de facto* captives placed there against their will by unfeeling parents, devoid of persons seriously committed to religious devotion, and dominated by male clerics bent upon maintaining an immoral status quo. The new historical analysis of religious women in the era, when taken together with careful consideration of the writings of Gaetano, suggests that convent reality was far more complex.

Historians studying the social context of women engaged in or assigned to religious pursuits have found that in Italy claustration sometimes became a convenient means for control of the growing surplus female population. That control was judged necessary especially in the Renaissance era, as patrimonial and dotal resources were decidedly strained and often demanded determined strategies for conservation. Convents served elite families as a destination for daughters too numerous to be dowered adequately in pursuit of desirable marital alliances. The problem, apparently, was of vast proportions, especially in cities, where statistics available indicate that fully 3 percent of the Venetian population, for example, was registered in convents by the mid-seventeenth century. Whether the basic motivation for this solution that favored the interests of fathers more often than the interests of daughters was economic or wrapped up with considerations of family honor can be debated, and contributors to the debate are certainly not lacking.[76] The debate still needs to be enhanced through consideration of pertinent literary sources. For example, Maria Carafa—one of the women with whom Gaetano corresponded—sought monastic life against the wishes of her parents. Her experience raises another issue associated with the general picture of convent life, for she also pursued more rigorous devotional practice than she originally found in her newly chosen career.

Indeed, studies focusing on the religious devotion of women in convents have identified a general conclusion that can be summed up in one word: laxity. At best, convents were rather uneven in religious commitment and practice, and if anything was "typical," it was weak adherence to the rules and practices set up for religious women in medieval rules and guidelines. Travel by nuns outside the confines of the convent—and visits by family members and lovers within—rendered the concept of "cloister" meaningless. Similar subversion of regulations on prayer, fasting and other devotional matters was common. Although the term "laxity" implies dedication to forms of behavior considered dissolute or immoral, ignorance and the absence of continuing education among the professed was likely an important source of the disintegration of religious life as well. Where reform initiatives existed, it was often secular authorities, not religious ones, who pursued them.

The general laxity, however, can be viewed from a different perspective, one that challenges rather than reinforces the typical picture of early-modern convent life. Women religious found themselves far from dominated by male counterparts seeking to keep them isolated in silence and obedience, and they did so throughout the sixteenth century. Instead, they carved out for themselves a unique place in reaction to the gender-based social stratifications that influenced religious life. The women accomplished this through mysticism, as did their medieval forebears, but also through direct opposition to those who would "reform" their practices, through literary activities and language, and through resources not always associated with the struggle for social independence and mobility—like food.[77]

Some sixteenth-century clerics undoubtedly believed religious women needed direction and sought to restrict their activities and devotions. The women affected were not just nuns in monasteries, but also "bigots" or "house nuns." Dressed in black and pacing in Italian *piazze*, they were common at that time, and can be identified even now, in Italian society. Among nuns, Paola Antonia Negri (1508–1555) suffered under such restriction and control. First considered an oracle and dominant for a short time in leadership of the religious groups known as the Barnabites and the *Angeliche*, the charitable activity she encouraged was cut back by a combination of Venetian civic leaders and Roman religious authorities. She was even forced to live in the cloister of Santa Chiara in Milan after an attempted flight in 1552.[78]

In the end, only one conclusion is possible: male interaction with female religious and their institutions was not by any means comprehensively repressive or supportive. Women who enjoyed mystical experiences, for example, sometimes received encouragement from men, and at other times did not. The determining factor behind this particular difference may have been the nature of the message an individual woman believed she had received. When it simply contained devotional import for the woman (or the women and men with whom she was associated) male confessors and directors tended to encourage. When the mystical experience contained a prophetic message, especially if the prophecy held significance for the reform of institutions or of the church at large, they did not. Recent investigation of the legislation on claustration and other issues connected with convent life, to provide another example, reveals that there were no comprehensive Tridentine policies; rather, practice varied by diocese and in accord with the views of the current pope. The pope most firmly dedicated to the claustration some historians consider tantamount to imprisonment was Pius V. On the local level, it is clear that zealous post-Tridentine bishops pursuing any reform initiatives, especially revival of cloister restrictions, encountered substantial female opposition and had to seek change through standard "political" means: negotiation and compromise.

One of the more interesting aspects of the complex interaction between men and women in sixteenth-century religious practice revolves around the relationship of confessor/confessee or spiritual director/directee. The relationship was certainly not one-sided, for although men exercised considerable power in such relationships, at times they were profoundly dependent upon the women they "directed." For men and women in Mediterranean cultures, a good part of the relationship revolved around the image of the Spanish *beata* (devout laywoman) or the Italian *divina madre*. The holy woman/holy mother of sixteenth-century Italy stood perhaps as the logical culmination of the proliferation of opportunities for women in religious roles and in medieval mysticism that occurred between the twelfth and fourteenth centuries. Spiritual mothers served as hosts, in a way, for rapport with God the Father, Jesus, and various saints that could inform and direct the work of individual and institutional reform. During the era, males increasingly considered the duty of undertaking any such work as pertaining to themselves (to the exclusion of female action), but many sought their first advice on religious matters from a *divina madre*. These women found their own models in the character of religious persons from the past, like Catherine of Genoa and the Blessed Virgin Mary. They apparently saw themselves as spiritual almsgivers, supporting the devotional life of others. They stood as symbols of purity and goodness to those they advised, at least according to the writings of their "spiritual sons," who felt encouraged to imitation of the same qualities.

Although it is dangerous to attempt to psychoanalyze persons at a distance of five hundred years, one might argue that the men involved in relationships with "holy mothers"—and Gaetano was one—could have found in them a psychological support reinforcing their commitment to the priesthood. Above all, it is important to recognize that some women served as real directors in their own right through these relationships and developed images used in devotional literature, such as the utility of frequent communion, abnegation of the will and spiritual combat. In the end, this too calls into question the legitimacy of the image of male dominance as one that accurately describes religiosity in general or specific developments in the history of spirituality during this era. Early-modern women, especially those deserving of the term *divina madre*, simply are not best understood as persons constrained by a social norm that relegated them to "inferior" status.[79]

Gaetano maintained relationships with women that reinforce the complexity of this context, but ones that are in some ways exceptional and unique. To begin with, he reflected the basic shift in mid-sixteenth century Italy away from male solicitation of the spiritual advice of women to male direction of the spiritual lives of women. Nonetheless, we must not ignore the significance of the mutuality of his relationship with Mignani just because we lack her side of their correspondence. Neither is it useful to ignore the importance of the fact that he was, in a sense, "assigned" to care for the spiritual needs of the other woman with whom he had most frequent correspondence, Maria Carafa. Her brother, co-founder with Gaetano of the Theatines and soon to be cardinal, after all, had suggested that Gaetano look after her and her fellow nuns. The letters he drafted to Maria later are indeed remarkable in comparison with the earlier group to Mignani. He did not solicit Maria's advice concerning his own spiritual development, despite the conviction he apparently held in her religious zeal and devotion. His letters also reflect the struggle or implicit contradiction between humility and the pursuit of spiritual gifts through prayer. At the same time, however, they reflect a mature conviction on his part that women were capable of both and ought to pursue both.

In a similar way, Gaetano's relationship with his niece, Elisabetta Porto, appears to have been complicated by ties with other persons, yet it can still be suggestive of his character. It is dangerous to base an interpersonal analysis on a handful of letters, but it seems he must have appeared almost as a father to her. Gaetano apparently worked hard to ensure not only her dowry and the arrangement of a suitable marriage, but also attempted to protect her from relatives like Ferdinand and Girolamo Thiene, whom he did not seem to trust. His letter to them of 1524 represented an attempt to ensure that they might never make a legal claim to any of her resources, which in that era would have been her dowry. He even used his status as a priest and as one who understood (and taught) the process of salvation to buttress his appeal. He urged them to remember that in the end they would be accountable to God for their actions. Gaetano's letter to Elisabetta in 1522, of course, is filled with language more normally found in correspondence between fathers and daughters than between uncles and nieces. Here too he urged a female recipient actively to seek a relationship with God through her own actions that might help her gain eternal life. The letter is remarkable in that it suggests Gaetano believed one could cement that relationship, and eternal life in the long run, through devotional pursuits in everyday life, outside of a monastery or convent, and in an extraordinarily "human" event—childbirth.[80]

The relationship Gaetano maintained with Laura Mignani is most remarkable of all, for it suggests a number of things about both him and her. His letters indicate that he entertained serious questions about his own ability to lead the life of a priest. As a result, the letters suggest something of the way he perceived his own needs as a young priest. He apparently possessed real determination to improve his spiritual life at that stage in his career, and he shared with others in the early sixteenth century a conviction that religious women could provide important guidance and advice on such matters. But even without the other side of the correspondence, these letters suggest something about Mignani as well. She must have believed that she had something to offer a person like Gaetano. Women like Mignani could become, and did become for Gaetano, objects of devotion, not just direction. And in the end, even without her letters, it is possible to conclude that relationships between men and women with "spiritual" interests could be, and at least in some cases were, mutual. Struggling to be a person growing in spiritual devotion as well as a priest, preacher, teacher, director and confessor in the vibrant context of the Tridentine Reformation, Gaetano may well have found a way to fulfill some of his religious, devotional and spiritual needs through his relationships with women.

LORENZO SCUPOLI AND HIS TEXTS:
IL COMBATTIMENTO SPIRITUALE AND *AGGIUNTA AL COMBATTIMENTO SPIRITUALE*

Born about 1530 at Otranto, in the peninsula of Salento—the spiked heel of the boot of Italy—Scupoli received the name Francesco from his parents.[81] Otranto was the site of a massacre of local Christians in 1480, and that event of heroic martyrdom must have figured prominently in the local lore during his childhood. Little else is known of Scupoli's early life, or of a good chunk of his adult life, until he somehow came to Naples and entered the Theatine house of San Paolo Maggiore in 1569. His name, given as Franciscus de Hydrunto, can be found in a brief mention in the records of the general chapter of the Theatines convened that year.[82] The records from such meetings are preserved at the Roman headquarters of the order.

Scupoli, although relatively close in age to the founders and early members of the order, was really a second-generation Theatine. This is mainly due to his relationship with those other Theatines. Perhaps he came to the house in Naples as a result of his knowledge of these men and their charitable activities, which apparently became renowned in the city. Members of the order who resided in that house figure prominently in the history of the order and in the devotional history of early-modern Catholicism. Two considered "blessed" (Giovanni Marinoni [+1562] and Paolo Burali d'Arezzo), plus two saints (Gaetano and Andrea Avellino [1521–1608]) lived in the house in the mid-sixteenth century. At any rate, it was there that Scupoli became a student of the spiritual and religious life under a number of prominent Theatines, including one of the founders. Gaetano's influence and the possibility that Scupoli became familiar with the sources behind the founder's spirituality—like Battista da Crema—cannot be discounted, despite the fact that Scupoli directly revealed almost none of his sources at all. Andrea Avellino must have been a continual influence upon Scupoli, however, because of their years of residence in the same houses and the relationship that would have developed between them.[83]

Avellino, who received canonization in 1712, was ordained a priest in 1545 and became acquainted with the Theatine order through the house in Naples two years later. He also came to know early members of the Jesuit order, especially their second superior general, Diego Lainez, under whose direction Avellino followed the meditative program embodied in the *Spiritual Exercises* of Ignatius Loyola. That experience apparently had a profound impact upon Avellino, as he encouraged the same practices recommended there to his Theatine directees and even wrote a set of "spiritual exercises" for himself and for them sometime between 1560 and 1590. He must have promoted the approach with considerable intensity, since there are striking similarities between the recommendations found in Scupoli's writings and those earlier practical guides for meditation and prayer. Avellino entered the Theatine order in 1556 and led a busy religious life in administration of various Theatine offices, including master of novices, and through spiritual correspondence with such figures as Francis de Sales (1567–1622) and Carlo Borromeo (1538–1584). He also wrote extensively. For the most part he composed texts on prayer, but added scriptural commentaries and treatises on particular virtues.[84]

Scupoli made his novitiate, beginning on 1 January 1570, under the direction of Avellino. After five months, he received a transfer to Milan, where he completed the training under Girolamo Ferro (d. 1592). His study with Avellino continued both in that city and elsewhere. After a profession in January 1571, when he adopted the name Lorenzo, Scupoli lived for most of the next ten years in Theatine houses where Avellino was superior, including the house of San Antonio in Milan, and one in Piacenza. He was ordained a priest in Piacenza, late in 1577. No records survive indicating his program of studies, but it is reasonable to assume that it was extensive and demanding, given the original project of the Theatines to promote improved clerical preparation and behavior. It is also reasonable to assume that as superior Avellino would have continued to promote his own views on the importance of prayer, Scripture, and spiritual exercises like meditation in young clerics like Scupoli. He, along with some others, attended Avellino in his final illness and death in 1608 in Naples, and this further reinforces the probability that Avellino served as the formative influence in Scupoli's religiosity.

After ordination, Scupoli worked in a variety of different places. He was assigned to a house in Milan in 1578, along with Avellino again, and there he took part in the diocesan reform activity promoted and directed by Carlo Borromeo. Newly converted—both as an individual and as cardinal-nephew—to the concept of reform in 1563, Borromeo became a tireless diocesan innovator in the long process of application of the Tridentine decrees. He used Theatine priests, among others, to undertake the work he considered so important.[85] In 1581, Scupoli moved on to Genoa, where he worked on behalf of plague victims. Soon thereafter, his life took a different turn, being marked not by reforming pastoral work in Italian cities but by obscurity and denigration.

In 1585, for reasons that still remain unknown, Scupoli faced a trial before the general chapter. It ended in his conviction and imprisonment. The chapter deprived him of his priestly status, reduced him to the position of lay brother in the order, and promised a final adjudication of the matter at the next yearly meeting. Records from the early chapters of the Theatine order are notoriously sketchy, as I have noted. In most cases, the description of the meeting is given in just one paragraph, and a decree of 1572 that was confirmed in 1578 suggests that paper work was routinely burned immediately after the general chapter acted on matters like this. The chapter records covering the years of Scupoli's trial and imprisonment provide no exception to the policy. There are no records that provide any details concerning the case, and no indication of any reconsideration of Scupoli's case in the 1586 summary. It appears that he remained a prisoner for about three years, although he lived under the condemnation much longer. Historians have argued that the harsh treatment was due to reasons ranging from heresy to some personally motivated calumny, but still, only conjectures can be made. In any event, the unnamed offense must have been viewed as extremely serious to result in such punishment. Even though Scupoli lived in other Theatine houses later, his life and activities from this point on remain obscure, if not altogether hidden. Some commentators, especially other Theatines, have suggested that this experience stood at the heart of Scupoli's teachings on humility and patience, but this cannot be firmly demonstrated, although considering the span of time over which he wrote *Il combattimento spirituale*, it is certainly possible.[86]

The chapter did not lift its condemnation until shortly before Scupoli's death, and between 1588 and 1610 he moved through a number of Theatine houses. He apparently also spent a good deal of time writing. He went to San Niccola da Tolentino in Venice in 1588, and in 1589 the first edition of *Il combattimento spirituale* appeared. The author was identified only as "a servant of God," and another priest, referred to on the title page as "Girolamo Conte di Porci il Vecchio," served as editor and agent. It was he who delivered the text to the printing house of Giolito for publication, and he who dedicated the first edition to the sisters of the convent of San Andrea in Venice. Scupoli may never have intended that the text be published, but the dedication made sense in light of the fact that he had a female audience in mind. Apparently an unknown "sister in Christ" solicited his advice and thereby inspired the text. In addition, textual evidence in the original points clearly to a female audience (he used feminine pronouns and forms of address in *Il combattimento spirituale*). Over the years, however, Scupoli must have come to realize that his writings could and would be used by more than just female religious. In his later writings—like the *Aggiunta*—he omitted use of the earlier, feminine forms.

Scupoli visited Padua on several occasions between 1589 and 1591 and took up residence in Naples for the last time in 1598, rejoining his old teacher Avellino. Scupoli was living there when the chapter general decreed him rehabilitated on 29 April 1610, and when he died in the same year, on 28 November.

The first edition of *Il combattimento spirituale* contained thirty-three chapters, but Scupoli continued to add to the text, and it gradually grew, in editions published between 1589 and 1657, to comprise sixty-six chapters. The first edition published in Naples appeared in 1599, and it added a considerable amount of material. Twenty-seven additional chapters were joined to the original text, whose chapters now numbered sixty. The new edition also provided an opening dedication to Jesus and a separate second part: six chapters entitled *Modo di apparecchiarsi agli assalti del nemico nel tempo della morte* ("The way to prepare oneself for the attacks of the enemy at the time of death"), and thirty-seven chapters entitled *Modo di consolare ed aiutare gli infermi a ben morire* ("The way to console and assist the sick to a holy death").[87] Although other texts were erroneously attributed to Scupoli (like Camilla Battista da Varano's *Dolori mentali di Gesù Cristo* ["The mental anguish of Jesus Christ"] and Juan de Bonilla's *Il sentiero del Paradiso* ["The path to heaven"]) and included in some editions of his work, the last substantial and apparently genuine additions were made in the final edition published prior to his death. It came from a publishing house in Naples and indicated that the author was a Theatine priest. It also added a thirty-eighth chapter *Aggiunta al combattimento spirituale* ("Addition to the Spiritual Combat") and a five-chapter *Modo di recitare la Corona della Madonna* ("How to recite the rosary"), considered the last of Scupoli's writings.[88]

Final changes bringing us to the modern edition of sixty-six chapters with Scupoli's name on the title page began soon after his death. The first edition naming him as author appeared on 19 December 1610, from a Bolognese printing house. The text was actually attributed to a variety of others over the years. In addition to the quasi-anonymous attributions to a "servant of God," an unnamed "Theatine," and to the Theatines as a group, four others were at one time or another named as the author: the man who originally brought the text to press, Girolamo Porcia; a Benedictine named Juan de Castañiza (+1599); the Jesuit priest Achille Gagliardi (+1617); and a Greek monk named Nicodemus the Hagiorite (1748–1809). Verification of the attribution to Scupoli was provided by two Theatine superiors general, Andrea Castaldo Pescara (+1629) and Francesco Carafa (+1658), as part of a project to issue a definitive, authentic text. In 1655, a Theatine named Carlo De Palma received the commission of Carafa to edit the new version. He allegedly based his version upon Scupoli's original manuscripts and published it in Rome in 1657 through the printer Vitale Mascardi. There the six-chapter *Modo di apparecchiarsi* from the 1599 Neapolitan edition was added to *Il combattimento spirituale*, and all subsequent editions included sixty-six chapters.[89] Most historians analyzing the text have considered it to be comprised of six basic parts: 1) on distrust of self

INTRODUCTION

(Chaps. 1–2); 2) on confidence in God (Chaps. 3–6); 3) on combat for the correction of faults (Chaps. 7–26), for victory over Satan and his assistants (Chaps. 27–32), for acquisition of virtues (Chaps. 33–43); 4) on prayer and meditation (Chaps. 44–52); 5) on communion (Chaps. 53–56); and 6) practical advice, especially on death (Chaps. 57–66).[90]

To some extent before, and certainly after 1657, *Il combattimento spirituale* became a runaway best-seller. Some six hundred editions have been published over the nearly four centuries since Scupoli's death. The modern editions, like some of the earlier ones, proliferated in part because of what editors have considered its timeless and practical spiritual program. That view of the text constitutes a mixed blessing. Although the main result was the availability of Scupoli's writings in virtually every language, there were some undesirable effects upon the text and its comprehension. When the Greek monk Nicodemus undertook a translation, he sought to adapt the text to his own Orthodox Christian audience. He even gave it a different title—*Unseen Warfare*. That text was re-edited and translated by Theophan the Recluse (1815-1894) for a different Orthodox audience in Russia. These Orthodox adaptations are markedly different from Scupoli's original. Orthodox editors made technical changes, inserting references to parallel scriptural passages, for example, and substantive changes, such as the introduction of hesychastic methods of prayer.[91]

In the final analysis, of course, adapted versions are ahistorical and hold the danger of moving the reader away from the original message of the author. The most recent editions of *Il combattimento spirituale* provide further examples. Convinced that Scupoli's message is "vigorous, realistic and full of keen insight," providing *any* Christian with the means to battle "passions and vices" and to avoid "running around blindly beating the air," an American publishing company recently picked up a defective English translation from 1945 and reissued it. Even the brand-new Italian version seeks to provide not a truly critical edition, but rather a version in modern prose.[92] Such use of the text, although expressing the noble purpose of rendering it relevant to a wider twentieth-century audience, requires simple but meaningful changes: the feminine nouns, pronouns, and forms of address have to be eliminated and the generic "you" or "Christian" must be substituted. The overall result, unfortunately, is to tear the text from its rich sixteenth-century context and to make Scupoli, as a Theatine author affected by that background, virtually incomprehensible. Therein lies the basic motivation for yet another translation of this already well-worn text: to return *Il combattimento spirituale* and the *Aggiunta* to their intellectual context and Scupoli to his historical context in Tridentine Italy. My hope is that all three—the texts, Scupoli and Tridentine Italy—can, as a result, be better understood.

For his audiences, first one sixteenth-century Italian nun and now all Christians in both the eastern and western traditions, Scupoli developed a complex spiritual message that went beyond that of the earlier Theatine writers like Gaetano. To begin with, Scupoli wrote at the height of the development of Protestant-Catholic controversialist literature, and while it was then forbidden to treat such matters in vernacular writing, he did so indirectly, but only insofar as they impinged upon his spiritual program. He cautioned against interest in "the novelties and changes of the world," in what may have been an oblique reference to current theological debates. He linked this point and all interest in such "unnecessary" matters to the snare of pride, urging the reader to become "completely dead" to them, for they represented "self-love . . . and a trap of the devil." Toward the end of his main work, Scupoli encouraged readers to address retorts and verbal challenges to devils who assault their faith. He even suggested specific responses in *Il combattimento spirituale*, all of which contained references to either the "holy Catholic faith," or that which the "Roman Church believes." Here again, Scupoli maintained his primary focus upon the battle against temptation and did not engage doctrinal controversy directly. He employed some references in the *Aggiunta* to the real presence of Christ in the Eucharist and to the Mass as a true "sacrifice." In these passages he came closest to polemical matters. In one case he presented the concept of the real presence only as a piece of evidence to demonstrate God's continual action on behalf of human beings. In two later chapters in the *Aggiunta* he elaborated at greater length, even employing medieval scholastic theological terminology to explain that "the consecrated Host and Chalice . . . the true Body and Blood of Christ . . . are hidden under those accidents of bread and wine."[93]

Although not especially focused on Protestant-Catholic controversy, Scupoli outlined a spiritual message that contained a substantial scriptural component. He offered few quotations and citations from the Bible in which he referred directly to specific books, but he quoted indirectly, paraphrased Scripture and alluded to its themes and stories often. When he provided direct quotations, they most often came from Old Testament books. Referring to spiritual enemies at the conclusion of *Il combattimento*

48

spirituale, for instance, he quoted the first book of Samuel: "Fight against them until they are consumed." He frequently employed the Psalms, perhaps in part due to his familiarity with them, and that of his original audience, through the divine office. In the *Aggiunta*, Scupoli employed the book of Ecclesiastes (1:2 and 2:11) to reinforce one of his favorite themes—rejection of worldly things. "We will take as our beginning and conclusion," he explained, "that which the most wise Solomon said, . . . 'vanity of vanities, all is vanity and striving after wind.' " Scupoli even more frequently utilized New Testament sources, but mainly through indirect quotations and allusions that seem designed to immediately recall original passages to the mind of readers familiar with the Gospels and epistles. Often, the material paraphrased came from the life of Christ, especially from the passion narratives. Scupoli also frequently used Jesus' parables. In material on the importance of conversion for the sinner, he alluded to two parables. The reason one must turn back to God after sin, he explained, "is the great obligation of the sinner, since the conversion of the son and his return to the house [brings] honor to the Father and rejoicing to all His house, to the neighborhood, and even to the angels in heaven." He reinforced this point by warning of the consequence of lack of conversion: "If he is not converted in time, the winter and the day of judgment will surely come [and] . . . he shall fall into the pains of hell, . . . without hope that even one time . . . water . . . might soothe him, not even as much as one can carry on the tip of the finger." Scupoli apparently knew such language would remind the reader of the parables of the prodigal son and of the rich man and Lazarus.[94]

In accord with this scriptural focus, Scupoli defined a spirituality that was both Christocentric and Marian. Although he made almost continual references to the teachings of Christ in parables, Scupoli clearly pointed to images and narratives of the passion as a basic source for meditation on the life of Christ. The imagery he used was descriptive, forceful and even graphic. He described the "bloody divine rain" that came "oozing" from Jesus in the garden early in the text, and then later provided two point-by-point descriptions of the passion, from the scourging and crowning with thorns to the actual crucifixion, urging readers throughout to apply their senses to smell "the stench of dead bodies that He smelled on Calvary," and to feel the "bitter agony and sharp pains" Christ endured, in an immediate, intense and personal experience. Scupoli clearly intended to shock the reader through this description, but saved the worst for last. He argued that for Christ, the physical pain was little compared to the mental anguish of receiving such brutal treatment from creatures he loved.[95] Imitation of the overwhelming patience of Christ in this ordeal was for Scupoli the key to identifying the means toward victory over our own passions. But as Christ provided an example of patience and adherence to the will of God in that event, so too did Mary. Scupoli tried to focus attention on her as well. He wrote, once again in very graphic physical terms, of the closeness between Mary and Jesus. She carried him, "sheltered . . . kissed . . . [and] nourished" him, and endured anguish for her love and special relationship. Scupoli recommended her as intercessor, as he believed she would come to the aid of those battling passions. He hoped his readers would, like her, come to conform themselves to the will of God.[96]

Given the Marian focus and his original female audience, it should come as no surprise that among the human virtues, Scupoli centered his spirituality on humility. He hoped his readers would attain this through distrust of themselves, and he made that point the principal message of the opening chapters of *Il combattimento spirituale*. Humility, or recognition of our real character and position relative to God, he believed, constituted the essence of genuine spiritual devotion. "Daughter," he explained, "the spiritual life . . . consists in nothing other than knowledge of the goodness and greatness of God, and of our nothingness and inclination toward every evil." He urged his audience to remember "that every grace and virtue in us derives from Him alone," and to be careful, because undue confidence in "mortification . . . flagellation . . . fasting and other similar vexations" can cause persons to "persuade themselves that perfection in all persons depends upon attendance in choir, silence, solitude and regular discipline." That could lead to excessive focus on external things, which can be of assistance, but only, for Scupoli, when sufficient attention is given to the proper inner relationship with God and confidence in him. Elsewhere, Scupoli contrasted comments on humility with virulent criticism of its opposite, pride and self-love. A frequently unrecognized trap of good works, he explained, is "the hidden worm of self-love and pride [that is] rotten and hateful to God." We ought to pursue good works by "humbling" ourselves and by seeking "to carry them out more perfectly," through "frequent recourse to Christ, who . . . teaches and helps [us] to be humble of heart."[97] Scupoli may have picked up part of his view on humility from the teachings and traditions related to Gaetano. In his compendium on the spiritual life apparently addressed to other Theatines, Gaetano discussed two kinds of humility—one that was identical to the truth, and another aided through the practice of charity.[98]

In this matter of humility, Scupoli utilized a distinction between internal and external things that stood behind one of the other principal elements of his spirituality—a limited rejection of the world and its values.

He viewed the world generally, as well as the particular persons and situations that an individual might confront, as a possibly dangerous distraction and source of temptation. In cautions on excessive verbosity, he urged persons to "flee eloquence," for "persuading ourselves [that] we know much" can leave us "pleased with our own ideas." He went even further to recommend that as a result his readers "remain distant from conversations," because in the long run "instead of men" they "will have angels, the saints, and even God himself as company." This is not to say that he believed all must comprehensively shun the world through monastic withdrawal. He prescribed an approach that was individual and capable of adaptation to persons in non-monastic settings. Scupoli made this point nowhere more clearly than in his cautions on over-reliance upon monastic penitential practices. It is perhaps best to say that in this matter we recognize an ambivalence and lack of surety on his part. After all, the same persons who could tempt one to give in to passion, to use his own example, could also provide an opportunity for self-mortification that might contribute to the development of greater love for God. He saw the world and "the persons and places" one might encounter, at least in part, as aids. Through them, a person might be able to predict occasions of sin and thereby begin to guard against them. Adversities and disagreeable persons are a form of blessing sent by God, he argued, "so that enduring . . . through His love, He may more purge, draw near and unite you to Himself."[99]

The spirituality of Scupoli was personal in another way—the goal he sketched was total defeat of one's individual passions. The process, according to him, began with prayerful self-evaluation, which led to recognition of internal weakness. Truly spiritual persons, he said, "praying and meditating upon the life and passion of our Lord, . . . understand above all their own malignity." Those without such self-knowledge, he indicated, have it given to them from God "by way of failures, . . . so that thus coming to understand, they learn to be suspicious of themselves." With that preliminary information and outlook, he argued, "if you will undertake to press down and kill all your disordered appetites, desires and wishes, even the smallest, you will give greater pleasure and service to God."[100]

Scupoli provided developed analysis of the process of battling the self through individual experience of passions in his recommendations concerning sensual and sexual impulses. The former he clearly distinguished from the latter, as the sensual ones could be defeated through both vigorous resistance and a process of excitation and repression. He defined "sensual" passions apparently as anything one might "feel," including mental states like impatience or anger. To defeat a personal weakness toward impatience, he urged the reader to consider where the occasion for impatience might come from—a person who holds one in contempt, for example. In order to become truly patient in this situation, he argued, one must not just resist the impulse and then "excite [it] again" in order to repress it, but in addition, one must "wish to love the contempt itself, desiring . . . waiting and intending to endure even greater contempt." Such "contrary acts" he considered especially helpful. The process of excitation and repression of impulses seems to indicate considerable confidence on the part of Scupoli in the spiritual prowess and essential goodness of his readers.

He exhibited nothing of the sort in regard to sexual impulses, or what he referred to as "the vice of the flesh." In his opinion, when handling that vice, no confrontation was advisable, but only flight, whenever possible, "from all occasions and persons whatever, from which there may come to you [even] a minimal danger." For Scupoli, this vice took on independent action and almost human qualities. He believed that it "concocts its plots secretly" so that "it harms and wounds incurably . . . the more it appears calm and unsuspicious." He saw concupiscence as a force possessing the power to subvert completely the relationship between a spiritual person and God. In the lengthy chapter he devoted to this weakness, Scupoli indicated that mortifications and honest confession to the spiritual father were all helpful, but that flight was the only real solution. Flee the temptation and the source of temptation, he said, and also idleness and complacency. Without such flight, he argued, "the fire will, little by little, dry up the water of good intentions with its heat," such that "one will not fear God, or consider honor, or life, or all the pains of hell."[101]

The insistence with which Scupoli recommended flight in the battle with sexual impulses provides evidence for another of the characteristics of his spirituality—its practicality. His message was simple, and theological or philosophical reflection was virtually nonexistent. He wrote a set of guidelines that were, above all, meant to be put into practice. He urged his readers to avoid the idea that they could mechanically, consistently repeat spiritual exercises and proceed to virtue in a logical, necessary progression. "Never . . . be persuaded," he said, "[that] virtue can be gained from . . . spiritual exercises that, as if from a printing press, as they say, have determined days of the week, one for [each] virtue." He recommended that his followers similarly avoid setting particular periods of time for the acquisition of spiritual gifts, "neither in days, nor weeks, nor years." Each one requires its own time, he suggested, and "it is not possible for me to determine it, since this has to be regulated by the condition and need of the individual, by the progress one is making on the path of the spirit." He cautioned readers to be "prudent and discreet" in the matter of physical mortifications, suggesting they too must be adjusted to individual needs. This approach was at the heart of his message on the acquisition of spiritual "arms," and behind his discussion of strategies to defeat Satan. In one of the closing chapters of *Il combattimento spirituale* he gave sample responses designed "to make him burst with rage," and to thwart his attempts "to make us fall into the trench of desperation."[102]

Scupoli apparently adopted this practical approach, at least in part, in order to construct a spiritual program for persons with a simple, basic education. This is clear when considering his almost-complete rejection of complex theological issues and his focus on a personal, affective approach, but it can be further demonstrated through the literary methods he employed in the text. He often used, for example, that now-unfashionable pedagogical technique known as repetition. Whole chapters repeat information and recommendations contained in earlier ones, sometimes even repeating material from the chapter immediately preceding. In Chapter 38, for example, Scupoli instructed the reader to welcome, rather than run from, vexations that are particularly distasteful, because of their usefulness in the process of acquiring virtue. In the previous chapter he made precisely the same point in other words, indicating that virtually all afflictions are of use in bringing one closer to God, along with all the pain that accompanies them. This "technique," and others, may or may not actually have been chosen by Scupoli, especially when one considers those points in the text where method seems to be lacking or forgotten. He often engaged in redundancy and sprinkled the text with phrases like "to an infinite degree, superabundant," "completely uncovered and naked," and "infinite and with no limit whatsoever."[103] In these cases, he appeared to be creating redundancy for emphasis, but the reader is still left with the impression that he was a less-than-critical writer. This is reinforced through his sometimes confusing use of pronouns. At times he even interchanged "I," "you" and "we," in addition to shifting back and forth between feminine and masculine pronouns. This practice, plus his excessively convoluted syntax, shows that Scupoli was no stylist.

Scupoli appears to have been unsure about some other important things besides syntax and grammar, such as the nature of human freedom. In this he was not at all unlike his contemporaries, especially ones who lived, worked and wrote in a religious environment. He undoubtedly believed in the existence of real human choice, but in virtually every chapter of *Il combattimento spirituale*, and at a number of points in the *Aggiunta*, he tried to assert a balanced, two-sided approach to this problem. On the one hand, he emphasized the importance of human action through recommendations on how to "make yourself" the possessor of virtue, through self-exertion and the performance of certain exercises, prayers and especially "contrary" actions to oppose vice.[104] On the other hand, he sought to assert simultaneously the necessity of God's intervention as crucial to the ability of the individual to act. Scupoli wrote his conclusions on the nature of freedom in Chapter 32, which also happens to be the longest in *Il combattimento spirituale*. There, he seemed to take for granted the idea that human beings could successfully complete the good works he had described in earlier chapters, but he also harbored concern that such activity and success would lead to vanity and self-confidence. He therefore asserted the preeminence of God's action behind our good works. "Consider yourself always with what is yours and not [with] what pertains to God," he said, adding that God with "His omnipotent hand drew you" from nothingness. "Where the well-being of grace and doing good are concerned, what good and meritorious works," he asked, "could your nature, stripped of divine aid, ever do by itself?" He urged the reader to speak mentally with good works completed in the past, saying, "I do not know in what way you appeared and began to exist . . . because I am not your origin; rather the good Lord and His grace have created, nourished and sustained you." After reading this chapter, one might come to the conclusion that Scupoli held a cooperative notion of the connection between the human will and divine grace in good works, with grace and God's action as the most important factor. Yet, one must attempt to balance this with the overall message behind the whole book, in which he pushed his audience first to choose to engage the spiritual conflict, and then to fight, to battle, to wage war actively against oneself, against sin and against Satan. It seems undeniable that he committed himself to the idea of free will in human action, but equally undeniable that he saw a danger in overemphasis upon this conviction.[105]

In the matter of free will, Scupoli not only reflected sixteenth-century philosophical ambivalence and tension, but also directed attention to one of the crucial sources of his thought: the *Spiritual Exercises* of St. Ignatius. Although it is not known if he ever underwent the full program of that retreat, there can be no doubt that he was profoundly affected by Ignatian spirituality, as related to him, in all probability, by Andrea Avellino. The military symbolism behind the concept of "spiritual combat" echoed the military experience and focus of Ignatius, even if that was just one among many sides of Jesuit spirituality.[106] In his discussion of spiritual combat and his emphasis on human action in choosing to engage the conflict and to serve among the forces of Christ, Scupoli echoed the central meditation of the *Spiritual Exercises*—the Meditation on Two Standards. There, Ignatius urged his readers to consider how Christ, the commander of all good people on the one hand, and Lucifer, the commander of all evil ones on the other, both call upon individuals to join them. Further meditation concerning the message and plan of each commander, Ignatius hoped, would lead the person engaging in the exercise to choose the former in battle against the latter.[107] Scupoli reconstructed the scene, complete with the "smoke" Ignatius imagined hovering around Satan and the "invincible captain," Christ, in his dedication of *Il combattimento spirituale* to Jesus. Numerous other points of comparison between the *Exercises* of Ignatius and Scupoli's work can also be identified in material on discernment of spirits, on avoidance of worldly attachments, on application of the senses during meditation, on seeking the "greater glory" of God, and on working actively against vices through contrary actions.

For Scupoli, the object of all the action and the spiritual program he recommended contained a particular spiritual goal—nothing less than Christian perfection—defined through the individual's relationship with God. There can be no doubt that Scupoli urged action upon his readers. But he addressed, at least originally, an audience that lived in a convent, and virtually all his recommendations on action seem directed toward the promotion of charitable behavior that also happens to be useful in community life. He gave directives not to develop charitable work for the assistance of those outside the convent, but ones designed to mute criticism of the practices of others, to provide effective control over the tongue and its impertinent utterances, and to encourage, above all, patience.[108] Although in the long run these actions could be considered charitable, the first, and perhaps primary, beneficiary was the individual performing them. The primary purpose was to improve the relationship of the individual with God, and thus to contribute to the mystical transformation of practitioners. Ultimately, it seems, that was Scupoli's definition of "Christian perfection."[109]

Scupoli maintained that a mystical transformation of the person was possible for followers of his program through a variety of different means. He indicated that one could pass to the state of contemplation by use of the senses, despite the dangers implicit there, which he analyzed in detail. One could do so by considering examples of perfection found through the senses in physical reality and then by moving forward to reflect on the infinite source of those finite blessings. "You see the harm," he explained, "[so] look after the remedy, [and] separate by thought the created thing from the spirit that is in it, [for] all is the work of God." From that point, fix your attention, he said, "on the supreme Creator there present who has given it being . . . taking all delight in Him alone." Then, "recollected in itself, [the soul] can unfurl its powerful wings toward heaven and the contemplation of God." This reflects a form of prayer that required use of the mind as well as use of the senses and that echoed the "contemplation to attain the love of God" found in the Fourth Week of the *Spiritual Exercises* of Ignatius.[110] In a similar process, he urged readers to proceed to contemplation through prayer to the Virgin Mary. This had the effect, for Scupoli, of utilizing her "secure and powerful" intercession, but it was also a means of convincing God to answer one's prayer, once the individual had "enter[ed] into the eternity and mind of God." "Remind [Jesus]," he suggested, "of the virgin womb that carried Him for nine months," of her "compassionate eyes," "sweet lips," "and the toils and anguish . . . she endured for Him." Then, he concluded, "you will do sweet violence to the divine Son, so that He may answer you."[111]

Prayer stood at the heart of another method Scupoli found useful in achieving mystical union with God—communion, either sacramental or "spiritual." Scupoli, like Theatines before and after him, was a proponent of frequent reception of the Eucharist. He devoted four chapters near the end of *Il combattimento spirituale* to the topic of communion, and asserted that it was more powerful than the other four weapons useful in defeating spiritual enemies he described earlier. In Chapter 56, he even identified spiritual, imaginary reception of God (rather than actual reception of the Eucharist) as a means by which the reader could remain continuously focused on God, especially at times when actual reception of communion was impossible. In his earlier chapter on preparation for the Eucharist, however, he described most explicitly the union with God that he considered possible in this life. He urged his readers to imagine Christ transforming them into himself, and he indicated one should explain the process to the soul, mentally. He instructed his followers to address Christ as well, saying, "It is for no other reason that you give me your entire self for food than to transform me wholly into You." With "You living in me and I in you," the reader was to continue, "I shall become yourself through a loving union, and . . . out of the lowliness of my worldly heart You [will] . . . make a single divine heart with You . . . and by this means I will come to open my heart to You, I invite You and will do You sweet violence so You will enter it." Between the vague language in this passage, where it is difficult to be certain who would be doing what to whom, and the topic itself—that is, mystical union—Scupoli's writing undoubtedly had the effect of giving free rein to the imagination of his readers.[112]

For Scupoli, the method of choice to achieve mystical union with God lay in transformation of the will. In the very first sentence of the opening chapter of *Il combattimento spirituale*, Scupoli defined Christian perfection as a process of "drawing . . . near to your God, [to] become of one same spirit with Him" (cf. 1 Cor. 6:17). From that point through the fourteenth chapter, he filled out his description of the process of transforming the human will and fusing it with the divine, even in chapters whose titles do not explicitly suggest analysis of the will is to follow. He wanted readers systematically to disentangle themselves from the desires of their own will through "renunciation" and an opposite "resignation to His divine pleasure." He promoted distrust of self and confidence in God (Chaps. 2–4, 6) as crucial steps in the process, just like careful use of the intellect. This latter approach helped one, in his view, to recognize the distinction between things valued out of human considerations and those things truly worthy of value (Chaps. 7–9). In Chapter 10, he began specific discussion of the use of the will, reiterating time and again over the next few chapters that the goal was to recreate it "conformed in everything to divine pleasure." When "some desirable thing . . . offers itself to you," he said, "do not incline the will to desire it, if first you have not raised the mind to God, to see that it is His will that you desire it, . . . [for] by this will He moves and draws yours." He then distinguished between two different wills within the individual, the "superior," "reasonable" will, and the "sensual," "inferior" one. The reasonable will was left "as if in the middle" attempting to choose and decide between the urgings of the divine will above and of the inferior will below. Each of these attempted "to draw [the superior will] to itself and to render it subservient and obedient." He viewed this as the very essence of the spiritual conflict, as well as the means by which human beings can rise to "union with God." By mortification and acts contrary to the desires of the inferior will, it becomes broken and weakened, and the individual can then aim, in rejecting sensual impulses, as well as "in every other thing," as he explained, at "the will of your God, . . . like His faithful and generous warrior, in order to correspond to Him in love."[113]

Scupoli drew upon many sources in outlining his spirtuality. There is, nonetheless, a good deal of speculation required to identify the actual sources, as he made no references to other works within his writings. He used few direct quotations, and those were exclusively to Scripture, with the exception of two passages he took from Thomas Aquinas: one cited in the first chapter of *Il combattimento spirituale* and the other in Chapter 24 of his *Aggiunta*. The general topic of spiritual conflict, of course, has a number of scriptural referents, as does the concept of the will as site of the battle. These are mainly from the writings attributed to St. Paul.[114] Scupoli employed Scripture as a source in a far more general sense, and that can be persuasively argued through analysis of his language, in the many places where it is apparently derived from Scripture.

Analysis of the language Scupoli used can also point, though again not conclusively, toward other possible sources. Passages reminiscent of the *Spiritual Exercises* of Ignatius are legion, but he drew on a long tradition of earlier authors as well as on contemporary writers concerned with the spiritual life. Given the sixteenth-century context in which he lived and received his priestly training, it is reasonable to assume that he possessed solid familiarity with authors like Bernard of Clairvaux, Aquinas, and John Cassian, even in the absence of direct quotations. It is possible to identify language in Scupoli reminiscent of the teachings of Augustine, as well. The bishop's pessimism concerning the natural state of human beings and their inclination toward evil, for example, could well be reflected in statements Scupoli made on the same matters in Chapters 11, 32, and 35 of *Il combattimento spirituale*. Most authors who have studied the sources of Scupoli's thought have seen it as part of a movement among contemporary writers linked to the *devotio moderna* and its expression in *The Imitation of Christ* through such late fifteenth- and sixteenth-century authors as Catherine of Bologna (d. 1463), Alonso de Madrid (dates unknown, but works first published in 1521), Battista da Crema, Serafino da Fermo (1496–1540) and Ignatius of Loyola. The movement culminated in authors like Luis da Granada (d. 1588) and Scupoli. There is little doubt that Scupoli's experience as a Theatine, first as a student of someone like Andrea Avellino, who was committed to the value of both contemporary and patristic spiritual literature, and then as a prisoner and outcast for so many years, naturally served as source for the reflections and focus on humility present in his texts.[115]

Scupoli employed a variety of images in these two works to drive home the main points of his spiritual message. At times he used theological images, especially the fire of divine love, in a fashion similar to his fellow Theatine, Gaetano. He described the crucified Christ, after a lengthy description of his sufferings, as a book to be read, "from which you will be able to draw the true portrait of every virtue," and thus he indicated that the reader should see Christ himself as "the book of life."[116] Still, the most strikingly obvious set of images Scupoli utilized was military, as in the very title of his major work. Throughout that text and the *Aggiunta*, he improvised with military imagery, and even manipulated words at times to make the image applicable to his original female audience, where it might not naturally translate. He was not consistent in this, however, for although he sometimes used the very unusual form *guerriera* to refer to a female warrior (in Chapters 14 and 28 of *Il combattimento spirituale*), he used the same imagery while retaining masculine referents, telling his audience in Chapter 45, for example, to "manfully" (*virilmente*) resist those who battle against them.

Scupoli also employed mercantile and financial imagery. Some was convention, as in the reference to himself as "purchased" by Christ's blood in the introduction to *Il combattimento spirituale*. Elsewhere, Scupoli went beyond conventionalities, as when he equated commitment to self-directed will as a disadvantageous sort of "ownership" traceable to interior blindness and ignorance. In a section on avoiding rash judgment of peers, he argued that it would be useful to view persons with any "defect" as under a different sort of divine guidance. God permits the fall of some, he explained, in order that by holding "himself lower in his own eyes, and . . . with the disdain of others, he may profit from humiliation and make himself more acceptable to God." The image is all the more powerful if one reflects on the personal humiliation Scupoli himself endured. An even more striking use of this imagery can be found in the section where Scupoli was most creative: in his discussion of the Eucharist and mystical union. In gratitude after receiving communion, he instructed his readers to ask the Lord, "Who has led You within me?" Scupoli added the words they could expect to hear from Christ. "Nothing," he would say, "but love, . . . [for] I am asking you to despise yourself in order to give you my love, for your heart in order so it will unite with mine." Scupoli expected Christ to complete the message with reference to a most remarkable transaction: "You see that I am of incomparable price and despite all my goodness, I am worth what you are worth. Buy Me now, then, my soul's delight, by giving yourself to Me."[117]

Perhaps most fascinating of all is Scupoli's use of sensual and sexual imagery. To begin with, as noted above, he encouraged toying with all sensual desires other than sexual ones in order to repress and drive them away more effectively. In addition, he utilized language that could suggest a sexual content to the message without explicitly stating it, such as in the words "fulfill your divine pleasure in me," which he urged his readers to use when commencing meditation.[118] When he came to describe pursuit and attainment of union with God, he utilized the imagery in a more developed fashion. A few passages, such as the one cited in the last paragraph, held notable sexual content simply by virtue of the suggestion of mystical marriage. In others, Scupoli went much further. In describing sacramental communion, he urged the reader to "open" the heart to Christ with "prayerful exclamations and loving aspirations." As was his custom elsewhere in the text, he even provided the words. "O most celestial food," she was to ask, "when may I sacrifice myself to You with nothing other than the fire of Your love?" He urged the reader to beg Christ to free her soul from earthly attachments, to "adorn it with Your holy virtues . . . because by this means I will come to open my heart to You, I invite and will do You sweet violence so You will enter it." She was to conclude by saying, "Then You, Lord, without resistance will work in me those effects that You have always desired."[119]

In addition to the connection between this imagery and that typical in the spirituality and hagiography of late-medieval women, the choice of words here is especially noteworthy. Scupoli used the term *violenza*, one of whose primary meanings carries sexual import. This phrase suggested a "holy rape" of Christ himself by the spiritual devotee, and Scupoli made use of the same word elsewhere. His use of the term in the first chapter, in a discussion of a variety of mortifications, seems designed to connote the more standard meaning of the term, "to do violence," in this case to oneself. On another occasion Scupoli used *violenza* with yet another set of suggestions in a chapter devoted to prayer through the Virgin Mary. The reader should "do violence" to Christ in a manner that would render him ready to fulfill a request. Scupoli told her to remind Jesus first of Mary's loving devotion and tenderness to him as a child, and then of the anguish and pain she suffered through his passion and death. Scupoli apparently believed memory of this contrast, and of Mary's undeserved suffering, would move him to pity the devotee and to grant the request.[120]

Scupoli's written work, like that of Gaetano, is thus important for the history of the relationship between religious men and religious women in early-modern Europe. It has been common in the past to consider religious women in this era as controlled, if not dominated, by men who were their religious counterparts, through a combination of widely accepted male superiority, exclusivist priestly authority, and conciliar-inspired repression. Recent historical analysis (such as that cited above in the section on Gaetano) has gone a long way to challenge that common view and to illustrate the far more interesting complexity probably behind that male-female relationship. Scupoli, like Gaetano before him, illustrates another twist on the problem, and his writings reinforce the notion that men and women in this era, especially ones committed to religious perfection, interacted in complicated ways.

What might appear at first glance as a denigratory attitude in Scupoli toward the intellectual capacities of his female addressee should not be overemphasized. We must note his recommendations to follow closely "the judgment of your spiritual father," for he indicated that the nun should "submit to the rule of discretion." We must note his other counsel to remain completely obedient in all things. In addition, for the most part, he modified this advice only in matters that seem miniscule. When giving specific directions on the use of the Angelus prayer and the particular meditations and devotions it should call forth, for example, he said, "In this I rely upon your own particular devotions and the opportunities that exterior circumstances permit," expressing only limited confidence that women could "control" their senses. He came even closer to denigrating the mental and spiritual faculties of women outright, suggesting they were prone to measure their spiritual profit through "sensible" devotions, whereas it is by "higher reason" that men distinguish themselves. Although "men" in the latter instance could certainly be read generically, the implication is clear when considering the text as a whole.[121] Still, all this must be counter-balanced with some noteworthy qualifications. The very existence of the text and its first intended audience suggest that Scupoli believed women to be persons capable of the height of spiritual perfection. He provided support for this view in those chapters he devoted to the attainment of contemplation and union with God, even his use of the Neoplatonic image of the soul "unfurl[ing] its powerful wings" in flight toward heaven.[122] In addition, he might have used the text to dictate a set of guidelines and directives if he considered his audience dangerous, suspect or subordinate in a general fashion, but in fact, he likely intended just the opposite. By employing the term *guerriera*, for example, he exhibited similarity to an author with whom he might not often be compared: Veronica Franco (1546–1591). In another context, that author and courtesan used the term—and the "Amazon" status it evoked—to warn male literary interlocutors with whom she battled in defense of her own poetic productions, and to call other women to find a voice and join in the fray. Whether or not Scupoli knew of Franco's work, it is interesting that he employed the same term and seemed to view "virtuous" women in the same way she did. Although they may have defined the term "virtue" differently, they both apparently recognized the abilities and powers of women, as well as the legitimacy of encouraging the growth and development of those strengths.[123]

INTRODUCTION

The writing of Scupoli related to women, and that of Gaetano before him, remains interesting in a larger context—the general history of Theatine contact with women. A Theatine branch for women received official status in 1633, when Pope Urban VIII placed a group known as the Sisters of the Immaculate Conception of the Virgin Mary under the care of the male branch of Theatines. This group was founded in the early 1580s in Naples by Ursula Benincasa (1547–1618). They gradually came under the influence of Theatines, as they apparently adopted the Theatine rule and constitution for religious communities published in 1628. Eventually, the female branch created its own, separate rule.[124] In addition, just as male Theatines gained a high reputation for sanctity and generated male emulators, they inspired female ones. An independent female group in Pescia, whose phenomenal growth in the late sixteenth- and early seventeenth centuries is reflective of shifting population and socio-economic exigencies as well as of Counter-Reformation religious fervor, became known as "Theatines" even before they were enclosed in an independent convent in 1620. The label was appended to them not because of adaptation of official Theatine practices, but because of their reputed sanctity and the fact that they received spiritual direction from a contemporary male group in Pescia. Likewise considered Theatines, the male group may well have exhibited sanctity and deep religious commitment, but it too lacked any tie with the real Theatine order. All this suggests that the small Theatine order was influential as much by reputation as by direct activity, and highlights the significant, if not central position that the Theatine order and its spiritual teachings held in early-modern Italy.[125]

CONCLUSION

The texts and the history of Theatine spirituality will, in the long run, interest at least three groups: students of the history of spirituality; those investigating the history of the relationship between men and women in the West; and those interested in the history of the Tridentine Reformation. For the first group, this study and the texts that follow should provide further evidence for things already fairly well known. The Theatine order and its spirituality stood in continuity with Christian religious currents and thinking rooted in Scripture and developed through the long era of medieval Christianity. More specifically, the order must be linked with late-medieval confraternal institutions devoted to spiritual perfection and active charity.

INTRODUCTION

Reference to the roots of their devotional teachings in Pauline, Augustinian, Franciscan, Thomistic and medieval reform literature is crucial for complete understanding of Theatine spiritual writers. These authors combined the Aristotelian and Thomistic focus on the will as a rational faculty with some engagement of the Augustinian notion of the will as love in defining their spiritual message and putting it into words. Gaetano appears to have given the Augustinian model more emphasis, and Scupoli the Aristotelian/Thomistic in straddling this intellectual and spiritual fence. They are also examples for those modern literary analysts who identify in the Renaissance a gradual shift toward use of the sense of sight over against that of hearing when they define discourse and techniques of discourse in the early-modern period. Theatine authors reflected an outlook toward language and discourse that they shared with others in the same period, just as they shared with contemporary spiritual authors an incarnational and sacramental outlook toward religiosity and devotional practice. Without consideration of these referents and context, the Theatines and their spiritual writings will remain either an enigma or part of the subject matter for an oversimplified, and hence unacceptable, picture of the "Counter"-Reformation.[126]

The Theatines and their writings are located in the middle of at least two early-modern historiographical issues generating much attention in the late-twentieth century. One of these revolves around the nature of male-female relationships in the period. Recent scholarship generated on this topic has forced reconsideration of earlier oversimplifications. No matter how widely accepted and imbedded as "fact" in western culture today, it is simply unacceptable to maintain that women were systematically and comprehensively repressed by men in this era, and that their spiritual and intellectual qualities were universally considered second rate. It is also unacceptable, however, to try to sweep away the misogynist character of large portions of western literature both in this period and after, as though it never existed. Neither extreme position helps us to understand persons who lived in the early-modern world for what they were—human beings.

The sources here edited can assist in just that process. In both Gaetano and Scupoli we can identify an ambivalent attitude toward women and their spiritual powers. Gaetano first sought advice from a woman on spiritual matters and only later turned to give direction on his own. Even when he did assume the latter role, he still expressed firm confidence in the spiritual prowess and essential goodness of the women to whom he addressed his letters. Undeniable, however, was his rapid, even rude, correction of women on particular points—such as the mechanical details concerning recitation of the divine office. Scupoli wrote in a manner that reflects similar ambivalence. The basic assumption behind the text, once understood as it was originally written—that is, to a woman—remains one of powerful confidence in the ability of women to attain the highest degree of spiritual perfection. Undeniable, however, are the passages in which he expressed limited confidence that women could find their own way in the spiritual life, as well as his apparent switch, especially in the *Aggiunta*, to address a wider audience. Gaetano and Scupoli together may serve as examples (to be verified by additional research) of broader ambivalence concerning women and relationships with women, as well as genuine inconsistencies in male Catholic clerical policies toward women in the sixteenth century. If such ambivalence and inconsistency can be identified, as recent historiography seems to be suggesting, there is an explanation for this as well. In the search for unfilled charitable needs—and therefore, opportunities to do "apostolic" work—a characteristic of both new and newly reformed orders around the time of the Council of Trent—the work of spiritual direction for female religious was enticing and needed. But it was also possibly dangerous. Male religious and the governance structures of their orders exhibited caution when considering the assumption of pastoral activities that could generate suspicion of impropriety, however true or untrue. Within this dialectic between desire to serve in an apostolate for the benefit of all and caution to appear publicly irreproachable, there is plenty of reason for ambivalence.[127]

All this should be of greatest interest to those committed to analysis of the second historiographical battle, over the real nature of early-modern Catholicism. Linked though they may have been to the late-medieval past and to even earlier trends in Christian devotional life, the Theatines were creators of a somewhat different spiritual response, one that reflects their cognizance of contemporary change and shifting needs. Their response was unique and not merely repetitive of the images, concepts and methods of the medieval past. If it had been such, their works would never have gained the prominence that they did, or, in the specific case of Scupoli, would never have become applicable to Christian audiences around the world. The Theatines developed complex answers to matters that were themselves quite complicated. Although intimately tied to the decidedly intransigent Counter-Reformation activity of Gian Pietro Carafa as Pope Paul IV and of Michele Ghislieri as Pius V, they were just as intimately tied to the work of Catherine of Genoa, Ettore Vernazza, and the Oratory of Divine Love. The former "counter-reformers" and their outlook help account for the repressive tone in portions of these texts and for the subsequent behavior of some Theatine clerics. The latter representatives of so-called Catholic Reform help account for Theatine writings and activity that reflected something altogether different: the desire for a broad clerical and lay reform. This shift of focus was toward an individual, immediate experience of God that would drive charitable activity and cooperate with the work of God to effect salvation both on the giving and receiving end of that charity. Hence, the Theatines stand as a microcosm of the larger Tridentine cosmos, motivated above all by a desire to change and reform the church and themselves in continuity with the medieval past and Renaissance humanism, and secondarily, by a desire to counter the spread of Protestantism at almost any cost. To some in the period, the two matters apparently worked hand in hand, for they hoped that serious reform would bring Protestants back to the fold. For others, one side of that dual program took precedence over the other. It should not surprise us to find representatives of both these approaches cooperating with each other at times, and in conflict at times. Neither should it surprise us to find both views represented in groups like the early Theatines. They were human, after all, and they created a new, but human, institution.

Rule of [Gian Pietro] Carafa[1]

(TRANSLATED BY BERNARD MCGINN)

I. All should live in a common way of dressing and clerical form of life according to the holy canons and the profession of the three vows of poverty, chastity and obedience.

According to the vow of poverty, so that no one has anything of his own, but everything is held in common and all live from the common store. They should not beg, because the canons forbid it, but they should live from alms freely given by the faithful. They can also live from tithes and first fruits, where this is fitting, freely serving the altar and the Gospel. We are not forbidden common possession of ecclesiastical revenues, neither through the canons, nor our own profession; but we have little concern for them for many reasons, as experience itself has taught us.

According to the vow of chastity, so that they may live not only in bodily integrity, but also in that of the senses, and of speech, and, insofar as possible, in purity of thoughts and inclinations. The same is true for frugality of food and sobriety. Association and conversation with women, even very upright and holy ones, are to be shunned, as the canons command. Where there is some inevitable necessity or the law of charity commands something different, the Superior should decide and others should obey.

Obedience is first of all owed to the Superior and the Elders, as to God's vicar and ministers. After that the brethren should be obedient among themselves, serving one another in charity. This should be done in such a way that everything takes place in order, as the Apostle says,[2] and no one should claim for himself the office of Superior or anyone else's office, or authority to give orders. The Superior should also be mindful that where no command of God or the Church exists, or where the force of one's own religious profession does not obligate someone, we hold that there is no command among us that binds under pain of sin.

II. The Superior is elected every year and is confirmed, if it seems right, up to a three-year term. The electors are those who have a voice in the Chapter. When the election has taken place, its confirmation is according to the canons and the whole Chapter, or by the larger portion of the Chapter. They first need to be summoned, and those who are absent should be waited for as long as is necessary.

III. No Novice is to be admitted to probation or profession without having been tested and proven by a long time, considerable experience, and patience over two or three years. This happens by consent of the whole Chapter. From the beginning the Novice is to be assigned to one of the brethren who with God's help will instruct him and teach him about the new life.

The Night and Day Office should regularly be said in choir only by clerics and priests according to the rite of the Roman Church, though with due respect to the custom of the church or diocese in which we happen to be, at least in matters not contrary to the Catholic Church. The Sacraments are to be freely administered through those the Superior has chosen and those persons he shall allow. They are to be administered with diligence and purity, faithfully observing the terms of the privileges and exemptions of the Apostolic See by not abusing the immunity that has been granted and always with due respect for the reverence of the Superior and the Ordinary Judge.[3] The manner of celebrating Mass and the Divine Office, as well as of reading, pronouncing and singing in choir and in church (aside from the authentic and ancient rubrics of the Missal and Roman Breviary) has been separately described for you and handed over in some brief and easy regulations where we even advise you when some Proper of the Saints is to be received or omitted.

IV. No specific color of dress or habit is commanded or forbidden us, as long as it is one befitting decent clerics and not against the sacred canons or obnoxious to the common custom of the city or diocese in which we dwell.

V. No priest or cleric should leave the house alone, but only after having taken a companion, first made a prayer before the altar, and after receiving the blessing of the Superior. The same rule is observed on returning. A lay brother, however, especially one who has the necessary care of running the household (even if he be a cleric), is not prohibited from at times going out alone when he has made the prayer and received the blessing, as stated.

RULE OF [GIAN PIETRO] CARAFA

We bow down in prayer twice a day when the signal is given, each in his own place or remaining in his cell, praying in silence and repose. This is in the morning when Lauds are finished and at Vespers in the beginning of the night. (In Summer, however, at midday.)

Let them keep in most diligent fashion the fasts proclaimed throughout the Church. We also customarily add a Friday fast through the entire year and an Advent fast, not far from precept but fasting freely and spontaneously.

Sacred reading must always be done at table, drawn either from the Holy Scripture or from the books of the Holy Doctors. The reading is to be heard in the deepest silence by all. No one save the Superior should dare to comment on it.

VI. Unless God's command and the Church's constitution are in agreement, or it is held to be observed before God from one's own profession of the three vows, we in no way permit something to have the force of law, nor do we wish to bind anyone in conscience with regard to custom or way of life, either in the things that pertain to divine worship and take place in some way in the church, or with regard to the things belonging to the common life that we are accustomed to observe within the house or outside it.

VII. It would take far too long to discuss the rest of the way in which we live point by point. Meanwhile, anyone who wants to know about it should do what the Lord says and hear Him inviting him when He says: "Come and see."[4]

Among other things he will learn how we receive guests; how we test Novices and how they are given exercises and finally are admitted to profession in lawful manner; how in the case of already professed lay brothers or clerics or priests some definite ministry or duty is required in which, out of love for Christ, they may serve either the common good or the necessity of individuals.

Furthermore, he will understand how devoutly and faithfully each one of us ought to conduct himself in his obedience, overcoming himself and looking to be helpful to others and obeying them, as befits God's servants. This is so not only in those matters that customarily take place in choir and in church and in the convent, but also in those that pertain to each one's private duty, such as sacristan, librarian, wardrobe keeper, janitor, gardener, prebendary,[5] or the ministers of other things, even the lowest. The same is true with regard to studies.

He will also understand what is the greatest and the most useful thing of all, that is, the force of the vows, the goal of those who make them, the purpose for which we have come together in unity in the name of the Lord Jesus Christ. And he will be taught daily through experience the Lord's word and its power as he says: "He who wishes to come after me, let him deny himself, take up his cross and follow me."[6] Let him enter through the narrow gate and walk through the sorrow of penitence until he comes to the bosom of widespread charity. He will judge everything to be vanity, even among us who have renounced the world, unless one is vigilant with every effort in overcoming concupiscence and gaining the charity of the Fathers. This charity, as St. Augustine says, is especially preserved if the way of life fits charity, the way of speech fits charity, and the way of appearing fits charity.[7] We also add: if the vows serve charity, the profession serves charity, and the whole religious life serves charity. Let us consider violating this virtue alone to be just as evil as violating God, knowing that charity was commended by Christ and the Apostles in such a way that if it be absent, as I said, everything is in vain, and if it be present everything is complete.

What remains to be said you will perceive far better by seeing and hearing than by the written word.

Letters of St. Gaetano da Thiene (St. Cajetan)

(SELECTED AND TRANSLATED FROM FRANCESCO
ANDREU, ED., *LE LETTERE DI SAN GAETANO DA
THIENE*, STUDI E TESTI, #177
[VATICAN CITY, 1954]. [FOOTNOTES DELETED.
END NOTES ARE MY OWN.])

---

1. TO SISTER LAURA MIGNANI, 31 JULY 1517, FROM ROME.

I hope that Life is most abundantly sprinkled into your heart, Mother in Jesus Christ, so that often, as if through windows, there may burst forth running streams with which I long to extinguish, if possible, this ardent flame in my life, and to make myself feel, through the meeting, the power of the blazing and illuminating fire of that holy food which alone is feeding me in this dark forest, so that everything in the world may become bitter to me.[1] In this heavenly meal and banquet, your Charity will always be remembered. Pray that your Spouse may not disdain prayers from me, but may answer me through you. I commend to you my soul, oppressed by wounds and enemies. To you I commend she from whose womb I was born.[2] I commend to you your spiritual son, my brother.[3] To you I commend this city, at one time holy, now Babylon, in which there remain so many holy relics. Today at Mass, at the altar of Sts. Lantia and Veronica, I remembered your Charity. I long to sense the effects of the power of such relics. Your letter shall always be close to my heart, for which your Spouse gives you thanks.

From Rome, on the last day of July, 1517.

Your favored son in Christ,
Gaetano da Thiene.

71

LETTERS OF ST. GAETANO DA THIENE

2. TO SISTER LAURA MIGNANI, 28 JANUARY 1518, FROM ROME.

JESUS

Venerable Mother in Christ,

The divine fire so lights up in you that not only those close to you, but we also, although both physically and morally distant, receive heat. In all your letters I see your sweet concern for miserable me, something most pleasing to me. But I am not able to give you a worthy or even similar offering, to such an extent that if it were good, I think I would not be able to forget your name and especially how I, worm-like and vile, even amid paradise itself and the persons of the most holy Trinity would presume to argue with the very Illuminator of the sun and Creator of the universe. Oh, what a wretched sort of blindness. It now reveals to me one of two alternatives: either to cease sacramental functions out of unworthiness and so to humble myself, or to serve the humble Lord as a faithful distributor and modest treasurer, that is, to always take up that which He proclaims to me. He calls me to be humble, and yet I am proud. That Illuminator and Way says, "You must follow me," and yet I remain in the world. I must take up that glowing blaze of which He says, "I have come to cast fire and discord upon the earth." Still I remain cold, lazy and tied to the affections of this miserable life.[4] And that infinite, paternal patience endures even me, but I do not know enough to tolerate difficult things for my Lord. For so many years, though, and in every moment, I have certainly tolerated mortal wounds delivered to my depraved soul—indeed I have thanked and praised the flesh, the world and my enemies. Now it is definitely time, Mother in Christ, that I undertake constant warfare against these, my three pestiferous enemies, and overcome them with the help of the cross. But no matter how good the desire, I will not be able to turn from them if there is not first given to me—from my Patroness—the ability to hold myself in contempt and the desire to be scorned. She indeed has both given me some lofty gifts and shown love for me, but all is for naught if she does not give me this ability and desire. It is well known that she says, "He has regarded the low estate of his handmaiden."[5] But I am ungrateful for the gifts, and I do not turn to serve her, but flee. The truth is that her will is carried out and not mine. I know that she wants the ministers of her sweet baby Jesus to be humble like her. Oh, why is this not accomplished in me? It is to her honor, it is her desire, it is in her power. I was attracted to her, loved and clothed by her. Oh, why did you abandon me? Cry, Mother, saddened since your light and teaching have become scarce and

72

distant from your creature. And what can be so inflamed that does not quickly lose heat if covered by many ashes? Such are my senses, my body, my heart—all ashes—such is my bruised, burning soul. It is to hope I turn, so that my Patroness and Star will be begged by you for the gift, making a bond and assurance out of me. If that gift is given to me, I shall never abandon her, no more than the vigilant spouse abandoned her with little Jesus. Rather I shall be with her through Egypt and the desert and her other struggles, to the cross and to the sepulcher.

Boldly, in the hour of His most holy birth, I found myself in that real and most holy manger. This desire was given to me by my father in love of the manger, the most blessed Jerome, whose bones are hidden under the entry to that manger.[6] And with the confidence of vigilant Joseph, I took the tender child, incarnation of the Eternal Word, from the hand of the cautious Virgin, newly my mother Patroness. Hard was my heart, and well believe it, for I am certain that the fact that it was not instantaneously melted is a sign that it is truly hardened. Similarly, I found myself there at the circumcision, but still my senses are not circumcised. Then, at the appearance of the Magi, I did the same—but nothing other than iron, waste and useless gifts was found in me. Within just five days I shall find myself in place and time with them yet again, to hear that sweet canticle of old Simeon and his tough, bitter words of prophecy.

Mother in Christ, I offered your name before, then in those instances, and always shall offer it, until grace shall be given to me from above, confiding not in myself, but in the victorious passion of Jesus. Moreover, if out of your Charity I will be assisted every morning, it is well known that it will not be useful to me alone, but to all redeemed persons past and present for whom I offer the suffering Lamb to His Father, whipped and pierced by thorns, nails and lance, who only permitted Himself to cry out, "Father, may all these sufferings pass away"; "forgive them, they know not what they do."[7] The Mass will be an aid to your dear son and the departed soul of his brother, for whom I shall not cease to offer it at the feet of those most holy and genuine imitators of Christ, whose merits assist us. I am certain that our pleasure and firmness of soul more quickly render thanks to God than our sadness: to your Charity it gives such aid and hope that your father must gain much.[8] And thus I believe, since it is done to the honor of the Lord, it is wonderful. Mother in Christ, your labors are well spent—they continue and they now beseech a wedding garment, so I hope you shall go in quickly to your Spouse in order never to come out again.[9] I see that you have written to both him and to me,[10] and that the letter to me was a great undertaking since I am so troubled, due to my many sins. Your

Spouse compels us to reply that truly I ardently desire (though mainly out of force) to leave for Venice after spending Easter here, in order to see if God wishes me to ease my mind so that I shall be able to serve my Lord in every way, freed from worry over my homeland and relatives.

I know that the death notice of a servant of God who was long distant from here was sent to you. In every moment I am able to be of service to my Lord, but I do not turn to it for such reasons, but only out of love, if I have grace from Him. The enemy is evil; I do not wish to be his creature. I am not able to flee; I am saved when the majesty of God gives me strength. Truly it pains me, since even though I have begun to serve, nevertheless it is not because I choose it.

If you are not annoyed at my coming, I shall visit you for three hours to give you knowledge of one saved by your Charity and of my brother Bartolomeo. And since I am poor in human perfections and even more so in divine qualities, I beg you, through the heart of Jesus Christ, to have faith in me as you do in your son Bartolomeo. And if I can gain something for your Charity or your monastery from the Pope before my departure, inform me about it, so that I will do all that I can and more.[11] And again, when departing I shall leave some worldly friend that always will be at your disposal whenever Bartolomeo shall require something again. It is true that I am poor in everything, but sometime Charity will make up for it. May the bond of your Spouse strengthen and be with you and with us.
From Rome, the 28th day of January 1518.

The unproductive servant of Christ and your son,
Gaetano da Thiene.

Postscript: Only now do I see that I have gone on too long. I'm sorry. Have patience, and give to me a little of your prudence.

3. TO SISTER LAURA MIGNANI, 16 JUNE 1518, FROM VICENZA.

Venerable Mother,
Your loving Spouse Jesus increases light and fire in your heart, and your delights burn every root of sin for us also. The letter of your sweetest Charity was the greatest joy to me, [as I was] longing to know of your condition, and I doubted that my letter had gone to waste. May our Lord be continually blessed by all, because He always consoles and helps us, never dwelling on our sins. You embarrass me and also offend God our Lord, and

even the Cardinal, in giving such attention to my little works and how they are carried out, which I see in demonstration especially in your letter. Today, these works are the subject of little concern by miserable mortals.[12] The name of God be praised, so that the prayer may be a little intercession for the needs of your Charity. It promised to be worth at least some forty or fifty ducats, and until reaching that sum, I am certain that I ought to be all yours. Never mind!—miserable also on that holy Wednesday was the price of your Spouse, who chose to make up for that which was lacking to you in temporal needs by changing them to spiritual goods, by having washed with His precious blood the souls that are going to the source of the treasure that is well-known only by those who are troubled in the limited but still most cruel fire of purgatory, or, on the other hand, by those very few to whom the Lord has revealed it today, in this life.[13]

Your very tender love toward me through the wounds of your sweet Spouse, Jesus Christ, is so pleasing to me that I believe I appear ungrateful to the Lord for such a benefit. Still, I console myself with the thought that your Charity has (and I am certain) the prize from Him. Through that prize comes your extraordinary love for me. I am not able to do anything for His divine Majesty on your behalf other than to remind Him of His spouse every day in the holy sacrifice of the Mass, and to work gratefully for Him, even if by means of sinners. I beseech your Charity to compel your dear Spouse not to reject my bold continuation in these works, because without life there is death.[14] I do not trust in any other defender from death. Beg Him so that now and forever He may place in this, His dwelling, some flowers and pleasing fragrance that are certainly to the honor of His great Majesty—and as much as necessary. You grieve with Him, like one jealous of His honor, but do not permit yourself to come into this shadowy, puzzling waste. He is husband to you, He loves you, while I am His dwelling place and treasurer, and yet you love me. Oh, who can understand this? I know that your Mother helps you, and I hope that you remind holy Monica of me and of the many others related to her.[15] Whether I wish it or not, He is Lord, and may I prefer His will to my own—this is honest. Have compassion for me, so that although so blind, I may desire from the Lord His virtues, though I am cold in first expelling my numerous vices, for amid them the virtues cannot be placed. I know that what your Charity writes to me is most true: tribulations are the fire that purges sins. The reason may desire it, but already having served and committed too much sin, it cannot breathe. My desires ought not to be my own, but those of my Lord; still, they are too often mine.

My mother, you are already old, but I hope you can regain your health somewhat for my arrival. I desire you to bind me in all things and to give me to your Spouse and lead me toward love of Him, not love for this life. I hope for your health—that the many afflictions you have in this life may, through hope, be converted into joy. May your Charity help me.

The most reverend Cardinal, placed amid the fires of this world, has had pity on me. It will be a holy work if your Charity offers him help. It is nowadays a difficult undertaking, but perhaps something easy for the Servants of Jesus.[16]

The day before I left (as he wrote to me), your dearest Bartolomeo dedicated his life to the cross of your Spouse. Your Charity enriched him with the infinite treasure of the heavenly King, to the honor of His Majesty, to the profit of souls lost and spent in human miseries, and to the consolation of those who especially love Him. Your Charity knows that you have provided the foundation for this building. May he follow you to perfection.

The gift of Your Charity was sent from your loving Spouse [and] accepted by me, and it is proof to me of how exhausted I was before consuming it. How could I wish to be in a sea of worldly food rather than placed in the eternal Kingdom?

O wretched me! I have no gift to send to your Charity. May the true Giver, the Creator of all, your dear Spouse, make up for this a hundred-fold, and assist your Charity and all those of your house in every necessity, under the sweet wood of the cloistered life that is a defensive weapon for all mortals against invisible and inaccessible enemies. May your Charity deign to accept our house and all of us at the service and disposal of your house, should it happen that any of you pass through this place.

From Vicenza, the 16th day of June, 1518.

The unworthy priest belonging completely to your Charity,
Gaetano da Thiene

4. TO SISTER LAURA MIGNANI, 7 AUGUST 1518, FROM VICENZA.

JESUS

Your loving Spouse gives us peace, Venerable Mother. Perhaps your Charity received one of my letters some days ago, in which I commended to you my sick mother. The Lord has brought her even to the door of death. Perhaps she is not lost, but well-cleansed of everything; may He always be praised. She is again bedridden, although out of danger, except for the fact that her age places her in danger of relapse. Please commend her (and me also) to your Spouse, Jesus Christ. It was my duty to write these few words in order to give you news of her condition.

Yesterday I received a letter, dated the 28th, from our Bartolomeo, who is well. He hopes that I may visit your Charity; he sees my need, and the desire for my need is not lacking. Now the times are apt and desirable, as the feast of the Assumption of our Patroness, Queen of the angels, has passed. But either my sins or my enemies make me fear that some impediment may arise. I beg your Charity from the heart not to tire the Mother of absent consolation that commends me there, and give me the means to come if it truly be to the honor of His beloved Son—your Spouse—whom I serve, at least outwardly. Three reasons compel me to come, and still I see my needs reflected in all of them. May the fiery knife of Divine Love cut through all obstacles so that I may come for the whole of August. May your Charity give some assistance on this feast to Bartolomeo, your dear son and my brother in the wounds of Jesus. We are novices, devoid of spiritual arms, and clothed with worldly attachments. The enemy never rests. On you, Mother, I call, so that such enemies be put to flight, even if we are sleeping; otherwise evil will be done to us.

Rejoice, Mother, that your Patroness has ascended to heaven in order to prepare a place for you, and reigns in eternity with Christ, your Spouse, whose wounds sweeten your own soul more and more every day. My mother and myself, most devoted to your Charity, humbly commend ourselves to you.

From Vicenza, on the 7th day of August 1518.

The ungrateful servant of your Charity,
and even more so of Christ,
Gaetano Thiene

5. TO SISTER LAURA MIGNANI, FROM VICENZA, N.D.
C.1518–1520.

JESUS

My observant Mother in the wounds of Jesus Christ, He gives me confidence in writing through the great love I have for Bartolomeo. Since your chaplain has already promised me his approval, you may read this letter with the permission of the reverend abbess alone. Otherwise, burn it. I say to your Charity that I think Bartolomeo has already told you that he has been ill. Some remnant of it remains, so that the past year was one of considerable pain, and he worried himself too much. I often consoled him over this, since he was ashamed that anyone should know it and that I might repeat it to our friends in Christ and make it known to all. So he endured the brief embarrassment, and he is no longer ashamed in front of us.[17] Now he has a little wound in one arm, but one easily healed. In his last letter he wrote to me that it causes him concern and that he treated himself. He has not had pain, except for mental disturbance, but already there has been much sorrow there.[18] Now I think that his peace of mind alone was lost; however, I believe it was very troubling to him. May your Charity, like his mother, take this concern from me. For that purpose may you urge your Spouse Jesus to give him health, along with increased service of Him. I am certain that he has been ill, that his soul has healed and may be useful. Nonetheless, when the Queen said, "They have no wine," and He responded to her, "What have you to do with me?," still then He did the favor, for even if it is not the hour, if the Queen wishes it, Jesus will do it all.[19] For myself, I wish him to be holy and healthy, joyful insofar as it is possible, and not sad. This sorrow he did not communicate to you in order not to trouble you. And I wished to do so only with confidence that whenever you write to him you speak no word of this, but only that you beg for the cure since you know of the illness. I say to you that your Charity ought not to trouble yourself, because neither the pain nor the continuation of it is of importance, but only the mental disturbance at times.

And now that I have shared this secret, I shall say four words about myself. The wars have brought about a situation that in order to marry my niece with a dowry and to pay our debts there remains for me only one affordable office, which costs 2600 ducats, the money on which I live.[20] I know that your Charity advised Bartolomeo not to buy one, and so I have done the same. I ask your Charity to beseech Jesus that He may give me strength to endure poverty, even if it must be endured in Rome, or, on the other hand, that He inspire me to sell all in order to have life.[21]

Your Charity knows that I am pressed by these family concerns. May Jesus live in your heart so that you may beseech Him on our behalf, to His honor and the health of our souls, since I am very unsure of what I ought to do. I desire nothing other than what the will of almighty God desires from me always. This I seek, this I desire. I ask your Charity to do me the kindness of enabling me to visit Brescia and stay for two days. Truly Jesus makes the request and beseeches you. For that reason may you understand me, the dregs of the priesthood, the very storage chest of ignorance, while I speak to one that I observe but do not comprehend.

Greetings in Jesus

[no signature]

Postscript: You know that I shall not come to you if you do not command me to do so, although I hope this may be the time, and if possible within ten days. May your Charity pardon my very presumptous familiarity. God and Mr. Bartolomeo are the causes.

To the venerable sister in Christ, Laura.[22]

6. TO SISTER LAURA MIGNANI, FROM VENICE, 8 JUNE 1520.

Observant Mother in Christ,

Jesus Christ sanctifies our life to the end through the sea of His blood. Regarding the two letters of your Reverence, most desirous mother in Christ, I say that you should not exhaust yourself in writing to me, since Bartolomeo and you always satisfy my thirst. I am certain through faith and your indications that I am yours, spiritually. It is something necessary for me and accomplished by Jesus in order to heal me. I have this faith, and I know it will not be in vain. I do not want the merits of your Reverence to assist me—they might more quickly harm me, for all that we are and all that exists in man is false and our justice is filth. I hope that God has given our souls some of the true light so that it comes to see such foulness. O great gift! But it is not given so that we might content ourselves in it, but in order that we might content ourselves in the will of the Giver, and that always enthusiastic to seek Him we might not fall into the abominable sin of sluggishness, which leads the soul to convince itself that it is not in the state of mortal sin. Many lie in this nowadays. No one bears a likeness to Christ our leader, myself in particular, either interiorly or exteriorly. I ask your Reverence to beseech that resemblance particularly for me, along with your beloved son Don Bartolomeo. He is good who has the light [necessary] to cry out in such times. It moves me to cry out, "Lighten my eyes, lest I sleep the sleep of death."[23]

I commend to your Reverence and to your sisters two sinners: my niece and myself, that you may be pleased to love us in Christ so that we may no longer be flesh, like animals, but completely spiritual. I am certain that Jesus Christ will fulfill this hope, if He is asked. God has given me such a condition that I do not know what to think or do concerning the sale of my office, concerning the marriage of my niece, or whether to stay or go to Rome. I will let the boat pass until I see sufficient light to know what to do. For now, I see only darkness. I wish Jesus Christ would purify my heart quickly so that I no longer may be a rebel to His holy will. I am certain that I do not yet desire to be where He pleases and to do as He pleases. The glory of my Creator lies in this obedience and death to myself—not in affective fervor, but only in that effective fervor that purifies souls. Whether such grace comes now or not, I do not know, since I do not know if there will be a tomorrow. From Rome I have received, through the service of a friar, two large *Agnus Dei*, one of which I am sending to you so that it may serve you and the others. The cardinal had them sent to me.[24] I say this so that your Reverence may not forget him in his continual needs, that he wishes to belong completely to Christ. To your Reverence and the other venerable mothers and sisters I commend myself.

From Venice, the 8th day of June 1520.

From the servant of your Reverence,
Gaetano, lowly priest.

7. TO SISTER LAURA MIGNANI, FROM VICENZA, 22 NOVEMBER 1520.

JESUS

Beloved God, sweet love: yet you make me thirst for Him, sweet mother. In the same hour that loving Mary divided her heart in the departure of her beloved Jesus, so that He might go to the Holy Supper—rather than having all her heart go with Him and her body remain without a soul—here, alas, is your sweet letter. It declares to me that the prince of angels, most holy Michael, along with the most venerable St. Monica, has presented the soul of my mother to the Virgin Mary. Loving and reverend mother, I cannot deny that I have always invoked Michael and holy Monica, and that it seemed to me that Michael promised he would give me aid. In the three deaths of dear relatives that I was faced with in the last six months, principally in that of my mother, Christ has been a great comfort to me, and has made me certain that some souls in this life helped me in that passing. I am certain that your Reverence was one of them. May glory be to my Lord. It is certainly to His glory, I say, that during the fifteen days that she was in bed, I never saw sadness in her face over those painful things that occurred to her. This pleased me much. About the rest she was silent. Every day she heard Mass in her room, and she received communion four times in bed. And alas, in those last three days when she was unable to, she was choked up with desire. She never lost her intellect, memory and will, with the exception of the final three hours. For three days she was continually anticipating death, having abandoned the doctors of the body, surrounded by servants of Christ in continual spiritual conversation, although she said very little. And only in the last three days would she sometimes say, "Alas, I can do no more." This I explain for your consolation. It is true that for ten days I have been of the opinion that she is certainly in Purgatory, if only for my sins and for the carnal affections in me. But I ask you to console me in the glory of Jesus by not ceasing to aid her, to give the highest glory to Jesus for her.

As for your Reverence, alas, have in your heart St. Paul and St. Martin in order to desire to remain here for the good of our neighbors. You must not seek more for yourself, mother, but rather seek to forget yourself in everything for Jesus Christ, and be only like Jesus, suffering for your neighbors. Desire, as I know you have, that all the world may be thrown upon you, so that they may be saved. Listen to the voice of the anger of God against the Christian people and cry out, "To me, to me you must convert yourselves."

My spiritual brother Bartolomeo and I, if we go to Rome as He has commanded us, need first to be armed from on high, because it seems to me to lead certainly to the cross. And, provided that Christ be with us, how blessed it will be. Still, just a sparrow can throw me to the ground.

On account of having received the letter of your Reverence and having left for Verona, I have made this letter close to my other in length. Pardon me, your Reverence. I commend myself to you, along with my household, with all love from the heart. I have five children and one woman—all relatives—in the house. I hope that Christ may be with them always.

From Vicenza, on the 22nd day, at the third hour.[25]

I remain poor priest and your unworthy son,
Gaetano, hurriedly.

Postscript: Thrown at the feet of all the holy sisters of Santa Croce, I beg, through the heart of Jesus, that you compel your Mother, sister

Laura, to take me as her son, since the soul of my mother has departed. I offer to always remember your holy monastery in my priestly devotions.

8. TO SISTER LAURA MIGNANI, FROM VENICE, 28 MARCH 1521/22.

Reverend Mother in Christ,

May the holy peace of blessed Christ and of His mother be in your heart and body and in those of all your daughters in these days. Offenses against God are in abundance, and He endures [them]. In order to give thanks for such goodness amid such sin, [and] in order to save some soul in this great storm, one ought to try [to do] something pleasing to His Divine Majesty. Our Gian Bartolomeo has for a long time now desired that the Lord might give light to certain places in and around Bergamo, and he has had, among other things, a relic of St. Rocco destined for that place. I am certain that it has come by a good and hidden way, since these gentlemen from Bergamo were not permitted to take anything from the body of Rocco, which is here. One of those who carried it then gave a piece of bone to a Servant of God.[26] Seeing an opportunity, he is sending this relic with other relics via his brother, who had the duty to try to do it when it seemed possible. In this way he plans to place it in your Reverence's hands since you are close by. I have held it for a year. May it please your Reverence to aid this plan and good intention since the land has need of it in order to maintain the people as good Catholics, and because of the war, the plague and famine. I commend this concern to your Reverence, and if it should be accomplished through our friends in those places, may you choose to give them help. I know that no word of this will drop from you. Bartolomeo will explain this more fully in May. It only remains for me to commend myself strictly to your prayers and those of your daughters, which never, unfortunately, live too long in me. I desire also that the Lord loose Bartolomeo from concern with relatives and created things, so that he may be more free. I know that your Reverence does not fail him; may it not happen at this time either. Our Spanish friend Gerolamo commends himself to you with his every holy intention, and so do I.[27] I am certain that if I were as I ought to be, then through me the Lord would serve Himself, that He be glorified in all the world.

From Venice, the 28th of March 1521.

Gaetano, unworthy priest of your Reverence, hurriedly.

9. TO ELISABETTA PORTO, FROM VENICE, 10 JULY 1522.[28]

JESUS, MARY

Dearest in Christ, who is, through Christ, my daughter,

I desire that as the Virgin Mary visited Elizabeth and—through her Jesus—sanctified both Elizabeth and the son that was in her womb, so may He deign, because of your goodness, to visit you and the fruit of your womb, in order that you, who are the tree, and the fruit you produce may now and forever live to the joy of the angels and to the glory of blessed Christ.[29] My daughter, I am a sinner. I make a low evaluation of myself, but I take recourse to the true servants of the Lord that beseech blessed Christ and His Mother on your behalf. But I remind you that even all the saints are unable to make you as beloved by Christ as you yourself are able. Will to be so, and if you wish Christ to love you and help you, then love Him, direct your will toward pleasing Him always, and never doubt that even if you are abandoned by all the saints and by all creatures, He will always help you in your need. Know that it is certain, my daughter, that here we are pilgrims on a journey. Our Father is in heaven, and whoever becomes intoxicated with this life loses the way and goes down to death. Being here, we must acquire the eternal life that we can no longer obtain on our own because of what we have lost through our sins. But Jesus Christ has acquired it. We always ought to give Him thanks, love Him, obey Him and remain close to Him as often as possible. He has left Himself in the form of food—oh, the unhappy Christian that does not know this gift! We are able to possess Christ, son of the Virgin Mary, and we do not desire Him. Trouble comes to the one who does not care to receive Him.

My daughter, the blessing that I hope for myself I desire for you, but in order for you to be able to have it, there is no other means than to pray frequently to the Virgin Mary that she may visit you with her glorious Son. Sometimes go and beseech her to deign to give you her Son, the true food for your soul, in the holy sacrament of the altar. She will give Him to you willingly, and He will come more willingly to fortify you and your children in this journey through the dark forest, where who knows how many enemies are always setting traps. But if we have such aid, the enemies remain far distant, like the fly from the fire; otherwise, they often give us some beverage that makes us sleep, and so they lead us down the path to hell unknowingly. And if this should be explained to us, we do not believe it, because we are so bewitched with this diabolical drink that one cannot digest it except by eating the flesh of the Son of the Virgin Mary,

83

the God-man Jesus Christ. Thus, I beg you, my daughter, to wash your soul with the holy confession of our Reverend confessor, Father Battista, and then receive communion one time out of your own free choice, without the pressure of impending delivery.[30]

Do not take Jesus Christ, my daughter, in order that He act as you desire. I want you to give yourself to Him that He may take you, and being your God and Savior, may do with you and give to you that which pleases Him. This I desire and beg from you, and even demand from you as much as I can. As soon as you can, I want you to make a gift of yourself and the fruit of your womb to the Son of the Virgin Mary, saying, "Here, Lord, I give You my whole self, make me forever yours, along with all the children You will give me." And how much more will He value this gift now than just before the birth. I compel you, if you love me, to enjoin yourself to this and to force your husband Giovanni to command you to do it. But also do it voluntarily, not just out of respect for him or me. Then, when you come to the delivery, I ask you to make the offering again, in order to give yourself anew to Christ and to His Mother, begging them to make you the good mother of a good son. I am certain that Father Battista, if you will ask him to visit you, will come willingly, for he loves you in Christ. If you wish me to be satisfied with you, do what I have said. I desire that Giovanni be happy both here and in Heaven, but I declare, because I have shown it through my infinite wickedness, that neither he nor even a king has ever had a bit of happiness in this life, if not through Jesus Christ. All other delights are from the sorcery and witchcraft that the Devil directs at those who obey him. Believe me in this, my daughter, because I have never deceived you, but rather love your soul as I love my own and your body more than my own, since I wish to despise my own just like the Devil. Comfort Giovanni, Lady Valeria and Lady Chiara in Christ.

From Venice, on the 10th of July 1522. Pray to God for me, and greet your mother and father-in-law along with Mr. Francesco for me.

Your loving father,
Gaetano, unworthy priest.

10. TO PAOLO GIUSTINIANI, FROM VENICE, 1 JANUARY 1523.[31]

Reverend and observant father in Christ,

I desire for your Reverend Paternity the holy, spiritual circumcision at which today heaven and earth rejoice, and I desire that it also be granted to me who can always use it. And in order that this may be your own day, I desire your Paternity to know me well, and not just through bodily eyes and ears. It is a bad thing when one's name exceeds one's virtue. This has happened to me, and my Lord, who acts like the Samaritan to me out of His incomprehensible goodness, out of the desire He has to make me no longer an empty reed, goes searching His servants that they may offer me the means to virtue.[32] May He be praised forever. Your Reverend Paternity has visited me through your kind letter and given me matter for thought and improvement, feeling that my Lord wishes it be like a credit and enrichment to me. Such admonition is often given to me, and still I remain the same. Since your Paternity lives in solitude, I know that you understand what this requires, and that there one remains in order to help those that are battling in the field. Ask the good Lord, my reverend Father, that He may make me follow my vocation and not my own selfish direction, and if it is so, then I shall not go in vain, but with purpose, to the glory of my Lord and no one else. Implore the Lord for me, my reverend Father, that He may make me worthy to be placed beneath His holy feet in the mystical Body, unseen but still united with almighty God, without whom and without whose union, alas, I am nothing. But enough of me. I say only that having been preceded by your greater charity, perhaps what I am and ever will be may be possessed in the heart. If ever my heart becomes inflamed, it will add fire to fire, and I thank your charity for the offer of assistance to my miserable soul. Thanks be to the Mover and Creator, and may He give recompense to Your Charity, a hundredfold.

I was certainly not the one that was renowned—even in the university—you were. I have often seen your Paternity in Rome, but not spoken to you. I do not wish to say anything to Your Paternity now, either, save that I desire that you be perfect in your vocation and more full of virtues than reputation. For myself, I am saddened to feel the difference that there is between Your Reverend Paternity and this other servant of the Lord.[33] And although He would forgive all, He still condemns both of us as ungenerous. May Christ, the king of peace, be praised.

Through different means I heard of Your Reverend Paternity, once by a letter that was read to me saying that you had begun to translate John Cassian, but that you did not keep at it.[34] And if I may be so bold, I must now spur on Your Reverend Paternity with a letter of my own. I shall not let such occasion pass, since Your Paternity offers himself so generously, and so I shall ask because it is a request of Christ, not my own. I beg that Your Reverence, pleasing to almighty God, might embrace and carry out such a useful and holy undertaking, in which, as I (though blind) understand it, is found a veritable meadow filled with real virtue, as well as a hoe and sickle to cut down and pull out the roots of vice. It is true that one worthy father, a true disciple of this master, told me something else when suggesting some learned person translate it. I am certain that whoever translates it well will first need to have practical intelligence; otherwise he will not succeed. I hope in the Lord that perhaps such work will be reserved to Your Reverend Paternity, who has acquired the skill and also the practice necessary to chew the large mouthfuls in such a way that they may satisfy even the inexperienced. I have great hope that from your work some tinder will be added to the tepid condition of our age. O God, what are You to do? You came and are coming, indeed, You exist in order to send fire, that it may burn, and behold there is coldness, hoar-frost and ice.[35] It is not possible that this blazing torch of the consecrated Host be changed in power, or even that the human creature be transubstantiated into Lucifer. Beg for me, my Father, this grace: that the Sacrament of the Eucharist, which is too often despised or not well attended, be profitable for us. But now we come to the real matter. Your Reverend Paternity, lover of Christ, master of virtue, may you create a garden of virtue, so that everyone can acquire it, and that it may no longer stand at such a great, high distance to those that do not have the strength to ascend there because of ignorance.

It remains for me to say to your Reverend Paternity that I desire those noble persons, your sister and brother-in-law from the Gabriele house, may be sanctified.[36] He has exerted himself very much for Christ through exterior works. I shall not be silent. I would not make an adequate account of all exterior works and financial contributions if I did not sweeten them with the sauce of that blood He shed with such fiery love. Alas, alas, He is weeping over this noble city.[37] Certainly there is none here who seeks Christ crucified. It is amazing that in such a city I have not found, perhaps because of my sins, even one noble who despises honor for the love of Christ. Alas, not one, one! Christ waits, no one moves. I am not saying that there are no persons with good intentions, but all of them stay put on account of fear of the Jews, and are ashamed to be seen confessing or receiving communion.[38] My Father, I will never be content until I see Christians going to the priest to feed themselves like famished ones, with great joy rather than shame. But enough. The noble Mr. Benedetto is sick with a slight but continual bodily illness. He is free of exterior bonds, and he is better and is eager to do good, as he was in the year 1522. I pray that Christ may make 1523 altogether different for His glory, Amen.

I am still uncircumcised and confused as usual.[39] Your Reverend

Paternity knows that I am the same in heart. May you deign to pardon me and take this evil and give it to sweet Jesus, the name which by itself feeds the angels. Goodbye, Reverend Father, and may I be as you, dead to the world and living in Christ.

May your Reverend Paternity be prudent, as usual, in building up and not tearing down your noble brother-in-law, praying for him.

From Venice, 1523, on the day of the Circumcision.

I, servant and son of your Reverend Paternity,
Gaetano, unworthy priest.

Postscript: Our Lord Jerónimo de la Lama is in Padova with some spiritual followers. I sent the letter of your Reverend Paternity there, which I know will be most pleasing to them, since he and I have held you in high regard for many months.

11. TO FERDINAND AND GIROLAMO THIENE, FROM ROME, 22 AUGUST 1524.[40]

JESUS, MARY

Honorable brothers,

May the peace of Christ be yours always. We ought to desire that He reign in us more each day, He who confessed to Pilate that His reign was not to be in this world, saying, "My kingship is not of this world."[41] His goodness has spurred me a great deal over the years to desire a part in that reign through His infinite goodness. And every day He makes me see more clearly how we cannot serve two masters—the world and Christ.[42] I see that Christ was poor and I am rich, He reviled and I honored, He in pain and I enjoying delight. I long one day before I die to take some step toward Him, so at this hour I am notifying you that I have decided to reduce my possessions and no longer be so rich. Perhaps blessed Christ will give me spiritual things in exchange for temporal things, out of His mercy. And I have resolved first to desert the thing that is most temporal, and then the others insofar as the Lord deigns to give me light. And I think that along with depriving myself of this portion of goods, I should give greater thanks to my Lord and yours. I do this first to restrain myself and my pride. Second, I write to quiet your mind in case at some time you may doubt my intention. Third, to assist the family and your children at present, not later when I am no longer able to enjoy them. Fourth, to honestly withdraw from you, through this action, any unworthy opinion held against me or my niece or between us and you because of damages from the division made among us forty years ago by my deceased father—your protector—or since. Jesus Christ knows that I have been of good faith and, I think, able to remain so to the salvation of my soul.

I raise God as my witness that I was not able to see marrying her to anyone else, nor did I do wrong to you when not choosing her husband from your relatives. Concerning the trusts, I neither fulfilled them nor was I able to break them; and if they were *boni*,[43] that was neither known to me nor is known; rather I see that they all were untouchable, both by law and in fact. It was said that whatever was done, was done with advice according to the correct and holy conscience of holy men, to whom I revealed all these things. If I am able to make you content in everything with the grace of God, I will do it, in all that my Lord gives me strength and the heart to do, just as I am doing now. I am sending, then, a proxy in the person of Baptista da Porto and in Zaninello, in order to cede to you two and your immediate heirs "feudal right," that is, my whole four-tenths from now onward, so that they be yours and no longer mine in law and in use, etc. And I seek from you only, if it pleases you, fifty ducats from the first return that flows to you in order to repay a debt. Divide the rest between you, like good brothers. And this is because, as I said, I desire to remain calm, never being disturbed over this matter again. I also wish to be contented about what you claim to have been left by my predecessors through guardianship and division. In addition, I hope that you yourselves may be content to cede every right and action which you can claim against me or my niece and her heirs by reason of that guardianship and division, because in the rest I am not reputed to have been able to injure you. So if the trusts were *boni*, I cannot make them the opposite for you, neither can I make them *boni* if they were not.

May Christ be that which will make you content and satisfied and good Christians—you and your children, just like my niece and her heirs—so that all, being friends here, may delight for eternity in heaven. What I seek for you is love of God, felt because you have reason to feel it. And so that Christ may make me understand that no anger is held against me, it is enough for me that you and your heirs specifically renounce any demands against me or my niece and her heirs on account of the guardianship and errors or damage that you said were done to you in the division, and not excepting the trusts, but from every challenge. And I ask you with charity and humanity to inform me of all that may be done so that I have reason to beg the Lord that I might do by other means the things that will provide you consolation. I know that you, Ferdinand, have care of a son, and Jerome has a grown daughter and no boys. Thus, I do not wish to divide the tenth except into equal portions, since they are all your children, and in time Jerome will undertake to marry off his daughter. I beg you not to utter unkind words or offense in dividing them, but you, Jerome, can take those that are easier for you, and some with less difficulty, since you have no burden. I place everything for you before Christ, that He may arrange this and every other thing for you. Remember that we all are mortal and act in such a way that when coming He may not say, "I do not know you," and close the door against us, because God may turn away.[44]

Exhort those of your house. May Christ be with you always, with His grace.

From Rome, 1524, 22nd day of August.

Brother Gaetanus, unworthy priest. I will arrange also that all the feudal documents be given to you.

Postscript: Since the courier departed suddenly and I could not have the proxy signed and notarized, I am sending at least this letter so that the gift be made and so that you have time to arrange what I am asking of you. By the first you will have the proxy.

12. TO BARTOLOMEO SCAINI, FROM VENICE, 26 MARCH 1529.

JESUS

Honorable brother in the peace of Christ,
I have your letter and I am always grateful to you, mainly in seeing that your holy desires remain. I wish I could say without flattery that they are growing, but I do not know, and I do not sense it through exterior acts. Still, the desires cheer me, but I will rejoice perfectly when your work will be perfect. I want to say that you are completing the course you follow, and also that you are among those servants whose works show that they belong to the Lord. But often works place such persons with the Lord in order to trick them, and I may thus become a false guide. You may know that Bernardo, dressed in sackcloth, has been in our house for the past three days, and he says he has never had a desire from God to place

himself under the advice of others until now, under our father Bishop.[45] Now, since he cured him with the medicine of truth, [Bernardo] has left. I don't know if the Lord will give him the grace to believe and to escape and free his soul from the hand of the Enemy, since it seems serious to us that he was obliged to cease from public or private preaching under the pain of mortal sin. And it seems especially difficult to excuse him from past mortal sins, even if they were not called such, because it was arrogant for him to do something his equals are not accustomed to do without the advice of good and learned Christians who are tied to Christ and to His spouse the holy Church. The Church condemns to mortal sin all laity who preach publicly or privately, and she wishes such to be punished with excommunication. If they do not desist, she punishes them. All the holy Doctors proclaim this.[46] Indeed, those who say they are sent by God need to show it with obvious, not imaginary signs. I believe this poor man is not of the opinion that he is a rebel against the holy Church, but I fear it is the case. If he is curable, and our sins now or those of others there do not hinder it, he will certainly cease from such a life and path. But if Christ shall send him to hell because he is a companion of the Devil, then it will be painful for him. Those who follow him will be confused, even if he be the messenger of truth, for it will be of him and of them that the Lord said, "And they will say to me, did we not prophesy in your name?" Wherefore He will say to them, "I do not know you, because you did not know me."[47] That is the day, my brother, in which we cry out, "Hasten in order to rescue me (and also so that we may be chosen), I who have been led into errors, that my days may not be shortened."

I beg you to bind yourselves with humility to the holy Church of Christ, itself without wrinkle, even if prostitutes are among its ministers. You possess Christ, you hear and you follow Him. Who else makes known to you the defeat of the world, who else makes you recognize the saints on earth? Do not heal yourself, I beseech you, since I fear that every day we are finding more false messengers of Christ in the world, and the shadows are growing, and whoever stays may see some of them fall. You seem to me too quick to promise yourself continued survival and the ability to remain among the chosen. Oh! We are strong against the pain, my brother, not in this place, but in heaven, seeing the promised Lamb preparing to descend to our brothers, left behind in this valley after us, who cry out and listen. It troubles me more that you also may become prophets about me, in saying that I will be among the workers to help others. I beg you, do not say this only about me, but may you also reckon others to be such. I have been swollen up by the wind that was not and is not to the honor of Christ, but to my own utility. Help me to give in, and quickly, because final for me is that day, the "day of wrath" in which we believe.[48] Pray, my brother, that my flight may not be in winter or on the Sabbath or while I am pregnant or nursing.[49] All of us must be daily expecting our day of judgment and not let ourselves go, because we will make ourselves great tomorrow even if we know ourselves to be small today. We can—or wish—to do it, but if we are not trustworthy to others, how shall we be trustworthy to ourselves? You know because these judgments are invisible and eternal to us, those of others are worldly, transitory and not ours. Forgive me—I am sorry for your ease in the great works, and to hear that the works promise you great success on the path of God, because you still are not taking it. If you wish to take the path, it is necessary to act, for perfect works search out the perfect master. Do not boast of it to me, or do any similar thing. Pardon me a second time and beseech Christ to His glory. May this be the last time. This present confused letter proceeds from my jumbled, ignorant and proud mind. It contains good wishes for your health and may it falsely declare your arrogance. You may be able to illuminate, mortify and help yourself against this arrogance, if you will also be humble. Pray for us.

From Venice, the 26th day of March 1529. I thought you knew that our brother Paulo Arigo, distracted by all those temporal goods that he possessed, departed and went to a place in which no one recognized him, in order to test if the grace of God is in him.[50] We are praying for him. He desires to appear no longer in these parts, if so shall be the will of God. Few know the place to which his journey was directed. Again, pray for us, and remember us thankfully to Stefano for his letter.[51]

Your unworthy priest in Christ,
Gaetanus

Postscript: He who was in hot water here, this poor Bernardo, is said to have been hanged in Romagna. It was ordered by the Patriach who seized him. Report of the execution has not been confirmed. The good Bernardo showed he wished to be obedient to what was ordered to cure him; however, until now I did not believe it, since I always said that he was not in spiritual health, and well I still fear it. Until, by divine grace, he believes himself to be in error, he will not be cured, and until he says that he wishes to obey, we despair for the health which he can gain much better with these admissions. Your messenger wanted me to speak of them in the present letter.[52] I did not, since it can do them nothing but harm—a harm of ruin to those guarded principally by your favor.

13. TO BARTOLOMEO SCAINI, FROM VENICE, 15 FEBRUARY 1530.

JESUS

My brother in Christ,

After I finished writing yesterday, probably the Lord did not allow Beltrami to come.[53] Today he has shown himself more open to our intention, that is, that he be similar to us as he desired: made worthy by the Lord to live in the justice of God, with His just scorn, our faces weak with sweat; and that when he would test himself, he should be in Venice in order to persevere in this Congregation, probably with an increase of personal devotion, virtue and freedom. May he be able, like St. Paul, to evangelize freely, expecting nothing from the Lord, neither salary nor sustenance.

It seems to me that the press may lead to such perfection. From an influential person we have now a hall with two rooms in it, and most apt for such an enterprise.[54] Our Luca, Paolo Arigon, has deferred the charity that he brings us.[55] Our father Mr. Paganini is worn out by the world, but most skilled, and a man with a very honest, recollected way of life. I have given them permission to write about the press when the Holy Spirit shall deign to speak to them. I also wished to advise you to tell us if the Lord shows you that it may be feasible. If so, send word, and stay with Paganini to discuss if it seems a proper venture for us. And if the Lord inspires them to do this pious work and to be the ministers of the Lord to stabilize this holy life in the fathers and ministers of the Gospel, then certainly it will be more highly esteemed than if he would give the thousand scudi—nay even ten thousand scudi—in alms. Because this work would be the better work, by providing long-term well-being.

There are now fourteen of us here, so perhaps from among these it will be possible to gain the necessary labor for such an enterprise. And from this the Lord may be able to point out still other works. If Mr. Paganini will be moved by the Lord to make the offer to come and teach them for one, two or several months, as Christ wishes, if he can consider having as many dependents as we are here, and if he will stay in a religious house, eating spiritual food according to our poor efforts, then when such actions follow freely, you, if necessary, may give him help through your charity, if he has need of it. (A word to the wise . . .) May the Lord direct all our actions to please Him always, and may the peace of the Lord be with you. Greet Mr. Paganini in the Lord on our behalf, offering anything we can do, and indicating that it is not because we seek something from him now, but because of the love we bear for him.

From Venice, 1530, the 15th day of February. And if it were possible for him to help along such an outcome, he shall advise you immediately by speaking of what he promised himself and what he will be able to lend—to our consolation and for raising up what is holy with the help of St. Paul. It will be good if you give him the letter if you are there, and speak with him personally. Otherwise, be content to send this to Brescia.

> *Your dearest brother,*
> *Gaetano, most hurriedly.*

14. TO SISTER MARIA CARAFA, FROM NAPLES, SEPTEMBER-DECEMBER, 1533.[56]

JESUS

Reverend Mother,

I think you are obliged by the indulgence granted to say some particular prayers.[57] And so that the thought of doing it and how to do it may not disturb you, and in order to remove difficulties from your Reverence, you can make all those that recite the Office before receiving communion, recite three times the ten words which, it is believed, our Lord said on the cross—first from the twenty-first psalm, until "into your hands, Lord, I commend my spirit," along with ten Our Fathers and Hail Marys.[58] Those who do not recite the Office can three times say thirty Hail Marys, along with the three Our Fathers in between them.[59] And you, Mother, should say just three Our Fathers three times, along with three Hail Marys. All should pray for the reformation of the holy Church, for the health of Pope Clement and for his eternal life. Greetings in the Lord. I always remember your daughters in prayer.

> *Don Gaetanus.*

Postscript: And I recommend that every day all say, after they receive communion, three Our Fathers and three Hail Marys as long as the Pope lives in Rome, for the health of his body and soul.

15. TO SISTER MARIA CARAFA, FROM NAPLES, DECEMBER 1534 OR 1545.[60]

If God grants you life until Monday, I shall come to hear confessions, with the intention of distributing holy communion on St. Thomas's day.

You must have patience through Christmas day, because it is necessary for the laity and to the members of this House.[61] After Christmas has passed I will be at your service. May the peace of the Lord be with you all. Perhaps I shall come tomorrow at about the 21st hour in order to be among you, if I can.

> *Yours in Christ,*
> *Don Gaetano.*

16. TO SISTER MARIA CARAFA, FROM NAPLES, DECEMBER 1535 OR 1546.[62]

JESUS

Reverend Mother,
Since I have not come to do the duty, I think it better that I come Thursday to hear confessions, and then Saturday—that will be the holy day of Christmas—to distribute communion, God willing. It remains for me only to desire that Jesus Christ be born and live to the end in all your souls, that He has brought you together as one, and that through such union I may be made worthy to care for such a treasure, as Joseph did. And beg for this grace from the most holy Mother of that little child, who suffered for us and not for Himself.

> *Your servant in Christ,*
> *Don Gaetano.*

17. TO SISTER MARIA CARAFA, FROM ROME, 24 NOVEMBER 1536.

JESUS

Reverend Mother in Christ,
May holy peace be with you and with your daughters forever. I felt that this peace characterizes the letter which St. Chrisogonus wrote to holy Anastasia. From that same peace I also ask you to help yourself, my Mother, through all the temptations that the Lord sends in order to test you and in order that He, with just mercy, may accept you into His heavenly kingdom. No other words will I speak to comfort your Reverence, because I am poor in both the comfort and aid of the most merciful Lord God.

The reverend father our bishop remains very weak, due to the serious illness he has, but he still piously continues to gain new strength.[63] He sends you greetings and encouragement to be constant and strong in this brief battle, desiring to make use of it (with patience, that is) whenever the great heavenly Father shall call you to it, like him. He commends himself to your prayers and those of your daughters. Do not restrain yourself too much in speaking or in resolving something, neither on account of yourself nor on account of us—even if I have given my opinion about it all—for when it pleases the Lord He will give the daughters the greatest strength of all, if it is to be resolved. I hear from our brothers that you are also ill. I beseech you to let yourself be governed by your daughters, as you govern them when they are ill. Greet the lord count in the name of our father, if he is there, along with the lady countess and all the children.[64] Similarly encourage Madame Beatrice and all his other sisters who are there—for all of them he desires eternal happiness, and holy peace in this life.[65] May Christ our Lord be always in your midst with His grace. I commend my soul to all of you. In Rome, the 23rd day of November, 1536.

I wrote to Mr. Ioan Bernardino saying that the father would like to see him for help in this illness.[66] I also hope that some person there will provide money for him to come. Make it known to Signor Don Antonio that if he does not set off on the journey, the father will be afflicted, finding himself not just ill, but also depressed. Today is the day of most holy Catherine, and I beg the Lord to accept Lady Catherine into His holy wounds, so that she may pray with humility for the father bishop and for me.[67] I did not forget to commend Lady Giovanna to the prayers of our father, and to praise her as her good outlook and attitude merit. He drew a deep breath and said, "Oh, may it please Jesus Christ to give them a clear sight of His mercy and grace, since He is sending her to the false world." I related this so Madame Beatrice would know that I kept my promise to her. I commend myself to the prayers of all.

Your son in Christ,
Don Gaetano.

18. TO SISTER MARIA CARAFA, FROM ROME, 23 DECEMBER 1536.

JESUS

Reverend Mother in Christ,
May holy peace be with all of you. The judgment of God is unknowable.[68] It has pleased the Pope to raise our father bishop, among others, to

the rank of cardinal. May Christ our Lord, who can raise up children to Abraham from stones, sanctify his soul in accord with the dignity he has received.[69] The poor man seriously doubts the strength of his body, feels the new weight and wails. His most reverend Paternity received your very welcome letter and has instructed me to respond. Although I do not have time, I will fulfill the assignment quickly. His most reverend Paternity sends you a thousand greetings and begs you to help him more than ever. We should strive to comfort him whenever possible, bound by the grace of the Lord. With your prayers and those of your daughters you can share this weight he has. And not seeing only the temporary exaltation, but also the responsibility implied, he will find the eternal reward beyond that burden. Do not rejoice with him, but rather pity him, so taking your joy in heaven and not in earthly things—as you ought—as servants of Christ, not servants of the world. Mr. Giovanni Bernardino entreats the other Carafa relatives. To you I commend my soul.

From Rome, the 23rd of December 1536.

Your son in Christ,
Don Gaetano, in haste, without proofreading.

19. TO GIAMBATTISTA SCAINI, FROM NAPLES, 25 MAY 1537.

JESUS

Honored one in Christ,
 I have had your letter and that of Bartolomeo for more than a day, and in addition to these, letters of yours came in the past days addressed to your representative, who has been in Naples for three days and stayed here with us. The letter was given to him, and he said to me that he had some difficulties, but that through the grace of the Lord, he hoped for a good end in your concern. He said that he will return a letter from us. Yesterday evening we received your letter of the 12th, sent from Pesaro, along with one devoted to that other matter. We are asking a citizen of Bergamo so that he might come here today. Even now he has not appeared, and we do not know where he is lodging. I am certain he will come, but I am writing you this in case you have not had earlier news of him, to inform you how much he has profited by drawing on your doubts and anxieties. It remains for us to all be continually prepared, through divine mercy, to strip ourselves of this most beloved clothing of mortal flesh that we may be made worthy—when

some of us shall go on ahead—to be able to pray for those who remain. And may those who remain have true joy for those departed, with genuine hope that they are with the Father and all the elect. In this way we are content always to groan under the heavy weight of this mortality, although it is above all the universal curse. Still, more thorns and afflictions grow for those who more greatly love that mortal reality, and those are pricked more often who pay attention to the thorns. Greet Bartolomeo, Stefano and all those dear to you and to us in Christ, on behalf of our father general and all of us others.[70] Please also remember us to our friends in Verona and elsewhere who are dear to us in Christ.

From Naples, the 25th day of May, 1537.

Yours in Christ,
Don Gaetano.

20. RECOMMENDATIONS TO THE NUNS OF THE *SAPIENZA*, FROM NAPLES, 6 MARCH 1540.[71]

JESUS

On the 6th day of March 1540. Summary of the best examples of the advice of Father Don Gaetano, composed at the insistence of us sisters of the *Sapienza*. Who will ever be able to give voice or pen to such holy teaching, first on charity and prayer and on all the other virtues? The monastery, the congregation, ought to be one body with many members, each member fulfilling her own duties—the feet neither serving as arms or head, nor the head as feet or arms. No one ought to depend on or place hope in any person other than Christ. One ought to believe that hell can be avoided if one does not attain satisfaction of self-will and does not miss Purgatory, thus purging and purifying one's own will. One ought to consider what Christ has demonstrated through His own actions as well as those of His glorious Mother.

21. TO SISTER MARIA CARAFA, FROM VENICE, 13 MARCH 1541.

JESUS

Dearest and reverend Mother in Christ,
May the joy of Jesus Christ fill us all. I ought to be able to stop and respond to your (as usual) kind letter. Although the spirit necessary to

respond adequately as I am obliged and as I desire is not in me, Christ will supply it, I hope, from that immense goodness that has bound us together through His most holy and closest ties. May His Majesty at least make us sense in heaven our home, and, if it pleases Him, here on earth a bit of jail. And although you are in one room together with the nuns and I in another, still we are separate but united as one. May you be comforted, my Mother, for He who holds us in prison and who releases us from prison so loves us that He died out of love. For our eternal salvation He died, was raised and now reigns in heaven. We groan and cry out, but we are not sorry. Find relief with tears for the infallible promise that the sadness of His saints will be converted into joy. Be saddened by the fact that many who are still in prison laugh in mad fashion as if they were already in heaven.[72] Be content, then, to remain without consolation here, and like the true Captain, although bodily strengths are being lost, your spirit shall grow stronger, giving courage to your daughters given by Christ. Comfort ill Sister Christina, whom Christ our Lord is calling to himself through this infirmity. Comfort Catherine, that loving woman, through the goodness of Christ, since the delay that men are making in consoling her will contribute greatly to her true consolation. Greet the sub-prioress along with all the others, one by one. I continually beseech our Lord to bless each one with His most holy peace.[73] To you, my Mother, along with all the rest, I commend my poor soul. I pray that divine mercy may be your light and guide.

From Venice, on the 13th day of March 1541.

Your son in Christ,
Don Gaetano.

22. TO SISTER MARIA CARAFA, FROM VENICE, 6 APRIL 1541.

Reverend and most excellent Mother in Christ,
  May holy peace be always with you. I know that you are weak in body and that you only write with difficulty. You know that my hand is so weak that I do not know if I may ever again write legibly to anyone. Still, I cannot fail to respond to you, although it will be in my wretched scrawl. Today I received your letter of the 12th of last month. I am always grateful, and the letters will be even more welcome to me if, from the mercy of our Lord, I shall be granted the favor to see myself never more divided from that blessed Kingdom that the Son of God and the Virgin

Mary have acquired for us with His most precious blood—there we must hope to enjoy ourselves in eternity. We comfort ourselves, my Mother, and we catch our breath a little, since we are fatigued and weary. But little time remains to us, and it will pass quickly. We must invoke the most holy advocate, the Mother of our Redeemer, that she may deign to cover our ugliness and present us to the just Judge, her Son. He will not refuse to assume from His Mother the greatest of our debts, and pay them before our common eternal Father. Encourage the Prioress—along with all the sisters and that dear daughter lady Catherine—to be courageous and to wash themselves in the bath which the heavenly Doctor makes for us these days.[74] Greet my dearest Mother Lady Aloisa, that she may be pleased to shed tears for me with her friend in Christ, Madonna Cassandra, along with the others joined to them in charity.[75] Oh, when will that day come where there will be no more night, when we shall see in the beautiful and only true light—that is, the light of the spotless Lamb? But enough—I am not suited to raise my eyes to such a light, but rather to cry out upon the earth, "be gracious to me, a sinner, for truly I am dung and not a man."[76] I greet all of you in our Lord, who always blesses you.

From Venice, on the 6th day of April, 1541.

Your son and servant through Christ,
Don Gaetano, as well as I am able.

Postscript: It has been some days since I have received news of our most reverend Father.[77] This morning I wrote to him. May the Lord make him happy always.

23. TO THE BROTHERS OF THE COMPANY OF SAN GIROLAMO IN VICENZA, FROM VENICE, 17 JUNE 1541.

Dearest brothers in Christ,

May holy peace be with you all. I am writing this letter with the desire to greet you. And I am gladdened by you, since His divine Majesty has made you worthy of election among so many other Christians and has given you such dignity by placing so welcome an undertaking in your hands—that is, to have care and responsibility for persons ulcerated and in bad health—while also to be engaged in the other good and pious works that our holy oratory and company practices, all works of real corporal and spiritual mercy. Thus I beg you, through the heart of my Lord, to consider this work of great importance and value, if you wish God in a similar way to consider and to care for your souls. Oh, my dear brothers, if you wish to comfort my soul, let it be said—and let it be in fact also—that the work of the hospital goes well, that it is well administered, and that your activities are a light and carry a good aroma throughout that poor city. So I beseech you, through the love of Jesus Christ and His most holy Mother, that all of you persevere in these holy enterprises unanimously and as one body. And pray to God for me, and accept this advice not from me as a sinner, but from me out of the love and obligation to you which Christ our Lord has entrusted to me, and out of the desire that His glory be increased through this holy company.

From Venice, on the 17th day of June, 1541.

Gaetano, priest.

24. TO CATERINA CARAFA, FROM VENICE, 1541–1543.[78]

My daughter in Christ,

Through the letters of the Reverend Mother I heard of your new anxiety. Because of the concern and duty I have to look after your health, I ask you to learn from the Lord, who separated from His Mother in order to serve the eternal Father. When found on the third day, realizing that His Mother and Joseph were grieved, [He] left and conformed himself to their will and was subject to them for eighteen uninterrupted years, so that it might never again be mentioned.[79] Apply yourself to the mortification of all your will and all your opinions, and I assure you that you will be near to your Lord Jesus Christ. I have time now to say nothing more. Pray to the Lord for me.

Your father and brother in Christ,
Priest Gaetano.

25. TO SISTER MARIA CARAFA, FROM VENICE, 28 JULY 1542.

JESUS

My reverend Mother in Christ,

I have received frequent news regarding your health and the fact that the Lord has knocked at your door, but has not chosen to take you with

Him. We must always be content with what will be. May that dear daughter in Christ, sister Caterina, be content with Christ her Lord on the cross. May she be thankful and eternally praise the sanctifier of that cross, where the most holy mother, Virgin Mary, so devotedly stands.[80] I hope that through the name of Mary and her virtues, Caterina will be made wealthy in heavenly riches, powerful humility and humble strength, scorning like dirt the weak pride and proud weakness of the Traitor and the vain world, along with all his followers. Over these daughters you shed tears, along with the Lord Jesus Christ and the saints, serving them day and night, conceiving like twins, bearing in pain and nourishing with tears the daughters given to you in Christ by the eternal Father. I pray that my Lord may make you worthy, so that in heaven you may see the holy daughters of your holy daughters, and that they may beseech mercy for me.

From Venice, on the 28th day of July, 1542.

Postscript: Greet the Lord count of Montorio, the countess and the children for me in Christ. May the Lord God always be a guide and comfort to them all.

Your son in Christ,
Don Gaetano.

26. TO SISTER MARIA CARAFA, FROM VENICE, 30 SEPTEMBER 1542.

JESUS

My dearest and observant reverend Mother in Christ,
 Your letter was very welcome to me. (If we all go along with the flesh—toward the earth—we should be pleased, since our redemption is approaching and our deliverance is nearer than we believe.)[81] I greet you in Christ, along with all the dear Mothers and sisters, your daughters and our daughters, wishing that all be dressed, both in flesh and in spirit, with that only eternal and perfect virtue of holy charity, which is the daughter and mother of holy, willing obedience. To this condition and to this path I urge you, even until the moment of death, and you must not doubt that it will lead you to the door of salvation. Woe to the world today that is always nauseated by such a gift. The great pillars and vain, lofty ones are falling into the depths of the sea. My daughter, sister, Mother, be humble. Do not attribute even a dot to yourself, and be a

daughter of the Virgin Mary by refusing to believe some one or another new thing. Beg the most holy Mother that she might cover me, with her humility, from the just anger of her Son over my ingratitude, especially for the gift of the holy vows. I desire that the good daughter Sister Maria Caterina be crucified, first in spirit, and then, when the time comes, in her will and in her speech. Greet in Christ your noble relatives, and may the Lord himself always be with you and all the others. Pardon me, since I can only write poorly.

From Venice, the last day of September, 1542.

Yours in Christ,
Priest Gaetano.

Postscript: We hear that our brothers are moved to assume responsibility for San Paolo. If such vexations do not cease, I do not doubt that all will be lost. I say it to you so that if they wish to pursue this work in Naples, such intentions elsewhere may cease.[82]

27. TO BARTOLOMEO SCAINI, FROM VENICE, 2 DECEMBER 1542.

JESUS

Dearest in Christ,
I am unable to write because of cold hands, but I am constrained by charity to do this. The visitors of the poor, good persons with good intentions, are asserting to me that Jerome remains in prison at your insistence and, deservedly, in extreme misery. They also tell me there is no hope of him ever being able to make satisfaction or to pay. If that is so, I am certain you know it and do not want him to die there without hope of your mercy. I desire that he be justified to you in the heart of the Lord and in the hearts of men, and that the action which Christ our Lord would wish from us be done, and nothing else. So informed, may you do as it seems best to you in this matter, so that I can assert to these two visitors that you are Christian and just and pious. Goodbye, brother, greet all our friends in Christ.

From Venice, on the 2nd day of December, 1542.

Your brother,
Priest Gaetanus.

28. TO BARTOLOMEO SCAINI, FROM VENICE, 9 DECEMBER 1542.[83]

JESUS

Dearest brother—peace.

In relation to your letter, which I have had for some days, I want you to know that it was delivered that day to the clients. Concerning the recommendation of your son, since it would be subject to the Judge, we have no desire to do it, because he does not seem suitable to present for either the care of souls or other such office.[84] Second. Begging your pardon, but to judge is a holy office, and to be raised to be a judge is not proper for all, especially for us. In light of this fear of ours perhaps you will be able to purify your desires and follow Christ, that we may do the good because it is good. I send you and all our friends greetings in Christ.

From Venice, the 9th day of December, 1542.

Your brother,
Priest Gaetanus.

29. TO SISTER MARIA CARAFA, FROM NAPLES, 30 JANUARY 1544.

JESUS

Reverend Mother,

Since you have money beyond what you need for a few days, if God and your charity are willing, loan eight ducats of it (which will make twenty along with the twelve you already loaned), and give them to Antonio, our brother, the carrier of this letter.[85] May holy peace be with you.

From St. Paul's, on the 30th of January, 1544.

Yours in Christ,
Don Gaetano.

30. TO SISTER MARIA CARAFA, FROM NAPLES, 1545–1546.[86]

JESUS

Reverend Mother,
    You can say to Maria Cecilia that, God willing, tomorrow after Mass I will want to satisfy her request. May you be willing to present my one worry to the Lord again, if it be pleasing to His Majesty that you do it. And may holy peace be with you all. On the first day.

Yours in Christ,
Don Gaetano.

31. BRIEF COMPENDIUM ON THE SPIRITUAL LIFE. [NO PLACE OR DATE OF ORIGIN GIVEN][87]

    The true and inestimable delight of the spiritual person is to strive after likeness to the heart and person of Jesus, expecting no other prize, according to that saying of Paul: "I am ready not only to be imprisoned but even to die for the name of the Lord Jesus."[88]
    Likewise, the beginning and the end of every perfection is to know that we are unworthy of divine blessing and that the good that God does in us has no basis in ourselves, but proceeds only from the infinite goodness of the divine name.
    Humility is twofold, one which truth bears, and the other which charity strengthens. The true humility is that which comes from love of virtue and charity.
    The active life lies, 1) in taking up work and poverty, and 2) in scorn for the fame and honors of the world and in departing from its wisdom.
    The ingredients of true contemplation are three: purity of heart, closing off all the senses, and obedience to interior inspiration.[89]

32. TO SISTER MARIA CARAFA, FROM NAPLES. [NO DATE GIVEN][90]

JESUS

Reverend Mother in Christ,
    The mother of children in the flesh has pleasure in conceiving, and experiences pain in giving birth. The spiritual mother conceives with fear

LETTERS OF ST. GAETANO DA THIENE

and sorrow but gives birth with joy. Therefore I exhort you to be strong and composed through this illness and to conceive these two daughters with the Holy Spirit, in Christ, to the honor of the eternal Father, if it shall so please the most holy Trinity. And name whichever of them it seems best Paola, and the other Angela.

This evening call all those to whom you have given the habit and tell them that since you have the confirmation of your priorate from his Holiness the Pope, that you are giving them anew the holy habit of religious life. Beg them to give themselves anew to Christ with similar words. And this may be done anytime after Sister Giovanna has presented and read the brief, and lowers and places it on your head.[91] And then, if it seems proper to you and to Sister Giovanna to give the habit tomorrow to the two novices, call them individually and tell them that since it is customary—and if they are willing—it shall be given to them tomorrow morning.

I, God willing, shall desire to give holy communion tomorrow to all those that wish it.

May the grace of our Lord be in you always, praying and urging you to pray for me.

Your brother in Christ,
Don Gaetano.

33. TO SISTER MARIA CARAFA, FROM NAPLES. [NO DATE GIVEN]

JESUS

My Mother in Christ,
    See that you do not even think of giving your new daughter a place other than that described for all the other professed sisters according to their office. And if you do otherwise, you would snatch away glory from Christ, which is useful for you and for the others a reason for humility. It would also be a scandal to those close to you, and you would be in violation of your constitution.[92] If the Lord grants me the chance to give communion to you and the novice tomorrow, I will do so willingly; but since I am unable to promise it, I will not say so to you. Pray for me.

Yours in Christ,
Don Gaetano.

34. TO SISTER MARIA CARAFA, FROM NAPLES. [NO DATE GIVEN]

JESUS

My Mother,
    So, just as you ought to be obeyed by your daughters, it is also right that you obey those who have care of you. Thus I ask you to obey, as much as possible, all that the Doctor orders pertaining to the flesh, just as much as the other remedies.[93] And may Christ our Lord, with His most holy Mother, be attentive to the care of your body and soul, and those of all your daughters, whom I wish to visit tomorrow, if it shall please the Lord.
                                    Your Don Gaetano, servant in Christ.

35. TO SISTER MARIA CARAFA, FROM NAPLES. [NO DATE GIVEN]

JESUS

Reverend Mother,
    If you send a well-known person with your bill to Branchalion, you will get the six measures of salt through a faithful friend.[94] If the work of the craftsman of your tabernacle was appraised by the judges of that craft—and they themselves judge that twenty-eight carlini, plus three for the glass he had purchased, be given to him—then it is necessary to give them 31 carlini, that is, thirty-one. Therefore, whether you need help finding these carlini or not, make the completion of the transaction known to me, when it seems best to you.[95] My sins hold me bound,[96] so if the ill sister has the need or desire to confess, the father *preposito* can come. On my own I can promise myself nothing, except indeed when He, who is the Lord God, wishes. May He be our comfort and peace, light, and way and life. To the prayers of all I commend myself.
                                    Your servant in Christ,
                                    Don Gaetano

36. TO SISTER MARIA CARAFA, FROM NAPLES. [NO DATE GIVEN]

JESUS

Reverend Mother,
    I heard that the divine office was recited with a choral chant. If so, it was incorrectly done. Therefore, see that it is done in nothing other than a

low chant. You must correct whoever caused it, even though it is over with. And pray for me.[97]

> In Christ,
> Don Gaetano.

37. TO AN UNKNOWN ADDRESSEE. [NO PLACE OR DATE GIVEN][98]

JESUS

The great goodness of the Lord grants many graces and gifts that we blind ones do not recognize, due to our passions and worldly desires. Leaving behind everything else, it is a blessed soul who argues that these are the reasons for which we lacerate our soul, for which we mourn for it, for which we cry out and fail to consider immediately how obligated we are to give thanks for the excellent and supreme mercy of the great high God. Giving to this soul the true good, He desired that the prayers of the saints who are calling it to heaven have greater power than those of men who have sought to keep it on earth. And He truly enables the soul to believe that the glorious apostle St. Peter will beg his dear Lord and Master to break the chains of this miserable flesh and to open the prison of this dark life for that blessed soul, in the same way that the holy mother Church celebrates the fact that the Lord sent his angel, breaking his chains and freeing Him from the hands of Herod and the Jews.[99] Therefore, those who are now mourning, while silently thanking the Lord Himself, will listen. They will hear—with the ear of the spirit—the soft voice that echoes, "Now I truly know that the Lord sent His angel and freed me from the hand of Herod and from all the plans of the demons." That voice tells us that we indeed are that blessed soul in tears, so we may thank the Lord, bless the Lord and glorify the Lord, until we receive from Him a more perfect and accelerated cleansing. And if the Lord has cleansed and freed it out of His great goodness, through such gracious praises, it rejoices, every day increasing the glory and immense Goodness of His great Highness who grants it, through His grace. Amen.

38. TO FRANCESCO CAPPELLO, FROM VENICE, 17 FEBRUARY 1533.[100]

Dearest brother in Christ,
Recently, three of your letters were received. This one will respond to the letter in which you spoke of the request of our Mr. Marcantonio.[101]

We have understood and conferred together over what he asks and have presented his desire for our rule to the Lord in prayer. We then discovered together that it seems the Lord made it very clear to see that it is right and necessary for whoever puts a hand to the evangelical plow in our company to live in a manner common to all as regards the house, and in conformity in all other things, insofar as these servants of God are able, without detriment to the body or soul.[102] And as they carry the yoke of Christ in one flock, under one shepherd, so they ought to conform and flee every kind of distinction and unseemly difference.[103] Still, it happens that not all those who are congregated together are called at the same hour of the day, but rather according to the choice of that good father of the family who sometimes at the eleventh hour says to some, "Why do you stand here idle all day?"[104] In this way it happens that in the same company there may be found persons of different age, in different states of health, of different complexion, and with different degrees of goodness. Due to this, it is truly necessary to follow the rule of our holy Fathers—inspired by the Holy Spirit—that says, "They distributed them to all, as any had need."[105] Following upon and explaining that passage, Augustine said, "Not equally to all, because all were not equal in condition."

To come to this particular case. We say that if Mr. Marcantonio thinks that through this poor company some opportunity may come to free himself somewhat from the world and to make some progress in the way of God, it is in truth not possible to think or to hope for anything from us unless he first considers that we are governed and guided by the goodness of God, by the examples and teachings of the aforesaid holy Fathers, and by the aforesaid rule—not by our own inventions or by other human inclinations. And if he, in truth, believes that the goodness of God is only found in that which He has brought together and that which He governs and that which He maintains, he must believe also that if, for the service of the Majesty of God and his own salvation, he desires either perpetually or for some time to remain and live with us, then the same goodness of God will provide such understanding about him that we shall know what is necessary. He will also provide such charity that we are able to support the weight of his bodily or spiritual weaknesses, and such provisions that there will be enough to give him as much to eat as it will seem that he needs. Therefore, if he wishes to serve among us, he must think beyond the present to the time when God will want him to follow us by throwing himself freely and absolutely at the feet of Christ, and into our arms, without promising himself more freedom or more self-will than us, or more power to control forever his own goods, or more property than us—as if it were possible for us who are under the yoke of Christ to promise ourselves anything. And if this seems strange to him, it is clear he does not believe that God is among us, or that he may be governed by us. And if he thinks like this, he has no reason to desire to be among us. For by removing the protection and consolation of the goodness of God and the hope to serve and to please His Majesty by means of His grace, we have no reason anymore for fleeing and abhorring the world.

If he believes he wants to come among the servants of the Lord—even though his heart is not strong enough and he does not have enough faith to make him embrace the naked cross—still, in time, he may decide to prepare himself to live in the aforesaid manner and to arrange his matters in such a way that when he is among us, he will not even think about them. He must entrust himself to the Lord, because for our part we do not give any thought to desiring his possessions, neither as funds for charity, nor as a troublesome occupation, nor as the occasion of his own distraction. This would not be possible without reducing our peace of mind somewhat. Therefore, in conclusion, if he still wishes to be among us, he must not entertain even a thought about the rooms, or anything else, but only think of mortifying all his thoughts and desires in such a way that one day, between him and us, there may not be any other point of difference except that we are nailed to the holy cross and he chooses to enable himself to depart whenever it pleases him or us.

As regards teaching, we say that although his kind of learning is pleasing, still, the charity of Christ made learning more clear to all of us for another reason. The hope which we have that he may desire to humble himself and learn the alphabet of Christ may move him still further: from there to desire that some other comfort or fruit can come to him than from himself, or from learning, or from some other worldly good. Therefore, set forth the rule to him and then leave the rest to Christ. It seems best not to omit proper mention of our most reverend father the Bishop of Verona, of whom it would not be necessary to speak if the said Mr. Marcantonio had acted as a strong person and given himself freely to the service of Christ.[106] This is because in that case, no one would be able to deny his request, and I am unable to believe that our most reverend father Giberti wanted to recommend what is impossible and improper. Since the idea of Mr. Marcantonio is so faulty—and even beyond faulty to dubious, suggesting the danger of inconstancy— we do not see how it would be good to give him encouragement, let alone admission, without the proper grace and blessing of the most reverend father. With good wishes in Christ.

From Venice, 17 February 1533.

Your brothers in Christ,
The General[107] and brothers of the Clerics Regular, etc.

39. TO THE BROTHERS OF THE COMPANY OF DIVINE LOVE IN SALÒ, FROM VENICE, 5 OCTOBER 1542.

Dearest brothers in Christ,

It is indeed a pity, but it would be an incomparably greater pity if the delight and obligation that we have for you and for all in your city had proceeded from concerns of the world. That world possesses nothing if not a desire to make us see the pleasures and pains of the present. But since it has pleased the Holy Spirit to connect us with you through His most gentle but strong ties—ones that neither distance nor death can break—therefore we are comforted when both we and you are grieved in doing the will of our heavenly Father, imitating, through the mercy of God since we are poor and sluggish members, the head, our blessed Jesus Christ, who promised to all those dear to Him that He would convert their sadness into joy by entry into His body. This, we hope, the blessed Lord will certainly concede to you and to us. It remains for us to beg His infinite goodness, if it be to His glory, to concede us also the second promise in this mortal life, in order to increase our eternal joy, for as He said, "I will see you again and your hearts will rejoice."[108]

O most beloved brothers in Christ, we have prolonged the stay of those few of our brothers with you, in particular our brother Don Bernardino, as long as we could (and with some inconvenience for our Congregation). But we cannot any longer. It is necessary that we, and you, dearest in Christ, come together and that you and those brothers and all of us have patience. We have sent holy instructions in the name of God and of ourselves to the said brothers, so that it will be possible for them to more rapidly execute what the Lord requires when all three are here with us, if He shall deign to do it according to His pleasure. We are unable to give them more time than they need in order to depart from you, since the measurer of time does not lose time. May Christ our Lord deign to redouble the spiritual union and strength of our prayers for all of you over this physical distance, and may He be the great rewarder of all your charity directed toward us. We beseech you to convert our temporal subsidies and labors into continual prayers for this poor congregation.

From Venice, on the 5th day of October, 1542.

Yours in Christ,
The General [at that time, Gaetano] and the brothers of the Clerics Regular.

40. PRAYER COMPOSED BY GAETANO.[109]

Verse: That You will deem this city worthy to be defended, pacified, cared for and preserved.

Response: We beseech thee, hear us.

Look forth from your sanctuary and your lofty dwelling place in heaven, Lord holy Father, and see that Most Holy Victim that our High Priest offers to You for the sins of our brothers, Your holy Son our Lord Jesus Christ, and be appeased, even upon the multitude of our evils. Hear the voice of the blood of our brother Jesus cry out to You from the cross, "O Lord, hear; O Lord, forgive; O Lord, give heed and act; delay not, for thy own sake, O my God, because Your name has been invoked upon this city and this people."[110] And deal with us according to your mercy.

Lorenzo Scupoli
Il combattimento spirituale

(TRANSLATED FROM LORENZO SCUPOLI, *IL COMBATTIMENTO SPIRITUALE*, EDITED BY CARLO DI PALMA [ROME, 1657], WITH REFERENCE TO THE EDITIONS OF MARIO SPINELLI [MILAN, 1985] AND BARTOLOMEO MAS [ROME, 1992]. ALL SCRIPTURAL PASSAGES QUOTED FOLLOW THE REVISED STANDARD VERSION, UNLESS OTHERWISE NOTED.)

THE SPIRITUAL COMBAT

*T*o the supreme captain and most glorious victor, Jesus Christ Son of Mary:

Because the sacrifices and offerings of us mortals are always pleasing and pleasurable to your Majesty when they come offered from a pure heart and to your glory, I present this little treatise, the *Spiritual Combat*, dedicating it to your divine Majesty. I am not discouraged because this text is small, since it is well known that you alone are that great Lord who delights in humble things and who disperses the smoke and pretense of the world. But how can I, without offense and without damage to other persons, dedicate this to your Majesty, the King of heaven and earth? All of what this little treatise teaches is Your doctrine, having taught us that "distrustful of ourselves we trust in You, fight for You and pray to You."

In addition, if every combat requires an expert leader who guides the battle and inspires the soldiers, who fight the more generously the more they fight under an invincible captain, can this spiritual combat not require one? Thus they choose You, Jesus Christ (all of us who have previously resolved to battle and defeat every nemesis) for our captain, You who have overcome the world, the prince of darkness, and who with wounds and the death of Your most holy body have defeated the flesh of all those who have battled generously and are battling. Lord, when I arranged the *Combat*, I always kept in mind that saying, "Not that we are sufficient of ourselves to claim anything as coming from us; our sufficiency is from God."[1] If without You and without Your help we cannot think that we are good persons, then how can we battle alone against such powerful enemies, and avoid such hidden and innumerable snares? This *Combat* is Yours, Lord, from every perspective, since, as I have said, Yours is the doctrine and Yours are all spiritual soldiers, among which are we Theatine Clerics Regular. Therefore, we, all supplicators at the feet of Your highest Majesty, beg You to accept this *Combat*, moving us always and animating us with Your actual grace constantly to fight more generously, because we do not doubt at all that with You fighting within us, we shall be victorious for Your glory and that of Your most holy mother, the Virgin Mary.

> *Your most humble servant,*
> *purchased with your blood,*
> *D. Lorenzo Scupoli*
> *Cleric Regular*

THE SPIRITUAL COMBAT

"An athelete is not crowned unless he competes according to the rules." (2 Tm 2:5).

WORKS OF LORENZO SCUPOLI

CHAPTER 1: ON THE ESSENCE OF CHRISTIAN PERFECTION, HOW IT IS NECESSARY TO FIGHT TO ACQUIRE IT, AND ON THE FOUR THINGS NECESSARY FOR THIS BATTLE.

Desiring that you, most loving daughter in Christ, reach the height of perfection and drawing near to your God become of one same spirit with Him (which is the greatest and most noble deed that can be spoken of or imagined), you must first have knowledge of what makes up the true and perfect spiritual life. For many have immersed themselves in the rigor of spiritual life, in mortification of the flesh, hairshirts, flagellation, in long vigils, fasting and other similar vexations and corporal austerities without careful thought. Others, and particularly women, believe themselves to have attained great distinction when they engage in much vocal prayer, hear many masses and long offices, and frequent churches and communion. Many others—among whom at times is someone who wears the religious habit, living in cloister—persuade themselves that perfection depends completely upon attendance in choir, silence, solitude and regular discipline. And so one holds that the basis of perfection is in these, and another believes it is in other similar actions.

But it is not so, and since these operations are the means to acquire the spirit, and are fruit of the spirit, one cannot say that perfect Christianity and the true spirit consist in them alone. They are, without doubt, the most powerful means to acquire the spirit for those who use them well and discretely in order to gain force and strength against their own evil and weakness, [and] in order to arm themselves against the assaults and deceptions of our common enemies, [and] in order to provide themselves with those spiritual aids which are necessary to all the servants of God and to beginners especially. They are then, the fruit of the spirit in truly spiritual persons, those who punish the body because it has offended its Creator and in order to hold it subject and humble in His service. They are silent and they live only in order to flee the slightest offense against our Lord, and in order to hold conversation in the heavens. They attend to the divine office and to every work of piety, praying and meditating upon the life and passion of our Lord, but not out of curiosity or morbidity, but in order to understand above all their own evil, and the goodness and mercy of God, [and] in order to inflame themselves always more intensely in divine love and in hatred of themselves, following the Son of God with personal abnegation and with the cross on their shoulder. They frequent the Most Holy Sacrament for the glory of His divine Majesty in order to join themselves more closely with God and to gather new strength against the enemies.

But these exterior devotions can frequently present the occasion for ruin—sometimes even more than manifest sin—for those who place all their foundation in them, but not through any defect in the things themselves (since they are most holy), but instead through defects in those who use them. While intent upon them alone, they leave the heart abandoned in the hands of their inclinations and the hidden demon. Seeing that they have already left the straight path, he allows them not only to continue in these exercises with pleasure, but also to rove through the delights of paradise following their vain thoughts. They convince themselves they have been raised there amid the heavenly choir and that they hear God speaking within them. They sometimes find themselves all absorbed in certain meditations filled with high, strange and delightful points. Almost forgotten in the world and by creatures, it seems to them that they have been rapt to the third heaven.

One can easily understand from their life and morals in how many errors these entangled ones find themselves, and how distant they are from that perfection we are seeking, because in everything, great and small, they want to be favored and preferred over others. They are set in their outlook and insistent in all their desires, and blindly wrapped up with themselves; they are prompt, diligent observers and whisperers about others' words and deeds. If you criticize them a little for a certain vain reputation they hold of themselves—and in which they enjoy being held by others—and raise them from those rubber-stamped devotions, they all become disturbed and extremely agitated. And if God, in order to reduce them to true self-knowledge and to the way of perfection, sends them difficulties and infirmities, or permits them persecutions (which never come without His will wishing or permitting, and which are the touchstones of the loyalty of His servants), then they discover their false foundation and interior corruption. And thus they are spoiled by pride, because in every occurrence, whether it be sad or happy, they wish neither to resign themselves nor to humble themselves under the divine hand, calming themselves in the always just but secret judgments of God. Nor do they lower themselves beneath all creatures, in the example of His humiliated and impassioned Son, holding persecutors as dear friends, as instruments of divine goodness and aids to their own mortification, perfection and health.

Therefore it is certain that such persons are placed in grave danger. Having clouded the inner eye and looking at themselves and their good external works with that eye, they attribute to themselves many degrees of perfection, and filled with pride, they judge others. Through them no one is converted, except by extraordinary help from God. Therefore, it is a good deal easier to convert and bring to goodness an open sinner than one hidden and covered with the cloak of apparent virtue.

You see then very clearly as I have explained to you, daughter, that such things do not constitute the spiritual life. You must know that it consists in nothing other than knowledge of the goodness and greatness of God and of our nothingness and inclination toward every evil; in love of Him and hatred of ourselves; in subjection not only to Him but to all creatures out of love for Him; in the renunciation of our every desire and total resignation to His divine pleasure; and above all [in recognition] that all this is willed and done by us purely for the glory of God and for His satisfaction alone, and because He so wishes and merits being loved and served.

This is the law of love stamped by the hand of that same Lord into the hearts of His faithful servants; this is the self-abnegation that God desires from us; this is the sweet yoke and His light burden[2]; this is the obedience to which our Redeemer and Master calls us with voice and with example. Because you aspire to the height of such perfection, you have to do continual violence to yourself by bravely combatting and annihilating all your desires, either great or small. It is necessary for you to appear at this battle with all promptness of soul, since the crown is not given to any but soldiers of valor.[3]

Since this task is more difficult than any other—because in fighting against ourselves we are fighting at the same time with our very selves—so too the victory obtained will be more glorious beyond every other, and more dear to God. So, if you will undertake to press down and kill off all your disordered appetites, desires and wishes, even the smallest, you will give greater pleasure and service to God than if you voluntarily allow some to live, or were to scourge yourself until bleeding, and fast more than the ancient hermits and anchorites, or convert thousands of souls. Although the Lord Himself has more concern for the conversion of souls than for the mortification of a little desire, nonetheless you must neither desire nor work for anything, principally, other than what the Lord strictly seeks and wishes from you. And, without fail, He is more delighted that you tire yourself out in paying attention to the mortification of your passions than if you purposely set this aside and left the passions alive in you voluntarily, just to serve Him in some work, even if of greater importance.

So, in order that you see, my daughter, in what the perfection of the

Christian life consists, and that you acquire it, you have to undertake a continual and most bitter war against yourself. For this, four necessary things are to be provided to you—as very trusty, required weapons—in order to gain the palm [of victory] and remain the winner in this spiritual battle. These are distrust of self, confidence in God, spiritual exercise and prayer. All these we will discuss with the help of God and with approachable brevity.

CHAPTER 2: ON DISTRUST OF OURSELVES.

Distrust of yourself, daughter, is so necessary to you in this combat that without this you must consider it certain not only that you are unable to achieve the desired victory, but also to overcome one of the smallest of your little passions. And so let this be stamped well in your mind, inasmuch as we are far too prone and inclined by our corrupt nature to a false esteem for ourselves, while truly in ourselves we are nothing, though we convince ourselves that we are something important. Without any foundation, we presume vainly of our own powers. This defect is very difficult to recognize and very displeasing to the eyes of God, who loves and wishes to see in us a sincere recognition of this most certain truth—that every grace and virtue in us derives from Him alone, who is the source of every good, and that from us no single thing, not even a good thought, can ever be to His liking.

And it happens that this very important distrust is also a work of His divine hand, who wishes to give it to His dear friends at times through holy inspirations, at other times with harsh scourges and with violence and almost insurmountable temptations, and with other means we don't ourselves comprehend. Still, wishing that He may do His part together with us in what affects us, I propose to you four means with which, aided chiefly by divine favor, you may acquire such distrust.

The first is that you consider and understand your lowness and nothingness, and that on your part you can do no good sufficient to merit entry into the heavenly kingdom.

The second is that with fervent and humble prayer you request this often from the Lord, since it is His gift. And in order to obtain it, first you must demonstrate that you still do not possess it, and are completely powerless to acquire it by yourself. So, presenting yourself often before the divine Majesty with a secure faith so that through His goodness He may grant it to you, and awaiting it with perseverence through all the time His providence has arranged, there is no doubt that you will obtain it.

The third means is that you become accustomed to fear yourself, your own judgment, your strong inclination toward sin, the innumerable enemies against whom you are insufficient to raise even a minimal resistance, their long experience of battle and tricks, their transfigurations into angels of light and the innumerable artifices and traps that lead us secretly from the way of virtue.

The fourth means is that when you happen to fall into some defect, you then enter more deeply and more vigorously into consideration of your total weakness. It is to this end God has permitted you to fall, so that inspired by a much clearer light than before, knowing yourself well, you learn to despise yourself as something still too vile, and as such you also desire to be considered and despised by others. Without this desire it is not possible for you to be virtuously distrustful, [a quality] which has its very foundation in true humility and in this experiential knowledge.

It is clear that knowledge of self is necessary for those who wish to join themselves with the celestial light and uncreated truth. Divine mercy gives [this] ordinarily to the arrogant and presumptuous through failures, justly leaving them to fall into some fault from which they convince themselves they can defend themselves, so that finally reaching understanding, they learn to be suspicious of themselves in all things. But the Lord does not wish to use this wretched means, except when the other, more kindly means that we have spoken of above has not brought that benefit which His divine goodness intends. He permits more or less of these failures to befall a person as pride and self-esteem are greater or lesser, in order that where nothing of presumption is found—as in the Virgin Mary—so too nothing would have to happen. So, when you fall, run immediately to thoughts of humble self-recognition, and beg the Lord with insistent prayers that He give you true light to know yourself and to distrust yourself totally, so that you will not wish to fall again, especially into more serious harm.

CHAPTER 3: CONCERNING CONFIDENCE IN GOD.

Although so necessary in this fight, as we have said, nonetheless if we have distrust of self alone, we will either give ourselves to flight or be defeated and overcome by enemies. Therefore, in addition to this you also need total confidence in God, waiting and hoping for every benefit, aid and victory from Him alone. Since we ourselves are nothing, it is not licit for us to promise ourselves anything other than failings. Therefore, we ought to distrust ourselves completely, so that we will achieve every great victory safely through our Lord, provided that we arm our heart with firm confidence in Him in order to obtain His help. This can also happen in four ways.

First, by requesting it from God.

Second, by considering and seeing the omnipotence and infinite wisdom of God—to whom nothing is impossible or difficult—with the eye of faith. Since His goodness is without measure, He is ready and prepared to give, hour by hour, moment by moment, and with indescribable desire, all that is necessary for the spiritual life and the complete victory of we who turn to His arms with confidence. And how will it be possible for our divine Pastor, who ran back to the lost sheep for thirty-three years[4] with cries so strong that He became hoarse, and who shed all His blood for you and laid down His life for you by a road so laborious and sorrowful, to fail to rejoice with all His neighbors and the angels of heaven now that this sheep follows behind Him in obedience to His commandments? How could He hate or fail to allow to rest upon His divine breast she who has the desire (even if at the point of exhaustion) to obey Him, she who is calling Him and imploring Him not to turn away His eyes of life? If our Lord does not leave off seeking with great diligence and love and finding in the gospel drachma[5] the blind and mute sinner,[6] how could He abandon one who cries out and calls her pastor like a lost sheep? And who will ever believe that God does not want to enter you or be deaf to you, a God who knocks continually at your heart out of desire to enter and eat with you, giving His gifts, clinging to the heart and inviting it?

The third way to acquire this holy confidence is through the memory, by recollection of the truth of holy Scripture, that in so many places clearly shows us no one ever remains confused who confides in God.

The fourth means that will help to attain both distrust of oneself and confidence in God is this: when it occurs to you to do something and to strike some blows and defeat yourself, before you propose this to yourself or resolve that it be done, turn yourself in thought to your own weakness and completely distrust yourself. Then turn to the divine power, wisdom and goodness, and confiding in this, decide to work and fight generously. Then work and battle with these weapons in hand and with prayer, as I shall explain. And if you fail to observe this order, even if it seems to you that everything is done in the confidence of God, you shall find yourself deceived in large part. For presumption is so natural to man and so subtle that it almost always lives inadvertently in the distrust that we seem to have of ourselves and in the confidence we think we have in God.

In order that you may flee presumption whenever possible and work with distrust of yourself and with confidence in God, act in such a way that the consideration of your weakness comes before your consideration of the omnipotence of God, and both of these two before your efforts.

CHAPTER 4: HOW ONE CAN KNOW IF HUMAN WORKS ARE DONE WITH DISTRUST OF ONESELF AND WITH CONFIDENCE IN GOD.

Many times it seems to the presumptuous servant that he has obtained distrust of self and confidence in God, and it is not so. Therefore, the effect that failure shall produce in you will be obvious. If, when you fall, you become anxious, saddened and feel like calling out to someone in desperation because earlier you could go farther and do better, it is a certain sign that you confide in yourself and not in God. And the greater the sadness and desperation, the more you will have confided in yourself and the less in God. For those who distrust themselves and rely upon God are amazed by neither the sadness nor the sorrow when they fall, knowing that this occurred through their weakness and lack of confidence in God. In addition, the greater the distrust of oneself, the more humbly one trusts in God. For hating the fault and the disordered passions—the cause of the fall—above every other thing, one continues the enterprise with a great, calm and peaceful pain for the offense to God and pursues one's enemies until death with greater spirit and resolution.

I wish that these things were carefully considered by certain persons who call themselves "spirituals," for when they incur some fault, they are unable and unwilling to gain peace. They do not go immediately to find their spiritual father, at times more in order to free themselves from anxiety and worry born from self-love, not love for others. But, they ought to go, chiefly in order to cleanse themselves from the stain of sin and to take strength against it with the Most Holy Sacrament.

CHAPTER 5: CONCERNING AN ERROR OF MANY, AMONG WHOM COWARDLINESS IS CONSIDERED A STRENGTH.

Still, many are deceived who attribute the cowardice and anxiety that follow after sin to virtue, because they are accompanied by some sorrow, unaware that they are born from hidden pride and presumption and are founded in false confidence in themselves and their own powers. In these powers they have overwhelming confidence, because they value themselves above all things. Noticing from evidence of the fall that they are lacking something, they become agitated and marvel as if the shortcoming were something unforeseen. They turn cowardly, degenerating to a level that sustains the vain confidence they have placed in themselves.

This does not happen to the humble person, who, confiding in only God and presuming nothing about himself, does not become anxious or amazed when falling into any fault—even if he feels pain from it—knowing that all that happens to him through his own misery and weakness is made known for him by the light of truth.

CHAPTER 6: OTHER ADVICE IN ORDER THAT WE MAY ACQUIRE DISTRUST OF SELF AND CONFIDENCE IN GOD.

And because all the power to defeat our enemies is born principally from suspicion of ourselves and from trust in God, I am providing you with more advice, so that you can obtain it with divine help. You must know then, and consider it certain, that neither all gifts that exist, whether natural or acquired, nor all the graces freely given, nor the knowledge of all Scripture, nor long service of God, nor even making a habit of it, will make us do His will, if in any work we have to do that is good and acceptable in His eyes, or in any temptation we have to overcome, or in any danger we have to flee, or in any cross we have to carry in conforming to His will, our heart is not aided and raised up by the special help of God and does not also offer its hand [to God] to accomplish it.[7] We ought to have this resolution then, through all our life, every day, every hour and in every moment, for in this way, we can never confide in ourselves, not in any thought or in any fashion.

Thus, where trust in God is concerned, know that it is no more difficult for God to conquer many enemies than a few, nor old and crafty ones than the young and weak. And so, a soul may be loaded with sin, may have all the defects of the world as well, and be as faulty as one can imagine. It may have attempted what it wishes, and taken some measures and acted in order to leave sinfulness behind and to work for good, but it never was able to acquire even a dot of good. On the contrary, it may have leaned more heavily toward evil. Nevertheless, it should not lose confidence in God, or ever abandon spiritual weapons and exercises, but always battle generously. For you must know that in this spiritual war no one is lost who does not give up the battle and trust in God. His aid is never lost to His soldiers, although He permits some to be wounded. Fight on, since all that you need is here, because the medicine for the wounds is ready and efficacious for the soldiers who seek God and His help with confidence. When our enemies think the least of us, they find themselves dead.

CHAPTER 7: ON SPIRITUAL PRACTICES—FIRST, OF THE INTELLECT, THAT WE OUGHT TO KEEP GUARDED FROM IGNORANCE AND CURIOSITY.

If the distrust of self and trust in God that are so necessary in this war stand alone, we still will not gain victory over ourselves, but rather fall into many evils. Therefore, beyond these, spiritual exercise is necessary for us. That is the third item proposed above. The exercise has to be done primarily with the intellect and with the will. Regarding the intellect, we ought to guard it from two things that intend to contest it.

One is the ignorance that obscures and impedes the intellect from knowledge of the truth, that is, from its own object. Therefore, the intellect must be made lucid and clear with exercise, so that it can see and discern well what is necessary in order to purify the soul from disordered passions and to honor holy virtue. One can obtain this light in two ways.

The first and most important is prayer, beseeching the Holy Spirit that He deign to infuse it in our hearts. This He will always do, if we, in truth, will seek God alone and follow His holy will, and if we will properly subject everything to the judgment of our spiritual fathers.

The other means is continual exercise of profound and sincere consideration of things in order to see them as they really are—good or evil as the Holy Spirit teaches—not as they appear on the outside, as they represent themselves to the senses or to the judgment of the world. When this consideration is fittingly performed, it makes us understand clearly that all those things, which the blind and corrupt world loves and desires, and that one procures with various ways and means, ought to be considered as nothing, as lies and vanity; that the honors and pleasures of the world are nothing else than vanity and spiritual afflictions; that the injuries and disgraces which the world gives us carry true glory, and its tribulations give contentment; that to pardon one's enemies and to do good to them is noble-mindedness and one of the closer resemblances to God; that the more the world considers you hated, the more you are its master; that willingly to obey lower creatures out of love for God is something more magnanimous and generous than to command great princes; that humble recognition of ourselves ought to be valued more than the height of all the sciences; and that to conquer and mortify our own appetites, small as they may be, merit greater praise than to defeat many cities, to overcome powerful armed soldiers, or to do miracles and raise the dead.

CHAPTER 8: ON THE REASONS WHY THINGS ARE NOT DISCERNED BY US DIRECTLY, AND ON THE WAY ONE HAS TO CONSIDER THEM IN ORDER TO UNDERSTAND THEM BETTER.

The reason why all the things just mentioned, along with many others, are not perceived by us directly is because we attach either love or hatred to them at their first appearance. The intellect is clouded by that attachment, and does not judge them directly for what they really are. Whenever you can, be watchful to maintain your will purged—free from disordered affections about anything—in order to avoid this deception. And when any proposed object comes before you, examine it with the intellect, and consider it maturely before hating it if it is something contrary to our natural inclinations, or before loving it if it brings you pleasure—then show that you either desire it or reject it. The intellect, thus unencumbered by the passions, is free, clear and able to know the truth, to penetrate inside to the evil born under false pleasure and to the good covered by the appearance of evil.

If the will is first inclined to love the thing or has taken a hatred to it, the intellect cannot know it well, because the affection that is placed in between obscures it somewhat, so that it is considered something other than what it is. With the intellect representing it this way to the will, the will is moved either to love it or to hate it more strongly, against all order and the laws of reason. From that affection, the intellect becomes greatly obscured. Thus obscured, it makes the object appear once again to the will, more lovable or despicable than ever. So, if one does not hold to the rule that I have explained (which is of the highest importance in this exercise), these two powers, the intellect and the will, so noble and excellent, come miserably into a vicious circle, falling into greater and greater darkness, greater and greater errors.

So guard yourself with all vigilance, daughter, against all disordered affections of whatever kind that are not first well-examined by you and recognized for what they truly are, through the light of the intellect, and especially with the light of grace, prayer and the judgment of your spiritual father. This you ought to observe sometimes more in exterior works that are good and holy than in other things. In good and holy works there is more danger of self-made deception and indiscretion than in other works. Thus, through some circumstance of time, of place and of measure, or out of respect for obedience to yourself, sometimes you might bring no small harm to yourself, as many know who have endangered themselves through their most praiseworthy and holy exercises.

CHAPTER 9: ON ANOTHER THING ONE OUGHT TO GUARD THE INTELLECT AGAINST, BECAUSE IT CAN EASILY BE DISCERNED.

Curiosity is the other thing from which we have to carefully defend our intellect, because by filling it with harmful, vain and impertinent thoughts, we render it unfit and incapable of apprehending what pertains to our true mortification and perfection. Therefore, you must be completely dead to every trace of unnecessary earthly things, even those that are lawful. Always restrict your intellect as much as you can, and love making it foolish. The novelties and changes of the world, both small and great, must be nothing to you—as though they did not exist—and if they are offered to you, oppose and chase them from yourself. Render yourself serious and humble in the desire to understand celestial things, wishing for nothing other than to know the crucified Christ, both His life and His death, and what He asks from you. Hold all the rest at a distance, so that you will give great pleasure to God, for He has as His dear and beloved one the person who desires and seeks just necessary things from Him in order to love His divine goodness and to do His will. Every other question and investigation represents self-love, pride and a trap of the devil.

If you will follow this advice, you will be able to survive many dangers, because the cunning serpent, seeing that the will is vigorous and strong in those who attend to the spiritual life, attempts to battle their intellect in order to make himself lord of both the one and the other. Therefore, he often wishes to give high, lively and zealous thoughts, especially to those of sharp and great intelligence, and to those who are quick to raise themselves up to pride, so that while they are occupied in delight and discourse on those points in which they falsely persuade themselves to be delighting God, they forget to purify the heart and attend to self-knowledge and true mortification. Thus entering into the snare of pride, they fashion an idol out of their own intellect. From this it follows that even if unaware of it, they convince themselves little by little that they have no need of any counsel and instruction, being already accustomed in every occurrence to have recourse to the idol of their own judgment.

Pride in the intellect is a matter of grave danger and is very difficult to cure, since it is more dangerous than that of the will. Pride in the will, being manifested to one's intellect, easily can be cured in one day, through obedience to whom obedience is owed. But one who has a firm opinion that his view is better than that of others, how and by whom can that one be cured? How does one place oneself under the judgment of another, when he does not consider it as good as his own? If the eye of the soul— that is, the intellect with which one has to recognize and to purge the wound of the proud will—is sick, blind and full of the same pride, who can cure it? And if the light becomes darkness, or the habit fails, how will the rest not go likewise?[8]

By this means you must oppose that dangerous pride early on, before it penetrates you, to the marrow of your bones. Blunt the sharpness of your intellect, willingly subjecting your own to the opinion of others, becoming a fool for love of God, and you will be wiser than Solomon.

CHAPTER 10: ON THE EXERCISE OF THE WILL, AND ON THE END
TO WHICH ALL INTERIOR AND EXTERIOR ACTIONS MUST BE
ADDRESSED.

Beyond the exercises that you have to make concerning the intellect, it is necessary for you to rule your will so that it becomes conformed to divine pleasure in everything, instead of leaving it amid its own desires. And remember that it is not enough for you just to desire and procure the things that are most pleasing to God, but even more you have to seek them and do them as you are moved by Him for the goal of purely pleasing Him. In this too, even more than in the aforesaid, we have a great contrast with human nature, which is so inclined toward itself that in everything— and sometimes more in good and spiritual things than in others—it seeks its own convenience and pleasure, suiting itself, using and avidly consuming things as if they were unsuspicious foods.

And so, when things are offered to us, we immediately admire and desire them, not moved by the will of God, or to the end of pleasing Him alone, but through that good and contentment that derive from the desire for the things sought from God. This trick is more hidden the better that desired thing is in itself. Thus even in desiring God Himself we are subject to the deceptions of self-love, aiming more often at our interests and at benefits we expect than at the will of God. He is pleased through His glory alone, and wishes to be loved, desired and obeyed by us.

In order to guard yourself from this trap, which would block you on the path of perfection, and in order to accustom yourself to wish and do all as moved by God, with the pure intention of honoring and pleasing Him alone (who wishes to be the single beginning and end of our every thought and action), follow this method: when some desirable thing from God offers itself to you, do not incline the will to desire it, if first you have not raised your mind to God to see that it is His will that you desire it, that He so wishes it, and in order to please Him alone. Thus He moves and draws your will by His, so that yours may yield to desire as it pleases Him, to His satisfaction and honor. Similarly, while desiring to refuse things not willed by God, do not refuse them without first fixing the gaze of your intellect upon His divine will, which desires that you refuse them in order to please Him.

But you must know that the tricks of subtle human nature are little understood, for seeking itself always secretly, it often makes it seem that the motive and end of pleasing God are within us when it is not so. And thus it often happens that the thing one wishes or does not wish out of self-interest appears to us as desired or not desired according to the pleasure or displeasure of God. In order to flee from this deception, the proper and complete remedy would be purity of heart in divesting oneself of the old man and putting on the new, and so, to that end this entire *Combat* is addressed.[9]

In order to provide yourself with the needed skill, since you are full of yourself, remember to strip yourself at the beginning of your actions insofar as you can of every mixed motive,[10] where you can estimate that there is some self-interest. Do not desire, work for, or refuse anything, if first you do not feel yourself moved and drawn by the pure and simple will of God. If you cannot always feel this motive active in all operations, particularly in the interior ones of the soul and in the exterior ones that pass quickly, then content yourself with having it in each one virtually, always maintaining a true intention of pleasing only your God in all things.

In the actions that continue over some length of time, it is good for you to stir up this motive in yourself not just at the beginning. You are also

126

advised to renew it often and keep it aroused until the end. Otherwise, you would be in danger of running into another trap, also from our natural love. Our love, being more inclined and agreeable to itself than to God, often wishes to make us carelessly alter objectives and change goals over an interval of time.

The servant of God who himself is not very shrewd often begins to do some work with the thought of pleasing his Lord alone. Then, little by little and as if unaware, he becomes so pleased in it through his own sentiment that he turns, forgetting the divine will, and clings to the affected pleasure he feels about the work and to the utility and honor that can come to him as a result. Then God sends impediments to the work, with some sickness or accidents, or by means of some creature, so that he becomes completely disturbed and upset by it, and at times falls into murmurings about this and that, if not about God himself. This is a very clear sign that his intent was not completely on God, but was born from a spoiled and corrupted root and source. For whoever moves himself as moved by God and in order to please Him alone, does not desire one thing more than another, but only seeks something if God will be pleased that he have it, and in the manner and at the time that He will give it. And whether having it or not, he remains equally peaceful and content, since in every way he obtains his intention and reaches the goal, which is nothing other than the pleasure of God.

In this way you remain properly recollected in yourself and always on notice to direct your actions to this perfect end. And if sometimes you move yourself (while seeking the proper inclination of your soul) to do good work in order to flee the pains of hell, or through the hope of paradise, you can still propose as the ultimate goal the pleasure and will of God, who is pleased if you do not go to hell, but enter into His kingdom instead. When this motive has power and strength, no one can fully grasp it, since even a small or slight thing done to please God alone and for His glory is (as they say) worth infinitely more than many others of great price and value undertaken without this motive. Similarly, a single penny given to a poor person to give pleasure solely to His divine Majesty is more welcome to Him than if someone should strip himself of all he has, even of vast wealth, with another intention, even that of enjoying the blessings of heaven—which is not only a good aim but an exceedingly desirable one.[11]

This exercise of performing everything with the goal of purely pleasing God will seem difficult in the beginning, but one will render it simple and easy by the use of frequent desire for God himself, and by aspiring to

Him with deep affections from the heart as our singular and most perfect good. Above all things and by His very nature He merits the desire, service and love of all creatures. The more deeply and more often one will consider His infinite merit the more fervent and more frequent will be these acts of the will; and so we, more quickly and with greater ease, will come to acquire the habit of doing every work out of respect and love of the Lord who alone merits it.[12]

Finally, I advise you in order to obtain this divine objective that beyond what has already been said you should beg it from God with relentless prayers, and you should frequently consider the innumerable blessings that God has given us, and always does, out of pure love and without self-interest.

CHAPTER 11: ON SOME CONSIDERATIONS THAT INDUCE THE WILL TO DESIRE THE PLEASURE OF GOD IN ALL THINGS.

In order to reduce more easily your will to desire the pleasure of God and His honor in all things, remember often that He has first loved and honored you in various ways. In creation, by fashioning you in His image, out of nothing, and setting all the other creatures at your service.[13] In redemption, by sending not an angel, but His only Son to ransom you, and not with a corruptible price of gold and silver, but rather with His own precious blood, and with His painful and cruel death.[14] Thus, in every hour and at every moment He protects you from your enemies, fights for you with His grace, and keeps His beloved Son continually prepared in the sacrament of the altar for your defense and nourishment. Is this not a sign of the inestimable regard and love God holds for you?[15] Thus, no one is able to understand how this great Lord makes such an account of us poor wretched creatures in our lowliness and misery, or how, on the other hand, we are esteemed by so great a Majesty that He has done such and so many things for us.

If the great men of this world, when they are honored by poor and lowly persons, always feel themselves obliged to render some honor to them, what should our vileness do for the supreme King of the universe, by whom we are seen as so highly precious, who considers us so dear? Besides what was said above, always retain a vivid recollection that the divine Majesty in Himself merits infinite honor and service, purely for His pleasure, above all things.

CHAPTER 12: ON THE MANY DESIRES THAT ARE IN HUMANITY
AND THE STRUGGLE THAT EXISTS AMONG THEM.

And so, in this combat, it can be said that there are two wills in us: the will of reason (therefore called reasonable and superior); and the will of sense (thus called inferior and sensual). One signifies the latter with these terms—appetite, sensuality and passion. Nonetheless, since we are humans by virtue of reason, something we desire with the appetite alone is never understood to be truly desired by us unless we also incline ourselves to it with the superior will. Therefore, all of our spiritual battle lies principally in this: that the reasonable will is placed as though in the middle between the divine will that is above it and the inferior will, that of sense, below it. It is fought over continually by the one and the other, while each of them attempts to draw the reasonable will to itself and render it subject and obedient. Great pain and fatigue, especially at the beginning, test those used to doing evil who resolve to change their wicked life for the better, and who, stripping themselves of the world and of their sensuality, give themselves to the love and service of Jesus Christ.

Since the blows that the superior will suffers from the divine will and from the sensual appetite on every side in the combat are powerful and strong they are never sustained without great pain. This does not happen to those who already are accustomed to virtue or vices—and so are always intending to continue in the same way—because the virtuous easily consent to the divine will and the depraved bend themselves toward the sensual will without conflict.

But no one should presume the ability to pursue true Christian virtues, or to serve God as He wishes, if he does not wish to do himself true violence and endure the pain he feels in departing not just from great delights, but also from the little ones to which he first became attached through worldly affections. Because of this, very few arrive at the mark of perfection, for having overcome the major vices with weariness, they do not wish to mortify themselves. They continue to suffer the stings and toil that test their resistance to the seemingly infinite small examples of self-will and little passions of minor account. Those always prevail in them, gradually acquiring dominion and control over their hearts.

Among these are found those who do not take the goods of others, but are excessively attached to those they justly possess. They might not be procuring honors through illicit means, but neither do they abhor them as they should, nor cease to desire them. Sometimes they pursue them through different means. They might observe the obligatory fasts, but do not mortify the gluttony of eating excessively and of consuming delicate foods. Although living continently, they do not break away from certain practices they enjoy that constitute a great impediment to union with God and the spiritual life. Since these faults exist in all pious persons and are very dangerous (and more so in those who fear them less), they ought to be avoided as far as possible.

Because of these things, other good works are done with tepidity of spirit and are accompanied by ulterior motives, hidden imperfections, and a certain self-esteem and desire to be praised and cherished by the world. Those who do so fail to make progress on the road to health, and, by turning back, stand at risk of falling into the original illness, since they fail to love true virtue and demonstrate little thanks to the Lord who rescued them from the tyranny of the devil. They are ignorant of and blind to the danger in which they find themselves, while falsely persuading themselves that they live in security.

Here one discovers an error all the more harmful for being less noted. Many who devote themselves to the spiritual life possess more self-love than they need—although in truth they do not know how to love themselves. For this reason they practice those exercises that best suit their taste and leave aside other exercises that touch the very heart of their own natural inclinations and sensual appetites. All reason dictates that they should fight against those with all their strength.

Therefore, my beloved daughter, I advise and exhort you to fall in love with the difficulty and pain that carry victory over yourself along with them, because here they are everything. The more firmly you shall come to love the difficulty that virtue and struggle present to the beginner, the more certain and quick the victory will be. And if you will be a greater lover of the difficulty and of the pain of combat than a lover of victories and virtues, you will more quickly acquire everything.

CHAPTER 13: ON THE METHOD OF COMBAT AGAINST SENSUAL IMPULSES AND ON ACTS OF THE WILL NECESSARY TO ACQUIRE VIRTUOUS HABITS.

Each time your reasonable will is attacked by the sensual will on the one side and by the divine will on the other, you must exert yourself in various ways as each one seeks the victory so that the divine will prevails in you through it all.

First, when you are assailed and attacked by sensual impulses, you need to make vigorous resistance in order that the reasonable will does not consent to them.

Second, when these have ceased, stir them up in yourself again, in order to repress them with greater vehemence and force.

Then, call them back to a third battle, in which you will accustom yourself to drive them away with disdain and abhorrence. These two provocations to combat have to be carried out on all our disordered appetites, aside from the sexual desires, which we will discuss in a separate place.

Finally, you must perform actions contrary to all your depraved passions. It will all be made more clear with the following example. You may be afflicted by impulses of impatience. If you will be very attentive, staying within yourself, you shall notice that these struggle against your superior will continuously because it consents and inclines itself to them. And from the first encounter with such repeated desires, you must do as much as you can, opposing each impulse, so that your will does not give in to them. Never quit this battle until you perceive that the enemy surrenders, as if exhausted and virtually dead.

So you see, daughter, the cunning of the devil. When he realizes that we vigorously oppose ourselves to the impulses of some passion, he does not remain to stir them in us again. But since you are already excited, he then tempts you to acquire the impulses, so that we may fail to attain the virtue contrary to those passions, and beyond that, to make us fall into the trap of vainglory and pride. He deftly sets that trap by leading us to believe that we have quickly trampled our enemies through courageous combat.

Thus you will proceed to the second battle, recalling to memory and stirring in your thoughts what caused you impatience, in such a way that you feel yourself moved by this impatience in the sensual reason. Then repress its impulses with more intense desire and greater strength than before. And although we repulse our enemies because we know it is something good and pleasing to God, nevertheless, by failing to hold them in contempt, we run the risk of being overcome by them another time. Hence you must make yourself engage them in a third assault and drive them far from you, not only with disgust but with disdain, until you render them hateful and abominable.

Finally, in order to honor and perfect your soul with the habits of virtue, you must produce willful acts that are directly contrary to your disordered inclinations. For example, if, when you are desiring to acquire the habit of perfect patience, one should offer you occasion for impatience by holding you in contempt, it is not enough that you practice the three forms of combat I have explained. In addition, you ought to hope to love the contempt itself, desiring to be insulted again in the same manner, by the same person, waiting and intending to endure even greater contempt. The reason why such contrary acts are necessary in order to perfect ourselves in virtue is because the other acts, however many and strong, are not enough to eliminate the roots that produce vice.

Let us continue with the same example. When despised, even if we do not consent to the impulses of impatience and battle against them with the three weapons shown above, nonetheless, we will never be able to free ourselves from the vice of impatience if we do not also actively accustom ourselves to love the contempt and rejoice in it with many, frequent acts, for our inclination toward protecting our own reputation is based in the abhorrence of contempt. And when this root of vice remains alive it always comes to germinate in a manner that renders virtue sluggish, even to the point of suffocating it altogether. Besides this, it holds us in continual danger of falling again, on every occasion that presents itself to us. From this it follows that without the contrary acts we are never able to acquire the true habit of virtue.

Notice, moreover, that such acts have to be very frequent and great in number in order completely to destroy the habit of vice, for it has taken possession of our hearts through many detestable acts. Only with equally numerous contrary acts can one root them out of the heart in order to introduce the habit of virtue. And so I repeat that more good acts are necessary in order to create the habit of virtue, since they are not directly aided by the corrupt nature of sin as the vices are.

Beyond what has been said to this point, I add that if you would practice the virtue as requested, you must also make external actions correspond to the internal. Do this (staying with the same example) by using words of meekness and love with the one who is tiresome and contrary, and by serving the person in every way, if you can. And although these acts, both interior and exterior, may either seem or actually be accompanied by such spiritual weakness that you seem to do them against your entire will, you should not give them up by any means. Weak as they are, they hold you firm and steady in the battle and are helping you on the road to victory.

Be very shrewd and recollected in yourself in order to combat not just the great and efficacious desires, but also against the small, weak temptations to each passion. For these open the path to the greater ones whence the habits of vice are then generated in us. And due to the little care that some have taken to eradicate these small desires from their hearts, the less attention that they paid the more vigorously they were assailed and the more ruinously they were defeated by these same enemies, even after having overcome greater temptations to the same passion. Again I remind you to look after the mortification and annihilation of your desires, even, at times, for things licit but unnecessary. Many blessings will follow from it, and you will continuously render yourself more prepared and eager to defeat yourself in the other instances. You will strengthen yourself and become expert in the battle with temptations, you will flee the various traps of the devil, and you will make yourself most pleasing to the Lord.

Daughter, I say to you clearly: if you will proceed continually through these faithful and holy exercises for reform of yourself and victory over yourself in the manner I have described, I assure you that you will get accustomed to it in a short time and become truly spiritual, not spiritual in name only. But never convince yourself that you have acquired virtue and true spirit in another way or with other exercises, even though they may seem excellent and delightful to your taste, and even though it may seem that through them you are completely united to and in loving discourse with the Lord. This union and discourse (as I told you in the first chapter) does not consist in nor is it born from the practices that delight and conform to our nature, but rather from those that crucify our nature along with all its acts, and thus renew human nature by means of the habit of evangelical virtues, joining it to its Creator and Redeemer.

No one doubts that just as bad habits are acquired through many and frequent acts of the superior will giving way to the sensual appetites, so in the opposite fashion the habits of evangelical virtue are acquired by doing acts more and more often in conformity with the divine will. By that will we are first called to one virtue and then to another. For just as our will can never be depraved and worldly as long as it battles with our inferior will and with vice, or until it does not look up and surrender, so it will never be virtuous and joined to God—however deeply it may be called and struggle through the power of divine grace and inspirations—as long as it does not conform to the divine will with interior actions, and when necessary with exterior ones.

CHAPTER 14: WHAT ONE OUGHT TO DO WHEN THE SUPERIOR
WILL SEEMS DEFEATED AND OVERPOWERED IN EVERYTHING BY
ENEMIES AND BY THE INFERIOR WILL.

And if it seems to you sometimes that the superior will is powerless
against the inferior will and its enemies because you do not feel an effective interior inclination against them, remain firm and do not quit the
fight. You must consider yourself victorious as long as it does not seem
that you have openly surrendered. Just as our reasonable will has no need
of the inferior desires in order to produce its acts, so it does not want them
nor can it ever be constrained to surrender itself to them through defeat,
no matter how harshly they contest it. For God endowed our will with
such strength and freedom that if all the senses along with all the demons
and all the world would arm and band themselves together against you,
battling that will and pressing it with all their effort, it nevertheless can
choose or not choose, desire or reject all that it wants in order freely to
spite them. It can do so as often, for as much time, in whatever way, and
toward whatever end it finds more pleasing.

And if sometimes these enemies assail and press you with such violence that your will, as if suffocated, has not as they say breath to produce
any act of contrary desires, do not lose heart. Do not throw your weapons
to the ground either, but make use of the tongue to defend yourself in this
case, saying, "I do not yield to you, I do not want you," like one who
having attacked the enemy opposing him is unable to strike with the point
of the sword, uses the pommel instead. And just as a soldier first makes a
feint in order to wound with the sword point, you can withdraw into self-
knowledge, specifically of your weakness and nothingness. Then, with all
the faith in God that you can muster, give a blow to the enemy passion,
saying, "Help me, Lord, save me, my God; Jesus, Mary, help me to avoid
surrender to them."

Then, when the enemy gives you time, you can assist the weakness of
your will with recourse to the intellect, considering different points
through which the will can catch its breath and gather strength against the
appetites. For example, if you are so assailed with impatience over some
persecution or other trouble that your will seems unable to oppose it or
unwilling to endure it, then comfort it through discussion of these or other
points with the intellect.

First, consider if you deserve that evil you are suffering, because you
have given it an opportunity. For if you deserve it, justice demands that

you patiently endure the wound you have given yourself with your own hand.

Second, if you are blameless, turn your thought to the other failings for which God has still not punished you, and that you have not expiated as you should. And when you see that the mercy of God exchanges the penalty for them, a penalty that would either be eternal or else temporal in purgatory, for just a farthing in the present life, you ought to receive it not only willingly but with thanksgiving.

Third, when it seems that you have done much penance but little offense to the divine Majesty (this is something that you should never convince yourself of), you need to remember that no one enters into the kingdom of heaven except through the narrow door of tribulation.[16]

Fourth, even if you were able to enter heaven by another means, then by the law of love you should not, and should not even think of such a thing, since the Son of God with all His saints and friends entered there by means of thorns and crosses.

Fifth, in this and in every other thing what you must aim at is the will of your God, who through the love that He bears for you is indescribably pleased by every act of virtue and mortification that He sees you make, like His faithful and generous warrior, in order to correspond to Him in love.[17] Consider it certain that the more irrational and more shameful the source of the trouble, and therefore the more bothersome and serious for you to tolerate, the more will you give pleasure to the Lord by assenting to and loving His divine will and dispositions even in the midst of these disordered events because you love His will and dispositions more. Through this will and disposition everything that happens has perfect rule and order, no matter how disordered it may be.

CHAPTER 15: SOME WARNINGS ABOUT THE METHOD OF COMBAT, AND ESPECIALLY AGAINST WHOM AND WITH WHAT VIRTUE WE OUGHT TO DO IT.

You have already seen, daughter, the way that one must wage combat in order to overcome self and to adorn oneself with virtues. You know that to gain victory over your enemies with greater speed and ease you must agree to fight. And even more than that, you must battle every day, particularly against self-love, by training yourself to consider as dear friends all the loathing and contempt that the world can give you. As I hinted above, it has happened and still happens that victories are very difficult, rare, imperfect and unstable when persons do not heed this fight and take little account of it.

Again I warn you that your battle has to be performed with strength of heart. You will easily acquire this if you beseech God, and if noting the rage and eternal hatred of your enemies and the great number of their armies and squadrons, you will consider at the same time how infinitely greater is the goodness of God, how much stronger is the love with which He loves you, and how many more numerous are the angels of heaven and prayers of the saints that battle on our behalf. From this consideration many simple women have overcome and defeated all the power and wisdom of the world, all the assaults of the flesh and all the rage of hell.[18]

Thus you never have to be frightened, although at times it may seem that the attack of the enemies grows stronger and will last your entire life and that it threatens you with certain defeat from numerous sides. You must know, beyond what has been said above, that all the strength and knowledge of our enemies remains in the hands of our divine captain for whose honor one fights. He values us indescribably and calls us to the battle Himself. He will never allow violence to be done to you. Rather, by fighting for you Himself, He will defeat them for you when it pleases Him and with your greater profit, even if He delays until the final day of your life.

This alone pertains to you: that you do battle generously. Even if you are frequently wounded, never lay down your arms or give yourself over to flight. Finally, in order to fight with valor, you must know that no one can flee this battle, and whoever does not battle is necessarily caught and dies there. Even more, one has to deal with enemies filled with such evil qualities and hatred that there cannot be in any way either peace or hope of truce.

CHAPTER 16: ON HOW, EARLY IN THE MORNING, THE SOLDIER OF CHRIST OUGHT TO GO TO THE BATTLEFIELD.

As soon as you have woken up, the first thing that the eyes of your soul must observe is yourself inside an enclosure, locked in with this law: whoever fails to do battle there remains eternally dead. Within it imagine that you see your enemy before you—the evil inclination you have already undertaken to conquer. It is armed in order to wound and kill you. See on the right side your victorious captain, Jesus Christ, with His most holy mother, the Virgin Mary, together with her dearest husband, Joseph, with many legions of angels and saints, and particularly St. Michael the archangel. On the left side there is the infernal devil with his [troops] to rouse your passion, urging you to surrender to it.[19]

There you will seem to hear a voice, as if from your guardian angel, who says to you, "Today you have to battle against this and your other enemies." Do not let your heart become frightened, nor lose courage. Do not surrender to them through fear or any other consideration, because our Lord, your captain, remains here with you with all these glorious squadrons. He will fight against all your enemies, not permitting them to prevail against you by strength or oppression.[20] Hold firm, mortify yourself and endure the pain that you will sometimes feel in doing such violence to yourself. Shout from the depths of your heart frequently and call on your Lord, the Virgin Mary and all the saints, so that you will undoubtedly bring back victory. Even if you are weary and pessimistic, if your enemies are strong and numerous, many more numerous are the aids of Him who has created and redeemed you. Your God is exceedingly stronger, beyond comparison to anyone, and He has more desire to save you than the enemy has to ruin you. Battle then, and do not mind the pain, because from fatigue, from violence against your bad inclinations and from the pain that one feels through evil habits, both the victory and a great treasure are born, the treasure with which one purchases the kingdom of heaven and unites one's soul forever with God.[21]

In the name of the Lord you shall begin to fight and with the arms of distrust of self, confidence in God, prayers and spiritual exercises. Call to battle that enemy and your own inclinations, which you have resolved to defeat, following the instructions above,[22] first with resistance, then with hatred, and then with acts of the contrary virtue, wounding them more and more times, unto death, in order to please your Lord. He with all the Church triumphant stays to see your battle. Again I say to you that the battle must not trouble you, considering the duty that we all have to serve and please God and the necessity of the struggle. We cannot flee from this battle without wounds and death. And I repeat that when you wish to flee from God like a rebel and give yourself to the world and to the delights of the flesh, you must wage war against your vexation with so many contrary acts that the face will often sweat and the heart will be penetrated with the anguish of death.[23] Consider here what sort of insanity it would be to undertake that effort and pain, which leads to greater struggles and pain, not to mention the death that will never end, by fleeing from a quickly finished effort that unites us to eternal life and to the infinitely blessed, enjoying our God forever.

CHAPTER 17: ON THE ORDERS FOR COMBAT AGAINST OUR DEPRAVED PASSIONS.

It is very important to know the orders one must follow so as to battle properly, and not at random or automatically, as many do to their own detriment. The sequence of combat against your enemies and your evil inclinations is for you to discern. Entering within your heart, you must see through diligent examination what sort of thoughts and affections surround it and by what passions it is more often possessed and oppressed. Take up arms and fight against them in the main. And if you should happen to be attacked by other enemies, you must always fight against that which is actually then making war against you most closely, returning later to the principal engagement.

CHAPTER 18: ON THE WAY TO RESIST SUDDEN IMPULSES OF THE PASSIONS.

While still inexperienced in taking refuge against the sudden blows of abuse or of other difficult things, you must become accustomed to foresee and expect them time and time again, awaiting them with a heart fully prepared. When considering the condition of your passions, the way to foresee them is to consider also the places where and the persons with whom you deal. From that you will easily be able to guess which passion could befall you. And if any other unexpected, adverse problem crops up, beyond the help represented by keeping the soul prepared for passions you might anticipate, you can help yourself rather in the following other way.

As soon as you begin to feel the first stings of abuse, or any other pain, be alert and strengthen yourself by elevating your mind to God, considering the indescribable goodness and love with which He sends you that adversity, so that enduring it through His love, He may purge, draw near and unite you to Himself even more. And seeing how much He is pleased that you endure it, turn and reprimand yourself saying, "So, why did you not want to endure this cross that no enemy, but rather your heavenly Father, sent you?" Then turn back to this cross and embrace it with the greatest patience and happiness you can, saying, "O cross, built by divine providence before I existed; O cross, sweetened by the sweet love of my crucified Lord; nail me now upon yourself, because you can present me to Him who has redeemed me by dying on you."

And if you cannot raise yourself to God at the start, as the passion prevails on you and you are wounded, seek, nevertheless, to attempt it as much as before, as if you were not wounded. For an effective remedy against these sudden impulses, you must quickly remove the motive whence they proceed. Note, for example, that when you become worried due to the attraction that you have for something you usually fall into some sudden change of heart. The way to prepare ahead of time for such attacks is to take away the attraction. But if the change proceeds not from a thing but from some person who irritates you in her every single action because you two are not of one heart, the remedy is to force yourself to bend the will, to love her, and to consider her dear, because beyond the fact that she is a creature like yourself, formed by the same powerful hand, and reformed by the same divine blood as you, she is also presenting you an occasion if you will endure it to resemble your Lord, loving and kind with all.[24]

CHAPTER 19: ON THE METHOD FOR BATTLING AGAINST THE VICE OF THE FLESH.

Against this vice you must battle with special and different means from the others. And so, because you know how to fight methodically, you must pay attention at three moments: before we are tempted; while we are tempted; and after the temptation has passed.

Before the temptation, the fight will be against the motives that usually cause this temptation. You have to fight first not by confronting the vice, but by fleeing all occasions and persons whatsoever from which even a minimal danger may come to you, whenever you can. And when it is necessary at times to deal with persons [who place you in danger of temptation], do so very quickly, with a modest and serious countenance. And your words ought to be harsh, rather than excessively loving or kind.

Do not trust yourself if you do not feel arousal of the flesh, or even if you have failed to over many years of acquaintance. This accursed vice that may have done nothing in many years can do so in an hour, and it often concocts its plots secretly. And so, the more calm and unsuspicious it appears, the more it may harm and incurably wound.

Often there is more to fear (as experience has shown not a few times and always will show) where the contact continues under the cover of licit things, such as through family or a proper obligation, or else from virtue that may be in the person loved. For the poisonous delight of the senses is gradually mixed in through too many imprudent contacts. Oozing unnoticeably little by little, and finally penetrating into the very marrow of the soul, the reason is more and more clouded. Then dangerous things—the loving glances, the sweet words between one another, the delights of conversation—begin to be considered nothing harmful. And thus proceeding from one thing to another, one falls into ruin or into some troublesome temptation that is difficult to overcome.

I tell you again, you must flee in order to stop. Do not have confidence that you bathe in and are full of the water of goodness and strong will, resolved and ready to die rather than offend God. For with frequent contact, little by little the fire will dry up the water of good intentions with its heat and attach itself—when one is not even thinking of it—to such a degree that one will respect neither relatives nor friends. One will neither fear God nor consider honor, life, or all the pains of hell. Therefore flee— flee if you have any desire to avoid being taken, captured and killed.

Second, flee idleness, and be vigilant and alert with the thoughts and works that befit your position.

Third, never resist, but readily obey your superiors, promptly executing the things imposed. Execute even more willingly the ones that humble you the more and are especially contrary to your will and natural inclinations.

Fourth, never make rash judgments of those close to you, especially concerning this vice. If someone falls obviously, have compassion for him, do not disdain him or hold him in derision, but extract the fruit of humility and self-knowledge, recognizing yourself as dust and nothing. Approach God with prayers, and flee more than ever the practices where only the shadow of danger exists. For if you become ready to judge and disparage others, God will correct you against your will, permitting you to fall into exactly the same sin, so that you will recognize your own arrogance. Humiliated, you will procure the remedy for both these vices. And when avoiding the fall, or not changing your opinion [of someone], know also that there is always reason for you to question your own condition in a serious way.

Fifth and finally, take care that you do not adopt any vain complacency when finding yourself with some gift and delight in spiritual joys. Do not persuade yourself that you are something [great] or that your enemies shall no longer make war against you now that you seem to view them with nausea, horror and hatred. For if so, you will be imprudent, and you will fall easily.

In the time of temptation, consider whether it proceeds from intrinsic or extrinsic causes. Extrinsic I understand to be curiosity of the eyes or ears, excessive finery in clothing, and the customs and thoughts that lead to this vice. The remedy in these cases is honesty and modesty, wishing neither to see nor to feel things that lead to this vice; along with flight, as I said above. The intrinsic proceed either from the sensuality of the body or from thoughts of the mind that come to us from our habits or through suggestions of the devil. One must mortify the sensuality of the body with fasting, flagellations, hairshirts, vigils and other similar harshness, as discretion and obedience teach.

As for thoughts also coming from that part, the remedies required are these: occupation in different exercises suitable to one's position; prayers; and meditations.

The prayers may be in this fashion: when you begin to perceive not even the thoughts, but their warning signs just a little, immediately withdraw mentally to the crucified Christ, saying, "My Jesus, my sweet Jesus, help me quickly, so that I may not be captured by this enemy." At times embrace the cross from which your Lord hung, repeatedly kissing the wounds of His holy feet, and saying tenderly, "Beautiful wounds, chaste wounds, holy wounds, now wound this miserable and impure heart, freeing me from offending you."

When abandoning temptations to delights of the flesh, I would not suggest meditation around certain points that many books propose as a remedy, such as consideration of the vileness of this vice, the insatiability, the disgust, the bitterness that follow it, the dangers and ruin of property, life, honor and other such things. For this is not always a secure means of defeating the temptations. It can also bring harm, since if the intellect in one way drives away these thoughts, in another it presents to us the occasion and danger of delighting in them and of consenting to the delight. Thus the true remedy is complete flight, not only from the thoughts themselves, but also from all things—even their opposites—that represent them to us. Your meditation for this effect must center around the life and passion of our crucified Redeemer. And if while meditating, these same thoughts were to appear before you against your will, and were more annoying due to your solitude (as may easily prove true), you should not therefore be frightened or give up the meditation. Neither should you turn toward them by attempting to resist them, but you should continue your meditation, as intensely as you can, taking no heed of such thoughts as if they were not yours. For there is no better way to oppose them than this, even if they make continual war against you.

You will then conclude the meditation with this or a similar request: "My Creator and Redeemer, free me from my enemies, to the honor of your passion and your ineffable goodness." Do not turn your mind to the vice, because the memory of this alone is not without danger. Neither should you ever remain to dispute with similar temptations, whether you have consented or not. For under the guise of good this is either a trap of the devil to disturb you and to render you discouraged and cowardly, or on the other hand, to make you fall into some [vain] pleasure by keeping you occupied in such discourses. Therefore when consent is not certain in this temptation it is enough for you to confess all to your spiritual father, with brevity, remaining content thereafter with what seems best to him, without thinking of it further. And make sure that you uncover your every thought to him readily, so that the thought may never retain any of your respect or shame. For if we have need of the virtue of humility in order to defeat all of our enemies, so we ought to humble ourselves in this matter more than in others, since this vice is almost always a punishment for pride.

After the time of temptation what you have to do in order to be free or to prepare to be free and completely secure is to be mentally far removed from those objects that caused you the temptation, even though for virtuous or other good reasons you feel yourself moved to do otherwise. For this urge is a deception of our depraved nature and a trap set by our shrewd adversary who transforms himself into an angel of light in order to carry us off to the shadows.

CHAPTER 20: ON THE WAY TO BATTLE AGAINST NEGLIGENCE.

In order to avoid falling into the miserable servitude of sloth—something that not only would obstruct the way of perfection, but would also deliver you into the hands of enemies—you have to flee from every curiosity and worldly attachment, and from any occupations that do not suit your rank. Then you must strengthen yourself to do everything at the time and in the manner pleasing to your superiors, because this conforms with every good inspiration and their every direction.

Do not delay, even for a very brief instant, because that first, single delay brings the second closer, and that one the third and the others. Sense yields and cedes more easily to these hesitations than the first, being already attracted to them and near to the pleasure that it has tasted. Thus one either begins action too late, or abandons it as tiresome at every turn. And so, little by little, one creates a habit of negligence which reduces us to such a degree that at the same time we are held bound by it, we suggest to ourselves that we seek to be very solicitous and diligent at other times. Then we can recognize our very negligent condition only through our personal shame.

This negligence flows through everything. It not only infects the will with its poison, making it abhor work, but it also weakens the intellect so that it does not see how vain and badly founded are our resolutions for the future. Before long that which one ought to accomplish is left aside quite voluntarily, or else postponed to another time. It is not enough to undertake the work that you have to do quickly, but rather one must seek the quality and essence of that work at the proper time, and with all possible diligence, in order to gain every possible perfection.

It is not diligence but supreme laziness to do the work before the proper time and to finish it off quickly without doing it well. For then we quietly give ourselves over to slothful rest on which our thought remained fixed while the work was being rapidly done. All this great evil arises because one does not consider the value of a good work done at the proper time and with a heart resolved to meet the fatigue and difficulties that the vice of negligence brings to new soldiers.

You must repeatedly judge that a single elevation of the mind to God, or a genuflection in His honor, is worth more than all the treasures of the world. Any time we do violence to ourselves and to the vicious passions, the angels carry a crown of glorious victory to our soul from heaven. On the other hand, God takes the graces He has given, little by little, from the negligent and increases those given to the diligent, making them enter into His joy.[25] Regarding the fatigue or difficulty, if you cannot meet it generously from the beginning, you must hide it from yourself so that it may seem less [onerous] than the lazy consider it to be.

Your exercise requires many, many acts and toil over many days to acquire one virtue, and the enemies to be conquered may seem numerous and strong to you. Begin to produce acts as if you had to do few of them and as if you needed to toil for just a few days. Battle against one enemy as if the others did not need to be fought, and with great confidence that through the help of God you are stronger than they. For doing it this way you will then begin to weaken negligence and prepare yourself so that, hand in hand, the contrary virtue may enter there.

I say the same concerning prayer. Try to spend an hour in prayer during your exercise. And because this seems difficult to your negligence, begin as if wishing to pray for the space of an eighth of an hour, so that you will proceed easily to the next and from this to the others that remain. When in the second or in some other eighth you feel excessively violent repugnance and distaste, omit the exercise so that it does not annoy you, but take up the omitted exercise again after a short time.[26]

You also must maintain this same method in manual labor, whenever you become very annoyed because you have to do many things that seem difficult to your negligence. Begin courageously, nevertheless, and fulfill one assignment as if you did not have to do the others. Thus proceeding diligently, you will come to do them all with much less fatigue than you expected due to your negligence. For if you fail to work in this fashion and do not go out to meet your tasks and difficulties as shown, then the vice of negligence will prevail over you. The toil and difficulty that the first practice of virtue carries with it will not only be present, but even from far off it will render you anxious, impatient, fearful of assaults and attacks from the enemy, and you will view persons with distrust, lest something be imposed upon you. Thus you will live disturbed, even in rest itself.

And you know, daughter, that little by little this vice of negligence not only destroys the first, small roots that have to produce the habit of virtue with hidden poison, but also those of the good habits already acquired. Just like the worm in the wood, it comes secretly to gnaw and consume the marrow of the spiritual life. With this means, the devil lays an insidious trap for all persons, but especially spiritual ones.

Guard yourself then by praying and doing good, and do not wait to weave cloth for the wedding garment, since you ought to find it adorned in order to meet the Spouse.[27] And remember every day that the One who gives you the morning does not promise you the evening, and giving the evening does not promise the next morning shall come to you. Therefore, spend every moment of every hour according to the pleasure of God, and as if no other time was granted to you. Do so all the more because you will have to render a most detailed account of every moment.[28]

I conclude by advising you to consider any day as lost (even if you have finished off much business) in which you have not obtained considerable victory against your evil inclinations and self-will, or not thanked your Lord for His benefices, especially for the painful passion He endured for you, and for His sweet and paternal care in which He has made you worthy of the inestimable treasure of some tribulations.

CHAPTER 21: ON GOVERNING THE SENSES, AND HOW FROM THEM ONE CAN PASS TO CONTEMPLATION OF DIVINITY.

Great care and continual practice are required to rule and regulate our exterior senses well, because the appetite, which is the captain of our corrupt nature, is inordinately inclined to seek pleasures and contentments. Being unable to acquire them by itself, it makes use of the senses as its soldiers and natural instruments in order to take their objects, drawing and pulling imaginations of them to itself, printing these in the soul. From there, pleasure follows, and it is spread through all that portion of the senses capable of such pleasure by the affinity that exists between pleasure and the flesh. Thence it moves to the soul, as a common contagion in the body corrupts the entire person.

You see the harm, so look after the remedy. Be careful not to let your senses go freely where they wish, or to serve you by their custom, where only delight and no good end, usefulness or necessity moves you. If they wander too far without your notice, put them behind you, or rule them in such a way that where before they made themselves prisoners of vain pleasures in a miserable fashion, they now obtain a virtuous booty from each object and carry it into the soul. Then the soul, recollected in itself, can take wing with power toward heaven, to the contemplation of God. You can do it in this way.

When some subject is shown to any of your exterior senses, mentally separate the created thing from the spirit that is in it and remember that in itself it has nothing whatever that it presents to your senses, but that everything is God's, who with His invisible spirit gives it the being, goodness, beauty and every form of good that is in it. Then rejoice that your Lord alone is the cause and beginning of all the various perfections of created things, and that He contains all of them, eminently, in Himself. This being is nothing other than a most minute degree of His infinite excellence.

When you perceive yourself occupied in admiring things that have a noble essence, mentally turn to the creature's nothingness, fixing the eye of your mind on the supreme Creator there present who has given it being. Taking all delight in Him alone, you will say, "O divine essence, desirable in the highest degree, how I delight that you alone are the infinite beginning of all created being!" Likewise, when you notice trees, grass and other similar things, mentally see that life which they do not have from themselves, but from the Spirit that you do not see and that alone vivifies them. And you can thus say, "Here is the true life, from whom, in whom and through whom everything lives and increases.[29] O living pleasure of this heart!" Similarly, from consideration of the wild animals, raise yourself mentally to God who gave them sense and motion, saying, "O first mover Who, moving all things is immovable yourself, how much I rejoice in your firmness and steadiness!"

And when feeling attracted by the beauty of creatures, separate that which you see from the Spirit that you do not see, and consider that everything beautiful that appears outside is invisible against the one Spirit which gave rise to that external beauty. Say with all happiness, "Here are the streams from the uncreated source, here the droplets from the infinite sea of every good. Oh how I rejoice in my inmost heart, thinking of the eternal, immense beauty that is the origin and cause of every created beauty!" When perceiving goodness, wisdom, justice and similar virtues in other persons, make the same separation and you will say to your God, "O richest treasury of virtue that is my delight, every good wholly derives from You and through You, and in comparison to Your divine perfections, all are as nothing! I thank you, Lord, for this and every other good thing You have placed close to me. Remember my poverty, Lord, and the great need that I have of the virtue of N."[30]

When stretching out your hands to do something, judge that God is the first cause of that undertaking, and that you are nothing other than His living instrument. Raise your thoughts to Him and speak in this way: "Supreme Lord of all, how great is the contentment that I feel within myself from being unable to accomplish anything without You and from recognition that You are the first and main doer of all." When enjoying food or drink, recognize that God is the One who gives them flavor. Then, delighting in Him alone, you will be able to say, "Give thanks, my soul, that just as outside of your God no one has true pleasure, thus in Him alone can you delight in everything."

If you are pleased with the aroma of something pleasant to the sense of smell, do not dwell in that delight. Pass on in thought to the Lord, from whom that smell has its origin, and you will feel an internal consolation and say, "Alas! Grant, Lord, that as I rejoice because all sweetness proceeds from You, so my soul, stripped and naked of every earthly pleasure, may ascend on high and return a thankful aroma to your divine nostrils." When you hear some harmony of music and songs, turn mentally to your God and say, "How much I rejoice, my Lord and my God, over Your infinite perfections, which joined as one create not only a supernatural harmony in yourself, but also produce together a magnificent concert among the angels, the heavens and all creatures."

CHAPTER 22: HOW THE SAME THINGS HERE ARE THE MEANS TO REGULATE OUR SENSES, PASSING ON TO MEDITATION CONCERNING THE INCARNATE WORD OF GOD IN THE MYSTERY OF HIS LIFE AND DEATH.

I have shown you above how we can raise the mind from sensible things to contemplation of divinity. Now learn a motivation from the same things for meditation on the Incarnate Word, considering the most holy mysteries of His life and death. All things in the universe can serve this goal, when considering (as above) the most high God alone as their first cause. He has given them that being, beauty and excellence which they possess. Passing from this, then consider how great and immense is His goodness. As the one beginning and Lord of all creation, He wished to descend to such lowliness as to make Himself man and to suffer and to die for man, permitting creatures of His own hand to arm themselves against Him in order to crucify Him.

Many particular things may bring these holy mysteries before the eyes of our minds: weapons, ropes, scourges, pillars, thorns, reeds, nails, hammers and others, which were the instruments of His passion. Humble dwellings lead us to remember the stable and crib of the Lord. Falling rain will remind us of that bloody divine rain which watered the earth in the garden, oozing from His most holy body. The rocks we shall look at represent to us those that were split open at His death; the moving earth, that which He made move at that moment; the sun will represent the shadows that obscured it; and seeing water, we will come to remember that which poured from His most holy side. I say this equally of other similar things.

When enjoying wine or some other beverage, recall the vinegar and gall of your Lord. If the sweetness of aromas allures you, run back mentally to the stench of dead bodies that He smelled on Calvary. When dressing, remember that the eternal Word dressed Himself in human flesh in order to invest you with His divinity. When undressing, remember your Christ who was stripped naked in order to be scourged and nailed to the cross for you. Hearing the uproar and shouts of men, remember those abominable voices, "Crucify, crucify him, away, away," that echoed in His divine ears.[31] Every time the clock strikes, either remember the anguished beating of the painful heart of your Jesus, when in the garden He began to fear His imminent passion and death, or feel those heavy blows with which He was nailed to the cross.

On any occasion when sadness comes to you—either from your own pains, or those of others—remember that these are nothing compared to the incomprehensible anguish that afflicted and pierced the body and soul of your Lord.

CHAPTER 23: ON OTHER WAYS OF REGULATING OUR SENSES, ACCORDING TO THE DIFFERENT OCCASIONS IN WHICH THEY REPRESENT THEMSELVES TO US.

Having seen how one must elevate the mind from sensible things to divinity and to the mysteries of the Incarnate Word, here I will add various ways of drawing different meditations at that point, so that just as the tastes of individual souls vary, so they have many different foods. Besides that, it will be useful not only to simple persons, but also to those of higher learning and more advanced in the way of the spirit, since among them there may be someone not equally disposed and ready for more lofty contemplation.

You must not fear becoming confused by this variety, as long as you humble yourself before the rule of discretion and the counsel of others, understanding that you ought to follow with humility and confidence, not only in this matter, but in every other suggestion that comes to you from me. When admiring things which are beautiful to the eyes and valued in this world, consider that all are ever so vile and worthless[32] in comparison to heavenly riches, to which one may aspire with every affection by discounting the things of this world. When turning your face toward the sun, remember that your soul is even more bright and beautiful than that, if it remains in the grace of your Creator. Otherwise, it is darker and more abominable than the shadows of hell. When raising your corporeal eyes to the sky that covers you, penetrate even higher with the eyes of your soul to the heavenly kingdom. Fix your mind on the place that seems to you the most delightful eternal dwelling, if you want to live innocently on earth.[33] When hearing the singing of birds or other songs, raise your mind to those of heaven, where there echos a continual "alleluia," and beg the Lord to make you worthy to praise Him perpetually together with those celestial spirits.

When you notice yourself taking delight in the beauties of a creature, consider intellectually how the infernal serpent lies hidden within it, ready and fully intent upon killing or at least wounding you. Against him you can say, "O accursed serpent, how insidiously you appear ready to devour me!" Then, turning to God, you can say, "Blessed are you, my God, who has uncovered the enemy to me and freed me from his furious jaws." Flee immediately from this attraction to the wounds of the Crucified, occupying your mind with these and considering how the Lord suffered them in His holy body in order to free you from sin and make the delights of the flesh hateful to you. I remind you of another way to flee this dangerous allurement: enter deeply into yourself to consider what the object that then pleases you so much will be like after death.

While you walk, remember that you will come closer to death with every step you take. So, when observing the birds flying through the air and skimming along the water, consider that your life goes flying along to its end with even greater velocity. Impetuous rising winds, or lightning, or thunder, [should] remind you of the awful day of judgment. Drop to your knees and adore God, begging that He grant you the grace and the time to prepare yourself well to appear before His most high Majesty.

You should train yourself in the variety of problems that can befall a person. When you are oppressed, for example, by some pain or melancholy, or you suffer heat or cold or something else, raise your mind to that eternal Will which is pleased that you feel the inconvenience in such measure and over such time for your own good. Then be happy through the love that you show your God and through the hope of serving Him in everything that pleases Him more. Say from your heart, "Here in me [is] the accomplishment of the divine will which has lovingly and from all eternity arranged this affliction that I am currently suffering. May my most loving Savior be praised forever." And when the thought of some good thing is born in your mind, immediately turn to God, recognize that it comes from Him, and give Him thanks.

When you read, it may seem that you see the Lord beneath the words and receive them as if they were coming from His divine mouth. Gazing at the holy cross, remember that there lies the standard of His army. If you move away from it, you will fall into the hands of cruel enemies, and if you follow it, you will arrive in heaven loaded with glorious spoils. When you see the beautiful image of the Virgin Mary, direct your heart to her, she who reigns in paradise, thanking her who always was prepared for the will of your God. She gave birth to, suckled and nourished the Redeemer of the world, and in our spiritual conflicts, she never fails us with her favor and assistance. The images of the saints represent to you great champions who, having run their race valorously, have opened the path to us. By following that path in like manner, you will be crowned with perpetual glory along with them.[34] When you shall see churches you can consider—among other devout ideas—how your soul is the temple of God, and as His own house, you therefore ought to guard it, pure and clean.

When hearing the three signals of the angelic salutation at any time,[35] you shall make the following brief meditations, in conformity with the sacred words usually said before each of these heavenly little prayers. At the first signal, thank God for that messenger He sent to earth from heaven, who was the beginning of our redemption. At the second, give thanks with the Virgin Mary for the greatness to which she was elevated by her singular, most profound humility. At the third signal, adore the newly conceived Divine Child along with the happy Mother and the angel Gabriel. Do not forget to bow your head in reverence a little at each signal, and a little more on the last.

These meditations that are divided by the three signals are useful at all times. Those following below are separated according to the evening, the morning, and midday, and are related to the passion of the Lord. As great debtors, we ought to remember frequently the pains that our Lady endured through His passion. We demonstrate ingratitude if we fail to do so. In the evening, bring to mind the anguish felt by the chaste Virgin on account of the bloody sweat, the arrest in the garden, and the hidden pains of her blessed Son throughout that night.[36] In the morning, pity her for her afflictions during the presentation before Pilate and Herod, His death sentence, and His carrying of the cross.[37] At midday, consider the dagger of pain that pierced the heart of the anguished Mother in the crucifixion and death of the Lord and with the cruel piercing of His most holy side.[38]

These meditations on the sufferings of the Virgin can be undertaken from Friday evening until midday on Saturday; the others on other days. I rely on your own particular devotions and on the opportunities that exterior circumstances present. In order to sum up briefly the way you have to control the senses, be alert so that you are moved and drawn in everything and at every instance not by love or abhorrence of the senses, but only through the will of God. Embrace or abhor only what God wants you to embrace or abhor.

And take heed, for I have not given you these means of regulating the senses so that you occupy yourself with them. You always ought to be mentally absorbed with your Lord, who wants you to attempt to defeat your enemies with frequent action and your vicious passions by resisting them and through contrary acts of virtue. Rather, I have taught you these methods so that you know how to act when the need arises. For you must remember that one produces little fruit when undertaking many exercises, although they are most wholesome in themselves. They often become entanglements of the mind, self-love, instability and traps of the devil.

CHAPTER 24: ON THE WAY TO CONTROL THE TONGUE.

The human tongue needs to be well-regulated and held in check, because everyone is strongly inclined to allow it to run on and to speak of the things that are more pleasing to our senses. For the most part, speech is rooted in a certain pride. Persuading ourselves that we know much, and pleased with our own ideas, we strive to imprint them on other souls with much repetition in order to be masters over them, as if they needed to learn from us.

It is not possible to express with a few words the evils that are born from too many words. Loquaciousness is the mother of laziness, the proof of ignorance and insanity, the door to slander, the minister of lies, and what cools fervent devotion. Too many words give strength to vicious passions, and from there the tongue is induced much more easily to continue indiscreet conversation.

Do not engage in long discussions with one who wrongfully detests you, so as not to annoy her. Do the same with one who listens to you, so as not to exceed the limits of modesty.

Flee eloquence and raising your voice, as both the one and the other are very loathsome and give an indication of presumption and vanity. Never speak of yourself, of your affairs, or of your relatives, unless out of necessity, and then only as briefly and narrowly as you can. If it seems to you that others speak of themselves excessively, strive to form a good opinion of them, but do not imitate them, even if their words tend toward their own humiliation and self-accusation. You must think as little as possible about your neighbors and their business, except for speaking well of them when the occasion arises. Speak willingly of God, and particularly of His love and goodness, but also with fear of the possibility of error in this. Take care to remain more attentive when others speak of Him, retaining their words deep within your heart. Just the sound of others' voices may strike your ear and turn your mind to the Lord. Even if it is necessary to listen to conversation in order to understand and respond, do not as a result neglect to give thoughtful attention to heaven, where your God lives, and to gaze at His greatness, as He always sees your lowliness. You must first consider things in your heart that you want to say before they pass to the tongue, for you will notice many that would be good might not be if you spoke them aloud. But I warn you that no small number of those that you think good to say would be much better buried with silence. You know it when considering them after the occasion for discussion has passed.

My daughter, silence is a great fortress in the spiritual combat and represents sure hope for victory. Silence is a friend through whom one distrusts oneself and confides in God, a guardian of holy prayer, and a marvelous aid for the practice of virtue. In order to accustom yourself to silence, consider often the damages and dangers of loquacity, the great blessings of silence. Fall in love with this virtue. In order to make it a habit, be silent over some period of time even when it would not be bad to speak, provided that this would not be prejudicial to yourself or others. It will, therefore, also be useful to you to remain distant from conversations, for you will have angels, the saints, and even God himself, instead of men, as company. Finally, remember the combat that you have at hand. Seeing all that you have to do, you will need to leave excessive words behind.[39]

CHAPTER 25: HOW THE SOLDIER OF CHRIST OUGHT TO FLEE ANXIETY AND AGITATIONS OF THE HEART WITH ALL HIS POWER IN ORDER TO FIGHT WELL AGAINST THE ENEMY.

When inner peace has been lost we ought to do everything we can to recover it. You should know that no worldly mishap can occur that reasonably ought to take it away from us or otherwise disturb it. We have to be sorry for our own sins, but with a peaceful pain, as I have shown above in more than one place. So, one must pity all other sinners with the pious affection of charity, suffering under their blows without agitation of the soul, at least inwardly.

Although grave and troublesome occurrences like sickness, injury, death of those closest to us, plague, war, fires and similar evils are more resisted by the men of this world the more they are naturally bothersome, still, with the grace of God we can not only desire them, but also love them as the just penalty of the wicked and the occasion of virtue for the good. For in these respects our Lord God is also pleased by them. With His will favoring us, we shall pass amid the bitterness and misfortune of this life with a peaceful and tranquil spirit. And be certain that every agitation of ours displeases His divine eyes. If it is of the kind that we desire, it is never unaccompanied by imperfections and always proceeds from some evil root of self-love.

Therefore, keep your guard always ready. As soon as it discovers anything that can disturb and disquiet you, may it give you a sign so that you take up arms for defense, considering that all those evils and many others like them, despite their outward appearance, are not true evils, nor can they take true blessings away from us. And remember that everything God orders or permits to occur through these honest means or others unknown to us is without doubt just and completely holy. So one can do much good by maintaining the soul tranquil and peaceful in any accident, however sinister. Otherwise, all of our exercises are of little or no use.

Beyond that, as long as the heart is disturbed it lies always exposed to other blows of the enemy. Moreover, we cannot easily discern the straight path and secure road to virtue in such a state. Our enemy detests this peace beyond measure, as the place where the Spirit of God lives so that you perform great deeds. Under friendly guise he often attempts to take it away from us by means of different desires that have the appearance of good. Among other indications, one can recognize this deceit in the fact that desires seize our inner peace. When your guard warns you of some new desire, in order to take refuge from the danger do not open the entry of the heart if beforehand you do not bring it to God, free of any ownership or will. Confess your blindness and ignorance and beg insistently that with His light, He makes you see whether it comes from Him or from the adversary. Then have recourse, as soon as you can, to your spiritual father.

And even if the desire might be from God, mortify your excessive eagerness before you execute it, because the work that follows such mortifications will be much more pleasing to God than if done with natural eagerness. Sometimes the mortification will please Him more than the work itself. Thus, by driving evil desires from yourself, and failing to execute the good ones (unless you have repressed natural eagerness) you will hold the fortress of your heart in peace and security. And in order to protect it in complete calm it is also necessary to defend it and guard it from certain scruples and interior remorse against the calm that sometimes comes from the devil, even though it may seem the scruples and remorse are from God because they accuse you of some failing. You will know whence they proceed by their fruits.[40]

If they humble you, make you diligent in good works, and do not remove your confidence in God, you ought to receive them from God with gratitude. But if they confuse you, make you cowardly, diffident, lazy, and slow in good works, then consider it certain that they come from the adversary. In that case, complete your exercise, lending them no ear. Furthermore, because disquiet is more commonly born in our hearts from the occurrence of things contrary to us, you have to do two things to defend yourself from such blows. One is to consider and to see exactly what these notions [of disquiet] are contrary to—to the spirit, or to self-love and self-will. Those that are contrary to self-will and to love of self—

your capital, main enemy—you ought not to call "contrary things," but consider them favors and aids from the most high God. You ought to receive them with a happy heart, giving thanks. And those contrary to the spirit ought not thereby to remove inner peace, as you will be taught in the next chapter. The other thing to do is to raise your mind to God, accepting everything from the merciful hand of divine providence with closed eyes, without wishing to know anything else, as if it were full of different blessings which you are then just unable to recognize.

CHAPTER 26: ON WHAT WE HAVE TO DO WHEN WE ARE WOUNDED.

When you find yourself wounded, either out of weakness or, on the other hand, out of will and malice by falling into some defect, do not cower or disturb yourself on this account. Rather, turn immediately to God, saying, "Alas my Lord, I have acted in accord with my nature—one can expect nothing from me other than failure." And then, with a moment's pause, humble yourself in your own eyes, regret your offense against the Lord, and without confusing yourself, be enraged against your vicious passions, especially against the one that has caused you the fall. Then continue: "Not even here, Lord, would I have stopped myself if You had not sustained me through your goodness." And here render Him thanks and love Him more than ever, amazed by such clemency, for after being offended by you, He offers you His right hand so that you will not fall again.

Finally, with great confidence in His infinite mercy, you should say, "Act, Lord, in accord with Your nature: pardon me. Neither permit me to live separated from You or distant from You, nor to offend you again." And with this done do not speculate on whether God has pardoned you or not, because this is nothing other than pride, mental distress, loss of time and a snare of the devil, set under the appearance of different good pretexts. Therefore, leaving yourself freely in the merciful hands of God, continue your exercise as if you had not fallen.

And if you continue to fall many times a day and become wounded, do as I have told you—on the second, the third and even the last time with no less confidence than the first time. Despising yourself more the more hateful the sin, force yourself to live more cautiously. This exercise displeases the devil a great deal, both because he sees that it is very pleasing to God, and because he becomes confused, overcome by someone he had first defeated. Thus, he may adopt different, deceitful methods because we allow him to do so, and he obtains victory many times through our carelessness and lack of vigilance over ourselves. Therefore, if you find yourself in such difficulty, so much more must you do yourself violence, repeating this exercise more than one time, even after only one fall.

If you feel disturbed, confused and discouraged after the failing, the first thing that you must do is to regain inner peace, tranquility and confidence. Then turn to the Lord equipped with these arms, because the restlessness that one possesses because of sin has one's own damnation as an object, not offense against God.[41]

The method of recovering this peace is to forget having fallen for the time being and to set yourself to consider the ineffable goodness of God and how very ready and desirous He is to pardon any sin, no matter how grave. He calls the sinner through various means and by many ways, so that from there on, the sinner may come to Him and unite himself to Him with His sanctifying grace in this life and with the blessing of eternal glory in the next.

And since you will have pacified your mind with these and similar considerations, you will turn to your failure, doing as I have said above. Then at the time of sacramental confession—which I exhort you to frequent often—reprove all your failures. Uncover them honestly to your spiritual father with new pain and displeasure over your offense against God, promising never to offend Him again.

CHAPTER 27: ON THE PLAN THAT THE DEVIL FOLLOWS TO
BATTLE AGAINST AND DECEIVE BOTH THOSE WHO WISH TO GIVE
THEMSELVES TO VIRTUE AND THOSE WHO ALREADY FIND
THEMSELVES ENSLAVED BY SIN.

Daughter, you must know that the devil does not devote himself to anything other than our ruin and that he does not do battle with everyone by the same method. In order to begin to describe to you some of his actions, methods and deceits, I place before you the conditions of various persons. Some find themselves in servitude to sin without any thought of freeing themselves. Others wish to free themselves, but do not begin the enterprise. Still others believe themselves to be marching along the path of virtue and are really departing from it. And finally, others, after the acquisition of virtue, fall with greater ruin. We will clearly discuss all of them.

CHAPTER 28: ON THE COMBAT AND DECEITS THAT THE DEVIL USES WITH THOSE WHOM HE HOLDS IN SERVITUDE TO SIN.

While holding someone in servitude to sin, the devil endeavors above all to weaken him further and to remove him from any thought that might lead to knowledge of his most wretched existence. He not only removes thoughts and inspirations from the sinner that call him to conversion with other, opposite thoughts, but he also makes him fall into the same sins, or other greater ones, with readily prepared opportunities. By this means he renders the sinner more blind and ignorant of his blindness, readier to hurl himself down and become habitually sinful. So, if God does not provide His grace, the devil leads him through a miserable life in a vicious circle from one blindness to a greater blindness, from one error to a greater error.

As far as we are concerned, the remedy for one who finds himself in this most wretched state is to be ready to give rise to thoughts and inspirations calling him from the shadows to the light, crying out with all his heart to his Creator, "Oh, my Lord, help me, help me quickly, and leave me no longer in these shadows of sin."

Do not neglect to repeat this many times and to cry out in these and similar ways. And then run immediately to a spiritual father, requesting help and counsel, in order to be able to free yourself from the enemy. And if you cannot go immediately, quickly turn in mind to the Crucified, throwing yourself before His holy feet with your face to the ground, and also beg mercy and help from the Virgin Mary. Know that victory lies in the speed, as you will understand through the following chapter.

CHAPTER 29: ON THE CUNNING AND DECEITS WITH WHICH THE DEVIL BINDS THOSE WHO, UNDERSTANDING THEIR EVIL, WOULD WISH TO FREE THEMSELVES; AND WHY OUR RESOLUTIONS OFTEN DO NOT HAVE THE DESIRED EFFECT.

Those who already understand the diseased life they are living and who wish to change it are accustomed to being tricked and defeated by the devil with the following weapons: later, later; "Delay, delay," as the crow says.[42] I wish to first resolve and free myself from this or that business or affair, and later to give myself with greater attention to matters of the spirit. This is the snare with which he has taken and still takes many. The reason for that is our negligence and ineptitude, since in business which concerns the health of the soul and the honor of God, one does not quickly take up that most powerful weapon: "Now, now," why later? "Today, today," why "delay"? Say to yourself, "Since when is tomorrow guaranteed? So, fighting now shall be the path to health and victory, before the will receives wounds and causes new disorders."

Therefore you see, daughter, that in order to flee from this trap (that described in the preceding chapter) and in order to overcome the enemy, the remedy is quick obedience to divine thoughts and inspirations. The quickness, I say, is the remedy, not the resolutions, because these latter often fail and many remain ensnared in them for different reasons.

The first reason—also treated above—is that our resolutions are not founded on distrust of ourselves and confidence in God. Neither do they allow us to see our great arrogance, from which proceeds the trap and the blindness. The light required to know it and the assistance necessary for us to remedy it come from the goodness of God. He permits us to fall, calling us away from confidence in ourselves to Him alone and from our pride to understanding of ourselves through the failing. So, if you want your resolutions to be effective, they must be strong. And they will be strong when they contain none of our own self-confidence and are all founded upon confidence in God with genuine humility.

The other reason is that when we set about to make a resolution, we admire the beauty and value of the virtue to which our will is drawing itself. Because of the laziness and weakness that may be there, it then displays before itself the difficulties necessary for you to acquire it. Being lazy and changeable, the will withdraws and fails. Therefore, accustom yourself to love the difficulties which the acquisition of virtue brings to you even more than the virtue itself. Your will shall prosper, always nourished by these difficulties—first little by little, and later by leaps and bounds—if you truly want to make yourself a possessor of virtue. And know that as you more generously embrace all the difficulties (and even more) that virtue places upon you, so much more quickly and highly will you defeat yourself and your enemies.

The third reason is because at times our resolutions do not aim at virtue and the divine will but rather at self-interest. [When] one wishes to succeed in the resolutions customarily made at the time of spiritual delights and at the time when tribulations affect us greatly, we are to discover in these [resolutions] no other intention than to do everything for God and for the exercise of virtue.

In order to avoid falling in this regard, be very cautious and humble in your resolutions during periods of spiritual delight, particularly in making

157

promises and vows. When you find yourself troubled, focus your resolutions on patiently tolerating the cross according to God's will, and to exalt it, denying every worldly consolation, even sometimes those of heaven as well. Your singular request and desire must be for the aid of God, because then you can tolerate every hostile thing without blemish to virtue or patience and without the displeasure of your Lord.

CHAPTER 30: ON THE TRAP SET FOR THOSE WHO BELIEVE THEMSELVES TO BE WALKING TOWARD PERFECTION.

Having already defeated the enemy in the first and second assaults and traps as above, danger returns a third time. It consists in the fact that we forget the enemies who actually combat and injure us, occupying ourselves in desires and resolutions for high degrees of perfection. We are wounded continually by this, do not treat the wounds, and considering such resolutions as if they were actions, we become proud in different ways. So, unwilling to allow even one little thing or little word of objection, we consume time in long meditations, resolving to endure great pains and even purgatory for the love of God. And since the inferior will does not feel the disgust that is distant from it, in our wretchedness we convince ourselves that we are at the same rank as those who actually sustain great pains patiently.

In order to flee this trap, you must resolve to oppose and do battle with those enemies who truly and closely make war against you. Thus it will become clear to you whether your resolutions are true or false, strong or weak, and you will march toward virtue and perfection by the well-trodden direct path. But I do not advise you to take up warfare against enemies who do not often tempt you, unless you truly foresee from one moment to the next that they are about to assail you. In that case it is proper to make resolutions beforehand to be prepared and strong.

Therefore, never judge your resolutions according to the criteria of results already obtained, even if you have been exercising virtue by your own means for some time. In these matters be humble instead, fearful of yourself and your weakness. Confiding in God, appeal to Him with frequent prayers that He may fortify and guard you from dangers, especially from every slightest presumption and self-confidence. For in this case it is permissible for us to make resolutions toward a higher grade of perfection, although the resolutions cannot overcome any tiny defects the Lord sometimes leaves for our humble recognition and for protection of some advantage.

CHAPTER 31: ON THE DECEIT AND BATTLE THE DEVIL EMPLOYS SO THAT ONE MIGHT QUIT THE ROAD LEADING TO VIRTUE.

The fourth deceit proposed above with which the evil demon assails us when he sees that we are marching directly toward virtue is by exciting different good desires in us so that we fall from the exercise of virtue into vice.

A person finding herself ill can always endure the infirmity with a patient will. The shrewd adversary, who understands one can acquire the habit of patience by that means, places before her many good works that she would do in other circumstances and strives to persuade her that if she were healthy, she would serve God more perfectly, helping herself and others in the process. After he shows these desires to her, he increases them little by little, to such an extent that he renders her distressed because she is unable to carry them out as she would like. And the more these desires become greater and stronger in her the more he increases the distress. And thus, step by step, the enemy deftly leads her to lose patience with the infirmity, not as an illness, but as an impediment to those works that she anxiously desires to perform for a greater good.

When he has drawn her to this point, he takes the goal of divine service and good works from her mind with the same dexterity, leaving there the naked desire to free herself from the illness. When this fails to occur in accordance with her wishes, she gets upset to such a degree that she becomes completely impatient. And so it happens that from virtue practiced, one can fall into the contrary vice without perceiving it.

When you find yourself in a troublesome state, the way to guard against and oppose this trap is to take care to give no place to desires for any good that you cannot immediately carry out, for they probably would disturb you. And you ought to convince yourself through this, with all humility, patience and resignation, that your desires would not have the effect you believe they would, since you underestimated your weakness and instability. Or else, consider that God—either in His secret judgments or perhaps due to your faults—does not desire that good from you, but instead wishes you to lower and humble yourself patiently under the gentle and mighty hand of His will.[43]

Similarly, when impeded by your spiritual father or by some other reason from satisfying your desire for frequent devotions, especially holy communion, do not allow yourself to be disturbed and disquieted by desire for them. Instead, stripped of all your self-interest and dressed according to the pleasure of your Lord, reason with yourself, saying, "If the eye of divine providence had not seen ingratitude or defects in me, I would not now be deprived of receiving the Most Holy Sacrament. Thus may I, seeing that my Lord uncovers my unworthiness before me by this means, always bless and praise Him for it. I trust completely, my Lord, in your great goodness, that You desire me to open to You a heart disposed to Your every desire by leaning on You and pleasing You in all things. Then You, entering within it spiritually, can console and fortify it against the enemies that are trying to separate it from You. Thus may everything be done that is good in Your eyes. My Creator and Redeemer, may your will be my food and sustenance, now and always. I ask only this grace of You, my Dearest Love: that my soul, purged and free from anything that is displeasing to You, be always prepared with the ornament of holy virtue at Your coming, and to the degree that it pleases You to prepare me."[44]

If you will observe these recommendations, know for certain that in whatever desire for good you cannot carry out—whether it is caused by nature, or by the demon in order to disturb you and take you from the path of virtue, or even sometimes by God in order to test your resignation to His will—you will always have the opportunity to satisfy your Lord in the manner that is most pleasing to Him. The true devotion and service which God seeks from us consists in this.

I advise you again, so that you do not lose your patience in difficulties caused only by that part of you that desires them, to use the licit means that servants of God are accustomed to use. Do so not with the desire and intention of being freed, but because God wishes that they be used, since we do not know if it pleases His divine Majesty to free us by this means. If you do otherwise, you may descend into greater evils, because you either fall readily into impatience when action fails to succeed according to your desire, or your patience would be defective, unattractive to God, and of little merit.

Finally, I remind you here of a hidden deceit of our self-love that attempts on certain occasions to conceal and defend our faults. Some sick person, for example, having little patience for an infirmity, may hide her impatience under the veil of some zeal for an apparent good, saying that her anxiety is not actually impatience with the struggle of enduring illness but reasonable displeasure because the illness has given her occasion for it, or because others must care for her, or because she feels trouble and injury for other reasons. Similarly, the ambitious person who is troubled over dignity not obtained does not attribute this to her own pride and vanity, but to other motives which she knows well she would consider as nothing in other not so serious circumstances. So too a sick person cured may permit the same toil and labor to be done for someone else by the same persons that labored for her whose labor she said had pained her so much. This is a very clear sign that the root of their lamentation is in no respect anything other than abhorrence of things contrary to their will. You, therefore, in order not to fall into this or other errors, must always patiently tolerate whatever toil and pain comes from the cause of self-will, as I have told you.

CHAPTER 32: CONCERNING THE FINAL ASSAULT AND DECEPTION EXPLAINED ABOVE, WITH WHICH THE DEVIL TEMPTS US AND BY WHICH VIRTUES ACQUIRED BECOME AN OPPORTUNITY FOR OUR RUIN.

The crafty and malicious serpent never fails to tempt us with his deceptions, even with the virtues that we have acquired because they are for us the opportunity for ruin. While taking pleasure in those virtues and in ourselves, we come to raise ourselves on high, only then to fall into the vices of pride and vainglory. In order to guard yourself against this danger, do battle always after placing yourself on the level and secure field of true and profound knowledge that you are nothing, you know nothing, that you can do nothing, that you possess nothing but misery and defects, that you merit only eternal damnation. Confirmed and established within the terms of this truth, never allow yourself to be drawn, even a little, from whatever thought has come to you or from anything that has happened to you, recognizing as certain the fact that all are your enemies. If you fell into their hands, they would kill or wound you.

In order to train yourself well to go forward in this field of true knowledge of your nothingness, make use of this rule. Whenever you turn to consideration of yourself and of your works, consider yourself always with what is yours and not what pertains to God and to his grace, and then so will He appraise you as you truly are.

If you consider the time before you existed, you will see that in all that abyss of eternity you were absolutely nothing, that you have done nothing, and that you could do nothing to have being. In the present time, in which you have being solely by the goodness of God, leaving to Him what is His, namely the continual governance with which He maintains you in every moment, what are you in yourself, if not equally nothing? There is no doubt that you would instantly return to your initial nothingness, from which His omnipotent hand drew you, should He leave you for just the smallest moment. It is clear then that in this natural life, clinging to what is yours, you are mistaken to value yourself or to wish others to hold you in esteem.

Where the well-being of grace and doing good are concerned, what good and meritorious works could your nature, stripped of divine aid, ever do by itself? On the other hand, considering your many past failings, and beyond them the great other harm that might have come from you, had God not sustained you with His merciful hand you would find that your iniquities would have reached an almost infinite number by the multiplication not just of days and years but also of bad acts and evil habits since one vice calls forth and draws with it another. And so, if you do not wish to become a thief of the goodness of God, but rather to be always with your Lord, you must consider yourself worse day by day.

Take care that this judgment that you make of yourself is accompanied by justice, because otherwise it would do no small harm to you. For if anyone is better at recognizing your wickedness, even if he misses something in his blindness, you would still lose much and make yourself worse than he in voluntary exercises of will if you wish to be held in high regard by people and to be treated by them as something you know you are not.

If you want knowledge of your wickedness and cowardice to hold your enemies at a distance and to make you precious to God, be sure not only to hold yourself in contempt as unworthy of every good and deserving of all punishments, but be glad to be treated with contempt by others, despising honors, enjoying insults and inclining yourself at every opportunity to do whatever others despise. In not abandoning this holy practice, you must not consider the opinion of others at all, provided you undertake the practice for the sake of your abnegation and devotion alone, not with a presumptuous heart and the unconscious pride through which, sometimes for good reason, one pays little heed to the opinions of others.

If at times it happens that you are loved and praised for some good quality God has given you, be self-contained and do not be moved at all from truth and justice, but first address God, saying from your heart, "May I never, Lord, be the thief of your honor and grace. To you be honor, praise and glory, and to me be shame."[45] And then to whoever praised you say within your heart, "Why is it that she considers me good, if truly my God alone and his works are good?"[46] By doing this and by rendering to God his due, you will hold your enemies at bay and prepare yourself to receive greater gifts and favors from God. And when the memory of good works done places you in danger of vanity, immediately see them not as things of yours but as God's. As if speaking to them you can say in your heart, "I do not know in what way you appeared and began to exist in my mind, because I am not your origin; rather, the good Lord and His grace have created, nourished and sustained you. He alone you must then acknowledge as your Father, thanking Him and rendering Him all praise."

Remember then that all the works that you have ever done have been not only small in comparison to the light and grace conceded to you to recognize and pursue them, but also still very imperfect and far removed from the pure intention and proper fervor and diligence with which they ought to be accompanied and undertaken. And so if you think well of them, you ought to be ashamed rather than vainly pleased with yourself, because it is all too true that the graces which we receive pure and perfect from God are soiled by our imperfections in the execution of them.

Compare your works with those of the saints and other servants of God, because in comparison with them you will clearly perceive that the best and greatest of your works are adulterated small change. Compare them next with those of Christ, who in the mysteries of his life and continual cross labored for you. Considering them without the divine person who worked in them, and only for the affection and the purity of love with which they were performed, you will realize that all your works are naught. And finally, if you raise your mind to the divine and immense majesty of your God and to the service that he merits, you will clearly see that great fear, not vanity, derives from any of your works. And so in all paths, in all your works, no matter how holy they be, you should say to your Lord with all your heart, "God, be merciful to me, a sinner."[47]

I also tell you that you ought not to attempt to be too quick to disclose the graces that God has given you, since this is almost always displeasing to your Lord, as He tells you himself in the following example. He once appeared in the form of an ordinary creature, a child, to a pious and devout woman. He was sought by her with such simplicity that he recited the angelic greeting. He promptly began, "Hail Mary, full of grace, the Lord is with you. Blessed are you among women," but then he stopped, because he did not wish to praise himself with the words that followed. And while she continued to beg him to say something more, he disappeared, and left his servant consoled, having revealed this heavenly doctrine through His example.[48] You too, daughter, must learn to humble yourself, knowing yourself with all your works for the nothing you are.

This is the foundation of all other virtues. God, before we existed, created us out of nothing and now that we have being through Him He wishes to found the entire spiritual edifice upon this—our acknowledgment that in ourselves we are nothing. And the more we become immersed in that nothingness the higher that building will rise. The more we delve into the soil of our misery the more the divine architect can place firm building blocks to further that edifice. Nor should you persuade yourself, daughter, that you can ever humble yourself enough, but rather think this of yourself—that if it were possible for an infinite thing to exist in a finite creature, such would be your lowliness in you. With this knowledge well-rooted we possess every good thing. Without it we are little more than nothing, even if we should undertake the works of all the saints and ever be occupied with God.

O blessed cognition, which renders us happy on earth and glorious in heaven! O light that coming out of the darkness makes souls lucid and clear! O unknown jewel that shines amid our filth! O nothingness, knowledge of which makes us masters of all! I would never tire of speaking to you of it. If you wish to praise God, accuse yourself and long to be accused by others. Humble yourself with everyone and beneath everyone, if you wish to exalt Him in you and to exalt you in Him. If you wish to find Him, do not raise yourself up, because He will flee. Lower yourself, lower yourself as much as you can, so He will come to find you and to embrace you. And He will welcome you and clasp you to himself in love more dearly in proportion to how much you humble yourself in your own eyes and accept being lowered in the eyes of all, reviled as something despicable. Think yourself unworthy of so great a gift which your God, who was condemned for you, grants you in order to unite yourself with Him. Do not fail to give Him frequent thanks and to hold yourself obliged to whoever has given you such an opportunity, especially to those who have vilified you, or worse, who believe that you chafe under their scorn and bear it unwillingly. Should this happen, you must show no outward sign.

If in spite of such considerations, which are all too true, the cleverness of the devil, ignorance and bad inclinations prevail in us to such an extent that thoughts of our own exaltation do not cease to disturb us and make an impression on our hearts, then it is time to humble ourselves in our own eyes all the more, since we have proof that we have made little progress in the way of the spirit and faithful knowledge of ourselves and since we are not able to free ourselves from the troubles rooted in our vain arrogance. Thus we will draw honey from poison and health from wounds.

CHAPTER 33: SOME ADVICE ON HOW TO DEFEAT SINFUL PASSIONS AND ACQUIRE NEW VIRTUES.

I have told you much about the method you must follow in order to overcome yourself and to honor the virtues, but still I must advise you of other things.

First. In desiring the acquisition of virtue never let yourself be persuaded that it can be gained from those spiritual exercises that, as if from a printing press, as they say, have set the days of the week, one for one virtue, and the others for other virtues. The order of combat and exercise is instead to wage war on those passions that have always injured you and still assail and injure you, and to adorn yourself with the virtues contrary to them, as perfectly as possible. Once you acquire these virtues, you will quickly gain all the others with ease and with little action over occasions that are never lacking. For the virtues always come linked together, and whoever possesses one of them perfectly has all the others ready at the door of the heart.

Second. Never set time for the acquisition of virtues, neither in days, nor weeks, nor years. Instead, always fight and march persistently to the greatest perfection, like a new or recently recruited soldier. Do not stop for even an instant, because in a pause on the road to virtue and perfection no breath or strength is taken, but one either turns around or becomes weaker than before. By a "stop" I mean to convince yourself of having acquired the virtue completely and to take little account of small deficiencies and of the times and occasions that call us to new acts of virtue. Therefore be solicitous, fervent and attentive, so as never to lose even a small opportunity for virtue. Love every occasion that leads to virtue, above all those that are difficult to overcome. The acts made to overcome difficulties can more quickly and more effectively become habits, so love those that offer them to you. You have to flee to a great distance and with all skill and rapidity only from those that could lead you to temptations of the flesh.

Third. Be prudent and discreet in those virtues that can cause harm to the body, like those that afflict it with scourges, sackcloth, fasting, vigils, long meditations and other such things. These virtues ought to be acquired little by little, and by degrees, as we will explain below. With completely interior virtues, like love of God, disdain for the world, lowering oneself in one's own eyes, hatred of harmful passions and sin, being patient and tractable, love of all (even those who offend you) and other similar things, there is no need to acquire them little by little, or to climb to their perfection by degrees. Instead, force yourself to undertake every action, just as perfectly as possible.

Fourth. All your thought, desire and heart must think, seek and long for nothing other than to defeat the passion you are battling and to acquire its contrary virtue. May this be all the world, the heavens and the earth to you, this your treasure, and all to the end of pleasing God. Whether eating or fasting, at work or at rest, waking or sleeping, inside or outside the house, whether attending to devotions or manual labor, may all be directed to overcome and defeat the passion and to acquire its contrary virtue.

Fifth. Be a universal enemy of earthly delights and comforts so that you may be attacked with lesser force by all the vices that have pleasure as a root. Having cut this root through hatred of ourselves, those vices come to lose strength and meaning. On the one hand, if you wish to do battle against any particular vice and its delight, while on the other hand also indulging in various worldly pleasures, although your wounds may be light and not deadly the war will be long and bloody and victory will be very uncertain and infrequent. Therefore, always recall to mind those divine sentences: "He who loves his life loses it; and he who hates his life in this world will keep it for eternal life." "So then, brethren, we are debtors, not to the flesh, to live according to the flesh, for if you live according to the flesh you will die, but if by the spirit you put to death the deeds of the body, you will live."[49]

Sixth. Finally, I warn you that it would be good, perhaps necessary, that you first make a general confession with all the proper intentions that one should in order to more fully assure yourself of being in the state of grace before your Lord, from whom all graces and victories must be awaited.[50]

CHAPTER 34: ON THE VIRTUES ONE MUST ACQUIRE LITTLE BY LITTLE, PRACTICING THEM BY DEGREES, AND ATTENDING TO ONE AT A TIME.

Although a true soldier of Christ who aspires to the summit of perfection must never place any limit on his improvement, still some spiritual fervors are to be checked with a certain discretion, since if they are embraced firmly at the beginning with excessive ardor they are then often lost and leave us in mid-course. So, beyond what was said concerning self-moderation in external practices, in addition you must know that interior virtues also have to be acquired little by little and by degrees.[51] In this manner, the few quickly become many and long lasting. For example, we ordinarily should not rouse ourselves to gladness over adversities or the desire for adversities if we have not first passed through the lower degrees of patience. And I do not advise you to occupy yourself with all, or even with many virtues at the same time, but only with one and then another because in this way one may plant virtuous habits more easily and firmly in the soul. In fact, with continual exercise of only one virtue the memory leads one more and more quickly toward it in every occasion, the intellect becomes gradually more dextrous in finding new means and motives to acquire it, and the will is more easily inclined toward it. And all of this takes place with greater effect than if one were occupied with many virtues simultaneously.

In addition, the interior acts leading to one single virtue, due to the conformity they have among them, are completed with less fatigue by this uniform practice, since one act calls up another like it for assistance. Through this similarity they make a greater impression upon us, finding a place in the heart already prepared and disposed toward receiving those newly produced as the older ones give over first place to them. These reasons have greater strength the more one is convinced that each person well-practiced in one virtue also learns the means of exercising another. Thus, through the increase of one virtue, all grow together by the insepara-ble conjunction they have among them, like rays proceeding from the same divine light.

CHAPTER 35: ON THE MEANS WITH WHICH VIRTUES ARE ACQUIRED, AND HOW WE OUGHT TO USE THEM TO ATTEND TO ONE ALONE FOR A CERTAIN PERIOD OF TIME.

In order to acquire virtues, beyond that which we have said above, one ought to cultivate a great and generous soul: one neither weak nor enfeebled, but resolute and of strong will, with a certain confidence of being able to endure many adversities and harsh things. In addition, one should maintain an inclination toward virtues and an affection for them. One should be able to obtain this by considering often how pleasing they are to God, how noble and excellent in themselves, and how useful and necessary to ourselves since every perfection begins and ends in them.

We must make serious resolutions every morning to exercise ourselves according to what we probably must do that day, and then frequently examine whether we have followed them or not, renewing them more heartily. This is particularly true of the virtue being pursued. Following the example of the saints, our prayers and meditations on the life and passion of Christ, so necessary in every spiritual exercise, must be applied principally toward that same virtue that we are attempting to cultivate in ourselves.

The same must be done in all other instances, as we will show in particular later on, even if they are different. We will seek to become so accustomed to inner and outer acts of virtue that we will come to undertake them with the same ease and readiness with which we earlier made our acts conform to our natural inclinations. And the more those acts are contrary to such inclinations (as I have explained elsewhere), the quicker will they produce a good condition in our soul.

The sacred words of Holy Scripture, spoken aloud or at least considered in the mind as may be convenient, have an astonishing power to help us in this practice. Therefore we must have ready many exercises pertaining to the virtue that we seek to practice and employ them daily, especially when a contrary passion stirs within us. So, for example, if we seek to acquire patience, we can say the following or something similar: "My children, patiently bear the anger brought on you by God." "The hope of the poor shall not perish forever." "He who is slow to anger is better than the mighty, and he who rules his spirit than he who takes a city." "By endurance you will gain your lives." "Let us run with patience the race that is set before us."[52]

In like manner, to attain the same effect we are able to speak the following or other similar little prayers: "When, my God, will this heart of mine be armed with the shield of patience? When, to content my Lord, will I endure every affliction with a peaceful heart?" "O too-sweet pains that make me like my Lord Jesus who suffered for me!" "Will it ever happen, only life of my soul, that I shall live for your glory, content among a thousand woes?" "Happy me, if in the midst of the fire of tribulation I will burn with desire to endure greater things."

We will make use of these little prayers and others conforming to our progress in virtue which the spirit of devotion will teach us. These little prayers are called ejaculations [*jaculatorie*], because they are like darts and javelins that are hurled toward heaven. They have great power to excite us to virtue and to penetrate to the very heart of God, if they are accompanied by two things which act as wings. The first is true cognition of our God's contentment at our exercise of virtues. The other is a truly burning desire to acquire them for the sole purpose of pleasing His divine Majesty.

CHAPTER 36: HOW PROGRESS IN THE EXERCISE OF VIRTUE REQUIRES CONSTANT ATTENTION.

One of the most important and necessary things for acquiring virtue, beyond those taught above, is that in order to arrive at the end that we are proposing here one must make it one's business to advance continually; otherwise, simply by stopping one retreats. This is because when we pause in our virtuous acts, it necessarily follows that many disordered passions are raised in us due to the violent inclination of our sensual appetites and of the other external things that motivate us. These disordered passions destroy or at least diminish virtues. In addition we remain deprived of many graces and gifts we might have had from the Lord if we had made progress. Therefore, the spiritual path is different from the path that the traveler follows on earth, inasmuch as when we pause on the latter no portion of the journey already made is lost, as is lost in the former. Beyond this, the weariness of the pilgrim on the earthly path is increased with continual bodily motion, whereas on the spiritual road, the more one moves forward the more strength and vigor one gains.

Since with virtuous practices the inferior part, which by its resistance made the path more harsh and wearisome, is continually weakened, the superior part, where virtue lies, is all the more sustained and fortified. And so with progress in goodness some of the suffering that one feels is diminished, and, through divine action, a certain secret cheerfulness is mixed with this same pain, growing with every hour. In this way, continuing to advance from virtue to virtue with ever-increasing ease and delight, one arrives finally at the summit of the mountain, where the soul made perfect labors without vexation, even with enthusiasm and jubilation. Having already won over and tamed disordered passions and standing above all created things, and even itself, it lives in felicity in the heart of the most high God, and there pleasurably working takes its rest.

CHAPTER 37: ON HOW WE ALWAYS OUGHT TO CONTINUE THE PRACTICE OF VIRTUE, AND NEVER FLEE OPPORTUNITIES TO ACQUIRE THOSE THAT ARE PRESENTED TO US.

We have seen very clearly that in the journey leading to perfection we should progress ever forward without stopping. In order to do so, let us be very attentive and vigilant not to let slip any opportunity for acquiring virtue that comes to us. Therefore, those who keep as far away as they can from contrary things fail to understand that they too could be of use in the acquistion of virtue.

Staying with the same example, if you desire to acquire the habit of patience, it is not good to withdraw from those persons, actions and thoughts that move you to impatience. And so, you do not have to take yourself away from some matters, even if they are disturbing you. Rather, by conversing with and handling whatever brings you annoyance, hold the will always disposed and ready to tolerate whatever disagreeable and disgusting thing comes to you. If you do otherwise, you will never accustom yourself to patience.

Similarly, if an activity brings you vexation—either in itself or because of the person who has imposed it upon you, or because it diverts you from doing another that would be more enjoyable—do not waver. Get started and keep at it, even if you feel disquieted and that you would find peace by quitting it. Otherwise, you would never learn to endure, nor would your quiet be genuine, since it is not proceeding from a soul purged of passions and adorned with virtue. I say the same to you regarding troublesome thoughts that sometimes torment and disturb your mind. You do not have to drive them all away, for they come together to serve you through the pain they give so that you may accustom yourself to tolerance of difficult things. And whoever tells you otherwise is teaching you how to flee the troubles you experience, not how to acquire the virtues you desire.

It is very true that it helps the new soldier to dally and fence with care and dexterity on such occasions—now thrusting, later parrying his blows—to the extent that he has acquired more or less virtue and strength of spirit.[53] But one should never turn one's back and retreat in such a way as to leave all instances of difficulty behind completely. Because if we save ourselves for now from the danger of falling, we may be exposed to the blows of impatience when greater risks come by failing first to arm and strengthen ourselves with use of the contrary virtue.

These instructions have no place, however, when it comes to sins of the flesh, which we have already considered separately.[54]

CHAPTER 38: HOW ONE OUGHT TO CONSIDER PRECIOUS ALL OPPORTUNITIES TO BATTLE FOR THE ACQUISITION OF VIRTUE, ESPECIALLY THOSE THAT INVOLVE GREATER DIFFICULTY.

I am not pleased, daughter, that you avoid the difficult opportunities to develop virtue that present themselves. I want you to seek them out sometimes. Always embrace them happily as soon as they appear, as things of great value, and consider them more precious and dear the more they displease your senses. This you shall do with divine aid, if you will carefully bear the following considerations in mind.

One is that the opportunities are the proportional and necessary means to acquire virtue. Therefore, when you request the latter from the Lord, ask for the former as well. Otherwise your prayer would be in vain and you would come to contradict yourself and test God, since He does not ordinarily give patience without tribulations, or humility without scorn. And one may say the same of all other virtues, for there is no doubt that these are attained by means of adverse occurrences. The adversities bring us much greater help by means of this effect: they have to be considered more valuable and pleasant the more troublesome they are, because the more we act generously and firmly in such cases the more easily and quickly they open the path of virtue before us. As a result, they are to be valued and their use is not to be omitted, even on the smallest of occasions, such as a single glance or word against our will. This is because these acts are done to you more frequently,[55] although they are less intense than those we produce in serious difficulties.

The other consideration (one I have also touched on above) is that all the things that happen to us come from God for our good and so that we can draw fruit from them. And although some of these, such as our defects or those of others (as we also said in another place), one cannot say are from God in the sense that He does not will sin, still they are from God in that He permits them and while able to impede them does not. But all afflictions and pains that come to us either through our defects or through the malice of others are both from God and of God, since He concurs in them.[56] Although He might prefer them not be done, because to His purest eyes the soul contains exceedingly hateful deformities, He wishes us to endure them for the blessing of virtue that we can draw from them and for other just reasons hidden from us.

Therefore, since it is more than certain that the Lord wants us to sustain willingly whatever trouble comes, either from others or from our unjust deeds, then to say (as many do in order to excuse their impatience) that God does not will and even abhors this form of evil action is nothing other than a vain pretext to cover up one's own guilt and to reject the cross that we cannot reject, the one that He wants us to carry.

And so that it may balance with the rest, I repeat that the Lord loves more our tolerance of those pains that derive from the iniquity of men, especially if they have first been of service and benefit to you, than our tolerance of the annoyances proceeding from other troublesome incidents. This is so because ordinarily vain human nature is more repressed in the former than in the latter. By enduring them we also willingly please and highly exalt our God, cooperating with Him in something through which His ineffable goodness and omnipotence shine brilliantly. We draw the precious and delicious fruit of virtue and goodness from the deadly poison of malice and sin.

Therefore you must know, daughter, that as soon as the Lord discovers in us the lively desire truly to succeed and to attend as we ought to this glorious acquisition, He prepares for us a chalice of stronger temptations and more difficult occasions than before so that we may take it up at His time. And we, as recognizers of His love and of our own good, ought to close our eyes to receive it willingly and quickly drink it to the very bottom with all confidence, since it is medicine put together by a hand that cannot err with ingredients so much more delightful to the soul as they are more bitter in themselves.

CHAPTER 39: HOW WE CAN TAKE ADVANTAGE OF THE EXERCISE OF THE SAME VIRTUE ON DIFFERENT OCCASIONS.

You saw above how the exercise of one virtue alone over some time is more fruitful than exercising many together, and that the opportunities that present themselves to exercise any virtue have to be regulated accordingly, despite the differences among them. Now you must learn how one can practice that more easily. It may happen in the very same day, and even at the very same hour, that we are reprimanded for an action that nonetheless was good and that someone else murmurs against us for another action. Perhaps some favor we request is harshly denied, or we are suspected of some tiny little evil for no reason, or we endure some bodily pain, or some bothersome trifle is imposed on us, or some badly seasoned food is served to us, or something else more serious and difficult to tolerate happens to us. Miserable human existence is chock-full of such things. Even though these and similar incidents might elicit a variety of virtuous acts, if we want nevertheless to hold to the demonstrated rule, we will proceed with acts that will all conform to the virtue we have in hand.

For example, if the occasions come at a time in which we hope to exercise ourselves in patience, we will produce acts to endure them all willingly, with interior happiness. If we hope to practice humility, we will recognize ourselves in all the misfortunes of every undeserving person. If we hope to practice obedience, we will place ourselves quickly under the most powerful hand of God, and for His contentment, as He so wills, under that of other rational creatures, and even under the inanimate objects from which these aversions come to us. If we hope to practice poverty, we will content ourselves in being stripped and deprived of every consolation of this world, either great or small. If we hope to practice charity, we will produce acts of love toward both our own neighbors as instruments of the good that we can acquire and toward the Lord God as the first, loving cause from which those inconveniences proceed or are permitted for our practice and spiritual profit.

And from what we say concerning the chance events that can occur each day, one can understand how we can proceed in either a singular occasion of infirmity, or in another difficulty that continues over a long time, making use of the virtue that we then happen to be practicing.

CHAPTER 40: ON THE TIME ONE MUST DEVOTE TO THE PRACTICE
OF EACH VIRTUE AND ON THE INDICATORS OF OUR
ADVANCEMENT.

It is not possible for me to determine the exact time over which one must continue in the exercise of each virtue. This has to be regulated by the condition and need of the individual, by the progress one is making on the path of the Spirit, and by the judgment of the one who guides us on that path. But if one would truly apply oneself with the diligence and the means we have described above, there is no doubt that one would profit more than a little in a few weeks.

The sign of having made progress in virtue is when one firmly continues in virtuous practices despite dryness, amid the shadows, distress and withdrawal of spiritual delights. There can be no clearer indication of this than the problem sensuality will cause us when producing virtuous acts. The more it diminishes, losing strength, the more one can consider having advanced in that virtue. When we do not experience contradictions and rebellion from the sensual and inferior part of ourselves, especially in the midst of sudden and unexpected assaults, this will be a sign of having already attained the virtue. The more our acts are accompanied by greater readiness and spiritual alacrity the more we can believe we have progressed in this exercise.

We should take care not to convince ourselves that we are certainly possessors of the virtues, or entirely victorious over any of our passions, even if after much time and many battles we do not feel its impulses. Here, the trickery and operations of the devil and our deceitful nature can again have a place, and so at that time vice can seem to be virtue, through hidden pride. Besides, if we aim at the perfection to which God calls us through the many changes we have made on the road of virtue, we still would not have to persuade ourselves that we had even crossed the threshold of His kingdom.

Therefore, like a new warrior, and like a babe just born to fight, you must always begin your exercises from the very foundation, as if you had done nothing before.[57] And I remind you, daughter, to attend more to marching forward in virtue than to scrutiny of your own progress, because the Lord God, the true and only searcher of our hearts, gives knowledge of this to some and not to others, according to whether mortification or pride follows from such knowledge. Like a loving Father, He removes the danger from the one and provides the occasions for growth and virtue to the other. And therefore, even if the soul does not perceive its progress, as long as it still follows its exercises it will see progress when it is pleasing to the Lord, for its greater good.

CHAPTER 41: HOW WE OUGHT NOT LET OURSELVES DESIRE
FREEDOM FROM TROUBLES WE MUST PATIENTLY ENDURE; AND
ON THE MEANS OF REGULATING ALL OUR DESIRES SO THAT THEY
BE VIRTUOUS.

When you find yourself in any painful situation whatever, endure it with a patient heart, take care never to let yourself be persuaded by the devil or by your self-love to desire liberation from it, because from this, two principal injuries would come to you.

One is that if this desire does not take the virtue of patience from you immediately, at least it would dispose you toward impatience little by little. The other is that your patience would become defective and would be rewarded by God only for the space of time that you suffered. If you had not desired liberation but left everything to His divine will, even if your suffering was in effect only an hour or even less, the Lord would have recognized it as service over an infinitely longer time.

Therefore, in this and in all things, as a universal rule, you have to hold your desires so distant from every other object that they aim purely and simply at their true and singular purpose, that is, the will of God. In this way they will be just and upright and you will not only be peaceful in any distasteful occurrence but also content. Nothing can occur without the eternal will; desiring that, you will come to wish and at the same time to possess all that you desire and seek, at all times. This does not refer to the sins of others or your own, since God does not will them, although He has a place in every suffering that comes from those or elsewhere, even though it be so violent and penetrate so far within that it comes to dry up the very roots of life, touching the foundation of the heart. For this pain is the cross with which God sometimes favors His closest and dearest friends.

What I say about the suffering you have to experience in every case you must understand as the part of each problem that remains. It is by the pleasure of the Lord that we endure, even after we have used licit means to free ourselves. And even these ought to be regulated by the will and disposition of God, who has arranged them so that we use them because He so wishes and not out of attachment to ourselves, because we love and desire freedom from troublesome things more than His service and pleasure.

CHAPTER 42: ON THE WAY TO OPPOSE THE DEVIL WHILE HE TRIES TO TRAP US THROUGH INDISCRETION.

When the crafty devil perceives that we walk directly on the path of virtue with lively and well-ordered desires he cannot, for this reason, draw us to himself with obvious traps. He transforms himself into an angel of light, and with friendly thoughts, quotations from Scripture, and examples of the saints, he persistently presses us to walk indiscreetly to the height of perfection in order then to make us fall from there into ruin. And so he encourages us to punish the body sharply with scourges, abstinence, sackcloth and other similar mortifications so that either we become elated for apparently doing great things—as frequently happens to women—or we become incapable of good works because of some infirmity that appears in us to such a degree that even spiritual exercises become annoying and abhorrent because we consider them too tiring and painful. And so, little by little, you become lukewarm in doing good, and give yourself over to earthly delights and diversions with greater interest than before. Many follow the impetus of an indiscrete zeal with spiritual presumption. Crossing the limit of their own virtue through immoderate exterior sufferings, they become lost in their own inventions and laughable to the malicious demons. This would not have happened to them if they had carefully considered those things said above. This type of painful action, although praiseworthy and capable of bearing fruit where there is corresponding physical strength and spiritual humility, must have a limit conforming to the quality and nature of each individual.[58]

For those who cannot struggle like saints in this painful mortification, other opportunities are not absent to imitate their lives: through great, efficacious desires and fervent prayers; by aspiring to the more glorious crown of true soldiers of Jesus Christ; by despising all the world and themselves as well; by giving themselves over to silence and solitude; by remaining humble and at the service of all; by enduring evil from and doing good to whoever is more contrary to them; and by guarding themselves from all faults, however small. This is something more pleasing to God than practices afflicting the body. In the latter I advise you to be discretely frugal, increasing them only as necessary, since with certain excesses you run the risk of abandoning them altogether. Of course I say this since I am convinced that you have not stumbled into the error of those otherwise spiritually strong who, flattered and trapped by alluring human nature, are too diligent in the protection of their physical health. These demonstrate such jealousy and anxiety over health that because of some trifle they are always doubtful and in fear of losing it. It is nothing for them to think more of that health or to maintain it more willingly than to manage this part of their life. Thus, they continually attend to procuring foods more in conformity to their taste than to their stomach, food that often weakens them through excessive delicacy. Under pretext of being better able to serve God, this is nothing other than an attempt to bring together two mortal enemies, the soul and the body, without advantage to either, but actually with damage to both. Care to the latter requires that which pertains to health, and care to the former that which pertains to devotion.

And thus a somewhat unfettered way of life is more secure and profitable in all respects, one that is not unaccompanied by the discretion I have spoken about, while maintaining consideration of the fact that not all are subject to the same rule because of different conditions and constitutions. And I add that we ought to proceed with some moderation not only in exterior mortifications, but also in the acquisition of interior virtues, as was demonstrated above in the step-by-step directions for gaining virtue.[59]

CHAPTER 43: HOW MUCH THE INSTIGATION OF THE DEVIL AND OUR OWN EVIL INCLINATIONS WITHIN CAN DO TO LEAD US TO RASHLY JUDGE OUR NEIGHBOR; AND HOW TO RESIST THEM.

From this vice of self-esteem and self-aggrandizement another is born that carries the gravest danger. This is the rash judgment that we make of our neighbors through which we come to despise them, criticize them and consider them base. This defect, since it is born of our evil inclinations and pride, is willingly fostered and nourished by them, because they increase together, pleasing and deceiving us imperceptibly. Thus, without realizing it, the more we presume to raise ourselves up, the more we lower others through our opinions. We consider ourselves far removed from the imperfections that we believe we can identify in them.

And the wily devil—who discerns this wretched disposition of soul in us—remains continually alert to open our eyes, and to keep us awake to see, examine and inflate the failings of others. The negligent do not believe and do not know how hard he works, even studies, to imprint on our minds the little defects (big ones being lacking) of one person or another. Therefore, if he is on the look-out to do you harm, you be alert too, in order to avoid falling into his traps. As soon as he puts one of your neighbor's shortcomings before you, stop thinking about it quickly. Even if you feel moved to pass judgment about it, do not let yourself be led into this, and remember that such power has not been given to you.[60] Even if it had been granted to you, you still could not make a correct judgment, since you find yourself surrounded by thousands of passions and far too inclined to judge badly without just cause.

As an effective remedy for this, I remind you that you should be occupied with consideration of the needs of your own heart, so that with every hour you will see more and more that you have much work and effort ahead of you and that you will have no time or inclination left to look after other people's business. Furthermore, by attending properly to such an exercise you will come to purge your inner eye more and more of the bad humors from which this pestiferous vice proceeds. And know that when you wickedly suspect a brother of any sin, some root of the same evil exists in your heart. When your heart is poorly disposed, it receives every like object that it meets.[61]

Therefore, when it occurs to your soul to judge others for some defect, then you say to yourself—and just as indignantly as against that guilty person—"How can I, miserably buried in this and other grave faults, be so bold as to raise up my head to see and judge those of others?" And thus the weapons that wounded you when they were pointed toward others, now turned against yourself, will bring healing to your wounds.

If, however, the error committed is clear and manifest, excuse it with pious affection, and believe that in this brother exist hidden virtues that the Lord protects by permitting him to fall, or that he has this defect for a certain time to humble himself in his own eyes. Perhaps with this and with the disdain of others he may profit from humiliation and make himself more acceptable to God, and thus his gain may be greater than the loss.

And if the sin is not just obvious, but also grave and from an obstinate heart, turn your thoughts to the awesome judgments of God. You will see people who at first were most wicked but later attained signs of great sanctity, and others who have fallen from the most sublime state of perfection which they seemed to have attained into misery. And so remain always in fear and trembling, and much more for yourself than for others.[62]

Remind and convince yourself that all the good and contentment that you feel within yourself for your neighbor is the effect of the Holy Spirit, and that all contempt, precipitous judgment and bitterness against him comes from your own malice and from diabolical suggestions. Therefore, if any imperfection in others makes an impression on you, never cower from it, and give your eyes no sleep until you can pluck it from your heart.

CHAPTER 44: ON PRAYER.

If distrust of ourselves, confidence in God, and practice are as necessary in this combat as has been demonstrated to this point, then prayer, the fourth objective and weapon proposed above, is necessary above all. With it we can attain from the Lord God not just these things, but every other good. This is because prayer is the instrument to obtain all the graces that rain down upon us from that divine source of goodness and love.[63]

With prayer—if you use it well—you can give the sword in your hand to God, so that He may fight and win through you. And in order to use it well, it is necessary to accustom yourself, even exhaust yourself, in observing the following things.

First, a true desire to serve His divine Majesty in everything and in the way that is more pleasing to Him must always live in you. In order to kindle this desire, consider well that God is worthy to be served and honored through His indescribably amazing excellence, goodness, majesty, knowledge, beauty and other infinite perfections, above all things. Consider how in order to serve you He suffered and labored for thirty-three years, and tended and healed your fetid wounds—poisoned by the malignity of sin— and not with oil, wine and strips of cloth, but with that precious liquid that flowed from His most sacred veins, and with His most chaste flesh, torn by scourges, thorns and nails. And beyond this, consider how important this work is, since through it we come to make ourselves masters over ourselves, superiors to the devil, and children of God Himself.

Second, you must have a lively faith and confidence that the Lord wishes to give you everything you need for His service and for your own good. This holy confidence is the vessel that divine mercy fills from the treasury of His graces and that will be just as enlarged and more capacious as prayer will more richly return to our breast.[64] If we call upon Him with faith and perseverence, how will the immutable and omnipotent Lord fail to give us a share of His own riches, having often commanded us to ask Him and having also promised us His Holy Spirit?[65]

Third, you must approach prayer with the intention of choosing the divine will alone and not your own. Ask accordingly to obtain what you are requesting, that is, to move yourself to pray because God wishes it. Desire to be satisfied with what He alone wishes. In addition, your intention ought to be to join your will with the divine will and not to lead God's to your own. This is because our will, being infected and spoiled by self-love, frequently errs, nor does it know what it requests. The divine will, however, is always joined to indescribable good and can never err. Therefore, it is the rule and queen of all other wills, and it both wishes and is worthy to be followed and obeyed by all. And so other wills must request things conforming to God's pleasure. Doubting that anything else could be,[66] you should ask with the condition of desiring something only if the Lord wishes that you have it. You shall request those things that you know will certainly please Him, such as virtues, more in order to satisfy and serve Him than for any other goal or end, even if spiritual.

Fourth, you must go to prayer adorned with works corresponding to the requests and after much more prayer you must exhaust yourself to become worthy of the grace and virtue that you desire. Prayer has to be equally accompanied with practice if we are to overcome ourselves, so that in time one follows the other. Otherwise, the request for some virtue without striving after it would be an effort to tempt God more than anything else.

Fifth, thanksgiving for benefits received must precede requests for more, in this or a similar manner: "My Lord, out of your goodness you

have created and redeemed me and freed me from the hands of my enemies such an infinite number of times that I myself do not know them all.
Assist me now, do not deny me that which I ask of you, even though I am
always rebellious and ungrateful to you." And if you are requesting some
particular virtue and you have at hand something contrary in order to
practice it, do not forget to render Him thanks for the occasions that He
has spared you, since this is not the smallest of His blessings.

Sixth, since prayer takes its force and power to bend God toward our
desires from His natural goodness and mercy, from the merits of the life
and passion of His only-begotten Son, and from the promise He has made
to answer us, you should conclude your requests with one or more of the
following phrases: "Grant me this grace through your infinite mercy,
Lord. May the merits of your Son close beside You beseech for me what I
ask of You. Remember, my God, your promises and hear my prayers."
And other times you should ask for graces again, through the merits of the
Virgin Mary and the other saints. They are very close to God and are
honored by Him greatly, since they honored His divine Majesty in their
lifetime.

Seventh, you must continue in prayer with perseverance, because
humble perseverance defeats the invincible. If the diligence and pleading
of the widow of the Gospel inclined a judge filled with every wickedness
to her request, how will it not have the strength to incline Him, who is
Himself the fullness of every good, toward our requests?[67]

Thus, although after prayer the Lord may wait to come and answer
us, and may even show signs to the contrary, still continue praying, maintaining firm and lively confidence in His help. For in Him there is nothing
missing, but rather, all those things necessary for you and other persons to
gain graces are superabundant, to an infinite degree. Therefore, if there is
no defect on your part, be confident of always obtaining everything that
you request or that which may be more useful to you, or even both
together.

The more it might seem to you that your prayers are unanswered, the
more you must humble yourself in your own eyes. Considering your
faults with your mind fixed on divine mercy, always increase your confidence in Him. If you keep your faith alive and firm, the more it is tested,
the more it will please our Lord.

Then always render Him thanks, recognizing Him as good, wise and
loving, even when some things are denied you, just as if they were granted
you. In any event, remain firm and happy in humble submission to His
divine providence.

CHAPTER 45: ON MENTAL PRAYER.

Mental prayer is an elevation of the mind to God with an explicit or implicit request for what one desires.

Explicit requests are made when we ask for grace mentally in this or a similar manner: "My Lord God, grant me this grace to your honor." Or, "My Lord, I believe that it may please You and be to Your glory that I ask and obtain this grace from You. Now, then, fulfill Your divine pleasure in me."

When you are actually attacked by enemies, you should pray in this way: "Be swift, my God, to help me, so that I may not surrender to the enemies." Or, "My God, my refuge, strength of my soul, assist me quickly, lest I fall." Continue the fight and also continue this form of prayer, always manfully resisting those who battle against you.

When the bitterness of the battle is over, turn to your Lord, present before Him the enemy you have fought and your weakness to resist, saying, "Behold, Lord, the creature of Your hands, redeemed out of Your goodness with Your blood. Behold Your enemy, who attempts to take away and separate the creature from You. To You, my Lord, I turn, in You alone I confide, for You are omnipotent and good. See my impotence, my readiness, without Your help, to make myself willingly subject to him. Help me then, my Hope and Strength of my soul."

An implicit request occurs when one raises the mind to God in order to obtain some grace, showing Him the need without otherwise speaking or conversing, as when I focus my mind on God and there in His presence recognize my powerlessness to defend myself from evil and to do good. Flushed by the desire to serve Him, waiting for His aid humbly with faith, I gaze and gaze again on this Lord. Such knowing admission of vivid desire or faith made before God is a prayer that implicitly requests what I need. The more clear and sincere that knowledge is, and the more intense the desire and more lively the faith, so much more efficaciously will one request.

There is also another sort of implicit prayer—more condensed— that one makes with a simple glance of the mind toward God so that He might help us. This glance is nothing other than a silent recollection and entreaty for the grace that we have earlier requested. Learn this sort of prayer well and make yourself familiar with it, because, as experience will show you, it is a weapon you can easily have at hand in every occasion and in every place. It is of greater value and advantage than I know how to explain.

CHAPTER 46: ON MEDITATIVE PRAYER.

When wishing to pray for some length of time, such as half an hour, or even an entire hour or more, you should add meditation on the life and passion of Jesus Christ to the prayer, always applying His actions to the virtue that you desire. If you wish to obtain the grace of strength and of patience, for example, you should undertake meditation on some aspects of the mystery of the scourging.

First. How after the order given by Pilate, the Lord was dragged by the ministers of wickedness to the assigned place for scourging, amid shouts and mockery.

Second. How He was stripped hastily and furiously by them: for they did not stop until His most chaste flesh was completely uncovered and naked.

Third. How His most innocent hands were tied to the column, fastened with a rough rope.

Fourth. How His body was all lacerated and torn by whips, and streams of His divine blood flowed down to the ground.

Fifth. How the wounds already inflicted became worse and worse, by the adding of blow upon blow to the same place.

So, having proposed these or similar points to yourself for meditation, then to acquire patience, you should first apply the senses. Feel, as vividly as you can, the most bitter agony and sharp pains your dear Lord sustained in each individual part of His most holy body.[68] Then, you should proceed to His most holy soul, comprehending as far as possible the patience and docility with which He suffered such afflictions, never satisfying the hunger to suffer greater and more atrocious torments for the honor of the Father and our benefit.

See Him flushed, then, with a lively desire so that you may wish to endure your own trials, and see how He prays for you by turning again to the Father so that grace may make you worthy to patiently carry the cross that now troubles you, and another besides. Thus, often bending your will to desire endurance of everything with a patient heart, turn your mind to the Father. First, thank Him that through His pure charity He sent His only-begotten Son to the world to suffer such severe torments and to pray for you, and then ask Him for the virtue of patience, through the merit of the works and prayers of His Son.

CHAPTER 47: ON ANOTHER FORM OF PRAYER THROUGH MEDITATION.

You should also pray and meditate in another way. Since you will have considered attentively the afflictions of the Lord and seen in thought the readiness of mind with which He sustained them, then from the greatness of His labors and His patience you can proceed to two other considerations.

One is on His merit, the other on the contentment and glory of the eternal Father through the perfect obedience of His impassioned Son. Representing these two things to His divine Majesty, you should ask for the grace you desire by virtue of them. And you should be able to do this not only in consideration of each mystery of the passion of the Lord, but in every particular interior and exterior act that He made in each mystery.[69]

CHAPTER 48: ON A METHOD OF PRAYER BY MEANS OF THE VIRGIN MARY.

Beyond the words above, I tell you there is another way to meditate and pray, turning the mind first to the eternal God, then to sweet Jesus, and finally to His glorious mother, and all by way of the Virgin Mary.

To turn to God, consider two things. First, the delight that He Himself took in Mary from all eternity before she was created out of nothing. Second, consider her virtue and actions since her birth into the world.

You meditate on the delight in this way. Rise high in thought above all time and all creatures and enter into the eternity and mind of God. Consider the delight that He took in the Virgin Mary, find God among these delights, and confidently ask Him, by virtue of them, for the grace and strength to destroy the particular enemies against which you are then fighting. Proceeding to consideration of the many and singular virtues and actions of this holy Mother—and offering now one of them to God, now all of them together—beg His infinite goodness, through them, for all your needs.

Then, turning the mind to the Son, you will remind Him of the virgin womb that carried Him nine months; of the reverence with which the little Virgin adored and recognized Him after He was born as true man and true God, her son and creator; of the compassionate eyes that beheld Him so poor, the arms that sheltered Him, the sweet lips that kissed Him, the milk that nourished Him, and the toils and anguish that in life and in death she endured for Him. By virtue of those things, you will do sweet violence to the divine Son, so that He may answer you.

Turning finally to the most holy Virgin, remind her that by eternal providence and goodness she was chosen as the Mother of graces and mercies, and as our advocate. And so, we have no more secure and powerful recourse than to her, after her blessed Son. Moreover, remind her of that truth written of her and known through so many astounding miracles: no one who invokes her with faith ever lacks a merciful response. Finally, you will place before her the sufferings that her only Son endured for our salvation, begging her that you may implore grace from Him, so that the sufferings can have the effect in you for which He sustained them, to His glory and contentment.

CHAPTER 49: ON SOME CONSIDERATIONS TO HELP ONE TURN TO THE VIRGIN MARY WITH FAITH AND CONFIDENCE.

If you wish to turn to the Virgin Mary with faith and confidence, you will be able to approach her by heeding the following considerations.

First. It is already known from experience that all vessels that have earlier contained perfume or some precious liquid for any length of time retain their odor, even after it is gone, and especially the longer it was there, and if some remains. But perfume has limited and finite qualities and so does every precious liquid. Similarly, something that remains close to a large fire retains the heat for a long time, even if it moves away from the fire. This being true, with what fire of charity, with what feelings of mercy and compassion shall we say that the vitals of the Virgin Mary burn and are filled? This is because for nine months she carried in her virgin womb and always bears in her breast and in her love the Son of God, who is charity itself, mercy and compassion, not of limited and finite virtues, but infinite and with no limit whatever. Thus, just as whoever goes near to a great fire cannot but receive some of its heat, so and even more every needful person who with humility and faith draws near to the fire of charity, mercy and compassion always burning in the breast of the Virgin Mary, will receive help, favors, graces and more, and all the more the more often he draws near with firmer faith and confidence.

Second. No single creature ever loved Jesus Christ so much, or conformed more to His will than His most holy mother. So if this same Son of God, who spent all His life and all His being for the needs of us sinners, has given us His mother for our mother and advocate so that she may help us and be, after Him, the means of our salvation, how could it ever be possible that our mother and advocate would fail us and become a rebel against the will of the Son?

Daughter, turn with confidence to the most holy mother Virgin Mary in your every need, because this confidence is rich and blessed, and refuge in her is secure, since she continually gives birth to graces and mercy.

CHAPTER 50: ON A METHOD OF MEDITATION AND PRAYER BY MEANS OF THE ANGELS AND ALL THE SAINTS.

In order to use the assistance and favor of the angels and the saints in heaven for meditation, you can employ two means.

The first is that you turn to the eternal Father and present Him with the love and praises with which He was exalted by all the celestial court and the labors and pains that the saints suffered on earth for love of Him. By virtue of these things, ask His divine Majesty for all that you need.

The other is to take recourse to these glorious spirits as those who long not only for our perfection, but also that we might be placed in an even higher position than their own. Beg their assistance against all your vices and enemies, and also for your defense at the moment of death.

Sometimes you will begin to consider the many and singular graces that they have received from the supreme Creator, rousing in yourself a lively affection of love and happiness for them because they are rich in many gifts, and as if the gifts were all your own. And you should praise God and give Him thanks as often as possible, more for those who possess the gifts, not for yourself, since such was His will.

To perform this exercise in order and with ease, you can divide the regiments of the blessed among the days of the week in the following manner. Sunday, you will take up the nine angelic choirs; Monday, John the Baptist; Tuesday, the patriarchs and prophets; Wednesday, the apostles; Thursday, the martyrs; Friday, the popes with the other holy bishops; Saturday, the Virgin with the other saints. But never let a day go by without running often to the Virgin Mary, Queen of all the saints, to your guardian angel, to St. Michael the Archangel, and to all your holy advocates.

Pray every day to the Virgin Mary, to her Son, and to the celestial Father that they might concede to you the favor of giving you St. Joseph, spouse of the Virgin, as a principal intercessor and protector. Then turn to this saint with prayers and confidence that he may receive you under his protection. All those who have held him in reverence and had recourse to him, not only in spiritual needs, but in temporal ones also, and especially in directing the devout in the way of prayer and meditation, say that many graces and blessings have been received from this saint. For if God holds high regard for the other saints because when living among us they rendered Him obedience and honor, how much more ought we to believe that He values this most humble and fortunate saint and that thus his prayers come close to God? After all, he was honored on earth by that same God to such a degree that He made himself subject to the saint and obeyed and served him as a father.

CHAPTER 51: ON MEDITATIONS CONCERNING THE PASSION OF CHRIST IN ORDER TO DRAW DIFFERENT AFFECTIONS FROM IT.

What I have said above about the passion of the Lord is useful for praying and meditating by way of petition.[70] Now I am adding how we can draw different affections from the same meditations. If you intend, for example, to meditate on the crucifixion, then among other points to consider within that mystery are the following.

First. How the Lord, on the hill of Calvary, was brutally stripped by those enraged folk, tearing to pieces the flesh that adhered to the clothing because of the recent scourging.

Second. How the crown of thorns was raised from His head, and then replaced, causing new wounds.

Third. How He was cruelly affixed to the cross with nails and the blows of a hammer.

Fourth. How His holy limbs, failing to reach the width required, were pulled from their sockets with such violence that all the dislocated bones could be counted one by one.

Fifth. How His most holy wounds were enlarged and worsened with indescribable pain, because of the weight of the body, since the Lord was hanging from that rough wood with no other support than the nails.

When desiring to rouse feelings of love in yourself, study these or other points through meditation, and pass from mere acquaintance to greater knowledge of the infinite love and goodness of your Lord, Who chose to suffer this way for you. The more this knowledge increases in you, the more love will equally increase. From the same knowledge of the infinite goodness and love that the Lord has shown to you, you will easily draw contrition and pain for so often and ungratefully having offended your God Who was maltreated and torn in such ways for your iniquities.

In order to move yourself to hope, consider that so great a Lord fell into this state of calamity to extinguish sin, to free you from the snares of the devil and from all your personal guilt, to render you right before the eternal Father, and to give you confidence to resort to Him in all your needs. You will feel happiness in passing from His pains to their effect. Through them He purges the sins of the whole world, satisfies the wrath of the Father, confounds the prince of darkness, kills death and refills the chairs of the angels. Move yourself to joy even more by the contentment that the most holy Trinity, along with the Virgin Mary and all the Church triumphant and militant, receives from this.

In order to incite yourself to hatred of all your sins, apply all the points on which you must meditate to this end only: as if the Lord had suffered for no other reason than to lead you to hatred of your evil inclinations and of the fault that dominates you and very seriously offends His divine goodness.

In order to move yourself to wonder, consider whether anything could be greater than this—seeing the Creator of the universe Who gave life to all things being persecuted, even to death, by His creatures; seeing the supreme Majesty oppressed and reviled, justice condemned, the beauty of God spat upon, the love of the celestial Father despised, that inner and inaccessible light given over to the power of darkness. For glory and felicity itself was deemed a dishonor and disgrace by the human race and buried in unbelievable misery.

In order to pity your suffering Lord, even beyond the meditation on His physical tortures, mentally penetrate to the unequaled internal pain that tormented Him. For if you are distressed by the former, physical tortures, it would be strange if the latter did not break your heart with pain. The soul of Christ saw the divine essence then just as that soul sees God now in heaven. The soul of Christ knew that essence to be most worthy, above all, of every honor and service. The soul desired that all creatures direct themselves to this through the ineffable love of God, and with all their strength. Seeing the contrary—God so unimaginably offended and dishonored through the infinite guilt and abominable wickedness of the world—the soul of Christ was then pierced by unbearable pains. The more His creatures crucified Him, the greater was His soul's love and desire that the most high Majesty be honored and served by all.[71]

Just as the greatness of this love and desire is incomprehensible, so there is none who can know how bitter and grave this internal distress was for the crucified Lord. Loving all creatures ineffably, He suffered exceedingly for all their sins in proportion to this love. Through sins they sepa-

187

rated themselves from Him, because by every mortal sin that all men who ever were or ever will be have committed and will commit, as often as each one sinned, just as often did each separate himself from the Lord with whom he was joined by charity. This separation is more painful than that of parts of the body when they are dislocated from their natural place. Because the soul is a pure spirit and therefore more noble and perfect than the body, it is capable of experiencing greater pain.

Among all the sufferings creatures caused the Lord, the most bitter came from the sins of the damned. Forever unable to reunite themselves with Him, they must suffer eternal, incomparable torments. If the tender heart of your sweet Jesus comes before you for contemplation, you will find in Him for your compassion the most unbearable pains imaginable. These pains were not only because of the sins committed, but also because of those that never were committed, for there is no doubt that our Lord earns for us the forgiveness of the former and our preservation from the latter only at the high price of His own effort.

You will not lack other considerations, daughter, to lead you to grieve over your impassioned, crucified Lord. This is because there never was nor ever will be any pain in any rational creature that He has not also felt within Himself. The soul of Christ is troubled by the injuries and temptations, penances, shame, and every anguish and trouble of every person. His soul is even more vividly troubled than those who actually suffer anguish. Our most merciful Lord understands all of their afflictions, great and small, those of the soul and those of the body, even the smallest headache or prick of a needle, perfectly. Through His unbounded charity He wishes to pity them and to imprint them upon His heart.

But no one is able to explain how much the sufferings of His most holy Mother grieved Him. The holy Virgin ached and suffered in every way and in every respect that the Lord ached and suffered. Perhaps not so intensely, but just as bitterly. And these, her own sufferings, renewed the internal anguish of her Blessed Son, becoming like so many burning arrows of love, wounding His sweet heart. Through such torments as I have described, and through the almost infinite others unknown to us, it could well be said that His heart became a loving inferno of readily accepted pain, as one devout soul used to say with holy simplicity.[72]

Daughter, if you consider carefully the reasons for all these torments that your crucified Redeemer and Lord endured, you will find nothing other than sin. Thus it follows clearly that the true and highest compassion and offering of thanks that He seeks from us, and that we infinitely owe Him, is our grief. Purely out of love for Him and for having offended

Him, we must hate sin above everything else and battle generously against all His enemies and our evil inclinations. Then, stripping ourselves of the old man and his actions, we may put on the new, adorning our souls with evangelical virtue.[73]

CHAPTER 52: ON THE PROFITS ONE CAN DRAW FROM MEDITATION ON THE CRUCIFIED AND FROM IMITATION OF HIS VIRTUES.

There are many advantages you ought to extract from this holy meditation. Among others, you should not only grieve over your past sins, but you should also be troubled because the disordered passions, those that put your Lord on the cross, live on in you.

Another advantage is to beg Him for forgiveness for your sins and the grace of perfect self-hatred so as never to offend Him again. Do it also in recompense for His great love for you in order to love and serve Him more and more perfectly. That is impossible without this holy hatred.

The third advantage is to persecute to the death every one of your wicked inclinations, however small it may be, and with delight.

The fourth is that you strive with all your strength to imitate the virtues of the Savior who has suffered, not only in order to redeem us by making satisfaction for our iniquities, but also in order to give us the example of His holy footsteps to follow.

Here I propose a method of meditation that will serve you to this effect. If you desire to gain patience, for example, then in order to imitate Christ consider the following points.

First, what the soul of Christ did for God during His passion.

Second, what God did for the soul of Christ.

Third, what the soul of Christ did for itself and for His most holy body.

Fourth, what Christ did for us.

Fifth, what we ought to do for Christ.[74]

For the first, then, consider how the soul of Christ, being completely fixed upon God, understood that infinitely incomprehensible greatness, compared to which all created things are as nothing. The soul was astonished to see that greatness, although immovable, subjected on earth to the most shameful treatments through men from whom He had received nothing other than infidelity and injury. Consider how He adored and thanked God nonetheless, and offered Himself completely.

Second. Look then at what God did for the soul of Christ: how God chose it and induced it to sustain all the insults, the spittle, the blasphemy, the scourges, the thorns and the cross on our behalf, discovering His satisfaction in seeing it completely overwhelmed with every sort of dishonor and affliction.

Third. From this, proceed to the soul of Christ. Consider how He perceived with His most brilliant intellect how great this pleasure was in God, and how He loved His divine Majesty with affection burning beyond all measure, and how He was invited by God to suffer for our love and example, because of His infinite worth and out of a sense of the immense obligations that He had. He was content and happy to obey promptly the most holy will of God. Who can penetrate within those profound desires that this purest, loving soul possessed? Here it found itself in a labyrinth of tasks, seeking always and never finding (at least as much as it desired) new ways and means of suffering. And thus the soul of Christ freely gave itself and His most innocent flesh which could not follow its own wishes over to the power and pillage of wicked men and the demons of hell.

Fourth. After this, look at your Jesus. With merciful eyes turned toward you He says: "See, daughter, that whenever you did not want to do a little violence to yourself your immoderate desires were applied to Me. See how I suffer—and how happily—for your love in order to give you an example of true patience. Through all my pains I beg you, daughter, to carry this cross willingly and every other cross that pleases Me, leaving yourself completely in the hands of all the persecutors I will send you, however vile and cruel to your honor and your body they may be. Oh, if you could only know the consolation I would feel! But you can easily see it in these wounds I have chosen to receive with such joy in order to adorn your poor soul, one beloved by me beyond all your estimation, with precious virtues. And if I am reduced to such a pitiful state by this, then why, My dear spouse, do you not wish to suffer a little to satisfy My heart and to soothe those wounds caused Me by your impatience? That afflicts Me more bitterly than the wounds themselves."

Fifth. Think carefully about Who it is that so reasons with you and you will see that it is the King of Glory himself, Christ, true God and true man. Consider the enormity of His torments and insults, undeserved by the most infamous criminal in the world. Watch your Lord amid such tortures remain not only astonishingly imperturbable and patient but actually delight in them as if at His own wedding celebration. And just as a little bit of water tends to excite a fire further, so with an increase of afflictions that are small to His superabundant charity His happiness is always increased and the longing with which He endures them is greater. Consider how none of this that the most merciful Lord has undertaken or endured was by force or out of self-interest, but rather, as He himself has told you, out of charity toward you, and so that in imitation of Him you might exert yourself in the virtue of patience. Gradually gaining clear understanding of what He desires from you and the contentment you give Him by practicing this virtue, may you produce acts of burning desire to carry your current cross, and every other cross, even when more difficult, not just patiently, but with happiness in order better to imitate your God and to give Him greater comfort.

When placing before the eyes of your mind the dishonors and bitterness He tasted because of you, and His perseverance and endurance, you should be ashamed to recognize that your patience is merely a shadow, for yours are not true afflictions and disgraces. Fear and tremble, because even the smallest thought leading you away from suffering out of love for your Lord might find a place to establish itself within your heart.[75]

This crucified Lord, my daughter, is a book that I give you to read. You will be able to draw from it the true portrait of every virtue. Because it is the book of life, it not only instructs the intellect with words but also inflames the will with living example.[76] All the world is full of books, but nonetheless all of them taken together cannot so perfectly teach the way to acquire all virtues as the contemplation of a crucified God.

You know, daughter, that there are some who spend many hours weeping over the passion of our Lord, considering His patience, and then when adversities overtake them demonstrate impatience, as if they had thought of everything but the passion during prayer. They are like the soldiers of this world. They promise great things in their tents before the battle but then drop their weapons and take flight at the appearance of the enemy. What is more foolish and miserable than this—to see the virtues of the Lord with crystal clarity, to love and admire them, and then to completely forget or discount them when an occasion to exercise them arises?

CHAPTER 53: ON THE MOST HOLY SACRAMENT OF
THE EUCHARIST.

Up until this point, daughter, I have provided you, as you have already seen, with the four weapons necessary to defeat your enemies and with much advice on managing them well. Now, I must suggest another, that is, the most holy sacrament of the Eucharist. For just as this sacrament is high above the other sacraments, so this fifth weapon is superior to all the others.

The four described above take value from the merits and graces that the blood of Christ has earned for us, but this weapon is the very blood and body itself, along with the soul and divinity of Christ. With this one can battle against enemies with the power of Christ. With this we battle against them together with Christ, and Christ fights them together with us. Thus, whoever eats the flesh of Christ and drinks His blood remains with Christ and Christ remains with him.[77]

Since this most holy sacrament and weapon can be utilized in two ways—taken sacramentally once a day and spiritually at every hour and in every moment—you never ought to miss any opportunity to take it frequently in the second manner or to receive it in the first way when it is granted to you.

CHAPTER 54: ON THE WAY TO RECEIVE THE MOST HOLY SACRAMENT OF THE EUCHARIST.

We can receive this most divine sacrament for different purposes. In order to attain them we have to do different things at three different times: before communion; when we are about to receive communion; and after communion.

Before communion, and no matter for what end one wishes to receive it, we must wash and purify ourselves from any stain of mortal sin that may exist in us with the sacrament of Penance. We do so that we might give ourselves with all the affection of our hearts, with all our souls, with all our strength, and with all our powers to Jesus Christ and to what pleases Him, since in this most holy sacrament He gives us His blood and body, along with His soul, His divinity and His merits. Considering how small and insignificant our gift is compared to His, we ought to desire this sacrament in order to offer it to His divine Majesty, as all human and celestial creatures have always offered and given it to Him.

Since He wants you to receive so that your common enemies may be defeated and destroyed, then, from the previous evening or even earlier before you communicate, begin to consider the desire the Son of God has that you give Him a place within your heart through this most holy sacrament, so that He can unite Himself with you and help you erase all your depraved passions. This desire of our Lord is so great and immense that the created intellect cannot comprehend it.

In order that you may understand it somewhat, engrave two things upon your mind.

One is the ineffable pleasure of God in living with us. For although He is supreme goodness itself, He calls this His "delight."[78]

The other is the consideration that He hates sin above all other things, both as an impediment and obstacle to His longed-for union with us, and as completely contrary to His divine perfections. Since He is the supreme good, pure light and infinite beauty, He can do nothing else but hate and infinitely abominate sin, which is nothing other than an intolerable darkness, defect and stain upon our souls.

This hatred of our Lord for sin is so ardent that all the works of the Old and New Testaments were directed to its destruction, particularly that of the most holy passion of His Son. According to the enlightened servants of God He would have exposed Himself to a thousand more deaths if necessary in order to obliterate every guilt from us, no matter how small.

Once you have understood, even imperfectly, from such considerations the greatness of the desire that the Lord has to enter into your heart, then arouse a vivid desire in yourself to receive Him for the same purpose He has: in order to drive away and wage total war with your common enemies. Making your heart all generous and ready, out of hope for the coming of your celestial commander, call the passion you have resolved to defeat even more frequently into battle. Repress it with repeated, contrary desires, producing acts of virtue opposed to it. This is the way you should pass the evening and the morning before communion.

When you come to take the most holy sacrament, just a moment beforehand give a quick thought to your shortcomings since your last communion: how they were committed by you as though God did not even exist; as though He had not endured the mystery of the cross for people like you; how they made you rely more on vile self-satisfaction and upon your own will than upon the will of God and His honor. With the same shame of yourself and with a holy kind of fear, you should be confused by your ingratitude and unworthiness. But remembering then how the abyss of your ingratitude and lack of faith recalls the truly immeasurable abyss of the goodness of your Lord, draw near to Him confidently, giving Him a large place in your heart so that He may make Himself your complete master. You will give Him a large place when you drive outside of your heart any affection for creatures whatever. Then close it up, since otherwise your Lord will not enter there.

After you receive communion, turn immediately back into the secrecy of your heart. First adore Him, mentally saying to your Lord with all humility and reverence, "You see, my singular Good, how easily I offend You and how powerful this passion is against me. On my own I can do nothing to free myself. Therefore, this battle is mainly Yours and through You alone do I hope for victory, although it is also necessary for me to fight." Then turn to the eternal Father, offering to Him, in order to render thanks and to gain victory over yourself, His blessed Son whom He has given to you and Who you already hold within yourself. Fighting generously against the passion mentioned above, and with faith in God, hope for the victory. For you will not be deprived of it, although it may be delayed, as long as you do all that you can on your part.

CHAPTER 55: HOW WE MUST PREPARE OURSELVES FOR COMMUNION SO AS TO AROUSE LOVE OF GOD IN US.

In order to stir yourself to love your God through this most heavenly sacrament you should turn in your thoughts to His love for you, meditating from the evening before on how that great and omnipotent Lord, not content at having created you in His own image and likeness, or at having sent His only-begotten Son into the world to suffer thirty-three years for your iniquities and to endure the harshest trials and the painful death of the cross in order to redeem you, also wished to leave Him to you as your food and your need in the most holy sacrament of the altar.

Consider well, daughter, the incomprehensible excellence of this love, which rendered the sacrament perfect and singular in all its parts.

First. From the viewpoint of time, our God has loved you perpetually and without any temporal beginning. Just as He is eternal in His divinity, so also eternal is the love with which before all ages it was fixed in His mind to give us His Son in that miraculous fashion. Rejoicing within yourself out of inner joy over this, you will be able to say, "Then in that abyss of eternity my littleness was so valued and loved by the most high God that He was thinking of me, and with wishes of ineffable charity He yearned to give me His own Son as my sustenance.

Second. All other loves, great as they may be, have some limit, nor can they pass beyond it; but this love of our God is alone without measure.

Thus, wishing to satisfy Himself completely, He gave His own son, equal to Him in infinity and majesty, of one substance and nature. Thus the love is equal to the gift and the gift equal to the love—the one and the other are so great that no intellect can imagine anything greater.

Third. Nor was God drawn to love us by any necessity or force, but His intrinsic natural goodness alone moved Him to such and so much incomprehensible affection for us.

Fourth. No work nor merit of ours has been advanced to make that immense Lord show such excess of love toward our mediocrity, but through His generosity alone He has given absolutely everything to us, His unworthy creatures.

Fifth. If you turn in your thoughts to the purity of this love, you will see that unlike earthly love it is not mixed with any self-interest, since our Lord has no need of our goods, being in Himself most happy and glorious without us. And so, His ineffable goodness and charity was purely invested in us, not for His, but for our profit.

Thinking well on this, you will ask yourself, "How is it that such an exalted Lord bestows His love on such a lowly creature? What do You desire, King of glory; what do You expect of me, who am nothing more than a little dust? I see clearly, my God, in the light of Your fiery charity, that You have but one intention—that I might more plainly discover the purity of Your love for me. For it is for no other reason that You give me your entire self for food than to transform me wholly into You, not for any need You may have of me, but because You living in me and I in You, I shall become Your self through a loving union, and that out of the lowliness of my worldly heart You may make a single divine heart with You."

Then, full of joy and wonder, seeing yourself so highly esteemed and loved by God, and knowing that He with His omnipotent love intends and wishes from you nothing other than to draw into Himself all your love, removing from you first all created things and then even yourself, creature that you are, offer yourself wholly to your Lord in holocaust. Therefore, from this point on only His divine love and pleasure will move your intellect, will and memory, and control your senses.

Seeing that no other single thing can produce in you such divine effects as receiving Him worthily in the Most Holy Sacrament of the altar, open your heart to Him for that purpose with the following prayerful exclamations and loving aspirations: "O most celestial food, when will the hour come when I may sacrifice myself to You with nothing other than the fire of Your love? When, when, O eternal, uncreated love? O living bread, when shall I live from You, for You and in You alone? O when, my life, my beautiful, happy and eternal life? O manna from heaven, when will I, weary of every other earthly food, yearn for You alone; when will I feed on You alone? When will it be, my sweetness, when, my only good? O my loving and omnipotent Lord, free now this miserable soul from every attachment and from every corrupt passion! Adorn it with Your holy virtues, and to the pure end of doing all things purely to please you alone, because by this means I will come to open my heart to You, I invite You and will do You sweet violence so that You will enter it. Then Lord, without resistance, You will work in me those effects that You have always desired." You can practice these loving sentiments in the evening and the morning in preparation for communion.

When the time for communion then comes near, think about what it is you are about to receive—the Son of God, of incomprehensible majesty, before whom all the heavens and all powers tremble, the Holy of Holies, the spotless mirror of incomprehensible purity, in comparison to which no created thing is clean. This is He who, for your love, wished to be treated like a worm, like dregs, by the common people, rejected, trampled, deceived, spat upon and crucified by the malice and iniquity of the world.

You are, I say, about to receive God, in whose hands lie the life and death of all the universe.

And tell yourself that, in contrast, since you yourself are nothing, and that due to your sin and wickedness, you have made yourself inferior to even the most vile and unclean irrational creature, so you are worthy to be confused and deceived by all the infernal demons. And tell yourself that instead of gratitude for such immense and innumerable blessings, you have, in your capriciousness and whims, scorned such an exalted and loving Lord and trampled upon His precious blood. But still, in His perpetual charity and immutable goodness, He calls you to His divine table and even compels you to go to it by threats of death. Nor does He close to you the door of His mercy, nor does He turn His divine back to you, even if by nature you are leprous, lame, dropsical, blind, possessed, or have given yourself to many fornicators.[79]

From you he asks only these things:

First. That you sorrow over His offense.

Second. That above all things you detest sin most, the small as well as the large.

Third. That you offer and give yourself over completely to His will and obedience, continually in your heart and actually at every opportunity.

Fourth. That you always hope and have firm faith that He will forgive you, that He will cleanse you and guard you from all your enemies.

Comforted by this ineffable love of the Lord, proceed then to receive communion with a holy fear, and lovingly say, "Lord, I am not worthy to receive You, because so many times I have gravely offended You, nor have I wept for the offense done to You, as I ought."

"Lord, I am not worthy to receive You, because I am not entirely cleansed from the passions of venial sins."

"Lord, I am not worthy to receive You, because I still have not sincerely given myself over to Your love, to Your will and to Your obedience."

"O my omnipotent and infinitely good Lord, by virtue of Your goodness and Your word, make me worthy so that with this faith, my love, I may receive You."

After communicating, immediately shut yourself within the depths of your heart, and forgetting all created things speak to your Lord in these or similar words:

"O most high King of heaven, who has led You within me, who am miserable, poor, blind and naked?" And He will answer you, "Love." Then replying, you must say, "O eternal Love, O sweet Love, what do you wish from me?" "Nothing," He will say to you, "but love, nor do I want any fire than the one that burns on the altar of your love, and in your sacrifices and in all your works—that fire of My love that consuming every other love and all desires of your own gives me the sweetest aroma.

"This I have asked and shall always ask, because I desire to be completely yours and that you be completely Mine, which will never be as long as you fail to make that resignation that brings Me such delight, are attached to love of yourself, to your own opinions and to your own will and self-esteem.

"I am asking you to despise yourself in order to give you My love, asking for your heart in order that it will unite with Mine which for this purpose was pierced on the cross. And I ask all of you so that I may be all yours. You see that I am of incomparable price, and despite all My goodness, I am worth what you are worth. Buy me now, then, My soul's delight, by giving yourself to Me.

"I wish from you, my sweet daughter, that you want nothing, think nothing, intend nothing, see nothing outside of Me and My will, so that I may will, think, intend and see everything in you in such a way that your nothingness, absorbed in the abyss of My infinity, will be converted into that infinity. Thus will you be fully happy and blessed in Me, and I will be completely content in you."

Finally, you must offer to God his Son, first in order to give thanks, then for your own needs, for those of all the holy Church, for all those close to you, for those to whom you are obligated, and for the souls in purgatory. This offering you will make with recollection of and in union with the offering He made Himself when, all bloody, hanging on the cross, He offered Himself to the Father. And in this way you will be able to offer Him also all the sacrifices of the Mass that in that day are made in the holy Roman Church.

CHAPTER 56: ON SPIRITUAL COMMUNION.

Although it is impossible to receive the Lord sacramentally more than one time each day, as I have said, one can nevertheless receive Him spiritually every hour and in every moment. No created thing can take this from us, outside of our own guilt or negligence. At times this communion will perhaps be as fruitful and pleasing to God as many other sacramentals are, especially considering the defects of those who receive them.[80]

Whenever you are disposed and prepared for such a communion, you will find the Son of God ready, He who feeds you spiritually Himself, with His own hand. To prepare yourself, turn your thoughts to Him with this intention. With a brief glance at your failings, declare your sorrow for offending Him, and with all humility and faith beg that He deign to come into your poor soul with new grace to cleanse and fortify it against the enemy.

When you would do violence to yourself and mortify yourself in one of your appetites, or carry out some virtuous act, do everything toward the aim of preparing your heart for the Lord, as He continually asks you.[81] Turning again to Him, call upon Him with the hope that He might come with His grace to heal you and free you from enemies, so that He alone may possess your heart. Or, on the other hand, remembering past sacramental communion, say with a fervent heart, "When, my Lord, will I receive You another time? When, when?"

If you wish to prepare yourself and to communicate spiritually in a more proper way, however, direct all mortifications, all acts of virtue and every other good work, from the night before, to the end of receiving your Lord spiritually.[82]

Then, early in the morning, consider how goodness and happiness belong to the soul that worthily receives the Most Holy Sacrament of the altar, since in this action lost virtues are reacquired, the soul returns to its original beauty, and the fruits and merits of the passion of the Son of God are communicated to it. And considering how it pleases God that we receive Him and possess these blessings, teach yourself to kindle a great desire to receive Him in your heart in order to please Him.

To be fervent in this desire, turn to Him, saying, "Lord, since I may not receive you sacramentally today, then, O eternal Goodness and Power, forgive me for all my faults and heal me, that I may worthily receive you spiritually now, in every hour and every day. Give me new grace and strength against all enemies, and particularly against this one with which I am now waging war, in order to please you."

CHAPTER 57: ON GIVING THANKS.

Because all the good that we do and possess is of God and from God, we are debtors who ought to render Him thanks for our every good practice, every victory, and for all the blessings we have received from His merciful hand, both individually and collectively. In order to do this properly, one must consider the reason why the Lord is moved to send His graces to us. From this consideration and recognition one can learn how God wants to be thanked.

Since the Lord primarily intends His own honor and to draw us to His love and service in every blessing He gives, first reflect in this way: "With what power, wisdom and goodness has my God given this blessing and conceded this grace to me?"

And seeing how in you and from you there is nothing worthy of any blessing, and indeed nothing other than demerits and ingratitude, then, with profound humility you will say to the Lord, "And how is it, Lord, that You choose to care for such a dead dog, granting me such blessings? May Your name be blessed over century upon centuries."[83]

Finally, seeing that He wants you to love and serve Him in return for the blessings, inflame yourself with love toward that affectionate Lord with a sincere desire to serve Him in His way. And you shall add to this an overflowing offering, which you can make in the following manner.

CHAPTER 58: ON THE OFFERING.

So that your self-offering may be precious to God in all ways, you need to do two things.[84] One is to unite with the offering that Christ made to the Father; the other is to separate your will from any attachment to creatures.

For the first thing, you must know that while living in this valley of tears, the Son of God not only offered Himself and His works to the heavenly Father, but also us and our works along with Himself. So, our offerings are made in union with His and with confidence in Him.

Concerning the second thing, consider carefully if your will has any attachments before offering yourself. If it has any, you ought to separate first from every affection. Have recourse to the Son of God, therefore, with the intention that when separating yourself, with His right hand He can enable you to offer yourself to His divine Majesty, loosed and free from every other thing.

Be very careful in this regard, because if you offer yourself to God while remaining attached to other creatures, you offer not what is yours, but that which belongs to those others. And besides, you are not really yourself, but belong to those creatures to which your will is attached. This is something displeasing to the Lord—it is as if one hoped to trick Him. From this it happens that such offerings we make of ourselves to God are not only returned to us empty and without fruit, but then we also fall into a variety of defects and sins.

We can offer ourselves to God while attached to creatures, but only toward the goal that His goodness will free us, so that then we can give ourselves completely to His divine Majesty and His service. We ought to do this often and with great love.

May your offering, therefore, be without attachments and without any hint of your own will. Aim neither at earthly nor heavenly blessings, but only at the divine will and providence to which you should always submit completely. Offer yourself in a perpetual holocaust. And forgetting every created thing, say, "Here, my Lord and Creator, is the whole and entirety of my will, in the hands of your will and eternal providence. Do with me as it seems good and pleases you—in life, in death and after death, the same in time as in eternity."

If you sincerely work in this way, notwithstanding that you do not know when difficulties may befall you, instead of being a worldly trader you will become a most happy and evangelical one. You will be of God, and God will be yours, just as He is in all who remove themselves from attachments to other creatures and to themselves and give and sacrifice themselves completely to His divine Majesty.[85]

So here you see, daughter, a most powerful way to defeat all your enemies, because if you so unite your offering to God that you become all His and He all yours, what enemy and what power will ever harm you? And when you would offer Him one of your works—like fasting, prayers, acts of patience and other good things—first turn your mind to the offering Christ made to His Father through His own fasting, prayers and other efforts. With confidence in the virtue and value of these, then offer your own.

If you wish to make an offering of the works of Christ to the heavenly Father because of your own debts, you shall do it in this way.

Take a general or even particular look over your sins. Seeing clearly that it is impossible for you to satisfy either the wrath of God or His divine justice, take recourse to the life and passion of His Son, considering one of His actions, such as when He fasted, prayed, suffered and shed His blood. There you will see that in order to render you pleasing to the Father and to satisfy the debt of your iniquity, He offered Him those works, sufferings and blood, as if saying, "Here, eternal Father, that I may make satisfaction according to your will and your superabundant justice for the sins and debts of N.[86] May it please your divine Majesty to pardon her and receive her among the number of your elect."

Therefore, you may then offer this same oblation and these prayers to the Father on your own behalf, beseeching Him to remit your every debt by virtue of them. And you will be able to do this not only by passing from one to another mystery of the life of Christ, but also from one to another act within each mystery.[87] This manner of offering will be useful not only when praying for yourself, but for others as well.

CHAPTER 59: ON SENSIBLE DEVOTION AND DRYNESS IN PRAYER.

Sensible devotion is caused at times by our nature, at times by the devil and at times by grace. From its fruits you will be able to determine whence it proceeds. Thus, if there does not follow from it some improvement in your life, you have to suspect that it is from the devil or from your nature, and all the more as it is accompanied by greater enjoyment, sweetness and attachments, or by some greater esteem for yourself. Therefore, when you will feel your mind caressed by spiritual consolations, do not stop to dispute over the source from which they came, neither rest upon them nor allow yourself to withdraw from recognition of your own nothingness. Rather, train yourself with greater diligence and distrust of yourself to hold your heart free from any sort of attachment, even if spiritual, and desire only God and His gratification so that in this way the consolation, whether originally from your nature or from the devil, will become one of grace for you.

Dryness similarly can proceed from these three causes. From the devil, in order to cool devotion and to turn the mind from spiritual endeavors to the entertainments and delights of the world. From ourselves, by way of our faults, our attachments to the earth and our negligence. From grace, either to advise us to be more diligent in giving up every attachment and occupation that is not from God and does not have Him as its end, or so that we may know by experience that every one of our goods comes from Him, or so that we may value His gifts more highly and be more humble and cautious to protect them, or in order to unite us more closely with His divine Majesty, through total renunciation of ourselves, even in spiritual delights. This advice comes so that through attachment to our inclination we do not divide the heart that the Lord wishes all to Himself. It may also come because He is pleased to see us struggling with all our strength, and with the help of His grace, for our own good.

Thus, if you sense aridity, enter within yourself to see through which one of your defects sensible devotion was taken away. Then, engage it in battle. Do so, not in order to recover the feeling of grace however, but to remove from yourself what is displeasing to God. If you find no defect, may your sensible devotion be true devotion, that is, quick resignation to the will of God. Therefore, on no account whatsoever must you interrupt your spiritual exercises, but continue them with all your strength, even though they many seem fruitless and insipid to you, drinking willingly the cup of bitterness that the loving will of God places before you in this dryness.

If the dryness is sometimes accompanied by such a thick sort of mental darkness that you know not where to turn or which side to take, do not become dismayed as a result. Instead, remain alone and steadfast at the cross, far from every earthly delight, from the world and from the creatures that it offered to you. Conceal this suffering from everyone, except from your spiritual father. You must uncover it to him, not in order to relieve the pain, but for your training in the way to endure it according to God's pleasure.

One ought to use communions, prayers and other practices not in order to descend from the cross, but to receive the strength to exalt that cross to the greater glory of the Crucified. And when you are unable to meditate and pray in your usual way, due to mental confusion, meditate as best you can. And what you cannot do with your intellect, force yourself to achieve with your will and with words. Conversing with yourself and with the Lord will produce marvelous effects, and in that manner your heart will catch its breath and regain its strength.

In such a case, you will be able to say, "Why are you sad, O my soul, and why are you disquieted within me? Hope in God; for I shall again praise Him, my help and my God." "Why dost Thou stand afar off, O Lord? Why dost Thou hide Thyself in times of trouble?"[88] "Do not everywhere abandon me."[89]

And recall the holy teaching that God infused in His beloved Sarah, wife of Tobias, in the time of tribulation. It can also help you to say with a lively voice, "Each one who serves You knows for certain that if he sustains the trial, he will receive the crown; if he has been in tribulation, he will be freed; and if he is rebuked, he may always rely on Your mercy. For You do not delight in seeing us perish, because after the storm has passed You send calm, and joy after the tears and mourning. May your name, O God of Israel, be blessed forever."[90]

You must also remember that in the garden and on the cross, even in His greatest pain, your Christ felt abandoned by His heavenly Father. Enduring the cross with Him, you will say with all your heart, "Thy will be done."[91] If you act thus your patience and prayers will elevate the flames of your sacrifice into the presence of God, while you remain truly devout. For, as I have told you, true devotion consists in a lively readiness and firmness of will to follow Christ with the cross on your shoulder, along whatever way He is pleased to call you to Himself, and to choose God for God's sake, and sometimes to forfeit God for God's sake.

If many persons who pursue the spiritual life, especially women, would measure their profit by this and not by sensible devotions, they would be deceived neither by themselves nor by the devil. Neither would they grumble uselessly and ungratefully over the gifts given them by the Lord, and they would attend with greater fervor to the service of His divine Majesty. He arranges and permits everything to His glory and our own good.

Women who guard themselves from the occasions of sin with fear and prudence may be tricked in this matter. When molested at times by horrible, ugly and dreadful thoughts, and then by visions similarly most unseemly, they become confused and lose heart. They convince themselves that they have been abandoned by God and left at a great distance, unable to persuade themselves that it is possible for His divine Spirit to dwell in a mind prone to such thoughts.

And so they are very depressed, almost ready to despair, and they leave off all their good exercises and return to Egypt. They fail to understand that the Lord has given them these graces and lets them be assailed by spirits of temptation in order to lead them to self-knowledge and so that they might approach Him as often as they need help. They ungratefully grieve over what should move them to thank His infinite goodness.

What you ought to do in such instances is to immerse yourself more deeply in consideration of your perverse inclination toward every dangerous evil. God wishes you to recognize this immediately for your own good. Without it you would fling yourself into desperate ruin. From this consideration proceed to hope and confidence that He is there to help you, since He makes you see the danger and wants you to draw closer to Himself through prayer and recourse to Him. You ought to render the humblest thanks. And remember that similar spirits of temptation and evil thoughts are certainly better expelled with a patient toleration of pain and by turning your back than by over-anxious resistance.

CHAPTER 60: ON THE EXAMINATION OF CONSCIENCE.

For the examination of conscience, consider three things: the failings of that day; their cause; and the desire and readiness you possess to make war against them and to acquire their contrary virtues.

Concerning the failings, you must do as I have told you in the chapter on "when we are wounded."[92]

You should strive to beat down the causes of these and throw them to the ground.

You should fortify the will for this purpose—and in order to acquire virtues—through distrust of yourself, confidence in God, through prayers, and with the multitude of acts opposed to a particular vice and conducive to the contrary virtue.

The victories gained and good works you have done must be suspect to you. Beyond what many advise, consider them as an almost inevitable danger of at least some hidden motive of pride and vainglory. Whatever they may be, leave them all aside to the mercy of God, addressing your thoughts to the many more works that remain for you to do.

When it comes to giving thanks for the gifts and favors that the Lord has given you that day, recognize Him as the creator of every good. Thank Him because He has freed you from so many obvious enemies, not to mention the hidden ones, and that He has given you good thoughts and opportunities for the exercise of the virtues, and for all the other blessings that you did not notice.

CHAPTER 61: HOW IN THIS STRUGGLE IT IS ALWAYS NECESSARY TO FIGHT CONTINUALLY UNTIL DEATH.

Among the other things that are sought in this combat, one is perseverance. With this we always ought to check and mortify our passions, for they never cease to stir in this life. Like weeds, they always germinate. This is the battle; since it never ends unless life ends, we cannot flee. By necessity, whoever does not fight is either dominated or dead.

Beyond this, one must treat the enemies that bear continual hatred for us in such a way that they can never hope for peace or even a truce. This is because they kill more cruelly anyone who initially seeks to be their friend.

You never have to be frightened by their strength and number, however, because no one can be lost in this battle who does not choose to be. All the power of our enemies remains in the hands of the Captain for whose honor we must do battle. He will not only refuse to permit you to be overcome, but will even take up arms for you. And since He is more powerful than all your adversaries, He will put the victory within your grasp if you will fight manfully with Him and will confide in His power and goodness, not in yourself.[93]

If the Lord does not quickly concede to you the palm of victory, do not lose heart, because you have to be more confident than all those who act against you, and you must also fight confidently. Those things that seem to you far removed, even contrary to your victory, He will convert to your aid and advantage, if you will behave like a faithful and generous soldier.[94]

Following your heavenly Captain, who has defeated the world and has even accepted death Himself for you, you must apply yourself, daughter, with a generous heart to this battle and to the complete destruction of all your enemies. For even if only one of them is left alive, it would be like a straw in the eye and a lance in the side to you. It would block your path to glorious victory.

CHAPTER 62: HOW TO PREPARE ONESELF AGAINST THE ENEMIES THAT ASSAULT US AT THE MOMENT OF DEATH.

Although our entire life is a continual war on earth, the principal and most important part is in the last hour of that great passage, since whoever falls at that point never rises again. What you have to do in order to find yourself well prepared is to battle manfully in this time that is granted to you. The one who fights well in this life easily obtains victory at the moment of death through the habit of good already done.

Beyond this, give attentive and frequent consideration to death. Then, when it overtakes you, you will fear it less and your mind will be free and ready to do battle. Worldly men flee from such thoughts in order not to interrupt their pleasure in earthly things that they are voluntarily attached to with love. They would feel pain if they even thought of having to give them up. And so their disordered affections are not diminished, but on the contrary they continue, always gathering strength. Thus the separation from this life and from such precious things is a matter of inestimable worry to them, and even more so when they have enjoyed these things for a longer time.

In order to make this most important preparation more effectively, you should sometimes imagine yourself alone and in the pangs of death without any aid. Lead your mind to consider the following things that could then trouble you.[95] Here you must mentally consider the remedies I shall propose so that they may be of better service in that final anguish. It is necessary for you to learn long in advance how to strike the blow that you will have only one chance to strike, so as not to make a mistake when there is no possibility to correct it.

CHAPTER 63: CONCERNING THE FOUR ASSAULTS OF OUR ENEMIES AT THE MOMENT OF DEATH. FIRST, ON THE ASSAULT AGAINST OUR FAITH AND THE MEANS OF DEFENDING YOURSELF.

The principal and most dangerous assaults which our enemies choose to bring against us at the time of death are four. They are temptation against faith, despair, vainglory and other illusions, and the transformation of demons into angels of light.

Concerning the first assault, if the enemy begins to tempt you with his false arguments, pull back quickly from the understanding to the will, saying, "Get behind me Satan, father of lies, because I not only refuse to listen to you, but it is also enough for me to believe what the holy Roman Church believes."[96] However you are able, refuse to give any place to thoughts concerning the faith, no matter how friendly they may seem, considering them as grounds for the devil to lead you into vain disputes.

If you do not have time to draw your mind back in this way, remain strong and firm in order not to fall before any reasons or scriptural authorities that the adversary alleges, because even if they seem good, clear and evident, they are always twisted or incorrectly interpreted, or incorrectly applied.

If the crafty serpent should ask you what it is that the Roman Church believes, do not respond to him. Even if you see his deception and are willing to take up words against him, instead make an interior act of faith. On the other hand, in order to make him burst with rage respond to him that the holy Roman Church believes the truth. And if the evil one replies, "What is this truth?," insist again, "That which She believes."[97]

Above all, hold your heart intent always on the Crucified One, saying, "My God, my Creator and my Savior, assist me quickly. Do not depart from me, so that I may not separate myself from the truth of Your holy Catholic faith, and may it please You that as I was born into this faith through Your grace, so may I end this mortal life, to Your glory."

CHAPTER 64: ON THE ASSAULT OF DESPAIR AND ITS REMEDY.

The other assault with which the perverse demon strives to cast us down completely is the terror he inspires in us through the memory of our sins in order to make us fall into the pit of desperation.

In this danger, hold fast to this secure rule—thoughts concerning our sins are from grace and are for your health when they lead you to humility, to sorrow for offense against God, and to confidence in His goodness. But when they trouble you and place distrust and cowardice in you, even if they seem to you something true enough to lead you to believe that you are doomed and that there is no time to save you, recognize them as the work of the deceiver. Humble yourself more and confide more in God, so that in this way you will defeat the enemy with his own weapons and give glory to God.

Be sorry for offending God every time you remember it, but still ask Him for pardon, with confidence in His passion.

I say to you that even if it seems that God Himself told you that you are not among His sheep, you still ought not to depart on that account from true confidence in Him, but rather humbly say to Him, "You have good reason, through my sins, my Lord, to reprove me, but I had greater reason to believe in Your mercy, because You pardon me. Thus I beg You for the salvation of this, Your poor creature, condemned by her sinfulness, but redeemed at the price of Your blood. I wish, my Redeemer, to be saved to Your glory, and with faith in Your immense mercy I leave myself completely in Your hands. Do with me as You please, because You are my only Lord. Even if You were to kill me, still I would keep alive my hope in You."

CHAPTER 65: ON THE ASSAULT OF VAINGLORY.

The third assault is that of vainglory and presumption. You must never allow yourself, by any conceivable means, to be led even to a minimal satisfaction in yourself and in your works. Rather, your satisfaction must be purely in the Lord, in His mercy and in the works of His life and death.

You must always humble yourself in your own eyes, until your very last breath. Recognize God alone as the author of every good thing that you remember you have done. Take recourse in His help, but do not expect it on account of your merits or the many great battles that you have overcome. Maintain yourself always in a holy fear, sincerely confessing that all your undertakings would be in vain if your God did not shelter you under the shadow of His wings, in whose protection you will wholly confide.[98]

By following these recommendations your enemies will not be able to prevail against you. And so, you will open the way that leads happily to the heavenly Jerusalem.[99]

CHAPTER 66: ON THE ASSAULT OF ILLUSIONS AND FALSE APPEARANCES AT THE MOMENT OF DEATH.

If our obstinate enemy, who never tires of troubling us, should assail you with false appearances and transformations into an angel of light, remain firm and steady in recognition of your own nothingness. Boldly say to him, "Return, O unhappy one, into your darkness, because I am unworthy of visions and have need of nothing other than the mercy of my Jesus and the prayers of the Virgin Mary, of St. Joseph and of the other saints."

Even if it seems to you through numerous, apparently genuine signs that they come from heaven, still reject them and drive them as far from you as you can. Do not fear that this resistance, founded upon your unworthiness, displeases the Lord. If the image is from Him, He will make it clear to you and you will lose nothing, since He who gives grace to the humble does not take it away because of acts done out of humility.

These are the most common weapons that the enemy chooses to employ against us in that final passage. He comes to tempt each one according to the particular inclinations which he knows that one to be most subject. Therefore, before one comes to this hour of great conflict, we ought to arm ourselves well and battle valorously against our more violent passions, and even more so against those that dominate us, in order to facilitate the victory in that moment where every future opportunity for victory is taken away.

"Fight against them until they are consumed."
(1 Sm 15:18).

Aggiunta al combattimento spirituale

(TRANSLATED FROM LORENZO SCUPOLI, *OPERE* [MILANO, 1831]).

---

*T*he author, to the reader. Devoted reader. Having recovered among my notes some rules and suggestions whereby a man may give himself over from vice to virtue and from creatures to God, I gathered them in these few pages for me and for you, to whom I am no less a debtor. Therefore, I beg you to receive them as an *Addition to the Spiritual Combat*, exhorting you in Jesus Christ, to whom, as our chief and captain this *Addition* is dedicated, to use it, to meditate upon it attentively and frequently with the intellect, and to put it into practice with the will in the opportunities that are never lacking, from morning to evening and from evening to morning. May God be always with you, guiding all your thought, word, and action, so that you may do what pleases Him and to the end that pleases Him. Pray for me.

CHAPTER 1: ON CHRISTIAN PERFECTION.

Devout soul, in order that you may not tire yourself out in vain through spiritual exercises, as happens to many, and avoid running off without knowing where, you must understand what Christian perfection is.

Christian perfection is nothing other than a careful observance of the precepts of God and of His laws for the purpose of pleasing Him, without deviating to the right or the left, and without turning back. "And this is true for every person."[1]

And so, the aim of the entire life of the Christian who wishes to become perfect has to be a habitual study, forgetting oneself more each day, and weaning ourselves from doing our own will. We must do everything as moved by the will of God for the purpose of pleasing and honoring Him.

CHAPTER 2: HOW IT IS NECESSARY TO DO BATTLE IN ORDER TO ATTAIN CHRISTIAN PERFECTION.

With few words much is said that one can profess, so keep this in mind and undertake its execution: "This work, this is the real labor."[2] Since within us there is a law contrary to that of God, due to the sin of our first parents and our bad habits, we must battle against ourselves and also against the world and the devil, who are the impetus to battle and the opponents in our warfare.

CHAPTER 3: ON THREE THINGS NECESSARY FOR THE NEW SOLDIER OF CHRIST.

Warfare demonstrates to us, new soldier of Christ, that you need three things: a generous and resolute disposition to fight; weapons; and knowledge of how to use them.

The resolution to fight will be derived from frequent recollection that "soldiering is the life of humans on earth,"[3] and that this war has a law: whoever does not fight as one ought will certainly remain eternally dead.

You should first acquire the largeness of spirit to distrust yourself, and then you should confide fully in God, and consider it certain that He is within you so that you may free yourself from danger. Therefore, you must believe it certain that when you are assailed by enemies you will carry off the victory, if you discount your own strength and knowledge every time, taking recourse with confidence to the power, wisdom and knowledge of God, and then battle from that position.

The weapons are resistance and violence.

CHAPTER 4: ON RESISTANCE AND VIOLENCE AND ON THE ART OF WIELDING THEM.

Although they are serious and painful weapons, resistance and violence are always necessary and are conveyors of victory. One can wield these arms in the following manner.

When you are so beset by your corrupt will and wicked intentions that you do not choose or carry out the things God desires, you must resist, saying, "Yes, yes, may I desire to do it."

You should oppose your enemies with the same resistance when you are called and drawn to choices through bad habits and your corrupt will, saying, "No, no. I wish to do the will of God, always with His help. Oh! My God, help me quickly, so that this desire that I now have, through your grace, always to follow your will, may not later be choked by my old, corrupt will."

When feeling great pain and weakness in the will during such resistance, you must do every sort of violence to yourself, reminding yourself that the throne of heaven suffers violence, and that mortifications of self and of one's passions can capture that throne. And if the pain and violence become so serious that you feel affliction in your heart, proceed mentally to Christ in the garden of Gethsemane. Combining your anguish with His, beg Him that in virtue of His anguish He may give you the victory over your own. Thus, you can say to the heavenly Father from your heart, "Not my will, but thine be done," or "Thy will be done."[4]

In this way you will more and more frequently bend your will to that of God, wishing just what He desires you to wish.[5] Practice making every single act with such fullness and purity of desire as if all perfection and every pleasure and honor to God consisted in that one act alone. And so you can then do the second act, the third, the fourth, and others.

Moreover, recalling the times you have transgressed some commandment, be sorry for the transgression, and seize greater strength of heart to obey God in the precept that you have at hand, and in every other one, in the opportunities that are present. Because you should never abandon any occasion to obey God, no matter how small, remind yourself here that if you will be obedient to Him in small things, God will give you new grace in order to obey Him later in larger matters, and with ease.

Also, accustom yourself first to adore God when bringing to mind one of the divine commands, and then beg Him to assist you when you are tempted, so that you may obey Him.

CHAPTER 5: ON HOW WE MUST BE CONTINUALLY VIGILANT OVER
OUR WILL IN ORDER TO SEE WHICH OF THE PASSIONS MOVES IT.

Remain recollected within yourself as much as possible in order to
recognize which of your passions more often moves your will and by
which you are more likely to be tricked and rendered subservient. It is
impossible for the human will to remain alone, unaccompanied by one or
another of our passions. Thus, the will must either love or despise the
desires, either flee or be happy with them, either be saddened or raised to
hope in them, either fear or surrender to them, either be daring or angry
before them.

When finding the will impassioned not toward the will of God but
toward self-love, exert yourself so that you may turn from love of self to
love of God and to the observance of His commandments and laws. This
you ought to do not only in the moments of passion that move you toward
mortal sins, but also in those that lead you to fall into venial sins. Although
these may move one gently and by small steps, they always keep us weak
and without virtue. We remain in great danger of falling into mortal sin
whenever the venial ones are voluntary.

CHAPTER 6: HOW BY TAKING THE FIRST PASSION (THAT IS, LOVE
OF CREATURES AND OF SELF) AND GIVING IT TO GOD ALL THE
REST REMAIN WELL-ORDERED AND CONTROLLED.

So that you may free your will from disordered passions summarily
and in an orderly fashion, you must devote yourself to defeat and transform the first passion, that is, love of self. Once this is transformed, all the
others follow it with the same steps, since they are born from it and have
their root and life in it. One can see this clearly, since man proportionately
desires that which he loves and takes delight in. Similarly, one despises or
flees what saddens us, and hinders and offends the things considered dear.
Neither does one hope for anything other than valued things. And we
despair of these same things when the difficulties of pursuing them appear
insurmountable and invincible to us. No one fears, or becomes fearless or
irritated, save through what impedes or offends the beloved.

The way to defeat and transform the first passion is to consider the
qualities within the object that the soul loves and is attached to and what it
claims through the attachment and love. When you discover the qualities of

beauty and goodness and the claims of delight and usefulness, you will say to yourself repeatedly, "And how much greater is the beauty and goodness of God, Who is the single source of every good and perfection? And what is there imaginable that is of greater usefulness and pleasure than to love God, since by loving Him we transform ourselves into Him, taking delight and joy in Him alone?" Moreover, the very heart of man is of God, because the same God has created and redeemed him and beseeches him every day through new blessings, "Son, offer your heart to Me."

So, all human hearts that reach to God through such motives, and that profess themselves to be lower and quite unable to satisfy the obligations that they have before God, render every other competing motivation completely jealous. For such hearts love nothing other than God alone and the things that are pleasing to God, and they do so with the moderation and in the manner that pleases God.

One must also have the same jealousy in relation to the passion of hatred, since these two are the foundation for perfect construction of the Christian life. Then one hates nothing other than sin and what leads to sin.

CHAPTER 7: ON WHAT IS NEEDED TO REINFORCE THE HUMAN WILL.

Our uncontrollable will is too weak to resist and overcome its passions and to direct them to God and to His obedience, as experience clearly shows. For although it may desire and even intend self-mortification, whenever a new occasion arises it is choked by its passions and all its proposals and intentions, the prey of these passions, vanish. Thus it is not only necessary to reinforce and aid the will on occasion, but also to do it quickly. Taking strength against oneself in the process, one can defeat the passions and free oneself from slavery to them, giving oneself completely to God and to His pleasure.

CHAPTER 8: HOW THE HUMAN WILL CAN OVERCOME THE WORLD AND BE GREATLY STRENGTHENED.

Our passions become active and take strength from the world and the things of this world. So, while the world shows them some of its grandeur, richness and delights, surely it follows that by rejecting the world and all earthly things, the human will may catch its breath and turn itself elsewhere, since it is unable to exist without love and delight.

The way to reject the world is to consider profoundly what worldly things and their promises really are. So as not to err or even to be blinded by one of our passions in this effort, we will take what wise Solomon said as our beginning and conclusion. He had direct experience of them all. "Vanity," he said, "vanity of vanities, all is vanity and striving after wind."[6] This truth is demonstrated every day. For a person's heart, seeking to satisfy itself even amid all it has ever desired, is never sated but rather all the more hungry. This is for no other reason than because he who feeds himself on the goods of this world comes to feed himself with shadows, dreams, vanity and lies—things that give no nourishment at all.

The promises of the world are all false and full of deceptions. The world promises one thing and delivers another. It promises happiness and gives anxiety. It promises and fails to deliver more and more often, or else it actually gives but then quickly takes away. And if it does not take them away quickly, it later afflicts impassioned ones more seriously. They then have their desires trampled in the mud. To these one can say, "Sons of men, why are you always of heavy heart, why do you choose vanity and seek after lies?"[7]

In a certain way the world gives in to those for whom the apparent goods of this world are true goods. But what do they say of the rapidity with which human life passes away? Where are the delights, the grandeur, and the pride of princes, kings and emperors? They too have passed.

Since you must overcome the world to such an extent that it becomes abhorrent to you and you to it, or perhaps we should say that it becomes crucified to you and you to it, the way to do so is to consider deeply its vanity and lies before the will attaches itself to them.[8] Thus, since neither the will nor the intellect is then impassioned, you may despise it with ease and you will be able to say to every creature presented before you, "Are you a creature? Then remove, remove your attachment, since I wish to find the Creator in all creatures, the spiritual not the corporeal. I wish to desire and love Him who gave you action and powers, not you yourself."

CHAPTER 9: ON THE SECOND AID TO THE WILL.

The second help to the human will consists in driving away the prince of darkness, the author of every disordered flame of our passions. This enemy can be banished and beaten every time we defeat and overcome ourselves in our concupiscence and disordered desires. Therefore, if you want the demon to flee from you, resist all your passions, for this is the resistance that St. James wishes one to make.[9]

Here be advised that the demon so assaults us at times, inflaming the concupiscence and passions of the flesh, that it seems we may be constrained to give in to them. But do not be dismayed. Resist instead and consider it certain that God is with you so that the demon may not overwhelm you. Resist, I say, for certainly you will win by persevering.

I said "persevering," because it is not enough to resist one, two or three times, but every time that he shall tempt you. This is because the habit of the devil is to test tomorrow those whom he was unable to defeat today, and next week those he has not won over this week. And thus he proceeds continually, with great patience, time after time, now with rage, now with cleverness, until at last he succeeds.

It is necessary then, to be steady, with weapons always at hand, never trusting in oneself even if the victories are many, since the life of man is a continual battle whose victory does not take place today or tomorrow, but in the end.

If you experience pain during this struggle, know that the demon feels even more pain when one resists him. Thus, to your own consolation, you can say to him, "Off to suffering you go, infernal demon! But since you suffer wickedly and I suffer by refusing to offend God, your pain will be eternal, and mine, through the grace of God, will be changed into eternal peace."

CHAPTER 10: CONCERNING TEMPTATIONS TO SPIRITUAL PRIDE.

In the preceding chapter I spoke to you of the temptations which the devil is accustomed to give us through the attractions, riches and delights of the world, but now I shall speak of temptations to spiritual pride, complacency and vainglory. These are more dangerous and terrifying to us and more hateful to God the less they are understood.

Oh, how many generous soldiers and great servants of God, after many years and many victories, have been thrown to the ground by this pride and transformed into servants of Lucifer!

The means of escape from this terrible blow and hidden trap is constantly to fear pride and to undertake our good works with fear and trembling, so that they are not done because of some hidden worm of self-love and pride that is rotten and hateful to God. And so, humbling oneself in those works, one ought to seek always to carry them out more perfectly, as if one had accomplished nothing good beforehand. And when it appears to us that we have accomplished something, then, in order to avoid self-confidence, we ought to say with all our heart, "We are useless servants."[10]

Above all, make frequent recourse to Christ. While freeing us from every form of pride, He teaches us and helps us to be humble of heart. Similarly, make recourse often to the most humble Mother of God, asking her to beseech for you the gift of true humility which is the foundation of the virtues so that it may increase and accompany them in order that they be not lost, but rather be multiplied and reinforced.

I will say nothing else on this matter of humility, having treated it at length in the *Spiritual Combat*.

CHAPTER 11: ON THE THIRD AID TO THE HUMAN WILL.

We most often have to assist our will with the third aid, which is prayer. So accustom yourself, when under attack, to turn immediately to God, saying, "God, bend to help me, Lord hasten to aid me."[11]

Your combat then, will be with prayer and resistance in the presence of God, while always clothed with distrust of self and confidence in Him. If you will fight with this means and apparatus, consider the victory secure.

What can prayer fail to overcome and defeat? What is it that resistance, accompanied with distrust of self and confidence in God, cannot repel? And by what battle can one who remains in the presence of God, with the desire to please Him, be defeated?

CHAPTER 12: ON THE MANNER IN WHICH A PERSON HAS TO TRAIN HIMSELF IN ORDER TO REMAIN IN THE PRESENCE OF GOD WHENEVER HE WISHES.

In order that you might be able to remain in the presence of God whenever you wish, try to recall frequently the thought that before you existed God saw you secretly and considered each of your thoughts and deeds.

Or even recall that all creatures are like so many gates through which the hidden God watches you, and at times says to you, "Ask and you will receive. Everyone who asks receives, and to him who knocks it will be opened."[12]

You will also be able to place yourself in the presence of God when you meditate on creatures by departing from what is corporeal and returning in thought to the God Who gives them existence, motion and the power to act. Then, when you wish to pray while you are fighting or doing something else, represent yourself to God in one of the aforesaid ways, and pray, asking for help and assistance from Him.

And you know now, devout soul, that if you make yourself familiar with the presence of God, you will bring back victories and infinite treasures. Among other things, you will guard yourself from impulses, thoughts, words and actions that do not lead to the presence of God and to the life of His Son. And the same presence of God will infuse you with virtue so that you may remain in His presence.

If one can draw upon the qualities and powers of created things near to us, things that possess limited and finite power, how much more must one say about the power of the presence of God, Who is infinite and indescribable virtue?

In addition to the aforesaid prayer—"God, bend to help me, Lord hasten to aid me"[13]—that applies to every need, you can also pray in another, more particular way. For example, if you desire to know the will of God and to do it, your prayer can be one of the following, "Blessed are you, Lord; teach me to to follow your statutes." "Lead me, Lord, in the narrow path of your commands." "If only you would make straight my path to observe your statutes."[14]

In order to ask as much from God as one can, and to ask what it will please Him for you to ask, use the Lord's Prayer. You ought to say it with all your heart's affection and with complete attention.

CHAPTER 13: SOME RECOMMENDATIONS CONCERNING PRAYER.

First, you must notice that prayers (I am not speaking of meditations, on which I will speak later) ought to be brief in the manner mentioned, frequent and full of desire and firm faith so that God may come to aid you, if not at the time and in the way you desire, then with still greater help at a more opportune moment.

Second, they should always be accompanied, either actually or implicitly, by one of the following little thoughts: "Out of Your goodness." "According to Your promises." "To Your glory." "In the name of Your beloved Son." "By virtue of His passion." "In the name of the Virgin Mary, Your daughter, spouse and mother."

Third, at times they should be joined with rapid, prayerful utterances like, "Grant me Your love, Lord, in the name of Your beloved Son." "And when will it be, Lord, that I shall have it? When?" One can also do so after every request, or perhaps after all of them, in the Lord's Prayer. For example, "Our Father who art in Heaven, hallowed be Thy name. But when will it be, our heavenly Father, that Your name is known, honored and glorified throughout all the world? When, my God, when?," and so on after every request.

Fourth, when requesting virtues and graces, it will be good to consider even more often the value of the virtue and the need that you have of it, the greatness of God and His goodness, and the merits of the one who asks. It is in this way that one will ask with greater affection and desire, with greater reverence and confidence, and with greater humility. And one must also consider the final end of the request. May it be for the pleasure of God and to His honor.

CHAPTER 14: ON ANOTHER METHOD OF PRAYER.

If one also wishes to pray perfectly, remain silently in the presence of God, emitting sighs to Him from time to time. Turn to Him an eye and a heart desirous of pleasing Him, and a firm, burning desire that He aid you, so that you love, honor and serve Him with purity. Or, turn with a desire that He concede to you the grace requested in the preceding prayers.

CHAPTER 15: CONCERNING THE FOURTH AID TO THE HUMAN WILL.

The fourth assistance to our will is divine love. It aids and strengthens the will in such a way that nothing is impossible, and it cannot be defeated by passions or temptations.

The means to attain it are prayers, that is, by requesting it often from God; or meditation, by considering those points that are attainable with the grace of God; or action, by kindling it in the base of the human heart. The points to consider are: Who is God? What is the power and wisdom and goodness and beauty of God, and how many examples are there? What has God done for humanity, and what would He do in addition if it were necessary? With what intentions did He act? What things does He do every day for man? And what may He do for us in the next life if one should live here in obedience to His commands, and with purity of mind, strictly to please Him?

CHAPTER 16: CONCERNING MEDITATION ON THE BEING OF GOD.

When considering what God is in Himself, one should recognize that He has responded and spelled it out, saying, "I am who am."[15] This predicate of God is such that it cannot be attributed to any creature—not to princes, kings or emperors, neither to angels nor to the world itself—because everything has being dependent upon God and possesses from itself absolutely nothing.

From this it is apparent how vain is the man who loves and is attached to creatures, rather than loving the Creator through them and creatures themselves only insofar as the Lord wishes. He is vain, I say, because he loves vanity. He is vain because he thinks he can satisfy himself with those things that in themselves are nothing. He is vain because he tires himself in pursuit of the things that only take away and kill. If you wish to love as you ought to love, then love God, Who alone fills and satisfies the heart.

CHAPTER 17: CONCERNING MEDITATION ON THE POWER OF GOD.

You know that not just this or that worldly power, but even all of them together, when they want to build not a kingdom, not a city, but just one palace, need a variety of materials, skilled workers, and a great period of time. Not even then, with all of this, is the edifice completed according to their desire. But God, with His power, created the whole universe out of nothing in an instant, and He can create with the same ability an infinite number of others, then destroy them and reduce them to nothing. The more profoundly one meditates and will meditate upon this point alone, the more new surprises and motivations to love such a powerful Lord shall be uncovered.

CHAPTER 18: CONCERNING MEDITATION ON THE WISDOM OF GOD.

The wisdom of God is so high and inscrutable that no one can comprehend it. Still, since you have some knowledge of it, turn your eye to the ornaments of the sky, to the beauty of the earth and of the whole universe in order to discover nothing else than incomprehensible knowledge of the divine Architect. Turn your mind to the life of humans and to the various incidents that occur—there is nothing disordered that in the sight of God is not done with inscrutable wisdom. Meditate on the mysteries of the redemption in order to find them all filled with the highest wisdom. "Oh, the depth of the riches and wisdom and knowledge of God! How unsearchable are His judgments!"[16]

CHAPTER 19: CONCERNING MEDITATION ON THE GOODNESS OF GOD.

The goodness of God is incomprehensible in itself, like all His other infinite perfections, but it is so spread through everything outside it that there is nothing in the world in which it cannot be found. Creation is from the goodness of God. The preservation and ordering of the world is from the goodness of God. The ineffable and infinite redemption held out to us is from the goodness of God. He gave us here, for our ransom, His own Son, and likewise our daily food in the sacrament of the altar.

CHAPTER 20: CONCERNING MEDITATION ON THE BEAUTY OF GOD.

On the beauty of God it is sufficient to say this to all: when contemplating Himself from eternity, without ever turning elsewhere, God remains incomprehensibly sated and blessed, despite His infinite capacity.

O man, you now understand the dignity to which you are called by the goodness of God. Be no longer of heavy heart, despising this dignity, and no longer give your love to vanities, lies and the shadows. God calls you to love of His power, wisdom and goodness; to delight in His beauty and to entry into His joy. Why do you make yourself deaf? Think, think over your actions, so that the time in which repentance will be useless may not come too soon.

CHAPTER 21: WHAT GOD HAS DONE FOR HUMANITY AND WITH WHAT INTENTION. ON WHAT HE WOULD YET DO IF IT WERE NECESSARY.

One can see what God has done to and for humanity by meditating on creation and redemption.

The spirit with which He has done it and performed His salvation has overcome infinity. Infinite was the price of ransom, but His heart was greater, because He wished to suffer more—even to endure death over and over again—if it were necessary.

Even if you had to give yourself up to ransom an infinite number of times, how much more are you the debtor to the heart of God, Who goes beyond and surpasses this human ransom?

CHAPTER 22: ON WHAT GOD DOES FOR HUMANITY EVERY DAY.

There is no day, no moment, in which the human person fails to receive new blessings from God, because every day and every moment God creates him, holding him in being. God serves him in every moment through creatures, the heavens, the air, the earth, the sea, and through all that is in them.

Every day He gives man His grace, calling him away from evil to good, guarding him in order that he might not sin, and when sinning, aiding him so that he may not sin again. He waits for him, calling him to penitence. Coming after him, God pardons him more quickly than the sinner is quick to desire the pardon. Every day He sends us His Son, with all the riches of the mystery of the cross, and He keeps Him present in the sacrament of the altar.

CHAPTER 23: HOW GOD SHOWS GOODNESS BY WAITING FOR AND TOLERATING THE SINNER.

So that you may understand how God displays goodness by supporting the sinner, consider first that just as God indescribably loves virtue, so does He infinitely hate vice when He encounters it.

What a goodness, then, does God show in supporting the sinner? Before the eyes of God's purity and majesty, he commits wickedness not one, two or three times, but again and again. "It amazes me, my Lord," the sinner can say, "that when I sinned you said to me in the depth of my heart, 'We shall see which of the two of us will outdo the other—you by offending me, or I by pardoning you.' "

Careful consideration of this point, I believe, will fire the heart of the sinner with the grace of God so that it can be quickly converted to God. And if one does not do so, one must justly fear the high and inscrutable judgments of God. Heavy blows of retribution without any remedy should be issued very quickly.

CHAPTER 24: ON WHAT GOD DOES IN THE NEXT LIFE, NOT JUST FOR THOSE WHO CONSISTENTLY SERVE HIM BUT EVEN FOR CONVERTED SINNERS.

The favors and delights that are received from God in the heavenly kingdom are such that they cannot be imagined on earth, and neither can they be clearly and fully desired. Who will ever come to understand how someone shall be seated at the table of God, Who serves him and feeds him from His happiness? Who can imagine the entry of blessed souls into the joy of their Lord? And who can ever understand the love and esteem that God shows to the citizens of His kingdom, of whom St. Thomas speaks in Treatise 63: "Almighty God so subjects Himself to every angel and holy soul that He is like a servant bought for each individual: can He truly be the God of each one?"[17]

O Lord, O Lord, whoever frequently and deeply considers Your works on behalf of creatures finds You so inebriated with love that it seems Your happiness consists entirely in loving them, in doing good for them and in nourishing them with Yourself. O Lord, give us this consideration in such a way that then we shall love You, and by loving You, become You through loving union.

O human heart, where are you running? Close to the shadow? Into the wind? Into the abyss? Aside from that, Who is everything? The greatest power? The height of wisdom? The ineffable goodness? The eternal beauty? The highest good? The infinite sea of every perfection? He hurries close to you, calling you with such strong cries and bringing new blessings, not just the old ones. Do you know whence your defects are born? It is because you do not pray, because you do not contemplate. Remaining thus, without light and without heat, it is not surprising that you fail to move yourself from works of darkness. Enter, enter now, O soul, O tepid religious, into the school of prayer and meditation so that here you will learn to demonstrate that the true study of the Christian and the religious is to study denial of self-will in order to do the will of God, to despise yourself and to love God. Without this all other studies can be nothing other than fuel for presumption and pride—as are all the sciences in themselves. The more they enlighten the intellect, the more they blind the will of those who acquire them to the ruin of their souls.

CHAPTER 25: CONCERNING THE FIFTH AID TO THE HUMAN WILL.

Hatred of ourselves is a necessary aid to our will, because without this the aid of divine love, author of every good, will never come.

The way to attain it is first to request it from God and then to see the damages that self-love has done and always does to humans. There is no loss, neither in heaven nor on earth, that was not born from self-love. This love of ourselves is of such malignity that if its entry to heaven were possible, the heavenly Jerusalem would immediately become a Babylon. Or consider what this plague does within a human heart in this present life.

If you remove self-love from the world, hell itself will be shut immediately. And who will be so filled with it, against themselves, that when meditating on the being, the quality and the effects of self-love, they are not angered by it and do not hate it?

CHAPTER 26: HOW ONE MAY RECOGNIZE SELF-LOVE.

In order to understand how the kingdom of self-love is enlarged and extended in you, you must resort often to examination of the passions in your soul. Identify which one most frequently occupies your will so that you might never again meet it alone.

When you find that your will loves or desires, or that it is happy or sad, consider carefully if the thing loved or desired is virtuous and follows God's commands. Consider whether it brings happiness or sadness in equal proportion to those things by which God wants us to rejoice or be saddened. On the other hand, consider if it brings happiness or sadness as much as do all those things that are born of the world and from attachments to creatures. If so, then it depends upon dealing with creatures, not upon anything like necessity or the pursuit of need, or the will of God.

And if this is so, it is clear that self-love rules in your will and motivates everything.

If the dealings and concerns of the will are centered around virtue and the things that God desires, it is necessary to consider whether the desire for these matters was caused by the will of God or by some internal complacency or caprice. It often happens that someone is moved by an unknown whim and satisfaction and gives himself to various good works, such as prayers, fasting, communion and other holy practices.

The test for this comes in two forms. The first is if your will is drawn on occasion to all good works without distinction. The other is if, when reproving what impedes them, the will complains and is disquieted and disturbed, or, on the other hand, when it has gained its desire, it is pleased and delighted with itself.

To determine if the will was moved by God, one must also consider where and to what end one's works are more often addressed. For if the end is the pure pleasure of God, the business will go well, but not in such a way that the individual can be sure of the outcome. This is how subtle and hidden is love of ourselves in good works and acts of virtue.

When this totally savage beast of self-love appears manifest, devote yourself to persecuting it with all your hate, to the death. Do so even in the small matters, not just the large ones.

Always devote yourself to suspicion of hidden things. Therefore, humble yourself after every good work and place your hand over your breast, begging God that He pardon you and guard you from love of yourself.

It will be good to turn to the Lord early in the morning and profess that your desire is to never offend Him, particularly on that day. Rather, you always desire to do His divine will in every instance in order to please Him. You will often beg God to help you to hold your head up so that He may recognize you, and to do what is pleasing to Him in the manner that is pleasing to Him.

CHAPTER 27: CONCERNING THE SIXTH AID.

Attendance at Mass is the sixth aid to the human will, along with communion and confession. Since the grace of God is the principal and necessary assistance to our will, because it guards one from evil and leads toward the good, it follows that all those things through which one gains an increase of grace are an aid to the will.

Since you acquire an increase in grace by listening to Mass, you shall hear it in the following way.

The Mass is divided into three parts. In the first one that begins with the Introit and ends with the Offertory, you will try to kindle in yourself a great desire that just as the Son of God comes from heaven and is born in the world and kindled in our world the fire of His love, so He may deign to come and be born with His power in the depths of your heart. May your heart then burn, thinking of nothing other than pleasing Him in everything, forever.[18]

When the orations are said by the priest, your needy soul can also ask for the same graces, provided it has the requisite desire. And as the Epistle and the Gospel are read, mentally ask for understanding and power from God in order to understand their sense and notice everything.

In the second part, which begins with the Offertory and ends with communion, remove yourself completely from any attachment and thought concerning other creatures or yourself and offer yourself totally to God and to His will.

When the consecrated Host and Chalice are raised, adore the true Body and Blood of Christ in all His divinity. Contemplating it hidden under those accidents of bread and wine, give Him loving thanks that He deigns every day to come to us with the precious fruits of the tree of His cross and with the identical offering. To the same end that He made Himself an offering to the heavenly Father when transfixed on the cross, you should offer Him again to the same Father. When the priest communicates sacramentally, you should communicate spiritually, opening your heart to Him while closing it to all creatures, so that the Lord may kindle there the fire of His love.

In the third and last part, together with the priest, though he with the tongue and you with the mind, you should request exactly what he asks for in the prayers after communion.

CHAPTER 28: CONCERNING SACRAMENTAL COMMUNION.

Because you receive a great increase of grace in taking communion, the best dispositions are necessary. But we cannot gain them by ourselves. So say the following prayer with great affection: "We beseech you, Lord, to purify our consciences by visiting us, so that at the coming of your son Jesus Christ, our Lord, with all the saints, He may find us prepared for His dwelling in us. Who with you . . . , etc."

In order that we not fail on our part to do something in cooperation with the divine aid, your preparation should first consider the end for which Christ instituted the sacrament of the altar. Discovering once again that he showed us the mystery of the cross so that we should be mindful of His love, we should consider why He desires this memory. Since He desires the memory so that we might love and obey Him, our best preparation will be a fitting desire and wish to love Him and obey Him, plus grief because we have not loved Him in the past, but rather offended Him. We must prepare ourselves until the time to receive communion with this proper desire and longing.

Keep faith in that through which you communicate, for under the accidents of consecrated bread is the true Lamb of God, Who takes away sins. Adore Him profoundly. Beg Him to take every hidden sin from your heart, along with all other sins, and receive Him with the hope provided by His love.

Receive His love in order to possess it and to introduce it into your heart, asking Him again and again for His love and for every other need in order to please Him. Afterward, offer it to the heavenly Father as a sacrifice of praise for the immense charity that He has shown us in this blessing and in every other involved in the redemption, and because He gives you His love. Offer it also for the needs of the living and the dead.

CHAPTER 29: ON SACRAMENTAL CONFESSION.

To be done properly, confession requires a number of things.

First, a good examination of conscience concerning the precepts of God and the state of your soul. When you recall your sins, even if minor, mourn them bitterly, considering your offense to the majesty of God and the customary human ingratitude toward His goodness and charity. Reviling yourself, you should speak these words against yourself: "Do you return, foolish and simple one, to your Lord? Is not He your Father Himself Who possessed you and formed you and created you?"

Frequently, a proper will, one that has not offended God, says in reply, "Oh, if only I had not offended my Creator, my heavenly Father, my Redeemer, and that I had suffered every other evil!"

Then turn to God with embarrassment and with faith because He has pardoned you, saying to Him with all your heart, "Father, I have sinned against heaven and before You; I am no longer worthy to be called your son; treat me as one of your hired servants."[19] Recalling once again the pain of offending God and with a resolution to choose to withstand any pain rather than offending Him voluntarily, tell your sins to your confessor with shame and sorrow, exactly as you have done them, without excusing yourself or accusing others.

After confession, give thanks to God, because despite all the ways in which He is offended time and time again, there is still nothing that He is not ready to pardon more quickly than the sinner is ready to receive forgiveness. From that fact take the occasion for even greater sorrow at offending such a loving Father, and resolve with greater determination never to offend Him again, with His help, along with that of the Virgin Mary, your guardian angel, and the other saints and protectors to whom you are especially devoted.

CHAPTER 30: HOW ONE HAS TO DEFEAT IMPURE PASSIONS.

All the other passions are defeated by facing and battling against them, even if they are wounded, and by recalling them again and again to combat until they are overcome in all desires, both great and small. Impure passion, however, not only should not be directly engaged, but should also be placed at a distance from all those things that can engage it.

Temptations of the flesh are defeated and impure passions mortified, then, by fleeing and not battling face to face. Whoever is quicker to flee, and to a greater distance, more securely conquers them.

Good habits, sincere desires, past tests and victories, relatives, objects of small and crude appearance that do not threaten danger—and whatever other things seem to promise security—are no good reason not to flee. Flee, flee, beloved soul, if you do not wish to be seized.

Even if there may be persons who deal with very dangerous individuals all their life and do not fall, this is no concern of yours, but of God alone. Besides, where falls sometimes do not occur, one may already be very close to the ground. You must flee and obey the advice and example God has given you in Scripture, in the lives of the great saints and throughout every day by various events. Flee, flee without turning back to look or to think about what object you are fleeing, because there is danger even in this. Do not turn back.

Since practice is necessary, it should be curt and short and your behavior has to be rough rather than polite, because here also lies the snare, the flame and the fire. Here it is well to take that old advice, "An ounce of prevention is worth a pound of cure."[20] Do not wait to become sick, but flee early, because that is the healthy medicine.

And when weakness comes upon you through misfortune, all your health depends on this: that in the same instant that you feel it, "you seize and dash your indiscretion to the rock,"[21] running to the confessor, without hiding from him even the smallest sin pertaining to this passion, because the hidden thing can germinate and grow larger.

CHAPTER 31: HOW ONE MUST FLEE ALL THINGS IN ORDER NOT TO FALL INTO IMPURE VICE.

The flight has to be from many things so that the wings not give themselves over to the passion of impure love. The first and main flight is from persons who threaten evident danger. The second is flight from other persons also, insofar as possible. The third is flight from visits, message carrying, gift giving, and friendships, even if distant ones, since distant relations can sometimes bind one more easily than those that are not. The fourth flight is from discussion of such passions and from immoral music, songs and books.

The fifth flight, known and advised by few, and even less practiced, is complete flight from enjoyment of created things, like clothing, the various things that one keeps in a room just for enjoyment, as well as foods and other things. These delights, although frequently permitted, always accustom the human heart to pleasure and make it greedy for pleasure. And so, when offering itself impure pleasures—those that by nature are ready to wound and to penetrate even to the very marrow of your bones—a heart finds the road to mortification of pleasures only with difficulty, never having practiced it before. Therefore, at the moment of encountering licit pleasures, hearts must accustom themselves to flee, so that when they are offered illicit and impure ones, they may flee quicker and with great ease at the very mention of their name.

CHAPTER 32: ON WHAT ONE MUST DO WHEN ONE HAS FALLEN INTO THE VICE OF IMPURITY.

If it should happen through misfortune or trickery that you fall into sins of the flesh, in order not to add sin upon sin, the remedy is to run quickly to confession, with all speed, and without any other examination of conscience. There, leaving behind all human prudence, speak with openness and manifest all your illness, taking whatever medicine and advice the confessor chooses to give you, even if bitter and difficult.

Do not delay, for there are hundreds and thousands of excuses for delay, and because if you delay you will fall again. From such repeated failing there are born other delays, affected ones. With new delays proceeding from the failings, you will pass years before you confess and rise from the sin.

In conclusion, to avoid this impure vice, I advise you again that if you do not wish to fall, you must flee. In regard to impure thoughts that come to you, small though they be, consider them no less important than the great ones, and flee them too. Even if your lucidity sees they are slight after you have quickly fled them, confess them nonetheless and uncover your enemy to the confessor. And when you have fallen, run to confession, never allowing yourself to be defeated by shame.

CHAPTER 33: ON SOME REASONS WHY THE SINNER OUGHT TO BE
CONVERTED QUICKLY TO GOD.

The first reason why the sinner ought to return to God is the consideration of God Himself. Being all good, the greatest power, wisdom and goodness, He gives man no reason to have boldly offended Him. Not on account of prudence, since it is a bad choice to assume it in comparison with omnipotence and with the supreme Judge Who judges it. Not on account of dignity and justice, either, since the sinner is not something God should tolerate, but rather nothing at all. This creature, formed out of mud, offends his Creator. The servant offends the Lord, the receiver offends his Benefactor, the son offends his Father.

The second reason why one must quickly return to the house of his Father is the great obligation of the sinner, since the conversion of the son and his return to the house brings honor to the Father and rejoicing to all His house, the neighborhood, and even to the angels in heaven.[22] Whereas before, by sinning, the son offended the Father and scorned him, so when one returns with bitter tears for the offense and with determination to obey all His precepts in everything in the future, one honors Him, thanks Him and wounds Him in such a way that His heart is moved to mercy. Then it is not enough for Him to wait for the sinner with longing. Instead

230

He runs to meet him, He embraces him, kisses him, and clothes him in His grace, and His other blessings.

The third reason is self-interest. For every sinner must consider that if he is not converted in time, that winter and sabbath day of judgment will surely come through which he shall fall into the pains of hell. This ought to terrify him, since there the pains and the passions that are holding him in sin will be infinitely increased, without hope that even at a single time he would have some of the water that might soothe him, not even as much as one can carry on the tip of a finger.[23]

The intention to be converted at the very last moment of life, or even some few years or months before, is not a good hope, because this resolution is crazy and full of godless trickery. The intention to overcome a great difficulty at the moment that a person finds himself most exhausted is the product of a small mind.

The sinner who persists in sin becomes more sluggish to convert every day, as the habit of sin is increased and transforms his nature. He gains more and more indisposition to receive the grace of conversion. This also happens because by scorning God with impious malice in taking as much as possible from created things, and then at the last breath, if not later, giving the self to God in a selfish way, the sinner effectively removes from God any desire to help him.

This advice and intention is also insane because God concedes the sinner the power of conversion and the necessary efficacious grace. Who has given, or will give a sinner the assurance that he will not die suddenly or without warning, as has happened to so many and continues to happen?

Cry out, cry out, sinner—right now as you read—saying to your Lord, "Convert me, and may I be converted, because You are my Lord God."[24] Never cease such prayers until you are converted to your Lord and Father, copiously mourning offenses against Him with a resolution to do what pleases Him for His satisfaction.

CHAPTER 34: ON HOW TO OBTAIN GRIEF FOR OFFENDING GOD AND CONVERSION.

There is no better way to procure mourning over offenses against God than meditation on the greatness of the charity and goodness that God has shown to man. Sinning offends the highest good and ineffable goodness, that is God, Who knows nothing if not how to do good and has done and always does good, pouring out His graces and giving His light to friends and enemies. Anyone who considers having offended Him for nothing, on a whim, for a moment of false delight, cannot but mourn abundantly.[25]

You should then place yourself before a crucifix, imagining that He says to you, "Look at me, and consider My wounds one by one. It was due to your sins I was wounded and so mistreated, as you see. Yet I am still your God, your Creator, your gentle Lord and merciful Father. Therefore, come back to me with pure mourning, with a proper desire that I might not be offended, and with a firm determination to endure whatever pain necessary in order never to offend Me again. Come back to Me, because I redeemed you."

Then, taking this bloodied Christ into your imagination, with the crown of thorns on His head and with the reed in His hand, imagine that someone says to you, "Here is the man."[26] Here is the man Who, loving you with inestimable affection, has redeemed you through this mockery, these wounds and this blood. "Here is the man." This man was injured by you, after showing you such love, after such blessings. "Here is the man." This man is the very mercy of God and abundant redemption. This man, with all His merits offered Himself to the Father, in every hour and in every moment, for you. This man, sitting at the right hand of the Father intercedes for you and serves as your advocate. "Why then do you offend Me? Why do you not turn back? Come back to Me, because I dispersed your iniquities like a cloud, and your sin like smoke."

CHAPTER 35: ON SOME REASONS WHY SOME LIVE WITHOUT MOURNING OVER OFFENDING GOD, WITHOUT VIRTUE, AND WITHOUT CHRISTIAN PERFECTION.

The reasons why someone sleeps in lukewarm devotion—neither rising from sin nor giving himself to virtue as one should—are many, and among them are the following.

Since a person does not live within himself and fails to see what is done in his house and who possesses it, he passes his days eagerly and curiously in vain pursuits. Even if he remains occupied in things licit and good in themselves, he gives no thought to those that are necessary for virtue and Christian perfection. And even if he has such thoughts at times and recognizes his need and is called, indeed, inspired by God to change his life, he responds, "Tomorrow, tomorrow, later, later." "Today" and "now" never come, because having the vice of "tomorrow" and "later," in every "today" and in each "now," he brings forth another "tomorrow" and another "later."[27]

There is no shortage of others who, while believing that true change in life and the exercise of virtue consist in some of their devotions, spend almost all day saying Our Fathers and Hail Marys without ever taking up the mortification of their disordered passions that keep them attached to creatures.

Others give themselves to virtuous exercises, but are building without the necessary foundations. Each virtue has its own proper foundation. Humility, for example, has a foundation in the desire to be considered little, even nothing, to be ashamed before others, and to be despicable in the eyes of others. Therefore, whoever first lays and builds the foundation can then receive the stones for the building of humility with happiness. The stones consist of the low esteem in which various persons hold us and the opportunities to carry out humble duties. From there, the desire to be considered lowly increases, and one who willingly receives the low estimation that comes from others can then acquire humility, requesting it again and again from God in honor of His humiliated Son.

Even if all this is done by some people, it is not always done out of love of virtue or in order to please God. From this is born the condition in some persons where acts are not consistent. They are humble with some and arrogant with others, or humble with the others and arrogant with those who do not value them as highly as they planned.

There are still others who, desiring Christian perfection, instead procure useless things through employment of their own feeble strength and by their own industry and exercises, rather than from God and through distrust of themselves. Therefore, they are going backward rather than forward.

Nor is there any shortage of those who scarcely enter the road to virtue and suddenly allow themselves to believe that they have arrived at perfection. Thus, vain in themselves, they also grow weak in virtue.

To acquire virtue and Christian perfection, try as much as possible to kindle in yourself the desire first for distrust of self, and then for confidence in God, advancing this desire every day. Beyond this, be advised never to allow any occasion of virtue to escape your hands, whether it be great or small. And if it escape you, chastise yourself in some way, and do not ever give up this punishment.

For many who proceed toward perfection, every day relies upon what has already been done. You must try to do some act with such diligence as if the whole of Christian perfection consisted in that one alone. Then proceed to the second act, the third and so on. With this diligence you guard against little defects; the zealous use these in turn to guard against the greater.

Embrace virtue for its own sake, and in order to please God. In this way you will behave identically with all, whether you are alone or with others. And in this way you will also remember sometimes to leave virtue to virtue and God to God. Deviate neither to the right nor to the left, and do not turn back. Be discreet, accustomed to solitude, meditation and prayer, frequently begging God that He give you the virtues and perfections you are seeking. For God is the source of all virtue and He is the perfection to which He calls us in every hour.

CHAPTER 36: ON LOVE TOWARD ENEMIES.

Since Christian perfection is complete obedience to the commands of God, perfection itself proceeds mainly from the precept of loving one's enemies, because this rule so closely resembles the habits of God.

Therefore, if you wish to acquire this perfection summarily and briefly, try to observe completely how much Christ commands in the precept to love your enemies—to love them, do good to them, and to pray for them. Do not do so slowly or mechanically, but with such affection that you seem to forget yourself. Give all your heart to love and pray for them.

When doing good to them (in what pertains to spiritual blessings) take heed that their souls never have occasion to take offense from you. Through your physical gestures, words and works, always show them that you love them and hold them in esteem, and that you always have a readiness to serve them.

Concerning other, temporal favors that one must do, prudence and good judgment will suggest proper action when you take into account the status of the enemies, your own resources and the particular occasion. If you will attend to this, you will see that virtue and peace will enter and fill your heart.

This command does not contain the great difficulty that others believe. No doubt it is challenging to human nature, but to those who desire it and remain alert to mortify natural urges quickly, it will become easy, carrying them secretly into sweet peace and comfort. Still, in order to assist us in our weakness, you should use four most powerful aids.

One is prayer. Often request this love from Christ, on account of

Him, Who on the cross first remembered His enemies, then His Mother, and Himself only in the end.

The second aid will be for you to say to yourself, "The command of the Lord is that I love my enemies, so I ought to do it."

The third aid is to see in enemies the living image of God Who created them and thus to stir yourself to love and value the image.

The fourth is to see value in them through the ineffable ransom with which they were redeemed by Christ. It was not silver or gold, but His own blood. Strive in a manner that will not be in vain, lost and condemned.

CHAPTER 37: ON THE EXAMINATION OF CONSCIENCE.

Examination of conscience is necessary three times per day for the zealous: before dinner; before vespers; and before going to bed. This is impossible for some, but the examination at night must never be omitted. If God sees the works done by man twice, and if man will never see as clearly as God but must later render a strict account of his actions, should he not examine them more than once?[28]

The examination shall be done in this way. First, you will ask for light from God, so that you may know all your intentions and actions. Then you will begin to consider how closed and recollected you have been in your heart and how you have guarded it. Third, whether or not you have obeyed God that day through all the opportunities that He has given you to serve Him. Here I say nothing else, as this third consideration contains in itself the status and duty of each one.

For correspondence between grace and your good works, give thanks that God has not forgotten you entirely, remaining desirous to pave your path anew, as if you had done nothing to that point. For faults, defects and sins, turn to God, grieving for offenses against Him, saying to Him, "Lord, I have acted according to my nature. But here You will stop me, if your right hand holds me fast. For that I give You thanks. Act, then, I beg You, my Lord, according to your nature, in the name of your beloved Son. Forgive me, and give me grace, so that I may offend You no more."

In penance for your faults, then, and in order to inspire improvement, mortify your will in some licit enjoyment, so that this may please Him greatly. I say the same in regard to bodily mortifications. And do it. Do not give up these or similar mortifications unless you want your examinations of conscience to become rather mechanical, fruitless and conducive to lukewarm devotion.

CHAPTER 38: CONCERNING TWO RULES FOR LIVING IN PEACE.

Although whoever lives according to what is said here will always have peace of mind, I still want to give you two rules in this final chapter that are implicit in the material above. Observing them, you will, insofar as it is possible, live peacefully in this unjust world.

One is that you attend with all diligence to the effort to close the door of your heart to desire, since desire is the long wood of the cross and of the disquiet which will be as serious as the magnitude of the desire. The more numerous these desires the more the wood of the cross will be prepared. Therefore, seeing the difficulties and drawbacks implied, do not carry out the desire.

Whoever does not desire or seek out the cross must abandon desire when finding himself upon it. Then, at the moment he abandons it, he will descend from the cross. There is no other remedy.

The other rule is that when you are disturbed or offended by others, do not turn your attention to them but rather consider different things. Do not think about whether or not they ought to do this to you, or who they are, or who they think themselves to be, or any other such thing. These are all fuel for the kindling of wrath, disdain and hatred. Instead, return immediately in such cases to the goodness and commands of God, because you know what you ought to do. Thus you will not commit worse errors than they. In this way, you will return to the road to virtue and peace of mind.

If you will not do as you ought to do to yourself, then why should it surprise you that others do not do with you what they ought to do?

And if revenge against those who offend you seems pleasing, you should first take revenge against yourself, for you have no greater enemy and offender.

Notes

1. Historiography on any of these general views of the period or its component movements is enormous. The classic statement on the fifteenth-century Renaissance as the reawakening of sleepy medieval folk, and as the beginning of a
modernity temporarily snuffed out by late-sixteenth and seventeenth-century
Spaniards and Roman clerics, comes from the nineteenth century: J. Burckhardt,
Die Cultur der Renaissance in Italien: Ein Versuch (Basel,1860; in English as *The
Civilization of the Renaissance in Italy*, in numerous editions). For the opposing
landmark description of the importance of the decaying of an "over-ripe" Middle
Ages in setting the stage for growth and development in the early-modern period,
see J. Huizinga, *The Waning of the Middle Ages* (New York, 1949). For a somewhat
different approach, although still arguing that the Middle Ages represented a more
directly positive contribution to the sixteenth-century heart of early-modern Europe than Burckhardt would admit, two significant treatments can be found in H.
A. Oberman, *The Harvest of Medieval Theology: Gabriel Biel and Late Medieval Nomi-
nalism* (Cambridge, MA, 1963) and S. Ozment, *The Age of Reform, 1250–1550: An
Intellectual and Religious History of Late Medieval and Reformation Europe* (New Haven,
1980).

2. Even a basic bibliography of twentieth-century works that have spun
from, challenged and rethought the fundamental insights of Burckhardt concerning the Renaissance could fill dozens of pages. A useful set of volumes that provides an introduction to a variety of modern approaches to the Renaissance and
extensive bibliographical citations for further reading saw publication recently: A.
Rabil, Jr., ed., *Renaissance Humanism: Foundations, Forms and Legacy*, 3 vols. (Philadelphia, 1988). For the reissued classic study on northern "Christian" humanism
whose theses still dominate textbook literature on the Northern Renaissance, see
E. H. Harbison, *The Christian Scholar in the Age of Reformation* (New York, 1956;
most recent edition: Grand Rapids, 1984). Even more useful is Anthony Goodman
and Angus McKay, eds., *The Impact of Humanism on Western Europe* (New York,
1990). Evidence of the importance of Christian religious concerns in Italian Renaissance figures can be found in primary sources like Petrarca's *Secretum*, from the

NOTES

critical edition *Francesco Petrarca, Prose*, ed. G. Martellotti, et al. (Milan and Naples, 1955), 22–215, and in the poems of Lorenzo de' Medici, also in a critical edition: *Lorenzo de' Medici, Laude*, ed. B. Toscani (Florence, 1990). A number of scholars have argued that evidence for the continuing importance of humanistic methodology can be found as well in ecclesiastical figures around the time of the Council of Trent (1545–1563). The classic treatment in this regard is H. Jedin, *Geschichte des Konzils von Trient*, 5 vols. (Freiburg, 1950–75). See also G. Alberigo, *I vescovi italiani al Concilio di Trento* (Florence, 1959); E. Cochrane, *Italy, 1530–1630* (New York, 1988), 118–23; and my own *Marcello Cervini and Ecclesiastical Government in Tridentine Italy* (DeKalb, 1992), 13–17, 39–42, 94–111.

   3. Cochrane, *Italy*, 69–105. For additional background, see P. Toesca, ed., *Storia dell'arte italiana* (Turin, 1927), vols. 1–4; R. Oertel, *Die Frühzeit der italienischen Malerei* (Stuttgart, 1966); J. E. White, *Art and Architecture in Italy, 1250–1400* (Harmondsworth, 1966); M. Baxandall, *Painting and Experience in Fifteenth-Century Italy* (Oxford, 1972); R. Krautheimer, *The Rome of Alexander VII, 1655–1667* (Princeton, 1985); N. Pirrotta, *Music and Culture in Italy from the Middle Ages to the Baroque* (Cambridge, MA, 1985); *The Age of Correggio and the Carracci: Emilian Painting of the Fifteenth and Sixteenth Centuries* (Washington, DC, 1986), esp. pp. 213–35; C. V. Palisca, *Humanism in Italian Renaissance Musical Thought* (New Haven, 1986); F. W. Kent and P. Simons, eds., *Patronage, Art and Society in Renaissance Italy* (Oxford, 1987); W. Braunfels, *Urban Design in Western Europe: Regime and Architecture 900–1900* (Chicago, 1988); J. Southorn, *Power and Display in the Seventeenth Century: The Arts and their Patrons in Modena and Ferrara* (New York, 1988); M. D. Pollak, *Turin 1564–1680: Urban Design, Military Culture and the Creation of the Absolutist Capital* (Chicago, 1991); and P. M. Jones, *Federico Borromeo and the Ambrosiana: Art Patronage and Reform in Seventeenth-Century Milan* (Cambridge, 1993).

   4. Historians analytical of the impact of the discoveries generated a huge body of celebratory and critical literature during the Columbus quincentenary. For some examples, see W. D. Phillips and C. R. Phillips, *The Worlds of Christopher Columbus* (New York, 1992); A. Pagden, *European Encounters with the New World: From Renaissance to Romanticism* (New Haven, 1992); and K. Sale, *The Conquest of Paradise: Christopher Columbus and the Columbian Legacy* (New York, 1990). The twentieth-century analysis of virtually all post-medieval western economic history turns on comparison of the era under investigation with the twelfth-century "commercial revolution" as described by R. Lopez in *The Commercial Revolution of the Middle Ages, 950–1350* (Englewood Cliffs, 1971), and with R. de Roover's identification of capitalistic methods in the late-medieval Medici bank of Florence, in his numerous writings, especially *The Rise and Decline of the Medici Bank, 1397–1494* (Cambridge, MA, 1963) and *Business, Banking and Economic Thought in Late Medieval and Early-Modern Europe*, ed. J. Kirshner (Chicago, 1974). Another "classic" is by J. Delumeau, *Vie économique et sociale de Rome dans la seconde moitié du XVIe siècle*, 2 vols. (Paris, 1957–59). Among the legion of recent contributions on early-modern economic history are J. De Vries, *Economy of Europe in an Age of Crisis, 1600–1750*

NOTES

(Cambridge, 1976); J. D. Tracy, *A Financial Revolution in the Habsburg Netherlands: Renten and Renteniers in the County of Holland, 1515-1565* (Berkeley, 1985); A. De Maddalena and H. Kellenbenz, eds., *Le repubblica internazionale del denaro tra XV e XVII secolo* (Bologna, 1986); C. Cipolla, *La moneta a Firenze nel Cinquecento* (Bologna, 1987); J. Marino, *Pastoral Economics in the Kingdom of Naples* (Baltimore, 1988); H. Kellenbenz and P. Prodi, eds., *Fisco, religione, stato nell'età confessionale* (Bologna, 1989); and J. D. Tracy, ed., *The Rise of Merchant Empires: Long Distance Trade in the Early Modern World, 1350–1750* (New York, 1990).

5. Herbert Butterfield popularized the term and the concept "Scientific Revolution" in lectures and later in a book entitled *The Origins of Modern Science* (London, 1949). For more on the history of the concept, see I. B. Cohen, *Revolutions in Science* (Cambridge, MA, 1985). Volumes IV through VIII of L. Thorndike's monumental *History of Magic and Experimental Science*, 8 vols. (New York, 1923–1958) are another important starting point. Some recent studies on the understanding of the movement in relation to its past are A. G. Debus, *Man and Nature in the Renaissance* (Cambridge, 1978); T. Goldstein, *Dawn of Modern Science: From the Arabs to Leonardo da Vinci* (Boston, 1980); A. Funkenstein, *Theology and the Scientific Imagination from the Middle Ages to the Seventeenth Century* (Princeton, 1986); N. G. Siriasi, *Avicenna in Renaissance Italy: The Canon and Medical Teaching in Italian Universities after 1500* (Princeton, 1987); L. Schiebinger, *The Mind Has No Sex? Women in the Origins of Modern Science* (Cambridge, MA, 1989); A. M. Smith, "Knowing Things Inside Out: The Scientific Revolution from a Medieval Perspective," *AHR* 95 (1990):726–44; and D. C. Lindberg, *The Beginnings of Western Science: The European Scientific Tradition in Philosophical, Religious and Institutional Context, 600 B.C. to A.D. 1450* (Chicago, 1992).

6. Some recent works on early-modern politics: P. Prodi, *Il sovrano pontifice, un corpo e due anime: la monarchia papale nella prima età moderna* (Bologna, 1982); A. Cernigliaro, *Sovranità e feudo nel regno di Napoli, 1505–1557* (Naples, 1983); J. M. Headley, *The Emperor and His Chancellor: A Study of the Imperial Chancery Under Gattinara* (New York, 1983); G. Del Torre, *Venezia e la terraferma dopo la guerra di Cambrai: fiscalità e amministrazione 1515–1530* (Milan, 1986); P. Mack and M. C. Jacob, eds., *Politics and Culture in Early-Modern Europe* (New York, 1987); Cochrane, *Italy*, 33–54; R. Bireley, *The Counter-Reformation Prince: Anti-Machiavellianism or Catholic Statecraft in Early-Modern Europe* (Chapel Hill, 1990); H. Nader, *Liberty in Absolutist Spain: The Habsburg Sale of Towns, 1516–1700* (Baltimore, 1990); R. G. Asch and A. M. Birke, eds., *Princes, Patronage and the Nobility: The Court at the Beginning of the Modern Age, c. 1450–1650* (New York, 1991); T. Astarita, *The Continuity of Feudal Power: The Caracciolo di Brienza in Spanish Naples* (New York, 1992); and L. Nussdorfer, *Civic Politics in the Rome of Urban VIII* (Princeton, 1992).

7. I am referring, of course, to his series of "woes" to scribes, Pharisees and other Jewish authorities; to the Sermon on the Mount; to his clearing of moneychangers and merchants from the Temple in Jerusalem; and to his consideration of the question on whether or not Jews ought to pay taxes to their Roman, pagan overlords (cf. Mt. 23:1–33; Mt. 5:3–10 and 6:1–6; Mk. 11:15–19; and Mt. 22:15–22).

NOTES

8. Works covering the general history of Christianity prior to the Protestant reformation that I allude to in this paragraph and the next are legion. Among the better ones are K. S. Latourette, *A History of Christianity*, 2 vols. (San Francisco, 1953); R. H. Bainton, *Christianity* (Boston, 1964); P. Johnson, *A History of Christianity* (New York, 1976); and J. McManners, ed., *The Oxford Illustrated History of Christianity* (Oxford, 1992).

9. Although a long list of sources should be consulted in order to gain a full understanding of medieval reform movements, one of the better ones that is readily available in English exists in volumes 3 and 4 of the *Handbook of Church History*, 10 vols., ed. H. Jedin and J. Dolan (New York, 1965–1981; volumes 5–10 published under the title *History of the Church*). For the poems of Vogelweide, see *Die Politischen Lieder Walthers von der Vogelweide*, ed. F. Maurer (Tübingen, 1954). A small, but nicely representative portion was translated into English and published in *University of Chicago Readings in Western Civilization, Volume 4: Medieval Europe*, ed. J. Kirshner and K. F. Morrison (Chicago, 1986), 376–77.

10. For an excellent recent study on the context Luther found and criticized, see G. Fragnito, "Cardinals' Courts in Sixteenth-Century Rome," *JMH* 65 (1993):26–56.

11. For background on the Protestant reformation and some of the subtopics alluded to in this paragraph and the previous one, begin with G. H. Williams, *The Radical Reformation* (Philadelphia, 1962); M. U. Edwards, *Luther's Last Battles: Politics and Polemics 1531–1546* (Ithaca, N.Y., 1983); T. Brady, *Turning Swiss: Cities and Empire 1450–1550* (New York, 1985); C.M.N. Eire, *War Against the Idols: The Reformation of Worship from Erasmus to Calvin* (New York, 1986); J. M. Kittleson, *Luther the Reformer* (Minneapolis, MN, 1986); T. Scott, *Freiburg and the Breisgau: Town-Country Relations in the Age of Reformation and Peasants' War* (Oxford, 1986); W. J. Bouwsma, *John Calvin: A Sixteenth-Century Portrait* (New York, 1988); R. P. Hsia, ed., *The German People and the Reformation* (Ithaca, N.Y., 1988); L. Roper, *The Holy Household: Women and Morals in Reformation Augsburg* (Oxford, 1989); H. A. Oberman, *Luther: Man Between God and the Devil* (New Haven, 1990); T. Watt, *Cheap Print and Popular Piety, 1550–1650* (New York, 1991); and S. L. Hindman, ed., *Printing the Written Word: The Social History of Books, c. 1450–1520* (Ithaca, N.Y., 1992). These represent just the tip of a very large historiographical iceberg.

12. General, standard works on the Reformation, like H. J. Grimm's *The Reformation Era, 1500–1650*, 2nd ed. (New York, 1973) contain information on the so-called "Wars of Religion"—in this case, 343–465. For some recent work on the French conflict, see D. Crouzet, *Les guerriers de Dieu: La violence au temps des troubles de religion vers 1525—vers 1610*, 2 vols. (Paris, 1990); and B. Diefendorf, *Beneath the Cross: Catholics and Huguenots in Sixteenth-Century Paris* (New York, 1991). For the imperial conflicts, see G. Parker's two works *The Army of Flanders and the Spanish Road, 1567–1659* (Cambridge, 1972) and *The Dutch Revolt* (Ithaca, N.Y., 1977); plus F. Fernandez-Armesto, *The Spanish Armada: The Experience of War in 1588* (New

NOTES

York, 1988); and P. Pierson, *Commander of the Armada: the Seventh Duke of Medina Sidonia* (New Haven, 1989).

13. For an overview of the development of historiography on the Reformation, see A. G. Dickens and J. M. Tonkin, *The Reformation in Historical Thought* (Cambridge, Mass., 1985). For information on the development of Catholic historiography concerning the Reformation, and the controversy over periodization, see E. Cochrane, *Historians and Historiography in the Italian Renaissance* (Chicago, 1981), 445–78; H. Jedin, *Katholische Reformation oder Gegenreformation?* (Luzerne, 1946); E. Cochrane "New Light on Post-Tridentine Italy: A Note on Recent Counter-Reformation Scholarship," *CHR* 56 (1970):291–319; S. Seidel-Menchi, "Inquisizione come repressione o inquisizione come mediazione? Una proposta di periodizzazione," *Annuario dell'istituto storico italiano per l'età moderna e contemporanea* 35–36 (1983–1984):53–77; G. Alberigo, "Dinamiche religiose del Cinquecento italiano tra riforma, riforma cattolica, controriforma," *CnS* 6 (1985):543–60; A. Prosperi, "L'Inquisizione: Verso una nuova immagine?" *CS* 25 (1988):119–45; P. Simoncelli, "Inquisizione romana e riforma in Italia," *RSI* 100 (1988):1–125; G. Fragnito, "Evangelismo e intransigenti nei difficili equilibri del pontificato farnesiano," *RSLR* 25 (1989):20–47; P. Prodi, "Controriforma e/o riforma cattolica: superamento di vecchi dilemmi nei nuovi panorami storiografici," *Römische historische Mitteilungen* 31 (1989):227–37; W. Reinhard, "Reformation, Counter-Reformation and the Early-Modern State: A Reassessment," *CHR* 75 (1989):383–404; A. J. Schutte, "Periodization of Sixteenth-Century Religious History: The Post-Cantimori Paradigm Shift," *JMH* 61 (1989):269–84; C. Harline, "Official Religion—Popular Religion in Recent Historiography of the Catholic Reformation," *AfR* 81 (1990):239–62; and J. W. O'Malley, "Was Ignatius Loyola a Church Reformer? How to Look at Early-Modern Catholicism," *CHR* 77 (1991):177–93.

14. For arguments in favor of adopting this terminology, see E. Cochrane, "Counter Reformation or Tridentine Reformation? Italy in the Age of Carlo Borromeo," in *San Carlo Borromeo, Catholic Reform and Ecclesiastical Politics in the Second Half of the Sixteenth Century,* ed. J. M. Headley and J. B. Tomaro (Washington, 1988), 31–46; and my *Marcello Cervini,* 6–17; 161–74. Contarini, the focus of much Italian historical investigation, is now the subject of a biography in English: E. G. Gleason, *Gasparo Contarini: Venice, Rome and Reform* (Berkeley, 1993).

15. The most recent general work on the confraternities in English is C. F. Black, *Italian Confraternities in the Sixteenth Century* (Cambridge, 1989). See also V. Meneghin, "Due compagnie sul modello di quelle del 'Divino Amore' fondate da Francescani a Feltre e a Verona (1499, 1503)," *Archivum franciscum historicum* 63 (1969):518–64; M. Fanti, *La chiesa e la compagnia dei poveri in Bologna: una istituzione di mutuo soccorso nella società bolognese fra il Cinquecento e il Seicento* (Bologna, 1977); G. G. Meersseman and G. P. Pacini, "Le confraternite laicali in Italia del Quattrocento al Seicento," in *Problemi di storia della chiesa nei secoli XV-XVII* (Naples, 1979); V. Paglia, *"La pietà dei carcerati": confraternite e società a Roma nei secoli XVI-XVIII* (Rome, 1980); D. Zardin, "Le confraternite in Italia settentrionale fra XV e XVII secolo," *Società e*

NOTES

storia 19 (1987):81–137; R. Rusconi, "Confraternite, compagnie e devozioni," in *Storia d'Italia, Annali 9: La chiesa e il potere politico dal Medioevo all'età contemporanea*, ed. G. Chittolini and G. Miccoli (Torino, 1986), 469-506; D. H. Dieterich, "Confraternities and Lay Leadership in Sixteenth-Century Liège," *RR* 25 (1989):15–34; and Cochrane, *Italy*, 111–18. For their medieval forebears, the classic study is G. G. Meerseman, *Ordo Fraternitatis: Confraternite e pietà dei laici nel Medioevo*, 3 vols. (Rome, 1977). On the Oratory, see K. J. Jorgensen, "The Oratories of Divine Love and the Theatines: Confraternal Piety and the Making of a Religious Community," Ph.D. Diss., Columbia University, 1989; M. Impagliazzo, "I padri dell'Oratorio nella Roma della Controriforma (1595–1605)," *RSLR* 25 (1989):285–307; and D. S. Camillocci, "Le confraternite del Divino Amore: interpretazioni storiografiche e proposte attuali di ricerca," *RSLR* 27 (1991):315–32. The statutes of the Oratory are available in English translation: J. C. Olin, *The Catholic Reformation: Savonarola to Ignatius Loyola* (Westminster, Md., 1978; reprint edition, New York, 1993), 16–26. On the general problem of poverty in the early-modern era and its connection with the confraternities, see A. Carlino, "L'Arciconfraternita di S. Girolamo della Carità: l'origine e l'ideologia assistenziale," *Archivio della società romana di storia patria* 107 (1984):275–306; M. T. Bonadonna Russo, "Problemi e istituti dell'assistenza romana nel Cinque e Seicento," *Studi romani* 34 (1986):230–52; A. Pastore, "Strutture assistenziale nell'Italia della Controriforma," in Chittolini and Miccoli, *Storia d'Italia, Annali 9*, 433–65; and M. Flynn, "Rituals of Solidarity in Castilian Confraternities," *RR* 25 (1989):53–68.

16. The key texts in the early history of the Jesuit order are all readily available in published English translations: Ignatius of Loyola, *The Spiritual Exercises of St. Ignatius*, ed. L. J. Puhl (Chicago, 1951); idem, *The Autobiography of St. Ignatius Loyola*, ed. J. C. Olin (New York, 1974); idem, *The Constitutions of the Society of Jesus*, ed. G. E. Ganss (St. Louis, 1970). Portions of all these documents, as well as a selection of the letters of Ignatius are available in another volume in this series: Ignatius of Loyola, *Spiritual Exercises and Selected Works*, ed. G. E. Ganss (New York, 1991). The portions on early Jesuit history contained in all other, older general works, like J. de Guibert's *La spiritualité de la Compagnie de Jésus: esquisse historique* (Rome, 1953), and W. V. Bangert's *A History of the Society of Jesus* (St. Louis, 1972) have been supplanted by a new, definitive study: J. W. O'Malley, *The First Jesuits* (Cambridge, MA, 1993). The most recent biography of Ignatius goes beyond historical commonplace only to posit a suggestive but unconvincing psychoanalysis of the Jesuit founder: W. W. Meissner, *Ignatius of Loyola: The Psychology of a Saint* (New Haven, 1992).

17. A new *festschrift* in honor of John Olin examines many of these orders in their early-modern context and is complete with useful bibliographical essays. See R. L. DeMolen, ed., *Religious Orders of the Reformation* (New York, 1993). On the reform of the Augustinians in this era, see D. Gutiérrez, *The Augustinians from the Protestant Reformation to the Peace of Westphalia, 1518–1648*, trans. J. J. Kelly (Villanova, Penn., 1979), 43–80.

NOTES

18. Modern, critical studies are lacking of all these popes (with the exception of Marcellus), as well as most of those through the seventeenth century. Hence, the best and most readily available source on them remains volumes 11–20 of L. von Pastor, *The History of the Popes from the Close of the Middle Ages*, 3d ed., 40 vols. (St. Louis, 1938–53); originally published as *Geschichte der Päpste seit dem Ausgang des Mittelalters*, 21 vols. (Freiburg im Breisgau, 1866–1938). See also my *Marcello Cervini*, 151–60; and my "Countering 'the Turk': Papal and Genoese Naval Policy, 1535–1536," *AHP* 30 (1992):351–62.

19. Some of the more famous representatives of the late fifteenth and sixteenth-century interest in mysticism and union with God, such as Teresa, John of the Cross, Roberto Bellarmino, Catherine of Genoa and Ignatius of Loyola, are the subject of other volumes in this series. For information on the more obscure figures, one must consult a large and growing body of periodical and monographic literature, whose proliferation has been fueled in recent years by interest in the history of women in medieval and early-modern culture. See, for a few examples, A. Cistellini, *Figure della riforma pretridentina* (Brescia, 1948); R. Creytens, "La riforma dei monasteri femminili dopo i decreti Tridentini," in *Il Concilio di Trento e la riforma Tridentina*, 2 vols. (Rome, 1965), 1:45–84; R. M. Bell, *Holy Anorexia* (Chicago, 1985); C. W. Bynum, *Holy Feast and Holy Fast: The Religious Significance of Food to Medieval Women* (Berkeley, 1987); R. P. Liebowitz, "Virgins in the Service of Christ: The Dispute over an Active Apostolate for Women During the Counter-Reformation," in *Women of Spirit: Female Leadership in the Jewish and Christian Traditions*, ed. R. Ruether and E. McLaughlin (New York, 1979), 131–52; F. Lussana, "Rivolta e misticismo nei chiostri femminili del Seicento," *Studi storici* 28 (1987):243–60; K. Norberg, "The Counter Reformation and Women: Religious and Lay," in *Catholicism in Early-Modern Europe*, ed. J. W. O'Malley (St. Louis, 1988), 133–46; E. Schulte van Kessel, ed., *Women and Men in Spiritual Culture, XIV-XVII Centuries* (The Hague, 1986); J. C. Brown, *Immodest Acts: The Life of a Lesbian Nun in Renaissance Italy* (New York, 1986); R. L. Kagan, *Lucretia's Dreams: Politics and Prophecy in Sixteenth-Century Spain* (Berkeley, 1990); M. Firpo, "Paola Antonia Negri, monaca Angelica," in *Rinascimento al femminile*, ed. O. Niccoli (Rome-Bari, 1991), 35–82; and two works by G. Zarri: "Monasteri femminili e città (secoli XV-XVIII)," in *Storia d'Italia, Annali 9*, 358–429, and *Le sante vive: profezie di corte e devozione femminile tra '400 e '500* (Turin, 1990). These and more of this literature will be examined below, in the portion of the introduction dedicated to analysis of the Theatine message to religious women.

20. Any future reconsideration of the process of church reform undertaken at the Council of Trent will have to begin from the magisterial work of H. Jedin, *Geschichte des Konzils von Trient*, 5 vols. (Freiburg, 1950–1975), and the collection of sources on which it was primarily based: *CT*. The decrees are available in an English translation: H. J. Schroeder, trans., *The Canons and Decrees of the Council of Trent* (St. Louis, 1941).

21. A suggestive set of studies on the continuing attraction of prophecy and

millennialist expectation in early-modern Rome was recently published: M. Reeves, ed., *Prophetic Rome in the High Renaissance Period* (Oxford, 1992). For some recent studies on missionary activity in this era, see R. Ricard, *The Spiritual Conquest of Mexico* (Berkeley, 1974); J. P. Donnelley, "Antonio Possevino's Plan for World Evangelization," *CHR* 74 (1988):179–98; S. Poole, *Pedro Moya de Contreras: Catholic Reform and Royal Power in New Spain, 1572–1591* (Berkeley, 1987); C. E. Ronan and B.B.C. Oh, eds., *East Meets West: The Jesuits in China, 1582–1773* (Chicago, 1988); S. MacCormack, *Religion in the Andes: Vision and Imagination in Early Colonial Peru* (Princeton, 1992); and G. Minamiki, *The Chinese Rites Controversy from Its Beginning to Modern Times* (Chicago, 1985).

22. For more on the continuing importance of humanist methodolgy and ideology in Catholic circles, see Cochrane, *Italy*, 118–23; J. F. D'Amico, *Renaissance Humanism in Papal Rome* (Baltimore, 1983); B. Collett, *Italian Benedictine Scholars and the Reformation: The Congregation of Santa Giustina of Padua* (Oxford, 1985); J. M. McManamon, *Funeral Oratory and the Cultural Ideals of Italian Humanism* (Chapel Hill, N.C., 1989); and my *Marcello Cervini*.

23. The complete texts of the three versions of the *Index* mentioned here are published, with a lengthy and helpful introduction in J. M. de Bujanda, ed., *Index de Rome 1557, 1559, 1564: Les premiers Index romains et l'Index du Concile de Trente* (Geneva, 1990).

24. The closest thing to an adequate modern study of either Paul IV or Pius V can be found in L. von Pastor, *The History of the Popes from the Close of the Middle Ages*, vols. 14, 17, and 18 (St. Louis, 1938–53). The first biographies of Paul IV come from the seventeenth century: A. Caracciolo, *De vita Pavli quarti Pont. Max. collectanea historica* (Cologne, 1612); and G. B. Castaldo, *Vita del Sanctissimo Pontefice Paolo Quarto, fondatore della religione de chierici regolari* (Rome, 1616). For the early years of Paul's career in the curia and as a force behind the Theatine order, see P. Paschini, *San Gaetano, Gian Pietro Carafa e le origini dei chierici regolari teatini* (Rome, 1926), 28–40, and this introduction below. Information on both popes can be found in other works, especially in the always-proliferating field of inquisitorial studies. See A. Aubert, "Alle origini della controriforma: studi e problemi su Paolo IV," *RSLR* 22 (1986):303–55; M. Firpo and D. Marcatto, eds., *Il processo inquisitoriale del Cardinale Giovanni Morone*, 6 vols. (Rome, 1981–95); M. Firpo, *Nel labirinto del mondo: Lorenzo Davidico tra santi, eretici inquisitori* (Florence, 1992); and Simoncelli, "Inquisizione romana." The current authority on the change in papal policy toward the Jews under Paul IV is K. R. Stow. See his *Catholic Thought and Papal Jewry Policy, 1551–1592* (New York, 1977), xii–xxvi, 3–59; and his *Taxation, Community and the State: The Jews and the Fiscal Foundations of the Early Modern State* (Stuttgart, 1983), 53–70. See also S. Baron, *A Social and Religious History of the Jews*, 2d ed. (New York, 1952–83), 14:32–35; and my *Marcello Cervini*, 158–59, 236.

25. The literature, both fictional and historical, concerning Galileo, his career and the controversy, took on a life of its own soon after the conclusion of his second trial. The most reliable account of the trial remains G. de Santillana, *The Crime of*

NOTES

Galileo (Chicago, 1955). For some recent contributions in English, see S. Drake, *Galileo at Work: His Scientific Biography* (Chicago, 1978); O. Pedersen, *Galileo and the Council of Trent* (Rome, 1983); W. A. Wallace, *Galileo and His Sources: The Heritage of the Collegio Romano in Galileo's Science* (Princeton, 1984); M. A. Finnochiaro, ed., *The Galileo Affair, A Documentary History* (Berkeley, 1989); S. A. Bedini, *The Pulse of Time: Galileo Galilei, the Determination of Longitude and the Pendulum Clock* (Florence, 1991); R. J. Blackwell, *Galileo, Bellarmine and the Bible* (Notre Dame, Ind., 1991); M. Segre, *In the Wake of Galileo* (New Brunswick, N.J., 1991); and M. Biagioli, *Galileo, Courtier: The Practice of Science in the Culture of Absolutism* (Chicago, 1993). An interesting, but thoroughly discredited, thesis can be found in P. Redondi, *Galileo, Heretic* (Princeton, 1987).

26. For some useful reflections on the long-standing nature of the problems that the implementation of Tridentine legislation sought to solve, as well as on the process of implementation itself, see B. M. Hallman, *Italian Cardinals, Reform and the Church as Property* (Berkeley, 1985); G. Alberigo, "Studi e problemi relativi all' applicazione del Concilio di Trento in Italia," *RSI* 70 (1958):239–98; J. B. Tomaro, "San Carlo Borromeo and the Implementation of the Council of Trent," in Headley and Tomaro, *San Carlo Borromeo*, 67–84; F. M. Hernández, *Los seminarios españoles: historia y pedagogia, 1563–1700* (Salamanca, 1964); G. Liberali, *Le origini del seminario diocesano* (Treviso, 1971); N. Baillargeon, *Le séminaire de Québec sous l'épiscopat de Monseigneur de Laval* (Québec, 1972); T. Deutscher, "Seminaries and the Education of Novarese Parish Priests, 1593–1627," *JEH* 32 (1981):303–19; W. J. Callahan, *Church, Politics and Society in Spain, 1750–1874* (Cambridge, MA, 1984); P. T. Hoffman, *Church and Community in the Diocese of Lyon, 1500–1789* (New Haven, 1984); and Jedin and Dolan, *Handbook of Church History*, 5:499–534.

27. On the Oratory in the development of organized welfare, see Bonadonna Russo, "Problemi e istituti," 230–33. For the alleged miracle, see the document from the Vatican Archives entitled "Origine et sommario delle opere pie di Roma instituite dal pontificato di Leone X, sino a Paolo IV," transcribed in Pastor, *History*, 8:469–70. Historians drawing ties between the Oratory and the Theatines have been legion. For three examples, see G. Moroni, "Teatini," in his *Dizionario di erudizione storico-ecclesiastica*, 153 vols. (Venice, 1840–79), 73:109–48; P. A. Kunkel, "The Theatines in the History of Catholic Reform Before the Establishment of Lutheranism," Ph.D. diss., Catholic University of America, 1941; and Jorgensen, "Oratories and Theatines," 143–97. An excellent article that looks at the central role of Gaetano and Carafa in the new order is F. Andreu, "Camaldolesi e teatini nella riforma del Cinquecento," in *Eremiti e pastori della riforma cattolica nell'Italia del '500* (Fonte Avellana, 1983), 145–80.

28. For more information on the life of Gaetano as related in this and the next four paragraphs, see A. F. Vezzosi, *I scrittori de' chierici regolari detti Teatini*, 2 vols. (Rome, 1780; reprint ed. Farnborough, 1966), 2:341–44; Paschini, *San Gaetano*, 7–27; Andreu, *Le lettere*, xiii–xxxiv; Jorgensen, "Oratories and Theatines," 1–17, 143–298; and the biographical articles on him by B. Mas in *DS*, s.v. "Gaétan de

NOTES

Thiene," and by Andreu in *DIP*, s.v. "Gaetano Thiene." The earliest biography is by G. B. Castaldo, *Vita del B. Gaetano Tiene, fondatore della religione de chierici regolari* (Rome, 1612).

29. See below, letter #2.

30. On Stella and Mignani, see Cistellini, *Figure*, 56–103; Andreu, *Le lettere*, xv–xviii; and letters #1–8, below.

31. The major writings of Battista are his *Via di aperta verità* (Venice, 1523); *Della cognitione et vittoria di se stesso* (Milan, 1531); *La philosophia divina, ossia Historia de la passione del nostro Signore Gesù Cristo crucifixo et modo di contemplare quella per imitarla* (Milan, 1531); and *Lo specchio interiore* (Milan, 1540). On his life, see *DS*, s.v. "Carioni, Jean Baptiste," by I. Colosio, and *DBI*, s.v. "Carioni, Battista," by S. Pezzella. For the Barnabites, see V. Michelini, *I barnabiti: chierici regolari di S. Paolo* (Milan, 1983). For the life of Negri, see M. Firpo, "Paola Antonia Negri," 41–50. For a fascinating study involving even later employment of the ideas of Battista, see Firpo, *Nel labirinto*.

32. See below, letters #17 and 18.

33. Paschini, *San Gaetano*, 45–51.

34. Paschini, *San Gaetano*, 44–45. For the text of the letter, see R. De Maulde La Clavière, *San Gaetano da Thiene e la Riforma cattolica italiana, 1480–1527* (Rome, 1911), 151. The original letter (1 January 1533, from Gian Pietro Carafa to Gian Matteo Giberti) is in the Vatican Library: *Barberino latino* 5697, f. 35–37.

35. For the text of the brief, *Bullarum Diplomatum et Privilegiorum Sanctorum Romanorum Pontificum, Taurinensis Editio*, 25 vols. (Turin, 1857–67), 6:73–74.

36. For a list of the general congregation meetings, their dates, location and the person elected superior at each, see Jorgensen, "Oratories and Theatines," 250. The list covers the years 1524–1560.

37. Jorgensen, "Oratories and Theatines," 198. The lack of direct evidence is in itself an outgrowth of the procedures of the Oratory, as the Theatine order maintained the traditional secrecy characteristic of the earlier confraternity.

38. Mk. 8:34. The Latin text of this "rule" was originally published in G. Silos, *Historiarum Clericorum Regularium a Congregatione condita pars prior* (Rome, 1650), 73–75. An English translation is available: Olin, *Catholic Reformation*, 128–32. Cf. also F. Andreu, "La regola dei Chierici Regolari nella lettera di Bonifacio de' Colli a Gian Matteo Giberti," *RD* 2 (1946):38–53; Jorgensen, "Oratories and Theatines," 198–243; and P. A. Quinn, "Ignatius of Loyola and Gian Pietro Carafa: Catholic Reformers at Odds," *CHR* 67 (1981):386–400.

39. Paschini, *San Gaetano*, 60–63; Jorgensen, "Oratories and Theatines," 241–43.

40. Paschini, *San Gaetano*, 66–106; Jorgensen, "Oratories and Theatines," 244–98. The text of Contarini's *De officio* is available in English: Olin, *Catholic Reformation*, 90–106. See also my "Two Instructions to Preachers from the Tridentine Reformation," *SCJ* 20 (1989):457–70; my *Marcello Cervini*, 94–98; and Gleason, *Gasparo Contarini*, 93–102. For Flaminio and his ill-fated attempt to enter

NOTES

the Theatines in 1533, see G. Kaminski, "Marcantonio Flaminio ed i Chierici Regolari," *RD* 2 (1946):5–18; and below, letter #38. Flaminio's *Lettere* have recently been edited by A. Pastore (Rome, 1978), but virtually all of the letters postdate his attempt to enter the Theatines. On Miani and the Somascans, see C. Pellegrini, ed., *Vita del clarissimo Signor Girolamo Miani gentil huomo Venetiano* (Rome, 1970; reprint ed. 1985); C. Pellegrini, ed., *Le lettere di San Girolamo Miani* (Rome, 1975); and G. Landini, *San Girolamo Miani dalle testimonianze processuali, dai biografi, dai documenti editi ed inediti fino ad oggi* (Rome, 1947). For these last three references, I am indebted to Kenneth J. Jorgensen, S.J.

41. *DIP*, s.v. "Chierici regolari teatini," by F. Andreu. The text of Carafa's memorandum has been published: I. P. Carafa, "De lutheranorum haeresi reprimenda et ecclesia reformanda ad Clementem VII," *CT*, 12:67–77. It is also available in English translation: E. G. Gleason, *Reform Thought in Sixteenth-Century Italy* (Ann Arbor, Mich., 1981), 55–80.

42. Paschini, *San Gaetano*, 107–19. The Latin text of one of the briefs (21 January 1529) is published there too, 159–60.

43. Ibid., 120–34; see also Moroni, "Teatini," 126–28. Gaetano originally secured a house in Naples through the patronage of Giovanni Antonio Caracciolo, the count of Oppido, but apparently his wealth and his promise further to endow the order frightened Gaetano into seeking a place of their own near the hospital.

44. For the Latin texts of the briefs of Clement, see Paschini, *San Gaetano*, 160–61. Carafa received his promotion on 22 December 1536. For the text of the *Consilium de emendanda ecclesia*, see *CT*, 12:134–45. An English translation is available in Olin, *Catholic Reformation*, 182–97. The numerous articles in *RD* on Burali were capped by F. Molinari's *Il cardinal Teatino Beato Paolo Burali e la riforma Tridentina a Piacenza (1568–1576)* (Rome, 1957), and his "Epistolario del Beato Paolo Burali, Cardinale Teatino, vescovo di Piacenza, arcivescovo di Napoli," *RD* 32 (1976):2–430. Another Theatine who did similar work was Girolamo Ferro (1528–1592). On him, see R. de Maio, "Un riformatore teatino nel Cinquecento: Girolamo Ferro," *RD* 16 (1960):3–58. Documents relevant to the history of the Theatines deriving from an investigation into the finances of all monasteries and convents begun by Innocent X in 1649 have recently been published: *I teatini, L'inchiesta di Innocenzo X sui regolari in Italia*, vol. 1, ed. M. Campanelli (Rome, 1987).

45. On Theatines as bishops in this period, see Pastor, *History*, 10:418; and Jorgensen, "Oratories and Theatines," 4–5, 283–86, 302–5.

46. For general information on Theatine missionary activity, see B. Ferro, *Istoria delle missioni dei Chierici Regolari*, 2 vols. (Rome, 1704–05). For the east Indies, see A. Spalla, "Le missioni teatine nelle Indie Orientali nel secolo XVIII e le cause della loro fine," *RD* 27 (1971): 1–76; 28 (1972):265–305; 29 (1973):3–37; and R. M. Wiltgen, "The Evangelization Congregation at the service of Java, Borneo, Sumatra (1622–1815)," *RD* 29 (1973):122–41.

47. For a brief article tracing the rise and fall of the number of members in the

NOTES

Theatine order, see Francesco Andreu, "Appunti per una statistical generale dell'ordine Teatino," *RD* 30 (1974):74–83.

48. The standard source for the analysis of Theatine literary production in the first 250 years of their existence is Vezzosi, *I scrittori*. For general information on Theatine spirituality linking them to the rest of the Christian tradition, see P. Pourrat, *Christian Spirituality*, 4 vols., trans. W. H. Mitchell, et al. (New York, 1922–27, 1955), 3:230–71.

49. See below, letter #7.

50. See below, letter #1.

51. See below, letter #3.

52. See below, letter #2.

53. See below, letter #7.

54. See below, letter #5.

55. See below, letter #8.

56. See below, letter #10. For more on the relationship between the two, see Andreu, "Camaldolesi," 152–63.

57. See below, letter #12. For other examples of lay preaching that called lines of ecclesiastical authority into question, this time in a northern Italian devotional movement in the seventeenth century, see G. Signorotto, *Inquisitori e mistici nel Seicento italiano: l'eresia di Santa Pelagia* (Bologna, 1989).

58. Two members of the Carafa family held that archbishopric in 1530: Vincenzo (archbishop 1505–1530) and his nephew Francesco (archbishop 1530–1544).

59. For more on the *Sapienza* as well as Neapolitan convents generally, see C. Russo, *I monasteri femminili di clausura a Napoli nel secolo XVII* (Naples, 1970), 72–113, 133; and A. Illibato, "Pastoralità e riforma nella visita pastorale di Francesco Carafa nella diocesi di Napoli (1542–1543)," in *Eremiti e pastori della riforma cattolica nell'Italia del '500* (Fonte Avellana, 1983), 233–48.

60. See below, letters #33 and 36.

61. See below, letters #21, 22, 26 and 32. The image of holy women in this period as symbols of purity who produce purity while remaining free of carnal temptations in perpetual chastity has recently been analyzed. See G. Zarri, "Le sante vive: per una tipologia della santità femminile nel primo Cinquecento," *AIGT* 6 (1980):371–445.

62. See below, letter #20.

63. See below, letter #18.

64. See below, letter #13.

65. One writer who posited a connection between northern Christian humanism and the approach of Gaetano was B. Mas. See his "La spiritualità theatina," *RD* 7 (1951):3–18; 64–88; 191–204. A recent article highlights the connection between northern humanism and many of the themes I locate in Gaetano's spirituality. See S. F. Campbell, "Nicolas Caussin's 'Spirituality of Communication': A Meeting of Divine and Human Speech," *RQ* 46 (1993):44–70.

NOTES

66. See below, letters #11, 31 and 40.

67. For these uses of the image of fire, see letters #3, 4 and 10.

68. For the apparent contradictions in his use of imagery with Mignani, see letters #1 and 2. As regards the Neoplatonic reference, it is worthwhile noting that Giustiniani himself used the image in a treatise on mystical love. See L. Fortini, "Un trattato cinquecentesco sull'amore mistico:il 'Secretum meum mihi' di Paolo Giustiniani," *RSLR* 22 (1986):241–55.

69. For Paul's use of the theme, see 1 Timothy 1:18 and 6:12; 2 Timothy 4:7; and 1 Corinthians 9:24–27. For the quotations from Gaetano, see below, letters #2 and 4.

70. See below, letters #9 (to his niece, Elisabetta Porto) and 3 (to Mignani).

71. See below, letter #2. The gospel stories related can be found in Luke 2:1–35. The manger vision of Gaetano is celebrated in a painting by Mattia Del Mare in the mother church of the order, the church of Sant'Andrea della Valle, in Rome. See Jorgensen, "Oratories and Theatines," 299–300, 308–9. An interesting study on sixteenth-century use of the image of Mary as mediator is available: L. Accati, "Simboli maschili e simboli femminili nella devozione alla Madonna della Controriforma: appunti per una discussione," in Schulte van Kessel, *Women and Men*, 35–43. For a related iconographical study (on a depiction of the Circumcision) see J. M. Greenstein, *Mantegna and Painting as Historical Narrative* (Chicago, 1992).

72. For the quotations, see below, letters #9 (to Porto) and 26 (to Carafa).

73. The original text reads: "El che sperar volgo, se per Vostro Carità la mia Patrona et Stella serà pregata, facendogli di me qualche sigurta et promissione." Andreu, *Le lettere*, 16. See also below, letter #2.

74. See below, letter #5. One historian recently argued that citizens in Venice generally sought individual intimacy with saints and the Virgin Mary in their own neighborhoods. If true, Gaetano might simply represent a more educated example of the same desire. See E. Muir, "The Virgin on the Street Corner: The Place of the Sacred in Italian Cities," in S. Ozment, ed., *Religion and Culture in the Renaissance and Reformation* (Kirksville, Mo., 1989), 25–40.

75. The literature on women in this era is enormous, so I will cite primarily collections of essays in English. For the medieval background, see R. Bridenthal and C. Koonz, eds., *Becoming Visible: Women in European History* (Boston, 1977), esp. 90–118; R. Blumenthal-Kosinski and T. Szell, eds., *Images of Sainthood in Medieval Europe* (Ithaca, 1991), esp. 199–221; and C. Klapisch-Zuber, ed., *A History of Women in the West*, vol. 2: *Silences of the Middle Ages* (Cambridge, 1992). For the early-modern era, see Bridenthal and Koonz, *Becoming*, esp. 137–91; Zarri, "Le sante vive"; M. W. Ferguson, et al., eds., *Rewriting the Renaissance: The Discourses of Sexual Difference in Early Modern Europe* (Chicago, 1986); F. Pasqualone, ed., *La famiglia e la vita quotidiana in Europa dal '400 al '600: Fonti e problemi* (Rome, 1986), 277–93; Schulte van Kessel, *Women and Men*, esp. 17–90 and 213–23; G. Zarri "La vita religiosa femminile tra devozione e chiostro: testi devoti in

NOTES

volgare editi tra il 1475 e il 1520," in *I frati minori tra '400 e '500* (Perugia, 1986), 125–68; S. Marshall, ed., *Women in Reformation and Counter-Reformation Europe* (Bloomington, 1989); L. L. Coon, et al., eds., *That Gentle Strength: Historical Perspectives on Women in Christianity* (Charlottesville, Va., 1990), esp. 79–96, 149–75; M. L. King, *Women of the Renaissance* (Chicago, 1991); O. Niccoli, ed., *Rinascimento al femminile* (Rome-Bari, 1991); and N. Z. Davis and A. Farge, eds., *A History of Women in the West*, vol. 3: *Renaissance and Enlightenment Paradoxes* (Cambridge, 1993).

76. See R. Trexler, "Le Célibat à la fin du Moyen Age: les religieuses de Florence," *Annales: Economies-Sociétés-Civilisations* 27 (1972):1329–50; J. Kirshner, "Pursuing Honor while Avoiding Sin: The *Monte delle Doti* of Florence," *Quaderni di "Studi Senesi"* 41 (1978):177–258; J. Kirshner and A. Molho, "The Dowry Fund and the Marriage Market in Early Quattrocento Florence," *JMH* 50 (1978):403–38; idem, "Il Monte delle Doti a Firenze dalla sua fondazione nel 1425 alla metà del sedicesimo secolo: abbozzo di una ricerca," *Ricerche storiche* 10 (1980):21–47; E. Cattaneo, "Le monacazioni forzate fra Cinque e Seicento," in G. Vigorelli, et al., eds., *Vita e processo di suor Virginia Maria de Leyva monaca di Monza* (Milan, 1985), 145–95; King, *Women*, 81–84; and J. K. Brackett, "The Florentine *Onestà* and the Control of Prostitution, 1403–1680," *SCJ* 24 (1993):273–300.

77. For analysis of women in sixteenth- and seventeenth-century convent life, covering the themes and issues related in this and the next two paragraphs, see P. Paschini, "I monasteri femminili in Italia nel '500," in *Problemi di vita religiosa in Italia nel Cinquecento* (Padua, 1960), 31–60; R. Creytens, "La riforma dei monasteri femminili dopo i decreti Tridentini," in *Il Concilio di Trento e la riforma Tridentina* (Rome, 1965), 45–84; Russo, *I monasteri*, 72–113; Brown, *Immodest Acts*; G. Zarri, "Monasteri femminili e città (secoli XV–XVIII)," in Chittolini and Niccoli, *Storia d'Italia, Annali 9*, 359–429; V. Di Flavio, "I monasteri femminili della diocesi di Rieti nella visita apostolica del 1573–74. Il punto sulla riforma," *RSCI* 43 (1989):145–65; O. Niccoli, "The End of Prophecy," *JMH* 61 (1989):667–82; and C. Harline and E. Put, "A Bishop in the Cloisters: The Visitation of Mathias Hovius (Malines, 1596–1620)," *SCJ* 22 (1991):611–39. For women and their literary pursuits, see Kagan, *Lucretia's Dreams*; R. E. Surtz, *The Guitar of God: Gender, Power and Authority in the Visionary World of Mother Juana de la Cruz* (Philadelphia, 1990); A. Weber, *Teresa of Avila and the Rhetoric of Femininity* (Princeton, 1990); and M. F. Rosenthal, *The Honest Courtesan: Veronica Franco, Citizen and Writer in Sixteenth-Century Venice* (Chicago, 1992). On religious women and food, see Bell, *Holy Anorexia*; Bynum, *Holy Feast*; and I. P. Culianu, "A Corpus for the Body," *JMH* 63 (1991):61–80.

78. For the "bigots," see A. De Spirito, "L'esperienza mistica femminile nel Mezzogiorno. Il caso della 'divota' Diana Margiacco di Benevento (1592–1629)," in *Il Concilio di Trento nella vita spirituale e culturale del Mezzogiorno tra XVI e XVII secolo*, 2 vols., ed. G. De Rosa and A. Cestaro (Venosa, 1988), 1:211–41. On Negri and the action against her, see Zarri, "Le sante vive," 397–424; A. Erba, "Il 'caso' di

NOTES

Paola Antonia Negri nel Cinquecento italiano," in Schulte van Kessel, *Women and Men*, 193–211; and Firpo, "Paola Antonia Negri," 47–65.

79. On women and their relationships with confessors and on the *divine madre* image, see Erba, "Il 'caso,' " 194–201; A. Prosperi, "Dalle 'divine madre' ai 'padre spirituali,' " in Schulte van Kessel, *Women and Men*, 71–90; R. Guarnieri, " 'Nec domina nec ancila, sed socia': tre casi di direzione spirituale tra Cinque e Seicento," in Schulte van Kessel, *Women and Men*, 111–32; J. Bilinkoff, *The Avila of St. Teresa: Religious Reform in a Sixteenth-Century City* (Ithaca, 1989), 96–107; R. M. Bell, "Telling Her Sins: Male Confessors and Female Penitents in Catholic Reformation Italy," in Coon, *Gentle Strength*, 118–33; A. J. Schutte, "Subalternità e potere: una chiave di lettura per l'autobiografia di Cecilia Ferrazzi," in C. Ferrazzi, *Autobiografia di una santa mancata, 1609–1664*, ed. A. J. Schutte (Bergamo, 1990), 103–13; J. Bilinkoff, "A Spanish Prophetess and Her Patrons: The Case of María de Santo Domingo," *SCJ* 23 (1992):17–30; and J. Bilinkoff, "Confessors, Penitents and the Construction of Identities in Early-Modern Avila," in *Culture and Identity in Early Modern Europe: Essays in Honor of Natalie Zemon Davis* (Ann Arbor, Mich., 1994). I am indebted to Jodi Bilinkoff, who kindly permitted me read and cite the latter work in its pre-publication form.

80. See below, letters #9 and 11.

81. The very sketchy and basic information we possess on Scupoli and his early life can be found in the introductions to any number of the editions of *Il combattimento spirituale*. For the most recent, which includes a helpful bibliographical note, see B. Mas, "Introduzione," in Lorenzo Scupoli, *Combattimento spirituale*, ed. B. Mas (Rome, 1992), 7–59. See also Vezzosi, *I scrittori*, 2:276–301.

82. *AGT*, Acta capitulorum generalium, Anno 1569; see also Mas, "Introduzione," 9.

83. On Avellino, see *Analecta Bollandiana* 41 (1923):139–48; and the excellent article in *DS*, s.v. "André Avellino," by G. De Luca. The latter includes substantial bibliographical references.

84. The *DS* article on Avellino provides a guide to his writings. He composed approximately three thousand letters, some of which are published in a two-volume edition: *Lettere scritte del glorioso san Andrea Avellino a diversi suovi devoti* (Naples, 1731–32). His other works, like *Esercizio spirituale*; *Esposizione del Pater, dell' Ave Maria, della Salve Regina*; *Trattato sopra le parole dell' Apostolo nel III capo a i Colossensi*; *Breve compendio della materia dell' Epistola di San Paolo alli Romani*; *Trattato dell'umilta*, and more are found in his *Opere diverse*, 5 vols. (Naples, 1733–34).

85. The most recent work on Borromeo in English is found in the form of a collection of essays: Headley and Tomaro, *San Carlo Borromeo*.

86. AGT, *Acta capitulorum generalium*, Anno 1585: "Che Don Lorenzo d'Otranto si tenga in carcere per tutto quest'anno, e nell'altro Capitolo seguente si dia ultima sententia nella sua causa come meglio sarà giudicato." See also, *DS*, s.v. "Scupoli, Laurent," by B. Mas; Mas, "Introduzione," 10–11; Vezzosi, *I scrittori*, 2:277–78.

NOTES

87. Mas, "Introduzione," 15.

88. On these early editions see Vezzosi, *I scrittori*, 2:280–85, and Mas, "Introduzione," 14–15.

89. On editions from 1610 to 1775, see Vezzosi, *I scrittori*, 286–301; for the false attributions, see Mas, "Introduzione," 20–1.

90. *DTC*, s.v. "Scupoli, François," by J. Mercier; *DS*, s.v. "Scupoli, Laurent," by B. Mas.

91. The Orthodox version is now available in English translation: *Unseen Warfare*, trans. E. Kadloubovsky and G.E.H. Palmer (Crestwood, N.Y., 1987). For more on Nicodemus, see *DS*, s.v. "Nicodème l'Hagiorite."

92. *The Spiritual Combat and a Treatise on Peace of the Soul*, trans. W. Lester and R. Mohan (Rockford, Ill., 1990). The quotations come from the cover of the paperback edition. The 1992 Italian edition is Scupoli, *Combattimento spirituale*, ed. B. Mas.

93. See below, *The Spiritual Combat*, Chaps. 9 and 63; and *Addition*, Chaps. 22, 27 and 28.

94. For just two of the many examples of Scupoli's allusions to the passion, see below, *The Spiritual Combat*, Chaps. 16 and 23. For the material quoted here from the parables, see below, *Addition*, Chap. 33.

95. For these descriptions, see below, *The Spiritual Combat*, Chaps. 22, 46, 51 and 52; and *Addition*, Chap. 34.

96. For Scupoli's use of Marian themes, see below, *The Spiritual Combat*, Chaps. 23, 48 and 49. Bartolomeo Mas considered the description of Mary as one who assisted those in spiritual battle against the passions as the characteristically Theatine contribution to Mariology. See his "La spiritualità," 190–93.

97. See below, *The Spiritual Combat*, Chaps. 1 and 2, *Addition*, Chap. 10.

98. See below, letter #31.

99. For these quotations, see below, *The Spiritual Combat*, Chaps. 24 and 18.

100. See below, *The Spiritual Combat*, Chaps. 1 and 2.

101. See below, *The Spiritual Combat*, Chaps. 13 and 19.

102. See below, *The Spiritual Combat*, Chaps. 33, 40, 63.

103. See below, *The Spiritual Combat*, Chaps. 44, 46, 49.

104. See below, *The Spiritual Combat*, Chaps. 13, 14, 29.

105. Most recently, Bartolomeo Mas asserted Scupoli's commitment to the concept of human free will. See his "Introduzione," 29–31. For the quotations contained in this paragraph, see below, *The Spiritual Combat*, Chap. 32. Cf. also Chap. 20.

106. John Olin, for example, noted one of the themes forgotten in Ignatian spirituality due to overemphasis upon its military images. See his "The Idea of Pilgrimage in the Experience of Ignatius Loyola," *CH* 48 (1979):387–97.

107. Ignatius Loyola, *Spiritual Exercises*, 60–61; Ganss, *Ignatius of Loyola*, 154–56.

108. See below, *The Spiritual Combat*, Chaps. 1, 24, 34, and 35.

NOTES

109. The ascetic and mystical elements of Theatine spirituality and the history behind them are considered in a recent article: Andreu, "Camaldolesi e teatini." Cf. also Andreu, "La spiritualità," 158–59. It is clear that early Theatines were less focused upon charitable, apostolic works than some of the other new orders of the sixteenth century, like the Jesuits. Their decision to retain the divine office in choir limited the amount of charitable activity possible. See G. Bottereau, "Le 'lettere' d'Ignace de Loyola a Gian Pietro Carafa," *Archivum Historicum Societatis Iesu* 44 (1975):139–52.

110. For the quotation from Scupoli, see below, *The Spiritual Combat*, Chap. 21. For the comparable exercise recommended by Ignatius, see Puhl, ed., *The Spiritual Exercises*, 101–3.

111. See below, *The Spiritual Combat*, Chap. 48.

112. See below, *The Spiritual Combat*, Chap. 55; and *Addition*, Chap. 24.

113. For these quotations, see below, *The Spiritual Combat*, Chaps. 1, 10, 12 and 14.

114. 2 Tim. 2:3–5; Gal. 5:17; Eph. 6:14–17.

115. For more on Scupoli's sources, see Mas, "Introduzione," 26–27, 32, 41–46; Mas, "La spiritualità," 181–204; F. de Ros, "Aux Sources du *Combat Spirituel*: Alonso de Madrid et Laurent Scupoli," *RAM* 39 (1954):117–39; and Andreu, "La spiritualità," 157–61. For a recent article hinting at the wide-ranging patristic sources behind medieval and early-modern spiritual writings, see B. McGinn, "Love, Knowledge and Mystical Union in Western Christianity: Twelfth to Sixteenth Centuries," *CH* 56 (1987):7–24. That background picture will be filled in as McGinn completes the publication of his four-volume series entitled *The Presence of God: A History of Western Christian Mysticism*. Volume I has already appeared: *The Foundations of Mysticism* (New York, 1991). Another recent study describing the medieval and northern European sources of sixteenth-century devotional literature, specifically on meditation, is K. Erdei, *Auf dem Wege zu sich selbst: Die Meditation im 16. Jahrhundert* (Wiesbaden, 1990).

116. See below, *The Spiritual Combat*, Chap. 52.

117. For the quotations in this paragraph, see below, *The Spiritual Combat*, "Dedication," and Chaps. 25, 43 and 55.

118. These counsels can be found in *The Spiritual Combat*, Chaps. 13 and 45.

119. See below, *The Spiritual Combat*, Chap. 55.

120. See below, *The Spiritual Combat*, Chap. 48. For more on the metaphors utilizing images of food and transformation, as well as language with sexual overtones, in writings by and about late-medieval religious women, see Bynum, *Holy Feast*, 113–86, and consult the notes to the previous section of this introduction on Gaetano and his relationships with female correspondents.

121. See below, *The Spiritual Combat*, Chaps. 8, 12, 23, 41, and 59.

122. See below, *The Spiritual Combat*, Chap. 21.

123. Cf. Rosenthal, *Honest Courtesan*, 191–92.

124. Moroni, *Dizionario*, 73:31–109.

NOTES

125. A woman who served as abbess of the Pescian convent, Benedetta Carlini, underwent an inquisitorial investigation; the records are the subject of a controversial analysis. See Brown, *Immodest Acts*, 29–41. Early Jesuits often had to correct the misperception that their mode of operation connected them directly with the Theatines. See O'Malley, *First Jesuits*, 68–69, 81–82.

126. For a study that provides an example of another sixteenth-century theory of language reminiscent of that employed by these Theatines, see Campbell, "Nicolas Caussin." Campbell's work relies on the overviews of Augustinian and Renaissance language theory provided by Tzvetan Todorov and Walter Ong, respectively. Cf. T. Todorov, *Theories of the Symbol*, trans. by C. Porter (Ithaca, 1982), 15–59; and the works of W. J. Ong, especially *The Presence of the Word: Some Prolegomena for Cultural and Religious History* (New Haven, 1967), 17–110; and *Interfaces of the Word: Studies in the Evolution of Consciousness and Culture* (Ithaca, 1977), 121–44. For some powerfully argued and fascinating reflections on the incarnational and sacramental focus of early-modern religiosity, see J. W. O'Malley, *Praise and Blame in Renaissance Rome: Rhetoric, Doctrine and Reform in the Sacred Orators of the Papal Court, c. 1450–1521* (Durham, NC, 1979), 123–64; and L. Steinberg, *The Sexuality of Christ in Renaissance Art and in Modern Oblivion* (New York, 1983).

127. For a general work that suggests ambivalence characterized the overall approach toward women in Christian culture, see M. R. Miles, *Carnal Knowing: Female Nakedness and Religious Meaning in the Christian West* (Boston, 1989).

Notes to Rule of [Gian Pietro] Carafa

1. This translation is made from the text found in Paul A. Kunkel, *The Theatines in the History of Catholic Reform Before the Establishment of Lutheranism* (Washington, D.C.: Catholic University Press, 1941), 166–70. The numbering of sections is that of Kunkel and is not found in the original letter. I have introduced paragraphs to facilitate reading the text.

2. 1 Cor. 14:40.

3. That is, the bishop of the diocese in which the community is situated.

4. Jn. 1:46.

5. This is my rendition of the puzzling genitive *Loci* of the text. A *locus* can mean a prebend, that is, a stipend allotted to a particular cleric from ecclesiastical revenues, something that the Theatines allowed as we see in I.

6. Mt. 16:24. The Kunkel text is defective here in leaving out a portion of the quotation.

7. This appears to be a general reference to the *Rule of St. Augustine*, the traditional basis for the canonical life renewed by the Theatines.

NOTES

Notes to Letters *of St. Gaetano da Thiene (St. Cajetan)*

1. The "holy food" to which he referred is the Eucharist, of course. Gaetano had recently been ordained a priest and apparently said Mass that day in St. Peter's Basilica. Andreu, *Le lettere*, 12.

2. Here Gaetano referred to his mother, Maria da Porto, who died in 1520. See also letter #7, below.

3. The spiritual brother was Bartolomeo Stella (1488–1554), whose description of Laura and her convent in Brescia led Gaetano to initiate the correspondence. Stella later came to know Filippo Neri and Ignatius of Loyola, and he served for many years as secretary to Reginald Pole.

4. Here Gaetano paraphrased words attributed to Jesus, but the sense in English is better maintained with a direct quotation. Cf. Mt. 10:34–36; Lk. 12:49–53.

5. Lk. 1:48.

6. According to tradition, St. Jerome (c. 345–419/20) settled in Bethlehem in 386, died there, and was interred in the grotto where Jesus was born. His bones were transferred to the crypt of Santa Maria Maggiore in Rome.

7. Gaetano here paraphrased Gospel accounts of the words of Jesus in the garden and on the cross. Cf. Mt. 26:39; Mk. 14:36; Lk. 22:42 and Lk. 23:34.

8. This seems to be a reference to Gaetano himself as her "father," or "priest."

9. The imagery here recalls the parable of the ten virgins, not to mention the concept of mystical marriage. Cf. Mt. 25:1–13.

10. Undoubtedly "him" in this sentence referred to Bartolomeo Stella and not to Christ.

11. This appears to be a reference to some indulgence that might be attached to the monastery and its devotions.

12. The cardinal referred to here was Giambattista Pallavicino. The bishop of Cavillon in southern France, he was made a cardinal in the first promotion under Leo X (23 September 1513) and died on 13 August 1524. The author of the most recent critical edition of the letters of Gaetano considered the remarks in this paragraph on "works" to be oblique references to the indulgence controversy sparked by Luther in the previous year. The judgment seems quite reasonable, especially in light of the contents of the rest of the letter. Cf. Andreu, *Le lettere*, 19.

13. Among these "few," according to Andreu, would be Catherine of Genoa, with whose teaching Gaetano was certainly familiar. Ibid.

14. The language Gaetano used here is reminiscent of passages in the letter of James that state that "faith without works is dead." Cf. Jas. 2:14–17, 26.

15. Here Gaetano referred to Monica, the mother of St. Augustine, and, apparently, to others like himself who are related to her by following the rule of St. Augustine—that is, other canons regular. Cf. Andreu, *Le lettere*, 21.

NOTES

16. Pallavicino had apparently obtained a brief sought by Gaetano from the monastery of Santa Croce. Cf. ibid., 20.

17. The illness he apparently contracted was a venereal disease. Beginning in 1520 he worked at a hospital for "incurables" in Brescia as part of his action in establishing an oratory of Divine Love in that city. Andreu suggests that the incurable disease in question was syphilis. Cf. ibid., 24. The suggestion certainly helps explain Gaetano's apparent unease in writing this letter to Laura.

18. Apparently, among Bartolomeo's associates at the hospital.

19. A quotation here from the Gospel story of the wedding feast at Cana. Cf. Jn. 2:1–11.

20. He was apparently considering the possible purchase of some Roman curial office.

21. A reference here to the Gospel story of the rich young ruler. Cf. Mt. 19:21; Lk. 18:22.

22. An attestation proclaiming the authenticity of the letter in the absence of a signature was added to the manuscript by Bernardino Faino in 1659. Cf. Andreu, *Le lettere*, 27–28.

23. Ps. 13:3 (12:4 in Vulgate edition).

24. The cardinal, once again, was Giambattista Pallavicino. The *Agnus Dei*, a sacramental approved by the Catholic Church, is a wax oval, bearing on one side the image of the paschal lamb with the inscription "Behold the lamb of God who takes away the sins of the world" (Jn. 1:29), and on the other the image of one or more saints, or the coat of arms of the pope then in power. The name of the pope and the date of issue are inscribed at the bottom. The origin of its use may go back to the fourth century, but more probably to the ninth, when the archdeacon of the Lateran basilica in Rome would, each Holy Saturday, break the Easter candle of the previous year, melt it down, mix it with oil, and form ovals for blessing. The impressions were distributed to the faithful on the octave of Easter. Paul II (1464–1471) used sacred chrism in the mixture, and this rite was reserved to the popes in the first year of their pontificates, and in every seventh year thereafter, in addition to jubilee years. Late in the sixteenth century, under Clement VIII (1592–1605), the disks came to be distributed through Cistercian confessors at the church of Santa Croce in Gerusalemme, in Rome.

25. Andreu and others argue that on the basis of the contents and tone of the letter, the loss of Gaetano's mother must have been recent. She reportedly died on 2 November 1520, hence this letter must have been written toward the end of the same month. Cf. Andreu, *Le lettere*, 32–33.

26. St. Rocco (or St. Roch, c.1350–c.1380) was the son of a rich merchant family in Montpellier and spent much of his life on pilgrimage. He visited the plague-stricken in towns throughout Italy. He allegedly contracted the illness himself in Piacenza and was fed by a dog in the wilderness. The date and place of his death are uncertain, but miraculous cures experienced by plague sufferers were

attributed to his intercession. Franciscans venerate him as a tertiary, but there is no evidence to confirm this.

27. The reference here is to Jerónimo de la Lama, a Spanish priest who had apparently become friends with Gaetano in Venice and was probably a member of the Roman Oratory. Cf. Andreu, *Le lettere*, 35–36.

28. Elisabetta was Gaetano's niece, the daughter of his brother Battista Thiene and Elisabetta de' Chiericati. Despite the apprehensions Gaetano expressed in letter #5 above, he was able to arrange a marriage for her and to provide a dowry of 4550 gold ducats. She married Giovanni da Porto in April 1521. The dotal document itself is published in De Maulde la Clavière, *San Gaetano*, 242–44.

29. For the Gospel story of the visit of Mary to Elizabeth, cf. Lk. 1:39–56.

30. He urged Elisabetta to confession with his own spiritual director, Battista Carioni da Crema, a Dominican from the convent of Santa Corona in Vicenza.

31. Paolo Giustiniani (1476–1528) was a prominent Venetian nobleman who, along with his friend Vincenzo Querini (1479–1514), joined the strict Camaldolese order in 1510. They participated in the widespread clerical call for ecclesiastical reform and together drafted the famous reform memorandum entitled *Libellus ad Leonem X*. The text is in *Annales Camaldulenses*, ed. J. B. Mittarelli and A. Costadoni, 9 vols. (Venice, 1755–73), 9:612–719. Both of them, along with their friend Gasparo Contarini (1483–1542), as well as Gaetano himself, were students at the University of Padua in the first years of the sixteenth century, but it is unknown whether the three Venetians met Gaetano at that time. Giustiniani apparently invited Gaetano, whom he had heard about through relatives, to join the Camaldolese reform movement. Gaetano responded with the letter translated here. For more on Giustiniani, see A. Fiori, *Vita del B. Paolo Giustiniani istitutore della Congregazione dei PP. ermiti camaldolese* (Rome, 1729); P. Lugano, *La congregazione Camaldolese degli eremiti di Montecorona* (Rome-Frascati, 1908); J. Leclercq, *Un humaniste erémite: le bienheureux Paul Giustiniani* (Rome, 1951); H. Jedin, "Contarini und Camaldoli," *Archivio italiano per la storia della pietà* II (1960):51–117; and N. H. Minnich and E. G. Gleason, "Vocational Choices: An Unknown Letter of Pietro Querini to Gasparo Contarini and Niccolò Tiepolo (April, 1512)," *CHR* 75 (1989):1–20.

32. Cf. Lk. 10:25–37.

33. Himself, that is.

34. John Cassian (c. 365- c. 435) wrote two texts: *De institutis coenobiorum et de octo principalium vitiorum remediis libri XII*, and *Collationes XXIV*. These can be found in *PL*, 49:53–1328. The first text is probably the one referred to by Gaetano. A selection from the second text, the "Conferences," has been published in this series: J. Cassian, *Conferences*, trans. C. Luibheid, The Classics of Western Spirituality (Mahwah, N.J., 1985).

35. The reference to fire, common in Gaetano, here refers to the idea that Jesus came to "send fire" upon the earth. Cf. Lk. 12:49, and above, letter #2.

36. The brother-in-law was Benedetto Gabrielle, a collaborator in the

NOTES

Theatine work for the *incurabili*, who died on 8 November 1523. Given the adjective *magnifico*, which Gaetano applies to him twice in this letter, plus the fact that Gaetano, as director of the hospital, presided over Gabrielle's funeral, it seems reasonable to assume that he was an important patron of the institution. Cf. Andreu, *Le lettere*, 54.

37. Gaetano suggested a comparison here to Christ weeping over Jerusalem—Lk. 19:41–44; cf. also Mt. 23:37–39 and Lk. 13:34–35.

38. By quoting here from the Gospel of John, Gaetano compared these nobles to the apostles, still fearful and hiding, even after the Resurrection. Cf. Jn. 20:19.

39. Here Gaetano is referring to the "spiritual" circumcision he wished for Giustiniani at the beginning of the letter.

40. Ferdinando and Girolamo were the paternal cousins of Gaetano. Cf. Andreu, *Le lettere*, 58.

41. Jn. 18:36.

42. Mt. 6:24; Lk. 16:13.

43. That is, goods held without full right of ownership.

44. Another reference to the parable of the ten virgins. Cf. Mt. 25:1–13.

45. The Bernardo referred to was Bernardo da Todi, a self-proclaimed prophet who predicted the imminent end of the world on preaching tours throughout Italy, all without canonical permission. His name, of course, recalled that of his more famous fellow-citizen of Todi, Jacopone (d. 1306), the Spiritual Franciscan and mystical poet. The "father Bishop" whose advice Bernardo took was Carafa, who convinced him to give up the preaching. Bernardo joined the Theatine order at Venice, took the habit on 20 August 1529, and made his profession on 29 March 1531. He worked in the papal household of Paul IV and died in Rome on 30 November 1580.

46. Gaetano here provided a parenthetical footnote to the pertinent portions of canon law: Gratian's *Decretum*, Part I canon 12, Distinction 10; Part I canon 14, *de Haereticis*, Distinctions 5, 7. Cf. Andreu, *Le lettere*, 66.

47. All but the last phrase here come from Gospel passages: cf. Mt. 7:22–23; Mt. 25:12; Lk. 13:25–27.

48. Here Gaetano utilized the language of the "Dies Irae," formerly a sequence in the Roman missal for All Souls' Day, which has scriptural as well as medieval roots. For the scriptural roots, cf. Zeph. 1:14–15; 2:2–3; and Rom. 2:5–8. The sequence itself, probably of twelfth or thirteenth-century origin, was commonly attributed to the Franciscan Thomas of Celano (d. c. 1260), who was the first biographer of Francis of Assisi. Some historians have maintained, however, that the "author" only reworked a previously existing text. In its first section it contains forceful language about and vivid images of the Last Judgment, which many ascribe to the general apocalyptic mood of the age. The second section appeals to the mercy of Christ. It was accepted into the Roman Missal under Pius V, and was more frequently translated into the vernacular than any other sequence. The text was put to one of the most familiar melodies in all Gregorian

NOTES

chant. See M. Inguanez, "Il *Dies irae* in un codice del secolo XII," *Rivista liturgica* 18 (1931):277–87; K. Young, *The Drama of the Medieval Church*, 2 vols. (Oxford, 1933), 1:26, 187; and J. J. Jungmann, *The Mass of the Roman Rite: Its Origins and Development*, 2 vols, trans. Francis A. Brunner (New York, 1951), 1:439. For the complete text, see *Missale Romanorum ex decreto Sacrosancti Concilii Tridentini*, 2d ed. (Ratisbon, 1887), 78–79.

49. A paraphrasing here of Gospel passages concerning the day of judgment, all of which are linked to consideration of both genuine and false predictions of the end. Cf. Mt. 24:19–26; Mk. 13:17–23; Lk. 21:23.

50. Paolo Arigoni, a Venetian, took the name "Luca" after entering the Theatines. Little is known of him, except for brief notices in the records of the Theatines in Venice. He entered as a novice in Padua on 2 August 1529 and withdrew from the congregation on 21 April 1531. Cf. Andreu, *Le lettere*, 64–65; and Paschini, *S. Gaetano*, 89–96.

51. The reference here is to Stefano Bertazzoli, a priest from Salò, who was apparently close to the Scaini brothers. He graduated with the degree in both civil and canon law at Padua, was noted for his piety and hard work as a priest as well as for his teaching. He died in Salò, according to Andreu, when over the age of eighty. Cf. Andreu, *Le lettere*, x; see also Paschini, *S. Gaetano*, 88–89, 206–7; and F. Andreu, "Una lettera di G.P. Carafa a Stefano Bertazzoli," *RD* 3 (1947):53–59.

52. It is unclear who Gaetano was referring to with the pronoun "them" in this sentence, undoubtedly because of his reticence and due to the fact that the messenger would be returning to Bartolomeo. The messenger could relay Gaetano's message orally.

53. Beltrami family members were among the best supporters of the Theatine order in Venice. Andreu, *Le lettere*, 70; Paschini, *San Gaetano*, 193–94.

54. Andreu indicates that Gaetano hoped to found a press near the Theatine house in Venice for evangelical and anti-heretical purposes. He apparently invited the typographer Paganino Paganini (+1538) to Venice, promising him a staff of fourteen, made up of orphans and indigent persons already under Theatine care, and space in which to do the work, as is related in part in this letter. The outcome of the intended project is unknown. Andreu, *Le lettere*, 68–69; Paschini, *San Gaetano*, 95–96. The most recent studies of the Venetian printing industry in this period are C. Di Filippo Bareggi, *Il mestiere di scrivere: lavoro intellettuale e mercato librario a Venezia nel Cinquecento* (Rome, 1988), S. Pillinini, *Bernardino Stagnino: un editore a Venezia tra Quattro e Cinquecento* (Rome, 1989), and P. Grendler, *The Roman Inquisition and the Venetian Press, 1540–1605* (Princeton, 1977). In 1601 members of the Paganini firm were condemned, along with others from the Venetian printing industry, for errors in the Roman Missal they published in 1596. See Grendler, *Roman Inquisition*, 247.

55. Paolo Arigoni. Cf. above, letter #12.

56. Maria Carafa (1468–1552) was the older sister of Gian Pietro and became the founder and prioress of the Dominican convent called *Sapienza* in Naples. She

NOTES

and her brother attempted to run away from home to enter religious life on Christmas Eve, 1490. She succeeded, entering the Franciscan convent of San Sebastiano, but he did not. They also apparently shared a desire for ecclesiastical reform, as the Dominican convent she founded in 1530 followed a rigorous communal life and strict enclosure. When Gaetano left Venice in 1533 for Naples, he undertook direction of the convent, as both Gian Pietro and Maria desired. See Andreu, *Le lettere*, xxii–xxv, 71–72; G. M. Monti, *Ricerche su Papa Paolo IV* (Benevento, 1925), 201; F. Maggio, *Vita della Venerabile Madre Donna Maria Carafa* (Napoli, 1670), 373–74.

57. Andreu indicated that many indulgences and favors were granted to the *Sapienza*, especially through the intercession of Gian Pietro Carafa, and hence the specific one referred to here by Gaetano cannot be identified. Cf. Andreu, *Le lettere*, 72.

58. The words from Psalm 21(22) he probably was referring to are: "My God, my God, why hast thou forsaken me?" See also Mt. 27:46. The phrase he put in the letter comes from Lk. 23:46.

59. Gaetano's allusion here seems to be to three decades of the Rosary.

60. The confusion over the dating is due, according to Andreu, to the fact that Gaetano did not date the letter, and to the reference within it to the feast of St. Thomas the Apostle falling on a Monday. The feast is on 21 December, and that day was a Monday in just two years when Gaetano lived in Naples: 1534 and 1545. Cf. Andreu, *Le lettere*, 73.

61. Pastoral duties both inside and outside the community, it would appear, were going to keep Gaetano busy until then.

62. The date was again determined by Andreu on the basis of the calendar and internal evidence. Christmas fell on a Saturday in only two of the years Gaetano spent in Naples: 1535 and 1546. Cf. Andreu, *Le lettere*, 75.

63. Here Gaetano gave news of the illness of Gian Pietro Carafa, who had recently been called to Rome by Paul III to participate in the reform group that eventually drafted the famous *Consilium de emendanda ecclesia* (1537).

64. The brother of Gian Pietro was Gian Alfonso Carafa, count of Montorio. His wife was Caterina Cantelmo. Cf. Andreu, *Le lettere*, 76. Neither appear in the new standard Italian biographical dictionary, *DBI*.

65. Beatrice was Gian Pietro's sister, and the widow of Gianluigi della Leonessa. At her brother's suggestion she took up residence at the *Sapienza*. By the "other sisters" Gaetano probably intended Agnese and Costanza, other nuns in the monastery, and Giovanna, whom Carafa dissuaded from religious life. Agnese and Costanza were actually the daughters of Gian Pietro's nephew, Antonio Carafa (+1588), marquis of Montebello, the son of Gian Alfonso Carafa. See *DBI*, s.v. "Carafa, Antonio." Antonio and Giovanna are also referred to in the last paragraph of this letter. Cf. Andreu, *Le lettere*, 76–77.

66. Carafa hoped for a visit from a certain Gian Bernardino Fuscano, a Neapolitan and good friend.

NOTES

67. Catherine was the daughter of another nephew of Gian Pietro and count of Montorio, Ferrante Carafa. Cf. ibid. She was also the recipient of a letter from Gaetano, #24, below.

68. There are many scriptural quotations that refer to the wise and unfathomable thoughts and ways of God. For the ones that most closely resemble this one (*judicia Dei abissus*), cf. Ps. 92:5; Rom. 11:33.

69. Cf. Lk. 3:8.

70. The general of the order at the time was a cleric originally from Verona, Pietro Foscarini.

71. The document is a compendium of the advice given by Gaetano to the sisters of the convent, transcribed and abstracted by Maria Carafa, at the request of her nuns. Hence, the original manuscript is in the hand of Maria. Cf. Andreu, *Le lettere*, 84–86.

72. Here Gaetano used language suggestive of the words of Jesus on the secret rewards that may be expected in heaven for those who suffer and act justly here, from the Sermon on the Mount. Cf. Mt. 6:1–18. The words "in my Father's house are many rooms" are similarly evoked. Cf. Jn. 14:2–3.

73. The sub-prioress at that time was Giovanna Villani, who succeeded Maria as prioress in 1552 for two three-year terms. Cf. Andreu, *Le lettere*, 88.

74. The reference to a prioress other than Maria puzzled even Andreu. He suggested that Gaetano probably intended to write *sottopriora*. Andreu, *Le lettere*, 90.

75. He referred here to Cassandra Marchese (d. 1569) of Sannazzaro, and her relative, Aloisa. Little is known of the latter, but Cassandra entered the *Sapienza* in 1542 and was professed, taking the name of Elisabeth, in September 1544. Ibid., 89.

76. The first half of this phrase, "propitius esto mihi peccatori," is suggestive of Peter's response to the call of Jesus, as related in Lk. 5:1–11.

77. Gian Pietro Carafa.

78. Caterina (d. 1594) was the first-born daughter (and orphan) of Don Ferrante, the son of Alfonso Carafa, the count of Montorio. Her mother was Geronima Spinelli. Hence, Caterina was the grand-niece of both Gian Pietro and Maria Carafa. When Ferrante died, the child became a pawn in the dynastic dispute between Alfonso and his daughter-in-law for control of Montorio. For that reason, Maria took charge of her in 1535 (when Caterina was eight years old) at the *Sapienza*. She took vows in 1543, after renouncing her right to succession in favor of her grandfather. The dating of this letter is uncertain. Cf. Andreu, *Le lettere*, 92–94.

79. Cf. the Gospel story of Jesus teaching in the Temple: Lk. 2:41–52.

80. Some months after this, in February 1543, Caterina took the name "Maria Caterina" in her religious profession. Cf. Andreu, *Le lettere*, 93.

81. This appears to be another reference to Maria's ill-health. She probably related it with frequency in letters to Gaetano, if this letter and his other responses (see above, letters #17, 22 and 25) are any indication.

82. In this postscript, Gaetano referred to a controversy concerning parish administration after Theatines took up residence at San Paolo Maggiore in Naples in 1538. The clerics took it upon themselves to care for the spiritual needs of the parishioners despite the existence of a regularly appointed parish priest, Leonardo Angrisano. It seems clear that Gaetano believed the assumption of this apostolate at least undesirable, and perhaps counterproductive in relation to the other Theatine activities in Naples. During the reign of Gregory XIII (1572–85), the parish see was transferred elsewhere to alleviate the problem after the intervention of a Theatine cardinal, the archbishop of Naples, Paolo Burali D'Arezzo (+1578). Cf. Andreu, *Le lettere*, 98.

83. The original manuscript of this letter is unreadable, and only fragments of it are preserved. It was later sent to Theatine missionaries in Goa, where it is still kept in the cathedral church as a relic. Andreu transcribed the letter from an authenticated copy in the documents from Gaetano's investigation for sainthood. Cf. ibid., 100–2.

84. The person for whom Scaini requested the recommendation is unknown, but the office in question seems to have been a magistracy in Venice. Ibid., 100.

85. Antonio Prato, a Milanese member of the group, who made his profession in Venice on 14 October 1540 and died in Padua in 1600. Little else is known with certainty about him, although other Theatine documents seem to refer to him. Cf. ibid., 103.

86. Andreu estimated the date of this letter to be somewhere between mid-September 1545 and June 1546. He based this upon knowledge that Cecilia de Marinis (d. 1572) and a companion, Barbara (d. 1588), two Venetian noblewomen, visited Naples bearing a letter of introduction from Gian Pietro Carafa dated 15 September 1545. The two began their novitiate at the *Sapienza* in June 1546, and spent the rest of their lives there. Ibid., 105–6.

87. Andreu correctly assumes that Gaetano wrote this for an audience of his own Theatine followers, since he wrote another for the nuns of the *Sapienza* in Italian while this one is in Latin. Ibid., 107–9.

88. Acts 21:13.

89. In large part, Scupoli's *Spiritual Combat* reinforces and develops at greater length just these points.

90. Andreu suggested that it could have been 1535, but this is speculation. Cf. Andreu, *Le lettere*, 110–11.

91. Polisena Villani (d. 1558), who was earlier a nun at the convent of Sant'Anna di Nocera. In her religious profession at the *Sapienza* (November 1530), she took the name Giovanna. Apparently noted for her zeal and devotion, she succeeded Maria as prioress, from 1552 to 1555. Ibid., 111, 119–20.

92. Gaetano collaborated on a similar decision within his own order, affecting Marcantonio Flaminio. See below, letter #38.

93. With "doctor" ("*Medico*") capitalized, Gaetano seemed to suggest God, the "heavenly doctor." Indeed, the entire letter could be read symbolically, since in

NOTES

1543, Carafa sought and gained dispensation for Maria from the divine office and from regular fasting, in consideration of her health and responsibilities. Gaetano would certainly have been aware of the dispensation. Cf. Andreu, *Le lettere*, 115–16; see also Maggio, *Vita*, 202–5.

94. This was a yearly gift from the city of Naples to the monastery of *Sapienza*. Andreu, *Le lettere*, 116–17.

95. Gaetano seemed to be offering to provide the funds himself.

96. Apparently he judged his sins responsible for an illness. Andreu, *Le lettere*, 117.

97. This pithy, sharp response reflected Gaetano's anger over liturgical deviation. The monastery was to follow "Theatine" practice of the divine office, that is, recitation in a low, uninflected and non-musical chant. Dominican monasteries commonly utilized choral chant, and the nuns of the *Sapienza* were explicitly distinguishing themselves from that group. Cf. Andreu, *Le lettere*, 118–19.

98. Andreu considered this a lengthy fragment of a larger letter, given all the missing information and the fact that the paragraph seems to have been written in one long sentence. It is preserved only in the manuscript of the documents presented at Gaetano's canonization trial. Ibid., 120–21.

99. This is a reference to Peter's release from prison in Acts 12:5–12.

100. The authorship of this letter is the subject of some controversy. Earlier analysts, like Vezzosi and Carlo Bromato, attributed it to Gaetano, who may have written it on behalf of Gian Pietro Carafa. The original manuscript is signed by Carafa, and more recent historians, like Monti and Paschini, have suggested that he drafted it. Andreu included it in his critical edition of the letters of Gaetano without drawing any definite conclusion, and asserted instead, like Chiminelli before him, that Gaetano must have been at least partly responsible for its contents. Vezzosi, *I scrittori*, 2:343; C. Bromato, *Storia di Paolo IV, pontefice massimo*, 2 vols. (Ravenna, 1748–53), 1:225; Monti, *Ricerche*, 272; Paschini, *S. Gaetano Thiene*, p. 70; P. Chiminelli, *San Gaetano Thiene—Cuore della riforma cattolica* (Vicenza, 1948), 882; Andreu, *Le lettere*, 124–25. The original manuscript is in the Vatican Library: codex *Barberino latino* 5697, 40r–41r.

101. Marcantonio Flaminio (1498–1550), the celebrated lyric poet, who, in 1533, sought entry to the Theatine order. Cf. Kaminski, "Marcantonio Flaminio"; Paschini, *S. Gaetano*, 81–82; Andreu, *Le lettere*, 123–25.

102. Lk. 9:62. The qualification in the final phrase of the sentence can be found in the rules of other orders in the same period. Ignatius Loyola and other early Jesuits like Juan de Polanco, for example, created a set of recommendations concerning external necessities like food, clothing, and shelter in the Jesuit version of religious life with repeated qualifications that balance is needed, that common sense must inform decisions on matters such as fasting, and that, above all, the superior must look to the individual and apply recommendations with "discretion." For some particular instances of this practical and adaptable approach, see

NOTES

Part III of their *Constitutions*, which he entitled "The preservation and progress of those who are in probation": I. Loyola, *Constitutions*, 153–70.

103. Jn. 10:16.

104. Mt. 20:6.

105. Acts 2:45.

106. Gian Matteo Giberti, without whose knowledge, apparently, Flaminio made the request. Giberti would have told Flaminio, Gaetano believed, that admission under the conditions suggested in the letter was entirely inappropriate. Cf. Andreu, *Le lettere*, 124.

107. At that time, Gian Pietro Carafa.

108. From John's account of Jesus' farewell to his disciples: Jn. 16:22.

109. Most believe that Gaetano composed this prayer, based it upon a sermon of Bernard of Clairvaux (1090–1153) on the passion of Christ and on verses from Daniel, and encouraged its recitation during a civil war in Naples in 1547. Cf. Andreu, *Le lettere*, 131–33.

110. Dan. 9:19.

Notes to Il combattimento spirituale

1. 2 Cor. 3:5.

2. Cf. Mt. 11:30.

3. Cf. 2 Tim. 7–8.

4. Mt. 18:12–14; Lk. 15:4–7.

5. Cf. Lk. 15:8–10.

6. Cf. Mt. 12:22.

7. There is ambiguity in the final phrase, "e ne porga anco la mano per farlo." Some editors suggest that Scupoli's intention here was to indicate that the devotee must be willing to be aided by God. He may also have been instructing the reader to cooperate willingly in any action, if it would be done in true accord with the will of God. Cf. Spinelli, ed., *Il combattimento spirituale*, 44, note #1.

8. Cf. Mt. 6:22–23.

9. Cf. Col. 3:9–10.

10. The Italian term *mistura* carries a sexual connotation from its Latin form (also *mistura*). It means carnal intercourse.

11. Cf. 1 Cor. 13:3.

12. This paragraph contains terminology and rhetoric reminiscent of two elements in Ignatian spirituality: the "First principle and foundation," and the meditation on "The call of an earthly king." Cf. I. Loyola, *Spiritual Exercises*, 12, 43–45.

13. Gen. 1:26–28.

14. 1 Pet. 1:18–19.

NOTES

15. There is an oxymoron operating here in the original Italian: "inestimabile stima."

16. Mt. 7:13–14.

17. Here Scupoli consciously rendered "warrior," a normally masculine noun (*guerriero*) in feminine form (*guerriera*) to suit his audience. The effect would be to describe the woman as a "holy Amazon."

18. The subject here, "simple women" (*femminucce*), carries a second meaning in Italian: "cowardly men."

19. The latter two elements in this description bear strong similarity to the Ignatian meditation on "Two standards." Cf. I. Loyola, *Spiritual Exercises*, 60–63.

20. Mt. 16:18.

21. Mt. 13:44–46; Phil. 3:7–8. The active role of all participants Scupoli identified here is worth noting—the devil and his forces, God and the heavenly host, and the individual.

22. In Chapter 13, that is.

23. This is an obvious allusion to the image of Jesus in the Garden of Gethsemane: Mt. 26:38; Mk. 14:34; Lk. 22:42–46. More specific reference to this New Testament image is made below, in Chapter 23.

24. The noun *persona* in this sentence could, theoretically, signify either male or female, but the pronouns standing as direct object to "love" and "consider" ("amar*la*" and "aver*la* cara") are distinctly feminine.

25. Cf. Mt. 13:12 and 25:29; Mk. 4:25; Lk. 8:18.

26. These "eighths" are usually rendered in English translations of *Il combattimento spirituale* as "quarters" of an hour, but this is misleading as well as imprecise. It fails to reflect the recognition Scupoli seems to reflect of the difficulty many encounter in mental prayer and the continual self-surveillance he recommended as a solution.

27. Cf. Mt. 25:1–13; Lk. 12:35–40; 1 Thess. 5:6; Rev. 19:7–8.

28. Scupoli here alluded to the parable of the talents (Mt. 25:14–30) and the parable of the pounds (Lk. 19:11–27).

29. Scupoli here recalled to his readers the final doxology of the Mass.

30. Here one was to insert the name of the desired virtue.

31. Cf. Mt. 27:22–23; Mk. 15:14; Lk. 23:21.

32. The word in the original is even stronger—*sterco*—"excrement."

33. The final phrase here—*se in terra vivrai innocentemente*—is ambiguous. It could suggest that the dwelling can be gained only if one lives "innocently" on earth, or that one could live "innocently" if maintaining focus on the heavenly dwelling.

34. Cf. 2 Tim. 4:7; Heb. 12:1–2.

35. Scupoli referred here to the three bells that typically signal the Angelus, the Marian devotion which commemorates the Incarnation by recalling the Annunciation (cf. Lk. 1:26–38). The precise origin of the devotion is disputed, but it seems an outgrowth of thirteenth- and fourteenth-century monastic practice of the

NOTES

recitation of three Hail Marys at specified times—morning, noon and evening—in different traditions. These three customs were unified in the sixteenth century and indulgences were attached to the practice by Benedict XIV (1740–58), Leo XIII (1878–1903), and Pius XI (1922–39).

36. Cf. Mt. 26:47–75; Mk. 14:32–72; Lk. 22:39–65; Jn. 18:1–27.

37. Cf. Mt. 27:1–2, 11–26, 31–32; Mk. 15:1–15, 20–21; Lk. 23:1–26; Jn. 18:28–40, 19:6–16. It is curious that in this passage Scupoli chose not to include consideration of the crowning with thorns and the scourging of Jesus, events that receive considerable development elsewhere, in Chapters 46 and 51, for example.

38. Cf. Lk. 2:35; Jn. 19:34.

39. Implied here, although not literally present in the text, is the idea that such activities are a distraction and waste of time.

40. With the final line in this paragraph, Scupoli evoked a passage in the Sermon on the Mount: Mt. 7:15–20; cf. Lk. 6:39–45.

41. Scupoli here suggested that it might lead to despair, the "unpardonable" sin.

42. Scupoli here used onomatopoeia—*Poi, poi, cras, cras*— to imply that the devil's suggestions mimic the sound of a crow.

43. Cf. 1 Pet. 5:6.

44. The final sentence in the quotation recalls the parable of the ten virgins—Mt. 25:1–13. It also provides evidence of Scupoli's conviction that both human action and the grace of God are necessary for spiritual growth and progress.

45. Cf. Ps. 115:1.

46. Cf. Mk. 10:18.

47. Scupoli seems here to be recalling for his readers the Gospel narratives on the healing of Bartimaeus (Mk. 10:46–52; cf. also Mt. 9:27–29 and 20:30–34) and of the lepers (Lk. 17:11–19).

48. The source of this story has not been identified.

49. Jn. 12:25 and Rom. 8:12–13, respectively.

50. The practice of general confession of all one's past sins with the intention of gaining self-knowledge and a firmer conversion to God may have originated in the *devotio moderna*. In the sixteenth century it was certainly spread widely by the Jesuit order after it was recommended by Ignatius in the *Spiritual Exercises*. See I. Loyola, *Spiritual Exercises*, 24, and O'Malley, *First Jesuits*, 137–39.

51. Here, Scupoli contradicted his statement in the "third" point of the previous chapter, number 33.

52. The first of these quotations is from a deuterocanonical book: Baruch 4:25. Since this book is not part of the *Revised Standard Version*, the translation is from *The Jerusalem Bible* (New York, 1966). The other four are Ps. 9:18; Prov. 16:32; Lk. 21:19; and Heb. 12:1, respectively.

53. A masculine ending is given here in the original for the word "soldier"—*soldato*.

54. See Chapter 19.

NOTES

55. And hence assist in developing a good habit.

56. This distinction between the voluntary evil of sin, which God permits, and the suffering that God wills positively to perfect the soul is traditional.

57. The two important nouns in this sentence, "warrior" and "baby," are deliberately feminine in the original: *guerriera* and *bambina*, respectively. The use of a feminine form of *guerriero* is especially unusual.

58. Here, and in the next paragraphs, are some good examples of how Scupoli, like Gaetano and the early Jesuits, believed physical mortifications could not be legislated in any comprehensive fashion. Such practices had to be employed carefully, with recognition of the individual's particular strengths and weaknesses.

59. He was referring most explicitly to Chapter 34. Variations on the topic are handled also in Chapters 35–40.

60. Cf. Mt. 7:1; Lk. 6:37; Rom. 2:1 and 14:10; 1 Cor. 4:3.

61. Here Scupoli called to mind the principles of judgment attributed to God in the letter to the Romans, 2:1–11.

62. Cf. Phil. 2:12.

63. Prayer is the fourth of the items he described as absolutely necessary for spiritual combat, in the very first chapter of the text.

64. The word *seno* that Scupoli used here carries even heavier feminine and maternal allusions: it can mean "womb" as well.

65. A host of scriptural passages are suggested in this paragraph: Jer. 29:12–13; Mt. 7:7–11; Jn. 14:16–17, 26; Jn. 15:7; Jn. 16:7, 23–24; 2 Cor. 1:21–22; 1 Jn. 3:21–22; 1 Jn. 5:14–15.

66. That is, nothing can take place which is not permitted by, and therefore pleasing to God.

67. Scupoli here recalls to the reader the parable of the widow and the unjust judge: Lk. 18:1–8.

68. Scupoli adds a phrase, *ed in tutte insieme*, which is difficult to translate succinctly in context. He is urging the reader to feel the pain sustained by Christ in each part of his body, and then somehow, to add them all up and imagine the pain as a whole.

69. Scupoli seemed here to be encouraging the reader to increase the depth and variety of her meditations, that is, to go below the surface and consider the attitudes and actions of Christ within each particular event of his passion and death.

70. See Chapter 46.

71. English readers would be confused in this paragraph by Scupoli's use of pronouns designed to distinguish three entities: the "soul of Christ," Jesus in the crucifixion, and God the father (or "divine essence"). I have provided nouns and pronouns here in the interest of clarity.

72. This person has not been identified.

73. Here Scupoli recalled to the reader an image from the Pauline epistles. Cf. Eph. 4:22–24 and Col. 3:9–10.

NOTES

74. These last two points contain the essence of one of the central meditations in the Jesuit *Spiritual Exercises*, the "Contemplation to attain divine love." See I. Loyola, *Spiritual Exercises*, 99–103. Cf. also O'Malley, *First Jesuits*, 45–46, 165.

75. With the phrase "fear and tremble" Scupoli probably hoped to evoke a number of scriptural passages, perhaps specifically (considering the audience) that Gospel story concerning the woman healed of a flow of blood (Mk. 5:25–34). Cf. also Jer. 33:9; 1 Cor. 2:3.

76. Cf. Rev. 3:5.

77. Jn. 6:56.

78. Scupoli here recalled the scriptural self-description of Wisdom, who delights in mankind. Cf. Prov. 8:31.

79. The allusion here, of course, is to the list of those sorts of persons whom Christ healed or forgave in the gospel narratives. Cf. Lk. 4:31–37; Lk. 5:12–16; Lk. 5:17–26; Lk. 7:36–50; Lk. 8:26–33; Lk. 13:10–17; Lk. 14:1–6; Lk. 17:11–19; Jn. 8:3–11.

80. Scupoli here made a distinction that was familiar to his contemporary readers but less familiar to twentieth-century readers: the distinction between sacraments and sacramentals. The latter are blessings, ceremonies or sacred objects, utilizing the prayer of the church. Some examples are the blessing and procession of palms, religious profession, consecration of virgins, consecration of holy oils, and even prayers for health or for rain. Some may resemble sacraments and are used according to the customs of the church, but are not believed to have been directly instituted by Christ. The distinction as presented in this part of the text is frequently lost in other English translations of *Il combattimento spirituale*. Cf. Lester and Mohan, *Spiritual Combat*, 168.

81. In the phrase "do violence to yourself," Scupoli used language loaded with sexual imagery. The primary meaning of *violentare* is "to rape, or violate." Another similar image is found above, in Chapter 55, concerning the "sweet violence" the devotee should undertake in order to compel Christ to enter her soul.

82. Scupoli recalled here the preparation described in Chapter 55 for sacramental communion.

83. Scupoli's language here was colorful and direct: *un cane morto*.

84. The pronoun Scupoli used here, which I have rendered as "you" is feminine: *ella*.

85. Scupoli made an interesting (and difficult to translate) choice of words in this paragraph. When referring to what the practitioner of this advice might become, he said, *ti diventerai di terrena, evangelica negotiatrice e felicissima*. This is further evidence of the convent audience he intended. In addition, one of the phrases that follows, *e Iddio sarà tuo*, indicates how seriously he apparently took the possibility of union with God on earth for his spiritual daughters.

86. Scupoli apparently intended for the reader to imagine her name being spoken at this point.

87. Here Scupoli repeated a point made earlier, in Chapter 47.

NOTES

88. Ps. 42:5–6; and Ps. 10:1, respectively.

89. Scupoli added this line, *Non me derelinquas usquequaque*, which does not appear in the Vulgate edition of Psalm 10. The most closely similar scriptural passages are Ps. 37:33 and Acts 2:27.

90. From the book of Tobit. This deuterocanonical book is not included in the *Revised Standard Version*, and in addition, the quotation Scupoli here employed was apparently taken from some edition of Tobit pre-dating the Council of Trent. The passage is not found in the Vulgate edition, or in modern Bibles containing editions of Tobit, like *The Jerusalem Bible*. Other modern editions of *Il combattimento spirituale* take a variety of approaches in handling this passage. Some explain its origin, others refer the reader incorrectly to the third chapter of Tobit, which contains the prayer of Sarah, although not at all in this form, while still others omit all reference to the problem.

91. Mt. 26:42.

92. Chapter 26, that is.

93. Scupoli likely assumed that his audience would read the adjective *virilmente* as "courageously," but the literal translation is important as well.

94. The final noun Scupoli chose here is feminine—*combattitrice*.

95. Those "following things" are covered in the last four chapters.

96. The first two phrases in this quotation come from Scripture: Mt. 16:23 and Jn. 8:44, respectively. This sentence contains one of the few direct references to the church and to the leadership of Rome in religious matters found in *Il combattimento spirituale*. It is also one of few places in the text where Scupoli referred obliquely to the doctrinal controversies of his age.

97. Scupoli here recalled to the reader the questioning of Jesus before Pilate. Cf. Jn. 18:38.

98. Cf. Ps. 17:8; Ps. 36:7.

99. Scupoli here recalled the image of the heavenly Jerusalem from the book of Revelation, chapter 21.

Notes to Aggiunta al combattimento spirituale

1. A classical aphorism.

2. Vergil, *Aeneid* 6.129.

3. Job 7:1.

4. Mt. 26:39 and Mt. 6:10, respectively.

5. Scupoli promoted complete indifference both to adverse, unpleasant things, and to enjoyable, pleasing things, including spiritual delights. He described this indifference as rejection of the desire to possess or not to possess anything unless God wills the possession. He referred to the goal of indifference frequently in his writings. For other examples, see *Il combattimento spirituale*, Chapters 10, 58 and 59; and *Aggiunta*, Chapters 1, 6, 16 and 26. His explanation is

NOTES

reminiscent of the "three classes of men" described by Ignatius of Loyola. See I. Loyola, *Spiritual Exercises*, 64–65.

6. Eccles. 1:2; 2:11.

7. Ps. 4:3.

8. The word I have rendered as "abhorrent" is even more graphic in the original: *puzzi* ("stinky").

9. Jas. 4:7. This is one of the few times in his works that one could argue Scupoli may have been alluding directly to a Protestant-Catholic controversy: that over the effectiveness (or lack thereof) in human actions directed toward God and salvation. The letter of James is one of the New Testament works that specifically states the importance of works (Jas. 2:14–17), and Luther rejected the letter as authentic Scripture in his 1520 treatise *The Babylonian Captivity of the Church*.

10. Scupoli used language here reminiscent of the gospel parable of the talents. Cf. Mt. 25:26.

11. Ps. 70:1; 38:22; 141:1.

12. Jn. 16:24; Mt. 7:7–8; cf. also Mk. 11:24.

13. The prayer from the previous chapter, that is.

14. These phrases all come, in one form or another, from the Psalms: cf. Ps. 5:8; 27:11; 118:12; 118:35.

15. Ex. 3:14.

16. ". . . and how inscrutable His ways." Rom. 11:33.

17. This quotation comes from St. Thomas's *Opusculum* 63. This was Scupoli's only direct reference to this Doctor of the Church, although some see other echoes of Thomas in his teachings on perfection, on the passion of Christ, and on the sensual appetites. The opuscules dealt with particular philosophical and theological questions, this one with an issue that was the subject of a great deal of Thomas's writing on the nature of God: the inability of human conceptions and words to understand His unlimited essence. The opuscules are available in a number of editions, such as T. Aquinas, *Opuscula omnia*, 5 vols., ed. P. Mandonnet (Paris, 1927). See also E. Gilson, *History of Christian Philosophy in the Middle Ages* (London, 1955), 368–72; and Mas, "Introduzione," 43.

18. Scupoli's language here was reminiscent of Luke 12:49.

19. Lk. 15:18–19.

20. A modern saying roughly equivalent to Scupoli's *Ante languorem adhibe medicinam*.

21. Ps. 136:9.

22. Another reference here to the parable of the lost son: Lk. 15:11–32.

23. Here Scupoli recalled the parable of the rich man and Lazarus: Lk. 16:19–31, especially verse 24.

24. Jer. 31:18.

25. There is perhaps no other passage in the entire work of Scupoli that demonstrates his tortured syntax better than this virtually indecipherable paragraph.

26. Jn. 19:5.

NOTES

27. Here Scupoli used the phrase *Cras, cras; Poi, poi*, as he did earlier, in Chapter 29 of *Il combattimento spirituale*.

28. In this paragraph, Scupoli appears to reinforce his suggestion that recommendations in the text could be employed by persons outside a monastic cloister. The suggestion that God "sees" twice refers, of course, to (first) his observance of all things in his infinite foreknowledge and (second) to his observance in the actual occasion. The necessary rendering of a "strict account" of actions is a conventional scriptural allusion: Mt. 18:23–35; Lk. 16:1–13; Rom. 14:12. Ignatius of Loyola and contemporary Jesuits also promoted the practice of frequent examination of conscience. Theirs was based upon recommendations in the *Spiritual Exercises* and legislative directives in the Jesuit *Constitutions*. See I. Loyola, *Spiritual Exercises*, 23–34; and I. Loyola, *Constitutions*, 158, 184–86.

Selected Bibliography

I. Principal primary sources

Archivum Generale dei Teatini, Rome, Italy. *Acta capitulorum generalium*.
Biblioteca Apostolica Vaticana, Vatican City. *Barberino latino, 5697*.
Le lettere di San Gaetano da Thiene. Ed. Francesco Andreu. Vatican City, 1954.
Scupoli, Lorenzo. *Il combattimento spirituale*. Ed. Carlo Di Palma. Rome, 1657.
———. *Il combattimento spirituale*. Ed. Mario Spinelli. Milan, 1985.
———. *Il combattimento spirituale*. Ed. Bartolomeo Mas. Rome, 1992.
———. *Opere*. Milan, 1830–31.
———. *The Spiritual Combat and a Treatise on Peace of Soul*. Trans. William Lester and Robert Mohan. Rockford, IL, 1990.
Unseen Warfare: The Spiritual Combat and Path to Paradise of Lorenzo Scupoli. Ed. Nicodemus of the Holy Mountain and Theophan the Recluse. Trans. E. Kadloubovsky and G.E.H. Palmer. Crestwood, NY, 1987.

II. Other primary sources

Avellino, Andrea. *Lettere scritte del glorioso San Andrea Avellino a diversi suovi devoti*. Naples, 1731–32.
———. *Opere diverse*. 5 vols. Naples, 1733–34.
Bullarum diplomatum et privilegiorum sanctorum romanorum pontificum, Taurinensis editio. 25 vols. Torino, 1857–67.
Carafa, Ioan Petrus. "De lutheranorum haeresi reprimenda et ecclesia reformanda ad Clementum VII." In *Concilium tridentinum*. 13 vols. Freiburg, 1901–38, 12:67–77. English translation available in Elisabeth G. Gleason, *Reform Thought in Sixteenth-Century Italy*. Ann Arbor, MI, 1981, 55–80.

SELECTED BIBLIOGRAPHY

Carioni, Battista (da Crema). *Della cognitione et vittoria di se steno*. Milan, 1531.

———. *La philosophia divina, ossia Historia de la passione del nostro Signore Gesù Cristo crucifixo et modo di contemplare quella per imitarla*. Milan, 1531.

———. *Lo speccio interiore*. Milan, 1540.

———. *Via di aperta verità*. Venice, 1523.

Consilium de emendanda ecclesia. In *Concilium tridentinum* 12:134–45. English translation available in John C. Olin, *The Catholic Reformation: Savonarola to Ignatius Loyola*. Westminster, MD, 1978; reprint ed. New York, 1993, 182–97.

Contarini, Gasparo. "De officio viri boni ac probi episcopi." In Gasparo Contarini, *Opera*. Paris, 1571, 399–431. English translation available in Olin, *The Catholic Reformation*, 90–106.

Flaminio, Marcantonio. *Lettere*. Ed. Alessandro Pastore. Rome, 1978.

Ignatius of Loyola. *The Constitutions of the Society of Jesus*. Trans. George E. Ganss. St. Louis, 1970.

———. *The Spiritual Exercises*. Ed. Louis J. Puhl. Chicago, 1951.

———. *Spiritual Exercises and Selected Works*. Ed. George E. Ganss. New York, 1991.

I Teatini. L'Inchiesta di Innocenzo X sui regolari in Italia. Vol. 1. Ed. Marcella Campanelli. Rome, 1987.

Missale Romanorum ex decreto Sacrosancti Concilii Tridentini. 2d ed. Ratisbon, 1887.

Rule of the Oratory of Divine Love (Genoa), 1497. In Pietro Tacchi Venturi, *Storia della Compagnia di Gesù in Italia*. 2 vols. Rome, 1910–22, 1:423–32. English translation available in Olin, *The Catholic Reformation*, 16–26.

Theatine Rule (1526). In Giuseppe Silos, *Historiarum clericorum regularium a congregatione condita*. 3 vols. Rome, 1650–1666. 1:73–75. English translation available in Olin, *The Catholic Reformation*, 127–32.

III. Secondary sources

Alberigo, Giuseppe. "Dinamiche religiose del Cinquecento italiano tra riforma, riforma cattolica, controriforma." *Cristianesimo nella storia* 6 (1985): 543–60.

———. *I vescovi italiani al Concilio di Trento*. Florence, 1959.

Andreu, Francesco. "La regola dei Chierici Regolari nella lettera di Bonifacio de' Colli a Gian Matteo Giberti." *Regnum Dei* 2 (1946): 38–53.

SELECTED BIBLIOGRAPHY

————. "La spiritualità degli ordini di Chierici Regolari." *Regnum Dei* 23 (1967): 154–83.

————. "Una lettera di G. P. Carafa a Stefano Bertazzoli." *Regnum Dei* 3 (1947): 53–59.

Aubert, Alberto. "Alle origini della controriforma: studi e problemi su Paolo IV." *Rivista di storia e letteratura religiosa* 22 (1986): 303–55.

Bagchi, David V.N. *Luther's Earliest Opponents: Catholic Controversialists, 1518–1525.* Minneapolis, MN, 1991.

Bell, Rudolph M. *Holy Anorexia.* Chicago, 1985.

Black, Christopher F. *Italian Confraternities in the Sixteenth Century.* Cambridge, 1989.

Blumenthal-Kosinski, Renate, and Timea Szell, eds. *Images of Sainthood in Medieval Europe.* Ithaca, NY, 1991.

Bottereau, Georges. "Le 'lettere' d'Ignace de Loyola a Gian Pietro Carafa." *Archivum Historicum Societatis Iesu* 44 (1975): 139–52.

Bridenthal, Renate and Claudia Koonz, eds. *Becoming Visible: Women in European History.* Boston, 1977.

Bromato, Carlo. *Storia di Paolo IV, pontefice massimo.* 2 vols. Ravenna, 1748–53.

Brown, Judith C. *Immodest Acts: The Life of a Lesbian Nun in Renaissance Italy.* New York, 1986.

Bynum, Caroline W. *Holy Feast and Holy Fast: The Religious Significance of Food to Medieval Women.* Berkeley, 1987.

Camillocci, Daniela Solfaroli. "Le confraternite del Divino Amore: interpretazioni storiografiche e proposte attuali di ricerca." *Rivista di storia e letteratura religiosa* 27 (1991): 315–32.

Caracciolo, Antonio. *De vita Pauli quarti pontificis maximi collectanea historica.* Cologne, 1612.

Carlino, Andrea. "L'Arciconfraternita di S. Girolamo della Carità: l'origine e l'ideologia assistenziale." *Archivio della società romana di storia patria* 107 (1984): 275–306.

Castaldo, Giovanni B. *Vita del B. Gaetano Tiene, fondatore della religione de chierici regolari.* Rome, 1612.

Chiminelli, P. *San Gaetano Thiene—Cuore della Riforma cattolica.* Vicenza, 1948.

Chittolini, Giorgio and Giovanni Miccoli, eds. *Storia d'Italia, Annali 9: La chiesa e il potere politico dal Medioevo all'età contemporanea.* Torino, 1986.

Cistellini, Antonio. *Figure della riforma pretridentina.* Brescia, 1948.

Città italiane del '500, tra riforma e controriforma. Lucca, 1988.

SELECTED BIBLIOGRAPHY

Cochrane, Eric. *Historians and Historiography in the Italian Renaissance.* Chicago, 1981.

———. *Italy, 1530–1630.* New York, 1988.

———. "New Light on Post-Tridentine Italy: A Note on Recent Counter-Reformation Scholarship." *Catholic Historical Review* 56 (1970): 291–319.

Collett, Barry. *Italian Benedictine Scholars and the Reformation: The Congregation of Santa Giustina of Padua.* Oxford, 1985.

Il Concilio di Trento e la riforma Tridentina. 2 vols. Rome, 1965.

Coon, Lynda L., et al., eds. *That Gentle Strength: Historical Perspectives on Women in Christianity.* Charlottesville, VA, 1990.

D'Amico, John F. *Renaissance Humanism in Papal Rome.* Baltimore, 1983.

Davis, Natalie Z., and Arlette Farge, eds. *A History of Women in the West, Volume 3: Renaissance and Enlightenment Paradoxes.* Cambridge, 1993.

De Guibert, Joseph. *La spiritualité de la Compagnie de Jésus: esquisse historique.* Rome, 1953. English ed. *The Jesuits: Their Spiritual Doctrine and Practice.* Trans. William J. Young. St. Louis, 1964.

De Maio, Romeo. "Un riformatore teatino nel Cinquecento: Girolamo Ferro." *Regnum Dei* 16 (1960): 3–58.

De Maulde La Clavière, R. *San Gaetano da Thiene e la Riforma cattolica italiana, 1480–1527.* Rome, 1911.

De Molen, Richard L., ed. *Religious Orders of the Reformation.* New York, 1993.

De Ros, Fidèle. "Aux Sources du *Combat Spirituel*: Alonso de Madrid et Laurent Scupoli." *Revue d'ascétique et mystique* 39 (1954): 117–39.

De Rosa, Gabriele and Antonio Cestaro, eds. *Il Concilio di Trento nella vita spirituale e culturale del Mezzogiorno tra XVI e XVII secolo.* 2 vols. Venosa, 1988.

Dickens, A. G., and J. M. Tonkin. *The Reformation in Historical Thought.* Cambridge, 1985.

Di Flavio, Vincenzo. "I monasteri femminili della diocesi di Rieti nella visita apostolica del 1573–74. Il punto sulla riforma." *Rivista di storia della chiesa in Italia* 43 (1989): 145–65.

Edwards, Mark U. *Luther's Last Battles: Politics and Polemics 1531–1546.* Ithaca, NY, 1983.

Eire, Carlos M.N. *War Against the Idols: The Reformation of Worship from Erasmus to Calvin.* New York, 1985.

Elliott, Dyan. *Spiritual Marriage: Sexual Abstinence in Medieval Wedlock.* Princeton, 1993.

SELECTED BIBLIOGRAPHY

Erdei, Klára. *Auf dem Wege zu sich selbst: Die Meditation im 16. Jahrhundert.* Wiesbaden, 1990.

Eremiti e pastori della riforma cattolica nel'Italia del '500. Fonte Avellana, 1983.

Fanti, Mario. *La chiesa e la compagnia dei poveri in Bologna: una istituzione di mutuo soccorso nella società bolognese fra il Cinquecento e il Seicento.* Bologna, 1977.

Ferguson, Margaret F., et al., eds. *Rewriting the Renaissance: The Discourses of Sexual Difference in Early Modern Europe.* Chicago, 1986.

Ferro, B. *Istoria delle missioni dei Chierici Regolari.* 2 vols. Rome, 1704–1705.

Firpo, Massimo. *Nel labirinto del mondo: Lorenzo Davidico tra santi, eretici, inquisitori.* Florence, 1992.

Firpo, Massimo, and Dario Marcatto, eds. *Il processo inquisitoriale del Cardinale Giovanni Morone.* 6 vols. Rome, 1981–95.

Fois, Mario. "Il contesto ecclesiastico ed ecclesiale italiano alla nascità dei Chierici Regolari." *Archivum Historiae Pontificiae* 27 (1989): 401–18.

Fortini, Laura. "Un trattato cinquecentesco sull' amore mistico: il 'Secretum meum mihi' di Paolo Giustiniani." *Rivista di storia e letteratura religiosa* 22 (1986): 241–55.

Fragnito, Gigliola. "Cardinals' Courts in Sixteenth-Century Rome." *Journal of Modern History* 65 (1993): 26–56.

———. "Evangelismo e intransigenti nei difficili equilibri del pontificato farnesiano." *Rivista di storia e letteratura religiosa* 25 (1989): 20–47.

I frati minori tra '400 e '500. Perugia, 1986.

Gleason, Elisabeth G. *Gasparo Contarini: Venice, Rome and Reform.* Berkeley, 1993.

Greenstein, Jack M. *Mantegna and Painting as Historical Narrative.* Chicago, 1992.

Hallman, Barbara M. *Italian Cardinals, Reform and the Church as Property.* Berkeley, 1985.

Harline, Craig. "Official Religion—Popular Religion in Recent Historiography of the Catholic Reformation." *Archiv für Reformationsgeschichte* 81 (1990): 239–62.

Headley, John M., and John B. Tomaro, eds. *San Carlo Borromeo: Catholic Reform and Ecclesiastical Politics in the Second Half of the Sixteenth Century.* Washington, 1988.

Hudon, William V. *Marcello Cervini and Ecclesiastical Government in Tridentine Italy.* DeKalb, IL, 1992.

———. "Two Instructions to Preachers From the Tridentine Reformation." *Sixteenth-Century Journal* 20 (1989): 457–70.

SELECTED BIBLIOGRAPHY

Impagliazzo, Mario. "I padri dell'Oratorio nella Rome della Controriforma (1595–1605)." *Rivista di storia e letteratura religiosa* 25 (1989): 285–307.

Jedin, Hubert. "Contarini und Camaldoli." *Archivio italiano per la storia della pietà* 2 (1960): 51–117.

———. *Geschichte des Konzils von Trient.* 5 vols. Freiburg, 1950–75.

———. *Katholische Reformation oder Gegenreformation?* Luzerne, 1946.

Jones, Pamela M. *Federico Borromeo and the Ambrosiana: Art Patronage and Reform in Seventeenth-Century Milan.* Cambridge, 1993.

Jorgensen, Kenneth J. "The Oratories of Divine Love and the Theatines: Confraternal Piety and the Making of a Religious Community." Ph.D. Diss., Columbia University, 1989.

Kagan, Richard L. *Lucretia's Dreams: Politics and Prophecy in Sixteenth-Century Spain.* Berkeley, 1990.

Kaminsky, G. "Marcantonio Flaminio ed i Chierici Regolari." *Regnum Dei* 2 (1946): 5–18.

King, Margaret L. *Women of the Renaissance.* Chicago, 1991.

Kirshner, Julius, and Anthony Molho. "The Dowry Fund and the Marriage Market in Early Quattrocento Florence." *Journal of Modern History* 50 (1978): 403–38.

———. "I Monte delle Doti a Firenze dalla sua fondazione nel 1425 alla metà del sedicesimo secolo: abbozzo di una ricerca." *Ricerche storiche* 10 (1980): 21–47.

Klapisch-Zuber, Christiane, ed. *A History of Women in the West, Volume 2: Silences of the Middle Ages.* Cambridge, 1992.

Kunkel, Paul A. "The Theatines in the History of Catholic Reform Before the Establishment of Lutheranism." Ph.D. Diss., Catholic University of America, 1941.

Leclercq, Jean. *Un humaniste ermite: le bienheureux Paul Giustiniani.* Rome, 1951.

Lussana, Fiamma. "Rivolta e misticisimo nei chiostri femminili del Seicento." *Studi storici* 28 (1987): 243–60.

Maggio, F. *Vita della Venerabile Madre Donna Maria Carafa.* Naples, 1670.

Magnuson, Torgil. *Rome in the Age of Bernini.* 2 vols. Atlantic Highlands, NJ, 1983, 1986.

Marshall, Sherrin, ed. *Women in Reformation and Counter-Reformation Europe.* Bloomington, IN, 1989.

Mas, Bartolomeo. "La spiritualità teatina." *Regnum Dei* 7 (1951): 3–18; 64–88; 191–204.

Meissner, W. W. *Ignatius of Loyola: The Psychology of a Saint.* New Haven, 1992.

SELECTED BIBLIOGRAPHY

Meneghin, Vittorino. "Due compagnie sul modello di quelle del 'Divino Amore' fondate da francescani a Feltre e a Verona (1499, 1503)." *Archivum franciscum historicum* 63 (1969): 518- 64.

Michelini, V. *I barnabiti: chierici regolari di S. Paolo.* Milan, 1983.

Miles, Margaret M. *Carnal Knowing: Female Nakedness and Religious Meaning in the Christian West.* Boston, 1989.

Molinari, Franco. *Il cardinal Teatino Beato Paolo Burali e la riforma Tridentina a Piacenza (1568–1576).* Rome, 1957.

Monti, Gennaro Maria. *Ricerche su Papa Paolo IV.* Benevento, 1925.

Moroni, Gaetano. *Dizionario di erudizione storico-ecclesiastica.* 153 vols. Venice, 1840–79.

Niccoli, Ottavia. "The End of Prophecy." *Journal of Modern History* 61 (1989): 667–82.

Niccoli, Ottavia, ed. *Rinascimento al femminile.* Rome-Bari, 1991.

Nussdorfer, Laurie. *Civic Politics in the Rome of Urban VIII.* Princeton, 1992.

O'Malley, John W. *The First Jesuits.* Cambridge, MA, 1993.

———. "Was Ignatius of Loyola a Church Reformer? How to Look at Early-Modern Catholicism." *Catholic Historical Review* 77 (1991): 177–93.

O'Malley, John W., ed. *Catholicism in Early-Modern Europe.* St. Louis, 1988.

Ozment, Steven, ed. *Religion and Culture in the Renaissance and Reformation.* Kirksville, MO, 1989.

Paglia, Vincenzo. *"La pietà dei carcerati": confraternite e società a Rome nei secoli XVI-XVIII.* Rome, 1980.

Paschini, Pio. *San Gaetano, Gian Pietro Carafa e le origini dei chierici regolari teatini.* Rome, 1926.

Pasqualone, Fernando, ed. *La famiglia e la vita quotidiana in Europa dal '400 al '600: Fonti e problemi.* Rome, 1986.

Pastor, Ludwig von. *The History of the Popes From the Close of the Middle Ages.* 3d ed. 40 vols. St. Louis, 1938–53.

Pourrat, Pierre. *La spiritualité chrétienne.* 2d ed. 4 vols. Paris, 1947; English edition: *Christian Spirituality.* 4 vols. Trans. W. H. Mitchell. New York, 1922–27.

Problemi di storia della chiesa nei secoli XV-XVII. Naples, 1978.

Problemi di vita religiosa in Italia nel Cinquecento. Padua, 1960.

Prodi, Paolo. "Controriforma e/o riforma cattolica: superamento di vecchi dilemmi nei nuovi panorami storiografici." *Römische historische Mitteilungen* 31 (1989): 227–37.

———. *Il sovrano pontifice, un corpo e due anime: la monarchia papale nella*

SELECTED BIBLIOGRAPHY

prima età moderna. Bologna, 1982; English edition: *The Papal Prince*. Trans. Susan Haskins. Cambridge, 1987.

Prosperi, Adriano, "L'Inquisizione: verso una nuova immagine?" *Critica storica* 25 (1988): 119–45.

Quinn, Peter A. "Ignatius of Loyola and Gian Pietro Carafa: Catholic Reformers at Odds." *Catholic Historical Review* 67 (1981): 386–400.

Reeves, Marjorie, ed. *Prophetic Rome in the High Renaissance Period*. Oxford, 1992.

Reinhard, Wolfgang. "Reformation, Counter-Reformation and the Early-Modern State: A Reassessment." *Catholic Historical Review* 75 (1989): 383–404.

Rosa, Mario. *Religione e società nel Mezzogiorno, tra Cinque e Seicento*. Bari, 1976.

Rosenthal, Margaret F. *The Honest Courtesan: Veronica Franco, Citizen and Writer in Sixteenth-Century Venice*. Chicago, 1992.

Ruether, Rosemary, and Eleanor McLaughlin, eds. *Women of Spirit: Female Leadership in the Jewish and Christian Traditions*. New York, 1979.

Russo, Carla. *I monasteri femminili di clausura a Napoli nel secolo XVII*. Naples, 1970.

Russo, M. Teresa Bonadonna. "Problemi e istituti dell'assistenza romana nel Cinque e Seicento." *Studi romani* 34 (1986): 230- 52.

Schulte van Kessel, Elisja, ed. *Women and Men in Spiritual Culture, XIV-XVII Centuries*. The Hague, 1986.

Schutte, Anne J. "Periodization of Sixteenth-Century Religious History: The Post-Cantimori Paradigm Shift." *Journal of Modern History* 61 (1989): 269–84.

———. "Subalternità e potere: una chiave di lettura per l'autobiografia di Cecilia Ferrazzi." In Cecilia Ferrazzi, *Autobiografia di una santa mancata, 1609–1664*. Ed. Anne J. Schutte. Bergamo, 1990, 103–13.

Seidel-Menchi, Silvana. "Inquisizione come repressione o inquisizione come mediazione? Una proposta di periodizzazione." *Annuario dell' istituto storico italiano per l'età moderna e contemporanea* 35–36 (1983–1984): 53–77.

Signorotto, Gianvittorio. *Inquisitori e mistici nel Seicento italiano: l'eresia di Santa Pelagia*. Bologna, 1989.

Silos, Giuseppe. *Historiarum Clericorum Regularium a congregatione condita pars prior*. 3 vols. Rome, 1650.

Simoncelli, Paolo. "Inquisizione romana e riforma in Italia." *Rivista storica italiana* 100 (1988): 1–125.

Spalla, Antonio. "Le missioni teatine nelle Indie Orientali nel secolo

XVIII e le cause della loro fine." *Regnum Dei* 27 (1971): 1–76; 28 (1972): 265–305; 29 (1973): 3–37.

Stow, Kenneth R. *Catholic Thought and Papal Jewry Policy, 1551–1592.* New York, 1977.

—. *Taxation, Community and the State: The Jews and the Fiscal Foundations of the Early Modern State.* Stuttgart, 1983.

Vezzosi, Antonio F. *I scrittori de' chierici regolari detti Teatini.* 2 vols. Rome, 1780. Reprint ed. Farnborough, 1966.

Vigorelli, Giancarlo. *Vita e processo di suor Virginia Maria de Leyva monaca di Monza.* Milan, 1985.

Zardin, Danilo. "Le confraternite in Italia settentrionale fra XV e XVII secolo." *Società e storia* 19 (1987): 81–137.

Zarri, Gabriella. "Le sante vive: per una tipologia della santità femminile nel primo Cinquecento." *Annali dell'Istituto storico italo-germanico in Trento* 6 (1980): 371–445.

Index

INDEX

INDEX

INDEX

INDEX

INDEX

INDEX

Will, 57, 123, 125–35, 214–16,
217, 219–20, 224, 225–26
Women, 63; charitable work, 12;
Gaetano's relationship with,
38–42, 63–64; mysticism, 12,
39; religious life, 11, 12, 18,
38–42; Scupoli's relationship
with, 60–62, 63–64

Zaccaria, Antonio Maria, 11, 20

Other Volumes in this Series

Fakhruddin 'Iraqi ● DIVINE FLASHES
Menahem Nahum of Chernobyl ● THE LIGHT OF THE EYES
Early Dominicans ● SELECTED WRITINGS
John Climacus ● THE LADDER OF DIVINE ASCENT
Francis and Clare ● THE COMPLETE WORKS
Gregory Palamas ● THE TRIADS
Pietists ● SELECTED WRITINGS
The Shakers ● TWO CENTURIES OF SPIRITUAL REFLECTION
Zohar ● THE BOOK OF ENLIGHTENMENT
Luis de León ● THE NAMES OF CHRIST
Quaker Spirituality ● SELECTED WRITINGS
Emanuel Swedenborg ● THE UNIVERSAL HUMAN AND SOUL-BODY INTERACTION
Augustine of Hippo ● SELECTED WRITINGS
Safed Spirituality ● RULES OF MYSTICAL PIETY, THE BEGINNING OF WISDOM
Maximus Confessor ● SELECTED WRITINGS
John Cassian ● CONFERENCES
Johannes Tauler ● SERMONS
John Ruusbroec ● THE SPIRITUAL ESPOUSALS AND OTHER WORKS
Ibn 'Abbād of Ronda ● LETTERS ON THE SŪFĪ PATH
Angelus Silesius ● THE CHERUBINIC WANDERER
The Early Kabbalah ●
Meister Eckhart ● TEACHER AND PREACHER
John of the Cross ● SELECTED WRITINGS
Pseudo-Dionysius ● THE COMPLETE WORKS
Bernard of Clairvaux ● SELECTED WORKS
Devotio Moderna ● BASIC WRITINGS
The Pursuit of Wisdom ● AND OTHER WORKS BY THE AUTHOR OF THE CLOUD OF
    UNKNOWING
Richard Rolle ● THE ENGLISH WRITINGS
Francis de Sales, Jane de Chantal ● LETTERS OF SPIRITUAL DIRECTION
Albert and Thomas ● SELECTED WRITINGS
Robert Bellarmine ● SPIRITUAL WRITINGS
Nicodemos of the Holy Mountain ● A HANDBOOK OF SPIRITUAL COUNSEL
Henry Suso ● THE EXEMPLAR, WITH TWO GERMAN SERMONS
Bérulle and the French School ● SELECTED WRITINGS
The Talmud ● SELECTED WRITINGS
Ephrem the Syrian ● HYMNS
Hildegard of Bingen ● SCIVIAS
Birgitta of Sweden ● LIFE AND SELECTED REVELATIONS
John Donne ● SELECTIONS FROM *DIVINE POEMS*, SERMONS, *DEVOTIONS AND
    PRAYERS*
Jeremy Taylor ● SELECTED WORKS
Walter Hilton ● *SCALE OF PERFECTION*